The Great Broadening

The Great Broadening

How the Vast Expansion of the Policy-Making Agenda Transformed American Politics

BRYAN D. JONES
SEAN M. THERIAULT
MICHELLE C. WHYMAN

The University of Chicago Press
Chicago and London

The University of Chicago Press, Chicago 60637
The University of Chicago Press, Ltd., London

Published 2019
Printed in the United States of America

28 27 26 25 24 23 22 21 20 19   1 2 3 4 5

ISBN-13: 978-0-226-62580-5 (cloth)
ISBN-13: 978-0-226-62594-2 (paper)
ISBN-13: 978-0-226-62613-0 (e-book)
DOI: https://doi.org/10.7208/chicago/9780226626130.001.0001

Library of Congress Cataloging-in-Publication Data
Names: Jones, Bryan D., author. | Theriault, Sean M., 1972– author. | Whyman, Michelle, author.
Title: The great broadening : how the vast expansion of the policy-making agenda transformed American politics / Bryan D. Jones, Sean M. Theriault, Michelle Whyman.
Description: Chicago ; London : The University of Chicago Press, 2019. | Includes bibliographical references and index.
Identifiers: LCCN 2018045779 | ISBN 9780226625805 (cloth : alk. paper) | ISBN 9780226625942 (pbk. : alk. paper) | ISBN 9780226626130 (e-book)
Subjects: LCSH: Legislative oversight—United States. | Public administration—United States. | Legislative power—United States. | United States—Politics and government—20th century.
Classification: LCC JK325 .J654 2019 | DDC 320.973—dc23
LC record available at https://lccn.loc.gov/2018045779

♾ This paper meets the requirements of ANSI/NISO Z39.48-1992 (Permanence of Paper).

CONTENTS

PREFACE AND ACKNOWLEDGMENTS

This project builds on a key distinction that Frank Baumgartner and Bryan D. Jones made in *The Politics of Information*. There they distinguished between the broadening of government and its thickening. Thickening is just more government within the traditional public sphere. Broadening is more diverse government—that is, government addressing more policy areas. We realized that the distinction they made had much wider implications than the information-supply argument they offered. It had become increasingly clear to us that the broadening process, involving changes in the scope of what government does rather than just how big it is, was generally overlooked by scholars, political commentators, and policy activists. The powerful and rapid increase in the scope of government from the late 1960s to the late 1970s was so obvious in the US Policy Agendas data we examined that we began to call it "the Great Broadening." Those changes in the policy terrain from that broadening surely had a transformative effect on the US political system. Moreover, we thought that the Policy Agendas Project had the potential of being harnessed in the study of this transformation, not just in isolating the concept of broadening itself.

The first reactions to our early work on the project were critical. We focused on the effects of "the Great Broadening," but people naturally wanted to know what caused it. Adding the analysis of causes made the early work cumbersome and confusing, leading to a desk rejection from a major journal (thanks, Jeff!). Nevertheless we ploughed ahead, trying to learn from every comment we received and every new analysis one of us produced.

We've adopted an eclectic approach, but it is centered in straightforward graphical analyses of extended time series from the Policy Agendas Project. We aimed at making a set of plausibility claims centering on both the data and qualitative case material from the period. Our argument centers on extreme policy feedback in which an intense period of policy-making activity deforms the *policy terrain* (a metaphor used both by James Q. Wilson and Paul Pierson) so severely that the entire course of policy and politics is altered.

We know this book raises many questions and answers only a few. Social science is mostly about open questions. But we do hope to stimulate others to consider a different way of viewing politics and government, one based on seeing politics as a result of policies, where policies can deform the political space in a more profound manner than is currently appreciated.

We incurred numerous debts in the course of this project. An earlier draft was presented at the Duke University Book Symposium, Department of Political Science, Duke University, May 2017, where we received amazingly insightful comments. We particularly benefited from detailed commentary from John Aldrich, David Rohde, Jason Roberts, Sarah Treul, Andrew Ballard, and Bailey Sanders. We especially appreciated how John intuitively grasped the notion of broadening in an extemporaneous comment, when he cited both Bill Riker and Tom Ferguson in the same breath. We also benefited from comments on presentations at Arhus University, the University of Washington's Center for American Politics and Public Policy, the University of Geneva, the Interdisciplinary Center in Hertzliya (in Israel), and the University of Ljubljana.

We are indebted to Dara Strolovitch and Christina Wolbrecht, who kept reminding us that social movements must have been critical in the Great Broadening until we found a way to study their role. We hope that the idea of sequencing of social movements contributes to their integration into more standard party and public-opinion accounts of policy change. Others who were kind enough to provide comments that helped us clarify and modify our ideas include Bat Sparrow, Hans Noel, Lee Drutman, Clarence Stone, Roy Flemming, Dara Strolovitch, Jeff Isaac, and John Padgett, whose work Jones seems always to be borrowing. Trey Thomas provided invaluable help in the mechanics of calculating the major measures we used in this book.

We benefited enormously from four formal reviews from university presses. Their collective comments were generally supportive, always insightful, and incredibly detailed. We are awed by the time and care with which they reviewed our work, and this book is far better because of their inputs. Thanks to Don Kettl and Laurel Harbridge-Yong, who wrote reviews for the University of Chicago Press, and David Mayhew and Beth Leech, who reviewed it for Oxford University Press. In particular, we appreciate the care that the University of Chicago Press, especially Chuck Myers, gave our manuscript.

Given our heavy reliance on the Policy Agendas Project, we owe our deepest debts to the graduate students at Texas, Washington, and Texas A&M who served as project managers, and the other students, graduate and undergraduate, who participated in the construction of both the database and the website we developed for delivering that database (policyagendas.net). Even more importantly, they were critical in building the research community around the project and assuming responsibility for its health. In particular, we want to acknowledge our deep debt to Michelle Wolfe, who was both a project manager and a contributor to the political communications literature. Her "Stepping on the Gas or Putting on the Brakes" is one of the finest articles in that field. Michelle was tragically killed in September of 2016 by a bolt of lightning.

Our relationship with Michelle represents what we value most in this profession—teaching and learning from our students and our mentors. This book is a special collaboration between three authors at three different stages in their careers: one at the beginning of her career, one at the midpoint (hopefully!), and one who is enjoying the successes of a multi-decade career. In speaking for the latter two, we feel very confident that our mentorship was worthy if our students have learned even half as much from us as we've learned from them (and that most definitely includes the former).

While we prize the students with whom we've worked, we dedicate this book to our mentors. It is because of their time, energy, and effort that we are who we are today. We're humbled by their intelligence, kindness, and perseverance.

Bryan Jones owes his usual debt to Frank Baumgartner. But he owes many other debts to those who have tolerated his hardheadedness and left-handed way of viewing the world over the years. That especially includes both Sean Theriault and Michelle Whyman. And he owes a big debt to Diane for her feisty tolerance over the years.

Sean Theriault thanks Dan Palazzolo, Barry Weingast, Paul Sniderman, Dave Rohde, and Bryan Jones for showing him not only what a good political scientist is, but also what a good person is. They have each opened up their hearts (and even their homes) to him—and to Anthony, who has done the same, but on a more regular basis.

Michelle Whyman thanks Bryan Jones for encouraging her to pursue a PhD and offering unfaltering support throughout her education. She owes Sean Theriault her deepest thanks for his mentorship and sterling friendship. She is also thankful to John Aldrich and Dave Rohde for extending their wisdom, advice, and friendship to her. She could not ask for better role models or mentors.

ONE

The Great Broadening

Once in a great while, history's trajectory through time is deflected—direction, velocity, and acceleration can all be forever altered seemingly instantaneously. While these ruptures have received great attention in geology, paleontology, technology, and astrophysics, they also occur in human history. Not all ruptures occur instantaneously; rather, some involve an interconnected network of events, changes in variables, and reactions to earlier changes.

In this book we examine one of those great ruptures—a burst of political activity and policy enactment in the United States. We call it "the Great Broadening" because government got larger not by doing more of what it already was doing but by getting involved in new issues where it had only limited presence before. Beginning in the late 1950s, peaking in the late 1970s, and declining afterward, the United States experienced a vast expansion in the national policy-making agenda. Many have noted this great expansion; indeed it was hard to miss. In this brief period, government in the United States morphed from a targeted activist state centering on social insurance (the legacy of the New Deal) and foreign/military policy (a consequence of the permanent tensions of the Cold War) to a vastly broadened activist state in which few elements of civil society escaped intervention. Here we examine in detail the causes, internal dynamics, and consequences of this great, extended burst of activity.

We employ both qualitative and quantitative methods throughout our analyses. Qualitatively, we examine the available historical narratives used to explain the Great Broadening. Quantitatively, we use data series from the Policy Agendas Project and supplementary sources to establish the plausibility of causal orderings that are consistent with the historical narratives. We put aside attempts to develop sophisticated (or even unsophisticated) statistical models in favor of a more inductive but nevertheless disciplined approach to assess the nature of this great rupture in the development of American politics.

This period was so distinctively different that it must be approached holistically, as a separate and distinct phenomenon. Paul Pierson and Theda Skocpol (2007, 2) note that US politics were transformed between 1957 and 2007, "so much so that a Rip van Winkle who fell asleep in 1957 and awoke in 2007 would hardly feel it was the same polity." Pierson and Skocpol were correct, but we show in this book that the transformation was much more rapid and complete than they and their collaborators in their collection of essays on the transformation realized. For the most part, the transformation was over by the late 1970s.

This great rupture has not gone unnoticed, but observers have struggled with how to define it and assess its effects. Historian James Patterson (1996, vii) sees the period as one of "ever-greater expectations about the capacity of the United States to create an ever-better world abroad and a happier society at home." Samuel Huntington (1981) finds the answer in "creedal passions" that cause historical bursts of governmental activity. Pierson (2007) depicts a general rise in activist government. Skocpol (2007) views the transformation as a civic reorganization of group life and its influence on government. Campbell (2007) writes about the changing nature of party politics, while McCarty (2007) sees it as a period of partisan polarization with severe consequences for public policy. Scholars such as Zelizer (2007) and Teles (2007) define the period by the era of conservatism that followed it.

All of these astute observers are correct, but they miss the critical unifying component. All agree that the key general characteristic of the period is how the federal government changed. But no agreement integrates the diverse elements they discuss. Like Theodore Lowi (1967), we find the key in the shifting relationship between state and civil society. The federal government quite suddenly extended its scope into policy arenas previously left to civil society or the states and localities. Government did not grow much faster, at least according to standard measures relating expenditures to the size of the economy; however, it broadened, becoming much more intrusive across many more issues than in the past. As a consequence, we term this period "the Great Broadening."

Patterson's grand expectations cannot have defined the period, because expectations have been raised and dashed many times in history. Nonetheless, the raising and sustaining of these expectations is the key to the self-sustaining nature of the broadening process. Pierson's "activist state" was trivially about more spending; it was more essentially a vast increase in scope. It is the particular nature of activism that mattered. The transformation of civic society that Skocpol so astutely examines was mostly a consequence of the Great Broadening. Political parties adjusted to this shift in scope; they were involved in causing it as well, but less so than many political scientists imagine. The more fundamental causes can be found in the social movements that proliferated during the period. Huntington recognizes the creedal passions that motivate social movements, but he downplays the roles of institutions, which are critical. Polarization and interest-group politics were largely a consequence of the broadening, not a characteristic of it. And conservatism as it developed after the Great Broadening would not have taken the same path without it—it too was a consequence. We offer evidence for each of these propositions and more.

The Arc of the Great Broadening

With the approaches we deploy in this book, we are able to measure the beginning of the period, its peak, and its end with considerable precision. The period may be described as a great arc, or horseshoe, of intense activity with a distinct beginning and end. We use a variety of different measures to assess this arc based in the intensity of the period and the changing scope of government.

We start with a simple demonstration that illustrates both the nature of the period and our visual approach to understanding it. Political news coverage increased during the period as the pace of politics intensified. Here we examine two news sources, the *New York Times* and the *Congressional Quarterly Almanac* (*CQA*). The *Times* reports generally on politics, public policy, business, and social affairs, whereas the *CQA* focuses on "inside the beltway" activity, reporting exclusively on policy-making and politics. Simple counts of articles published show similar arcs during approximately the same period of time (see fig. 1.1).[1] Of course there may have been other reasons for the increases and decreases in news coverage, but the correspondence between the two series is striking. We'll see this arc or ones very similar many times in this book.

Politics, even in relatively quiescent periods, can involve senses of urgency and intensity. But during the Great Broadening, politics and policymaking each had a frenzy about them, and they moved in tandem, each influencing the other. Within the arc of the Great Broadening, causal processes differed from those prevalent either before or afterward. Moreover, the dynamics within the arc were generated endogenously—that is, they were not directly caused by an external event such as the Great Depression or World War II. Rather, changes within the polity itself caused the increase

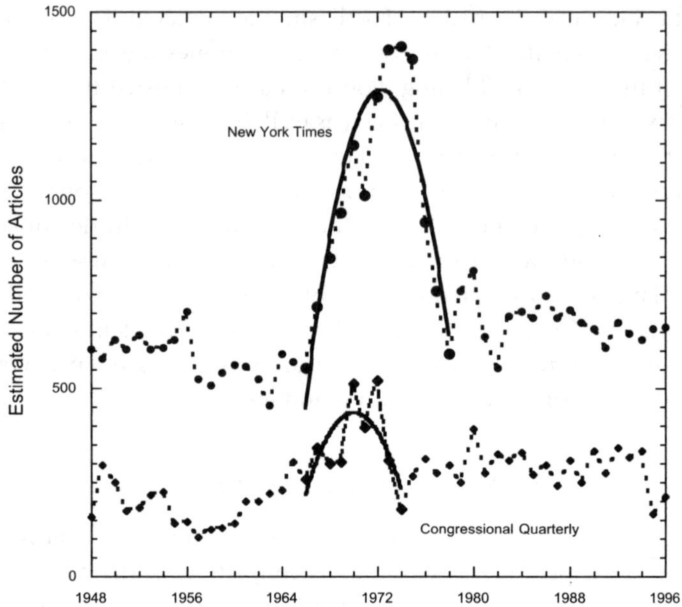

FIGURE I.1. Number of articles published annually in the *New York Times* and in the *Congressional Quarterly Almanac*

in intensity of policy-making activity. Part 1 of this book examines these internal dynamics, showing how the political processes within the arc were different in kind from those that came before and after.

Saying that the processes were different does not mean they were unique. Rather, the same factors used to explain politics in more normal times interacted more intensely, feeding on one another through emerging networks of activists and politicians. This pattern is not mystical. The processes inside the arc were generally similar to an arms race, a market bubble, or a trade war. Virtuous cycles also exist, of course. These sorts of self-sustaining processes are termed positive feedback systems. Outside the arms race, nations still arm. Outside a trade war, nations still pursue trade advantages. Supply and demand governs economic exchanges in or out of a bubble. The difference is how actors and groups key on each other's behaviors. In such self-sustaining feedback systems, external "shocks" are not required to explain change. Such systems are fundamentally unstable; they always end, but they sometimes end with a bang and sometimes with a whimper.

Part 2 of the book explores the causes of the Great Broadening—what set off the self-sustaining (for a time) dynamics that caused the rising phase of the arc. After pausing in chapter 7 to consolidate and reflect on what the empirical analyses have shown us, we embark on a study of the consequences of the broadening in part 3. Why did the arc decline, and what replaced it? The declining phase came about because actors who made gains during the period turned to consolidation, and those who lost mobilized against those policy changes.

In our analyses of consequences, we hope to establish the plausibility of a radical claim: much of American *politics* during the fourth quarter of the twentieth century and well into the twenty-first was strongly influenced by the *public policies* addressed during the third quarter of the last century. That policies cause politics is an old idea (Lowi 1964; Pierson 1993), but an important one that too frequently is underappreciated. We take this idea much further by demonstrating that the magnitude of the disruption of the Great Broadening was transformative to our entire system of governance. Its "downstream" effects dramatically influenced the functioning of Congress, the courts, political parties, interest groups, and voters, and they generated backlash and social movements that continue to reverberate even today. Congress shifted its primary focus from lawmaking to oversight, the interest-group system grew exponentially, social movements on the right responded to the left's policy successes, political parties in government polarized, the corpus of law grew much larger, and the docket of the Supreme Court expanded as Congress intensified its lawmaking during this period. Prior policy-making processes are as important as factors that are normally seen as critical, such as elections, public opinion, political parties, and the media.

The Two Paths of the Great Broadening

While many scholars and casual observers have detected large, transformative events in history, few have offered broader theories to explain these events. Nevertheless, two distinct approaches can be used to study such events. In the first, they are viewed as arising from the same causes that explain less extreme changes, but the independent variables are themselves extreme (see Barabasi 2010, 11, for a more general statement). We term this approach the *contemporaneous dynamics approach*. For example, political scientists hypothesize that changes in political party control of government lead to different public policies. If such a change is large, one might expect proportionately larger policy changes.

A second approach comes from historical institutionalism. It is also reflected independently in the study of American political institutions. In this approach, political institutions hold the trajectory of the political process within bounds; the process is path-dependent. It is not that change is precluded; rather, the costs of reversal are very high (Levi 1997, 28). Rarely, in what is termed a *critical juncture*, this path-dependency is disrupted. In this juncture, causation is different, because the bounds imposed by institutions have broken. As Capoccia and Kelemen (2007, 343) claim, "The freedom of political actors and impact of their decisions is heightened" during the critical juncture. This freedom of action leads to the creation of new forms of political rules and institutional arrangements. These new arrangements structure politics and are path-dependent and highly resistant to change unless they are disrupted by another critical juncture. Pierson (1996) has detailed some of these dynamics in the specific case of attempts to dismantle the welfare state; Hacker and Pierson (2014) expanded these ideas. Similarly, students of American political institutions have analyzed the resistance to change built into our constitutional design (Krehbiel 1998; Jones and Baumgartner 2005).

Our study shows that both contemporaneous dynamics and path-dependency face limits in explaining the Great Broadening. The contemporaneous dynamics approach fails most fundamentally because the standard political variables, even at high levels, cannot account for the Great Broadening. A quarter of a century ago, David Mayhew (1991) found that the passage of landmark legislation (including acts passed during the Great Broadening) could not be explained by the standard hypothesis of unified government, suggesting that a rethinking of the standard approach was in order. Put in context, though, the standard factors remain important.

As the historical institutionalism school would lead us to expect, we find distinct evidence that the Great Broadening altered American institutions of governing in important ways. It was indeed a great rift, permanently transforming the trajectory of politics and public policy in the United States. Second, we find evidence that the causation is different during the critical juncture than either before or after the rupture. But many intuitionalists assert that once the new trajectory is established, institutions reestablish constraints on actors within the new set of rules. We demur from this claim, at least partially, and we back up our dissent from the prevailing wisdom with data.

What actually happened is much more dynamic than the neo-institutionalists suggest. The Great Broadening did reset institutions, but it also set off counter-reactions and downstream consequences that continued to disrupt the historical path for decades after the peak of the Great Broadening. Most obviously, the actors who saw themselves as losers were unlikely to submit quietly to the new rules; rather, they were more likely to mount a counterattack on the system to keep it from becoming solidified.

We document two basic paths of the Great Broadening and its aftermath rather than the single path of the historical institutionalists. The first is indeed path-dependency—some parts of the system were shifted permanently in ways that we can assess and measure. For example, once Congress began to address the new issues that emerged during the Great Broadening, it continued to address them. The second is counter-mobilization, as opponents of the new policy direction tried and succeeded to halt the Great Broadening and have even reversed some of its effects. The intensity of lawmaking rose during the intense dynamics of the broadening period, subsequently falling as conservatives pushed back. We note that the first halves of both paths are the same, and it is that rise that we refer to as the Great Broadening. Once the agenda had broadened though, it could either persist, yielding the former path, or experience a downturn, yielding the latter.

Measuring the Great Broadening

Could it be that critical junctures in political systems are so rare that they must be studied by constructing narratives—guided by theory, but narratives nevertheless—as comparative neo-institutionalists recommend (Capoccia and Kelemen 2007; Bates et al. 1998)? Or, despite their rarity, can more quantitative methods be employed? We show here that quantitative study is both possible and productive, at least under some circumstances.

Our quantitative analyses are made possible by the availability of the Policy Agendas datasets that measure the occurrence of policy activity using a consistent and temporally compatible set of content codes from 1945 to the present (http://www.comparativeagendas.net/). The system is analogous to the National Income Accounts that economists use to track different sectors of the economy over time. The key to the system is backward compatibility and high reliability in coding, and the use of the same coding system on various policy-making activities (Jones 2016a).

The quantitative analysis based on the Policy Agendas Project is essential to understanding the Great Broadening, because the general conception of what the changes of the period were about is at least highly misleading. The whole process is often summarized as a growth of government, and most scholars of policy change examine government growth using expenditure data. If government spends more money relative to the growth of the economy, then one may conclude that government has grown.

If we look only at governmental expenditures, the Great Broadening would not seem particularly impressive. While many would claim that government grew greatly during the period, it cannot easily be detected through spending measures. Jones, Zalányi, and Érdi (2014) analyzed a newly constructed budgetary series from 1789 to 2010, finding disjoint shifts in budget trajectories associated only with major wars or economic collapse. Even an examination of post–World War II expenditure trends barely detects the vast initiatives of the Great Society. Some conservatives argue that these programs initiated an insatiable demand for government intervention and subsequent spending, an argument that would be better if Republicans had not contributed to the expenditure increases by supporting vast new spending on military and crime-control measures during the Reagan Administration. The supposed spending binges of the Great Society look like no more than a blip in a longer-term process of steady increases. Relative to growth in population and the size of the economy, the alleged "galloping big government" set off by the Kennedy-Johnson Great Society years was practically trivial.

These comparisons have led some observers to dismiss the claims of a huge growth in government as a gross exaggeration. It is not. Government intrusion into economic life is not always expensive. New regulations may cost the federal government little, but they may be quite costly for industries seeking to comply with new standards. They may also contribute to goals of equity and equality, as did the Voting Rights Act of 1965. To capture intrusion rather than expenditure, we develop a new measure of the growth in government that is independent of expenditure. Following Baumgartner and Jones (2015), the measure assesses how broad government has become: the number of new issues it has addressed across time. After a period of experimentation following World War II, broadening steadily increased in the mid-1950s, accelerated in the 1960s and 1970s, and peaked around 1978. Our analyses show how rapidly government moved into so many issues previously left to civil society that the very distinction between the public and private spheres nearly disappeared. On other issues, which had previously been the purview of state or local governments, the federal government also began to encroach. Moreover, we show that these processes, which we call broadening, work like a ratchet—once the federal government intervenes in an issue, it seldom moves out of that issue.

The 1960s and 1970s were transformative, but in a way typically unrecognized by scholars and pundits alike. The expansion of government consisted of a large increase in the *scope* of government, the number of issues that moved onto the national policy agenda. By the peak of the period, American politics had been radically and irrevocably transformed in a manner still ill-addressed and ill-understood by scholars and practitioners even today.

Thickening and Broadening Government

Government grew larger during this period, but what transformed government more than its thickening was its broadening. Some of these policies increased the public commitment to things it already did (thickening), while new issues crowded the agenda in a manner that broadened the federal government's scope (Baumgartner and Jones 2009). A *thickened* government is more active within established policy domains, often adding to previously established agencies with additional layers of bureaucracy (Light 1995; 2004). It spends more doing what it has done in the past. A *broadened* government takes on new responsibilities (Baumgartner and Jones 2015).

A fresh approach based on data from the Policy Agendas Project allows us to assess these two components with much more precision. We show that the broadening process traced a great arc through time, reaching its peak around 1978. Moreover, the new approach to assessing the broadening of government allows us to take a step back and show that the process is not strongly connected to the traditional understandings of the basis of policy change, such as elections and party control of government.

The arc seemed to have developed its own logic, *partially decoupled* from elections, parties, interest groups, and institutional changes. By "partially decoupled," we mean that the shape of the arc bore little direct relationship to the traditional variables that political scientists generally focus on first in any analysis of policy change. That does not mean that these standard variables are irrelevant to the broadening. They most definitely are relevant, but they interact in complex ways with other less prominent (at least to political scientists) variables. Particularly important are social movements, beginning with civil rights and including women's rights, environmentalism, consumer protection, and product safety, all of which accessed the policymaking agenda in a relatively short period. All of these movements spanned traditional issues and helped to cause feedback processes that expanded the broadening. During the Great Broadening, networks of actors crossing standard subsystems emerged, leading to self-reinforcing spillovers as similar ideas affected different, previously independent policy subsystems (Grossmann 2014).

Politics and policy were connected in a different, perhaps stronger, sense because the Great Broadening generated a powerful conservative counterreaction that succeeded in reversing the course of the arc in a fundamental manner. And once again social movements were an important component, as conservatives responded with an antitax crusade premised on shrinking government, a return to federalism as a first constitutional premise, a

"Southern strategy" by the Republican Party to capture the racial resentment of Southern whites, a demand for the restoration of the traditional role of women, and more general reactions to what they saw as the excesses of earlier waves of social movements. As strong as this counter-reaction was, powerful remnants of the transformation continued unabated, and indeed even strengthened, thereby permanently altering the course of American politics and government.

The Great Broadening swept away many of the distinctions between public and civil spheres in society and did so quite rapidly. Indeed, the distinction seems archaic in public discourse today. In an essay in the *American Political Science Review* in 1967, Theodore Lowi (1967, 5) noted that "the relatively small size of the public sector was maintained in great part by the constitutional wall of separation between government and private life." Lowi thought that the Great Society had swept away the distinction between public and private life and decried the lack of any agreed-on set of rules for arbitrating among contesting claims within the framework of a much larger state: "Statesmen simply no longer disagree about whether government should be involved" (10).

The broadening process was just getting underway when Lowi wrote his classic essay. Expansions into many more aspects of previously private life were occurring as he wrote. Statesmen and mere politicians did disagree about such issues. Indeed the failure of conservatives to be more vocal early in the broadening process could have been due to the weakness of conservative mobilization during the era rather than any inherent lack of disagreement. Perhaps Lowi may have written off the private-public distinction too soon, but it was not too early when, at the peak of the Great Broadening, James Q. Wilson (1979, 41) wrote, "Once politics was about only a few things; today it is about everything."

Despite the frequent criticisms of conservatives, the deconstruction of a civil society separate and distinct from government was a bipartisan effort. In major ways Republicans contributed to it. In the 1960s, the Republicans were more active earlier on some issues such as the environment, an issue that would later be coopted by the Democrats. But Republicans were not simply being the party of "me, too," as conservative activists claimed. By pushing for strict criminal justice policies in the 1980s (giving the Democrats their own opportunity to become the party of "me, too"), by leading the expansion of the national security state in the administration of George W. Bush, and by promoting moral strictures such as the restrictions on abortions, the establishment of school prayer, and, later, the prohibition of gay marriage, conservatives, too, expanded the scope of government and cheered its interventions into civil society. Nevertheless, as Lowi noted, political debates continue to be crammed into the same fundamentally meaningless private versus public debate that may have been relevant until the 1960s but was not afterward.

Governmental centralization was a strong second theme during the Great Broadening. Some of this centralization was close to consensual. It seemed inconceivable that a national transportation network could be built without the federal government, and early in the broadening period it took responsibility for a national highway system and a structure for promoting and regulating air transportation. Some was controversial, as it prohibited actions deemed discriminatory by state governments and private businesses in essential services, accommodations, and housing. Much of it, such as Medicaid and highway funds, involved federal grants-in-aid to the states, resulting in a complex network of arrangements broadly termed *fiscal federalism*. By the end of the broadening period, the relationship between the states and the federal government had been fundamentally transformed. The more the federal government broadened, the more it affected the leeway previously left to the states. It did so through prohibitions (as in the cases of open accommodations and housing) as well as inducements via the grant process, which involved regulations that irritated state governments.

We do not take a philosophical position in addressing the issue of the intrusion of government into areas of life in which that would have been unthinkable before the Great Broadening. Market failure is real; collective action can be necessary but difficult in the absence of government, and fairness is a strong norm in human societies. On the other hand, government can become oppressive and undercut not only personal liberties, but also the economic potential of a society. So we think these matters are best addressed on a case-by-case basis. These predilections are personal; our analysis holds whether one takes a conservative philosophical position on the role of government or a liberal one.

Nor do we claim that the end of government intrusion came in the late 1970s, although in this book we present evidence that the *broadening* process has changed little since then. Within the areas where government is established, *thickening* has occurred. Republicans led much of this thickening. President Reagan greatly expanded the military footprint in the United States and around the world. During the Reagan years, congressional Republicans led an assault on crime, and Democrats joined in, leading to excessive sentencing and overinvestment in crime control that is only being recognized today (Jones, Thomas, and Wolfe 2014). President George W. Bush led a vast expansion of governmental power into the areas of privacy and civil liberties after the coordinated terrorist attacks on 9-11-2001. He also proposed and successfully enacted great expansions of the federal role in education and health care. Presidents Bush and Obama led a bank bailout and re-regulation of finance in the wake of the Great Recession. And President Obama controversially expanded access and regulations in health care in the Affordable Care Act of 2010. Congressional Republicans in 2018 secured large expansions of the military. All of these actions took place within policy arenas that had previously been occupied by the federal government.

Moreover, within those areas, many political debates center on how government activity is to be conducted, not whether it is to be withdrawn. In education, advocates of "privatization" do not mean withdrawal of public funds; they mean allocating those funds to private schools, too. "Contracting out" governmental services to private companies similarly fails to reduce the size of the state and indeed may increase it—studies show that such arrangements are more expensive, and the freedom of such companies to lobby Congress means they are at least as able to defend themselves as government workers. President Bush expanded medical coverage under Medicare through a market-based mechanism, as did President Obama in the Affordable Care and Patient Protection Act. The issues involved changing incentives for major actors in these areas, not withdrawing from them.

Similarly, many of the moves of Republicans to decentralize and restore public authority to state governments were not designed to reduce government's power. Nixon used block grants to replace the specific grant-in-aid programs of the Kennedy-Johnson years, but this did not lessen the states' reliance on federal revenue streams. Block grants remain popular with conservatives today and appear in Republican proposals to reform health care. When conservatives control the national government, they quite readily interfere with state governments—for example, by requiring cooperation with federal immigration officials or imposing work requirements on welfare recipients. The very terrain on which political battles are fought has changed, yet in many ways the language has remained the same.

The Great Broadening altered much about modern American politics, from the content of political debates to the structure of the interest-group system to the conduct of legislative business. The transformation affected contemporary American politics profoundly, and it set both a new base for policy action and new rules for conducting it. Yet it is barely acknowledged in most modern accounts of politics and policy-making. In this book, we aim to right this imbalance.

Three Questions about the Great Broadening

Three seemingly straightforward questions about the Great Broadening will preoccupy us for the rest of the book: What was it? What caused it? What effects did it have?

What Was the Great Broadening?

That the federal government started doing more in the third quarter of the twentieth century is well known and well documented. Yet until Mayhew (1991) weighted laws by their importance, no attempts were made to assess this activity systematically. Mayhew's count of landmark enactments shows a clear burst of lawmaking that began with the 88th Congress (1961–62), continued at a high level until the 94th Congress (1975–76), after which the number of such laws dropped precipitously (see fig. 1.2).[2] Mayhew's count rose again during the G. W. Bush and Obama presidencies due to the passage of such initiatives as Medicare Part D, Obama's vast stimulus bill in response to the Great Recession, and the Affordable Care Act. But the count does not reach the levels of the earlier lawmaking surge. Interestingly, most analyses after Mayhew have failed to treat the surge as seriously as they should, mainly because his thesis about divided government producing as much landmark legislation as unified government was so captivating.

The arc shows how rapidly the surge in landmark legislation occurred and how quickly it declined. In a manner similar to the arcs of figure 1.1, we fit the arc to the data statistically for the congresses from just before to just after the surge.[3] We deploy this strategy to describe one of the two essential patterns in this book. This arc is what we would expect when expansionary forces meet increasingly strong resistance. The arc consists of three parts: the increasing stage, the leveling off stage, and the declining stage. During the rising stage, resistance is futile, but as resistance increases, the rate of growth in the broadening process decelerates and then ceases, leveling off for a few years. As the advocates for resistance gain ascendency, government action begins to dwindle.

It is unlikely that each landmark law was a result of different causes, but if they were the result of the same causes, it is not clear exactly what those causes were. The burst began in the 97th Congress (1961–62) and reached a peak in the 89th Congress under President Lyndon Johnson, with large Democratic majorities. The peak period for landmark legislation continued under two Republican presidents (Nixon and Ford), facing attenuated Democratic majorities, and ended during the tenure of a Democratic president

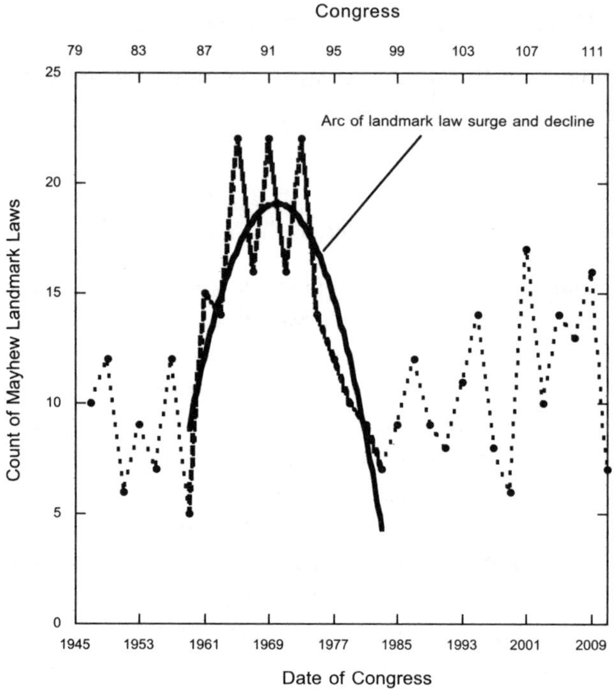

FIGURE 1.2. Count of laws rated by Mayhew (1991) as landmark, with an arc fit from just before to just after the lawmaking surge

(Carter), with large supporting majorities in Congress. The broadening process for landmark laws attenuated later, during the G. W. Bush presidency. It is difficult to associate the surge with the typical models of shifts in control of Congress and the presidency because of the shifting partisan compositions of Congress and the presidency.

A count of important laws does not really assess the Great Broadening. Mayhew's data show that the federal government is doing more, but it is silent on the policy scope of action. By categorizing Mayhew's list of landmark enactments into the number of Policy Agendas Project subtopics they address, we can get a measure of the broadness of the federal government's agenda (see fig. 1.3). Both series are quite similar in form. They contain an arc and both exhibit considerable congress-to-congress variability. Note that both series start increasing around the same time, but as the count measure peaks, the broadening measure continues to increase until the 105th Congress before subsequently declining steeply. As the last step in the

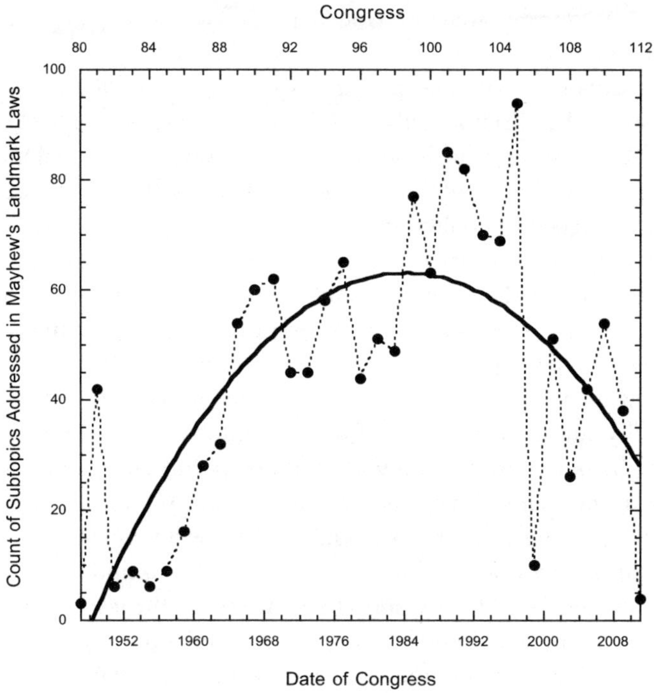

FIGURE I.3. Number of Policy Agendas Project subtopics addressed in Mayhew's landmark laws, by congress

policy-making process, enactments react later to the conservative counter-mobilization. The differences between theses series give us leverage in analyzing the Great Broadening and its aftermath.

The burst in the level of activity was accompanied by a burst in the scope of activity. After the 105th Congress (1997–98), landmark legislation mostly thickened government, and the expansionary curve declined. It is noteworthy that relative to the surge in landmark legislation alone, the broadening process in landmark legislation occurred over a much longer period, which is mostly a consequence of laws becoming more complex over time, containing more subtopics, as we show in chapter 8.

The arc of expansion in scope became self-sustaining through reinforcing feedback dynamics involving networks of political actors that crossed traditional policy subsystem boundaries. In this confusing and chaotic process, the limits on governmental action imposed by the old distinction between public and private spheres of action collapsed as the federal government moved into arena after arena previously left to civil society or to state and local governments.

When scholars observe these processes for a single issue, they use the term *issue expansion*. The idea is an old one. It is used "to discuss positive feedback effects that cause issues to move quickly among many decision-making units" (Baumgartner and Jones 2009, 17). Charles O. Jones (1979, 105) described the scramble over energy policy after the 1973 OPEC oil embargo as "Expansion is up, out, and over—up in public and institutional hierarchies . . . ; out to groups that declared an interest in energy policies . . . ; and over to decision making process in other nations or groups of nations, . . . forcing resource-based subsystem participants into considering each other."

We show later in this book that issue expansion happened in lots of issues virtually simultaneously, all of which reinforced each other and were influenced by boundary-spanning activities by policy entrepreneurs, social movements, and changes in political parties. These self-reinforcing processes leave traces in the historical record, both qualitative and quantitative. In the coming chapters, we examine these traces with new data and new measures, typically validated by older measures that have stood the test of time.

Part 1 of this book addresses the internal dynamics of the Great Broadening in detail. Chapter 2 examines the issue of the scope of government and how broadening required a readjustment of the traditional boundaries between public and private life. In chapters 3 and 4, we return to these figures of action and scope of action to show the various contours of when the government broadened and how. The argument has an important wrinkle that we introduce in chapter 3 about precisely what the laws enacted over the time frame contain. In chapter 4, we show how the step-by-step expansion happened and then how it stopped and even retreated.

The issue-expansion phase within a single policy arena can be sensibly viewed as a punctuated equilibrium in which a new path-dependency is established within the area, and a rich literature demonstrates the viability of this approach (Baumgartner and Jones 2009). These authors assert that "our principal claim . . . is that the course of public policy in the United States is not incremental, but rather is disjoint and episodic" (xvii), and they provide some indication of connections between changes in policy subsystems. Nevertheless, the punctuated-equilibrium approach does not generalize to the entire political system. It seems that the Great Broadening was a period of subsystem destruction on a grander scale. As Padgett and Powell (2012, 9) describe in their magisterial introduction of autocatalysis to social processes, new organizational forms "can appear as rapid 'punctuated equilibria' with unintended consequences for organizations in collateral domains."

The rapid punctuated equilibria across domains interconnected by coevolving social networks (Padgett and Powell 2012, 3) ensure that destabilization is more extended than the critical-juncture literature suggests. The reason is that feedback processes are much more complex than currently depicted in the public-policy literature, and we discuss these new conceptions of feedback politics in chapter 7.

What Caused the Great Broadening?

Part 2 of the book centers on causes of the Great Broadening. Causes of singular events such as the Great Broadening are difficult to disentangle because one cannot observe variability across similar events. Statistical analysis works by leveraging a large number of cases, but is less adept at handling extreme events—indeed, some analysts actually discard such "outliers." We find little evidence of simple causation; rather a set of interacting causes brought it about. These causes are difficult to disentangle because no one simple factor is responsible. Indeed, it is their complex interactions that likely account for the power and force of this phenomenon.

Many have taken note of this great expansion, but few have studied its causes systematically. On the one hand, some historians have claimed that a set of unique historical circumstances was responsible—the rebound from World War II, the necessities of the Cold War, the emergence of particular leaders both in and out of government. On the other, a few political scientists have deployed a more systematic approach. The success of these few systematic efforts has been limited at best. Their failures are likely a consequence of attempts to force-fit the expansion to a story involving *contemporaneous dynamics*—that is, it was caused by such institutional and exogenous factors as unified government, party control, and electoral alignments that occur at the same time as the event.

This approach, which we outline and test in chapter 5, is based on deconstructing the forces leading to an event independently and usually linearly in simple causal systems (Érdi 2008, 6). To build in history, context, and complex interactions, most quantitative analysts generally add a few lagged variables into a regression equation. This approach is not going to work very well in explaining extreme and very rare events born of complex processes such as the Great Broadening. Systems of causation are not usually so simple.

Such facets of politics as party control and public opinion are so natural for political scientists to consider that it is hard for us to recognize that in this critically important case they have failed to produce as expected. We don't mean to imply that they are unrelated to explaining the Great Broadening, but that they are only part of the story—and not even the most interesting part.

Focusing exclusively on contemporaneous dynamics is similarly damaging to our understanding of current politics. The historians have a point. History matters in a deeper sense than many political scientists realize, but the failure of historians to appreciate systematic causes leads them to bring a partial understanding to the table as well. We wrestle with combining contemporaneous dynamics with history in chapter 6.

Analytical narratives (Bates et al. 1998) provide a potential approach, but constructing a model of an extremely rare event in which qualitative comparisons to other events are impractical can lead to an over-reliance on theoretical expectations. When data are absent, theory guides too strongly.

Our approach to causation is to assess what factors may be important from a reading of the literature, including both contemporaneous dynamics and other more qualitatively assessed forces such as social movements. We use Policy Agendas data as well as other sources to eliminate simple causation while demonstrating the feasibility of our arguments. In complex systems, this is the best we can do at this point. While not perfect or, perhaps, even satisfying, it is far superior to a political science based solely on simple causation.

What Were Its Consequences?

The consequences of the extended burst of activity cannot be portrayed as a simple system-level punctuation that led to a new stable outcome. Rather, these consequences were complex, intertwined, and long-lasting. We examine these consequences in part 3. The conservative counter-mobilization, which has already been depicted as the right half of the arc in figures 1.2 and 1.3, had its roots planted in the 1950s, when conservatives were fuming about a state of affairs that simply did not exist, though it was soon to exist. The moderate Republican Party became the vehicle for these movement conservatives as they offered a new philosophy for practical Republican politicians. For conservatives, the Great Broadening served as a huge window of opportunity to push back at least some of the successes of the liberal reformists. Yet the unity of conservatives was always threatened by the tendency of many to demand more government in many areas, not less.

The Great Broadening and the conservative counter-mobilization that came after it had dramatic consequences throughout the political system. The broadening of laws changed the very nature of what laws looked like—they incorporated multiple issues as they got much longer (chapter 8). The

Great Broadening and the new nature of how law was conceived shifted Congress's attention from lawmaking to overseeing a larger and more complex bureaucracy (chapter 9). The broad historical trends (chapter 10) and piecemeal way in which Congress confronted new issues (chapter 11) helped ignite the party polarization that still pervades Congress today. Due to its sequencing, the rapid rise of interest groups was a consequence of the Great Broadening rather than a cause of it (chapter 12). Finally, the broadening contained the seeds of its own demise, as conservatives first succeeded in halting the liberal expansions, as was the case for the Equal Rights Amendment and further school desegregation measures, and then gained allies from across the political spectrum to dismantle aspects of the regulatory state, to construct a vast new intervention in crime control, and to initiate vast tax cuts, this time with fewer bipartisan allies (chapter 13).

Conservatives were successful in stopping the self-reinforcing dynamic of the Great Broadening, but success came at the cost of making many of its effects seemingly permanent. The new programs created during the broadening required massive increases in government agencies to implement them. It also created new constituencies who benefited from the programs and new targets of regulatory actions. Both groups subsequently organized for political action. Finally, this general process led to later transformations of our governing mechanisms, including Congress and our political parties (the subjects of chapters 8, 9, and 10), the regulatory state (discussed in chapter 11), the interest-group system (covered in chapter 12), and the very nature of electoral politics. *Lock-in* does not imply forever stable, as normal political dynamics continue apace. Indeed, we wish another term had been used for this. Moreover, we detect a final impact beyond the major two sketched above, and it does not imply the stability of lock-in. As it became clear that the new American policy system was going to stay, other parts of the system adjusted.

The general result was the second prominent pattern generated by the Great Broadening: the plateau, in which great growth occurred during the broadening period, but instead of declining after the peak, as occurred in the arc, a leveling off occurred. The broadening ceased, but important elements of it were not reversed. We find the plateau in many different data series, and we discuss them later in the book.

Feedback Politics and Plausibility Analysis

The analysis we present is firmly rooted in understandings of policy feedback developed by students of public policy over the years. The concept of feedback is best captured by Paul Pierson's (1993) essay title, "When

Effect Becomes Cause: Policy Feedback and Political Change." Policies cause subsequent reactions, but these reactions are varied (Mettler 2005; Campbell 2003; Campbell and Morgan 2005; Skocpol 1995; Hacker and Pierson 2014). In some cases, the policy disruption is so powerful that most elements of the policy-making system are strongly affected or even transformed.

Studying the Great Broadening and its aftermath offers a way to illuminate the fallacy of contemporaneous dynamics that a complex process can be caused by variables that occur simultaneously with the event of interest. For example, can changes in party control of government be associated with the Great Broadening? With each policy change, we immediately go to the "usual suspects" of partisan balance and other factors that occur contemporaneously with the policy change of interest. A focus on contemporaneous dynamics fails to predict the accretion of policy on which each "new" policy is built. Current political conflict is built on past policy changes—what else is there to fight about?

Even these feedback-based conceptions underestimate the great wake that flowed over U.S. politics following the expansion. Hacker and Pierson (2014, 644–48) develop the metaphor of "policy as terrain"—that is, contemporary politics is fought out on a terrain created by past policy decisions. To appreciate the effects of the Great Broadening on subsequent politics, we have to think of the policy terrain as subject to powerful "geologic" forces that radically alter the landscape in a short period of time.

Our analysis, of course, is by no means conclusive. We are observing a complex system in which cause and effect can intertwine like the double helix, and where complex nonlinearities are common; where autocatalytic processes (Padgett and Powell 2012) can self-sustain and create new organizational forms. In such a situation, the best we can do is a *plausibility analysis*. We rely on a combination of graphical presentations, historical analysis, theoretical connections, and, most importantly, the fundamental notion that an effect cannot precede a cause. To illustrate what we mean, we offer a simple example: the massive growth of the interest-group system cannot have caused the Great Broadening because it came after that expansion. This simple idea and graphical presentations of the variables of interest in our analysis lead to new perspectives on policy change.

Our graphical presentations adopt a minor but illuminating tweak on standard approaches. Most graphical programs depict the *X*-axis in extended form, with the *Y*-axis truncated, which has the visual effect of downplaying the relative size of changes in the *Y*-variable. This is particularly consequential if the *X*-axis is time. Here, we do the opposite. We truncate the *X*-axis, leading to an emphasis on the magnitude of changes in the *Y*-axis. For time series, this highlights the change rather than the passage of time (the figures in this chapter have this feature, which is continued throughout the book).

The Study of Extreme Events

Our study of the Great Broadening focuses on a single burst of activity. Is our study consequently unscientific, or, even worse, unsystematic? Political science is based in the search for the general, and it seems that we are arguing for the study of a unique event. But bursts of legislation and the expansion of the policy agenda (Ansolabehere, Palmer, and Schneer 2014; Whyman 2014; Huntington 1981; Schlesinger 1986) have occurred before in American politics and could do so again. Unfortunately, there is no general agreement on what defines the earlier periods, and scholars have come to different conclusions about what fundamentally characterizes them. The data from Ansolabehere, Palmer, and Schneer on US statutes indicate different historical bursts than the qualitative analyses of Huntington and Schlesinger.

Even if such events are historically unique, the underlying dynamics may not be. Treating our subject matter as outside the purview of social scientific analysis because of its uniqueness would be similar to cosmologists rejecting the study of the Big Bang, geologists rejecting the study of abnormally extreme earthquakes, and climate scientists rejecting the study of today's rapid global warming. Rather than being at the fringes of social science, understanding the causes and consequences of extreme events such as the Great Broadening should be at its core.

Furthermore, a specific extreme event is worthy of study in its own right, because such events may be pivotal in the development of a system. Social scientists used to eliminate "outliers" in their analyses on the grounds that they were atypical of the processes they were studying. The standard tool was (and still is) regression analysis, in which a dependent variable is caused by a series of independent variables, and the quality of the causal model is assessed by its fit to quantitative data. An outlier is a data point that is considerably beyond the typical range of the data used to fit the model. While the outlier could simply be an error in measurement, it also could be real, signaling something that should not be ignored.

It has become increasingly clear that such outliers are critical to understanding a process, not irrelevant to it. Indeed, a vigorous literature now studies extreme values, mostly from a stochastic-process vantage point. Unlike regression approaches, scholars employing stochastic-process methods start with a simple frequency distribution of a dependent variable and postulate models that are consistent with the observed distribution.

The Normal (or Gaussian) distribution is by far the most famous and generally the most useful of the probability distributions that underlie observed frequency distributions. For example, the classic incrementalist model of budgetary change, in which a budget for a government agency is simply an increment from last year's budget, generates a Normal distribution of budget changes if we aggregate across years or agencies (Padgett 1980).

It turns out that lots of distributions of interest to students of policy change are definitely not Normal. Budget-change data are not Normal (Padgett 1980; Jones and Baumgartner 2005). There are too many extreme budget changes and too few moderate budget adjustments. As a consequence, modern budget theorists have rejected the incrementalist model in its pure form and replaced it with models that incorporate both incrementalism and extreme changes in a single approach (Jones and Baumgartner 2005; Jones, Baumgartner, et al. 2009).

The importance of extremes has become clearer in natural sciences studies. Nassem Taleb (2008) popularized the study of extreme values as "black swans" because they were supposedly unpredictable. Others have noted that oftentimes these events were predictable (in a probabilistic sense), but people overlooked key indicators and were blinded by biases (that led to ignoring outliers, for example). They called these predictable but extreme events "white swans."

At one time, major earthquakes would have been black swans, inexplicable and unpredictable, but better measurement and better science is transforming them into white swans. Plate tectonics and better measures of earthquake occurrences at all scales and pressure build-ups on the plates are leading to probabilistic predictions of future earthquakes.

Scholars often isolate extreme events using stochastic-process methods, which involve constructing simple frequency distributions of changes from period to period. For example, figure 1.3, which graphs the number of Policy Agendas Project subtopics in landmark legislation passed per congress, displays some extreme changes. Some of these big changes are important, but some are less so (particularly the up-down pattern in the 81st Congress of 1949–51). We construct a simple histogram of the congress-to-congress percentage change in the number of different subtopics in Mayhew's landmark statutes (see fig. 1.4). Values above 0 indicate expansions in the number of subtopics in the laws; values below 0 indicate that fewer subtopics were addressed. The tails of the distribution represent very large changes, both up and down. It is also easy to see how far the distribution deviates from the familiar Normal distribution.[4] These kinds of distributions with fat tails signal important changes, but they can include aberrant cases.

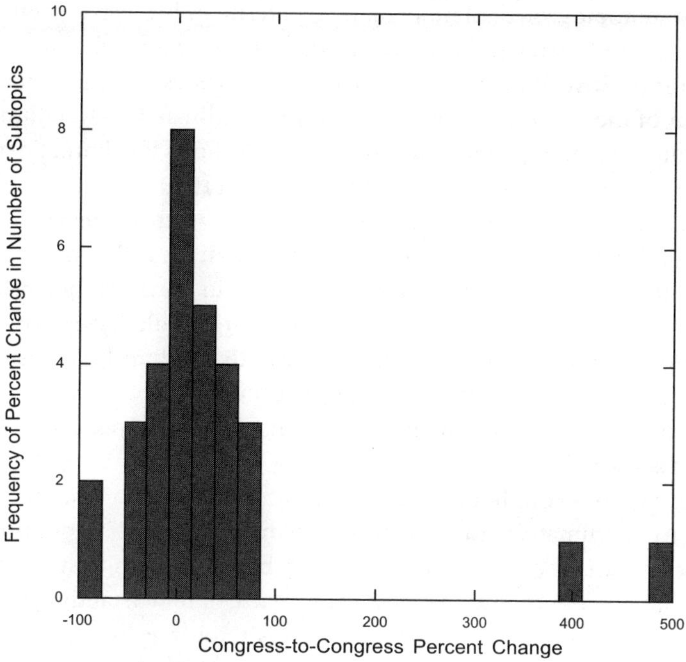

FIGURE 1.4. Congress-to-congress percentage change in the frequencies of Policy Agendas Project subtopics addressed in Mayhew's landmark laws

Rather than adopting the approach of ignoring or, even worse, deleting extreme observations, our study puts the focus on them. While normal year-to-year or congress-to-congress changes lend themselves to better systematic explanations, we think that approach focuses on the least interesting cases. Rather than studying the daily rain showers that make islands so tropical, we think it is more important to study the hurricanes that transform them. Even if the study of hurricanes is not as predictive as the study of rain showers, getting a handle on hurricanes, in the long run, will be at least as beneficial as understanding more typical weather patterns. By the end of the book, we hope that the reader agrees with us that the Great Broadening was a hurricane that dramatically changed the American political landscape.

What about the second issue raised by the study of the Great Broadening—that it was not a single event? While ignoring the extreme values and treating them as outliers, not worthy of study, quite obviously makes no sense, isolating extreme punctuations in policy change can underestimate the degree of change. Figure 1.4 shows three explosive changes (two in the positive direction; one in the negative) and some very sizable changes (six congresses involved subtopic growth of more than 60 percent; only one had reductions of more than 60 percent). The distribution is both fat-tailed and skewed toward the positive. We could examine these congresses in detail, but taking them out of the historical context would underestimate the overall magnitude of the lawmaking scope. After all, figure 1.2 shows the dramatic cumulative effect in the 86th through 90th Congresses (1959–68).

We can better understand what is going on if we treat this lawmaking bulge as a shift in the generating process rather than the action of politics as usual, with a couple of extreme events. By "a shift in the generating process" we mean that whatever caused the lawmaking surge could have been different in kind from the contemporaneous causes that political scientists typically use to understand political change. That generating process can involve interconnectedness among congresses that may not be properly assessed by standard statistical models.

Focusing on a couple of big changes rather than the broad arc would be akin to the climatologist focusing on the hourly rainfall amounts rather than the hurricane. While their models may be better at understanding the hourly rainfall amounts, doing so at the expense of understanding the hurricane would be a fool's errand. And so it is with outbreaks of policy activity, with the Great Broadening being the premiere modern example. Our variables for the big event may not be measured very well at present—such as social movements, networks of actors and groups that may wax and wane, and the contagion of ideas and emotions—in comparison to the standard suspects used by political scientists, such as elections and public opinion. The variables that we are interested in are likely to interact in extremely complex ways with each other and with standard political factors, leading to difficulties in assessing the causes of extreme processes such as the Great Broadening.

For naturally occurring extreme events, such as major hurricanes, surely we are as interested in effects as well as causes. Lives are lost, cities may be devastated, infrastructure is damaged, disease outbreaks are possible, all leading to potentially cascading events that can cause governments to collapse. Severe breaches in the normal policy process such as the emblematic Great Broadening surely lead to major consequences. But a focus on extreme changes in a time series of events can vastly underestimate the self-reinforcing processes that generate major shifts in the direction of public policy. These consequences can be transformative, and they in turn can have strong consequences. Or they may reinforce the changes more or less incrementally. In any case, we need better measures of interconnected, self-reinforcing processes than we have at present. Our use of plausibility analysis to gain some perspective on causal ordering, as described in the preceding section, is a first step on this journey.

As a consequence, the analysis we present throughout this book is highly suggestive of the argument we proffer; regrettably, we fall short of offering "proof." Scholars of American politics have gotten exceedingly good at knowing trees. By examining them in close detail and with a great deal of precision, we can usually arrive at a conclusion with a great deal of confidence. These analyses are valuable—indeed, we use their results for much of what underlies our analysis.

An examination of trees, though, does not provide a particularly good description of the forest. Individual elements are pinned down without much attention to the larger world in which they grow. Some analysis of the ecology of the forest is needed. A big, broad look at the forest does much for our understanding of how American politics operates today. More than that, we think that understanding the forest will help our tree analyses get even better.

Social scientists have figured out how to analyze trees; regrettably, we have not figured out much about how to analyze forests. In this book, we offer an analysis of the forest. Due to the nature of our enterprise, we are unlikely to present evidence as conclusive as that provided by scholars who examine trees. Over the broad sweep of tests that we present, though, we hope that we have captured a bit of what the forest is and how it operates. While some tree scholars may be unconvinced by our analysis, we are certain that we are adding to what is a paltry examination of the broader forest that we think is so badly needed. In the end, it is our contention that the forest plays a much bigger role in the growth of trees than an examination of the trees alone can possibly provide. Even if we cannot convince tree scholars that our specific, broader claims are true, none would ever suggest that the forest is immaterial to how trees grow. A wider examination of what has happened to the United States Government—both its broadening and its thickening—provides a perspective needed to appreciate how American politics operates today.

Summary

During the 1960s and 1970s, the United States experienced a great expansion of government involvement in society and the economy. In rapid succession, the federal government passed laws that limited the ability of businesses or local governments to exclude patrons based on race; ended discriminatory practices by state and local governments in voting; enacted major laws on health care, an area previously subject to little federal government involvement; initiated ongoing funding of cultural activities; vastly expanded environmental regulation and consumer protection; initiated urban and rural development programs; provided significant funding for primary and secondary education, ending a long-standing informal prohibition; passed major crime-control legislation, and much more.

Some of the programs of the Johnson and Nixon administrations *thickened* what was already within the provenance of government. While President Johnson initiated major new programs in transportation, the federal government had argued the wisdom of building transportation infrastructure since at least the construction of the Erie Canal. But other issues addressed during the period *broadened* government by initiating programs in areas where even proponents of federal intervention had feared to tread.

Just as important is what government considered, but failed to accomplish. Nixon proposed a guaranteed national income and universal health care, both of which died in Congress. The Equal Rights Amendment to bring about gender equality failed in the ratification process. Even a failed initiative indicates that the issue was no longer left up to civil society or state governments; rather, it had become part of the public debate on what the federal government ought to do about it.

Some programs suffered significant reversals, such as President Johnson's War on Poverty and many of the Great Society housing programs. But even though these initiatives were eliminated, public discussion about the issues did not end. Many times, an issue reappeared because participants saw the problem persisting, even though the particular solution may have faded in the minds of the participants. Once the barrier between what is proper for government and what should be left to the private sector or localities is breached, usually it is relatively easy to revive debate about it. That is why the agenda-setting process is so important in understanding the dynamics of the Great Broadening.

PART 1

The Internal Dynamics of the Great Broadening

Before the Great Broadening, the federal government was limited to far fewer activities than afterward. The new system exploded on a more tranquil system like a supernova, but its energy quickly faded. The result was a radically different system after the Great Broadening than before. What made this expansion possible? Causal processes differed more within the cauldron of the Great Broadening than they did before or after. The pace of policy-making increased, opening up many more opportunities for entrepreneurship. We explore these internal processes in the next three chapters.

TWO

Crossing the Legitimacy Barrier

Although the Great Broadening happened within a short period of time, it was a huge and complex event during which many issues came to be viewed as serious problems that required government action. What were the dynamics that fostered this explosion? We argue in this chapter that government faces two distinct kinds of issues: those that fit naturally into what government had already been doing and those for which government took responsibility for the first time. For simplicity's sake, we simply refer, respectively, to these as *old* and *new* issues.

We contend, and demonstrate later in the book, that different political dynamics underlie these two sets of issues. Old issues fit into preexisting frames based in partisan and ideological differences and interest-group politics. New issues do not immediately fit into such frames, and hence require some degree of recalibration as parties and groups adjust. Political leaders struggle to decide whether an issue should be addressed by the federal government or left to civil society or the states and localities. If the new issue is to be addressed by government, then how is it to fit in the preexisting frames structuring political conflict? One consequence of this dual struggle is that considerable organizational and policy innovation can emerge. During the cauldron of the Great Broadening, we would expect a great deal of such policy innovation to occur as new issues crowd the government's agenda. We provide both qualitative and quantitative evidence in support of this conjecture later.

The Two Faces of Policy Agendas

How the disadvantaged (or anyone else for that matter) get their policy proposals taken seriously (even if they are not adopted) is known in political science as the agenda-setting issue. The notion was born of the debate about the operation of American democracy that began in the 1950s and then exploded in a spirited and intense firefight about the extent to which the United States was democratic. But it was more: it was a debate about the very nature of political science, the scholarly discipline most concerned with power, rule, and authority (Dahl 1963).

Agenda-setting presents two distinct faces. The first face involves the simple selection of potential issues that could be addressed by policy-makers. Think of sitting at a window as traffic moves by. What attracts your attention? What do you notice? Certainly not everything. Just as individuals are limited in what they perceive in a complex and dynamic reality, so too are institutions (Jones 2001). Policy-makers can take cognizance of only a subset of the potential issues. Government decision-making institutions have limited capacities to access and react to issues, so there must be selectivity regarding which problems are addressed and which are ignored.

Examples of this issue-juggling aspect of policy selection abound. Both the press and members of Congress accused President Jimmy Carter of shoveling too many proposals at once onto the legislative branch. As Carter (1979, 371) admitted midway through his term, "Congress can only deal with so many issues simultaneously because, quite often, one of two committees in the Congress have to handle a series, a wide range, of issues." If one issue is addressed (i.e., is on the formal legislative agenda) the agenda space for other issues is more constrained. Though not particularly controversial, this understanding of agenda-setting is often unacknowledged in many models of legislative decision-making (Jones and Baumgartner 2005).

The second face implies that some issues are not viewed as legitimate for government to address, perhaps because the groups pressing those issues are viewed as less worthy than those already engaged in the process. Or perhaps the issues themselves are thought of as beyond the pale. This face of agenda-setting has a connotation of disadvantaged groups breaking through the barriers set by the powerful, who—consciously or not—acted to deny them access to serious consideration by government officials.

It is no accident that the agenda-setting debate in the academy took place as the Great Broadening gained steam. Political scientists and sociologists noticed how previously inactive groups were bombarding government with demands for action on issues that did not fit the mold of the issues inherited from long-standing political tradition. Some of these older issues had preoccupied the federal government since the founding of the Republic. Others were added over time—especially during the New Deal. Groups demanded policy action in areas previously left to civil society, asked for federal interference into discriminatory practices of state governments, and wanted expenditures in areas that the federal government had previously ignored.

The new issue revolution associated with the Great Broadening changed the intellectual debate over the role of government. It affected the nature of the discussion about American democracy, shifting it from a debate about balanced interests and the role of political parties to one based in the resistance of American institutions to the demands of the less fortunate and those excluded from the ongoing formal policy debate.

Over time many of the initiatives of the excluded gained serious attention, and in many cases stimulated real policy action. In some cases conservatives pushed back, stalling or even reversing policy momentum. Some of this push-back was bipartisan, as in the case for deregulation of some regulated industries during the Carter administration. In other cases, conservatives added to the broadening of government, particularly in areas such as criminal justice.

Nevertheless, in most cases the issues remained, if not on the center stage of government action, then at least in the close background. The question of denying some issues or groups access to the government's agenda has been replaced by the question of how much intervention is necessary. In short, the question of government involvement has shifted from "Whether to act?" to "How much to act?"

We make three critical claims in this chapter. The first, noted above, is that the American political system processes issues differently, depending on whether the policy-making system has regularly dealt with the issue before ("old issues") or whether it is a fresh issue that must be defined and understood ("new issues"). In the former case, the issues generally are understood according to earlier framings. These framings can be partisan, ideological, or group-based; the key is that they are stable. The system, in fitting the new issues into preexisting frames, often struggles to determine the proper fit. Is the issue a legitimate function of government? Or should it be left to civil society? If it is legitimate, should the federal government get involved, or should the issue be left to the states and localities? Should new agencies be established, or should the new function be assigned to existing bureaucracies? How do the parties decide what positions to take on the emerging issues?

The second claim is that the political system evolved under the pressure of the new issues that bombarded the system in the 1960s and 1970s. The entire political system changed as the new issues gained access to the system. In this chapter, we trace these changes by analyzing how political scientists and other observers evaluated the system during this period. Admittedly our examinations will be partial, but the flavor of the changing emphasis of the literature is undeniable. Later in the book we document this transformation quantitatively, showing just how policy changes altered the entire political system and how it operated.

The final claim is that the magnitude of new issues demanding policy attention necessitated rapid policy innovation during the relatively brief period of the Great Broadening. As a consequence, the entire system developed structures designed to foster such innovation. But those structures have been winnowed in the ensuing period, leaving the system less able to address current issues. These "downstream" changes include increasing partisan polarization and decreased analytical capacity.

Agenda Broadening and the Legitimacy Barrier

As we noted in chapter 1, Theodore Lowi (1967) argued that the old American public philosophy resting on the distinction between public and private spheres was dead. It had been replaced by a public philosophy based in the pluralist group struggle—what he called "interest-group liberalism." He decried this as an undemocratic public philosophy, as he saw policymakers delegating their policy responsibilities to organized interests. Lowi's analysis implies that it was the rapid increase in issues that caused the crisis in the old public philosophy. The choice of the mechanism that a political system uses to address issues is secondary to the overload of new issues. Other scholars confirmed Lowi's early diagnosis as the Great Broadening proceeded—the public-private distinction was dead.

James Q. Wilson (1979) emphasized what he termed the "legitimacy barrier"—what issues were treated as appropriate concerns of government. Like Lowi, Wilson saw a systematic destruction of the public-private distinction and went further to argue that this destruction had fundamentally altered the conduct of politics: "Once the 'legitimacy barrier' has fallen, political conflict takes a very different form. New programs need not await the advent of a crisis or an extraordinary majority because no program is any longer 'new'—it is seen, rather, as an extension, a modification, or an enlargement of something the government is already doing" (41). The strategies that groups use when they are dealing with a well-understood political terrain in which the conflict is about "how much" to intervene is different in kind than conflict about "whether" to intervene.

Wilson's analysis implies that once an issue is viewed as a legitimate one for government to address, that issue remains within the purview of government. The barrier becomes a floor. He also saw the accumulation of policies that addressed issues previously unaffected by government action, and how that would cause politics to infuse more and more issue areas.

The legitimacy barrier was certainly psychological and even philosophical. Wilson thought of it as a political barrier as well. Congress created new agencies to manage the new issues and to provide a bureaucratic rule base for the regular conduct of activity. Once they entered into the policy fray, the interest groups helped to cement the legitimacy of an issue as one appropriate for government action. Businesses first fought, and later found ways to profit, from the new normal. Political parties began to sort themselves on the new issue configurations as they determined their relative strategic advantages in the post-broadening world. Democrats moved to incorporate civil rights into their agenda, and Republicans moved to fill the vacuum by appealing to white Southerners. Environmentalism once split the parties, but over time Democrats adopted the pro-environment mantle, while Republicans defined environmentalism as antibusiness and hence antigrowth. Women's rights, more within the purview of Republicans initially, shifted toward the Democrats. The rapid increases in the breadth of government during the Great Broadening affected both interest groups and parties. This component of crossing the legitimacy barrier is so important that we spend a great deal of the latter chapters documenting it quantitatively.

Indeed, we show that the business of government was conducted differently before, during, and after the broadening period. Before the Great Broadening, government was conducted in relatively independent "silos," or subsystems, often consisting of relevant congressional committees, government agencies, and affected interest groups. During the broadening, issues spilled over from silo to silo as issues such as civil rights and the environment affected numerous policy areas simultaneously. Rapid changes within and between subsystems required innovative organizational and policy arrangements as networks of actors sprawled across traditional boundaries. Political parties presented innovative policy solutions to address the panoply of issues they faced. The Nixon administration, in particular, was bubbling with new ideas to consolidate and reduce the hand of government that was generated by the new programs of the Kennedy-Johnson years. Nixon proposed a guaranteed national income to replace the hodge-podge of welfare systems, a national health care system to replace the similarly chaotic health care approaches developed to address particularistic constituencies, and block grants to states and localities to consolidate the program-by-program approach of Kennedy-Johnson fiscal federalism.

The same year that Wilson published his classic essay, Aaron Wildavsky (1979) published his wide-ranging collection of essays in *Speaking Truth to Power*. In the chapter entitled "Policy as Its Own Cause," he detailed the changes in how policy-making was conducted after policies were enacted. Once enacted, policies may encounter problems because they were ill-designed in the first place or because the incentives of actors to shift required continual updating as times change. Agencies adjust to the changing reality by generating new regulations or proposals for new policies. "As problems grow, solutions create their own effects, which gradually displace the original difficulty. . . . Because policy is evermore its own cause, programs depend less on the external environment than on events inside the sectors from which they come" (62–63).

This line of thinking thrives today in the idea of policy feedback. After noting that policies may be thought of as institutions, because "policies clearly do establish rules and create constraints that shape behavior," Paul Pierson (1994, 44) continues: "Policies may create incentives that encourage the emergence of elaborate social and economic networks, greatly increasing the cost of adopting once-possible alternatives and inhibiting exit from a current policy path." Hacker and Pierson (2012) developed the idea of "policy drift" to denote the changes that nongovernmental actors make in response to economic and social trends that require a policy to be updated if it is to remain effective. This updating may not occur because of institutional friction or agenda crowding, leading to policies that do not fit either the current circumstances or the original intent of the policies.

These ideas transcended political philosophies. Both conservative and liberal political thinkers have noted that past policies strongly affect the process of current policy-making. Well-known theorists of the left, Lowi and Hacker and Pierson, join the neoliberals (conservatives) Wilson and Wildavsky in their understanding of how the very nature of politics is transformed by the substance of policy. Interestingly, both Wilson and Hacker and Pierson use the "policy as terrain" metaphor. Both see policy as occurring on a new landscape—the entire terrain of politics is deformed by policies.

Using the Policy Agendas Project to Measure the Great Broadening

Just how powerful was the Great Broadening? Was the Great Broadening merely rhetorical, or did it permeate all levels of the federal agenda, from debating nascent policies in hearings to passing laws and empowering federal agencies to promulgate new regulations? To assess the power and depth of the transformation we call the Great Broadening, we measure changes in the policy scope of government over time and across these different phases of the formal policy-making agenda using data from the US Policy Agendas Project (https://www.comparativeagendas.net/). The classification system, developed by Bryan Jones and Frank Baumgartner, was designed to be inter-temporally consistent, ensuring comparability across time in its categories. The system applies the same coding scheme to most of its datasets, allowing comparisons across different measures of activity. Activity within content categories in congressional hearings, for example, may be compared to activity on roll-call votes. The US Policy Agendas Project now publishes twenty different data series, eighteen of which are coded according to this same single, universal, and consistent coding scheme.

The Policy Agendas system codes policy outputs back to the early post-war period, enabling scholars to trace government activity designated by each code from the end of the war to the end of each data series (Baumgartner et al., 1998). The coding scheme currently consists of 220 subtopics nested within twenty major topics, each of which describes a discrete policy domain. For example, the major topic "Energy" is subdivided into nine subtopics, including "Coal," "Alternative Energy," and "Nuclear Energy," among others (see https://www.comparativeagendas.net/us for the complete list of subtopic codes nested within major topics).

As in almost any hierarchical scheme, topics are rarely identical in their scope—that is, the range of subtopics they cover. For example, Tax Code covers a wider range of content than does Consumer Safety. The coding scheme attempts to balance the inherent heterogeneity associated with too few topic categories with the promulgation of literally thousands of overly specific, but internally homogeneous, code categories that would have contained too few observations to make meaningful comparisons between topics (Baumgartner and Leech 1998). The originators of the coding scheme attempted to choose major topics that covered a roughly equal breadth of subtopics, and subtopics that covered a roughly equal breadth of subsidiary content.

The unavoidable reality that subtopics have different scopes is unlikely to affect our analysis. Given that we are interested in using the Policy Agendas Project data to pinpoint when new issues move onto the government agenda and for how long they remain there, perfectly equal scopes among categories are less important than inter-temporal consistency within a category (Jones 2016a). In a temporally consistent coding scheme, a topic code will have the same meaning, even if the language or key terms used to describe it have changed over time.

If a measurement system is not inter-temporally consistent, it cannot be used to generate reliable time series on government activities. A temporally inconsistent scheme adds new codes to represent an extant policy that is merely being discussed in new terms, thereby destroying the potential for it to be used as a temporally consistent measurement system. Adding new codes haphazardly may also introduce topics that have a much narrower scopes on average than extant categories.

If new codes are added or existing codes recombined into new subtopics, each observation in every Policy Agendas dataset is recoded to preserve inter-temporal reliability—ensuring what we call backward compatibility. This recoding ensures that each series, from beginning to end, has the same meaning throughout the period of measurement. Because the project applies the same codes to a variety of government outputs across time, we can use their datasets to trace the amount of attention government is paying to issues across several phases of the agenda-setting and policy-making process. For example, we can assess how much more members of Congress are talking about alternative energy in hearings in 2012 than they were in 1962, or how many more laws Congress enacted in the realm of nuclear energy in the late 1950s than it did in the 1990s.

Using the Policy Agendas database with its temporally consistent coding scheme also enables us to pinpoint the precise moment that a new issue crosses the legitimacy barrier and joins the mix of topics under discussion on the federal government's agenda. For example, using the hearings dataset, we can show that members of Congress formally began discussing federal involvement in parental leave and childcare in 1949. Over the next fourteen years, the bills dataset documents that members introduced sixty bills dealing with various facets of this policy area; none became laws. The public law dataset reveals that Congress moved from discussion to action in this domain for the first time in 1963, when it passed a law allowing child-care expenses to be tax-deductible for women who had been abandoned by and could not locate their husbands (Public Law 88–4). The genesis of the federal government's intrusion into all 220 subtopics can be mapped out in a similar manner as the parental leave and child-care example, illustrated above.

In addition to measuring the intrusion of new issues onto the federal agenda, the coding scheme enables us to capture the broadening of that agenda. To measure broadening, we use Baumgartner and Jones's (2015, 188–89) operationalization, which counted the number of subtopics in which a particular government activity took place. For example, Congress held no hearings on recycling and members introduced no bills on the subject until 1970; it was simply not on the agenda. Contrast that with the

Species and Forest subtopic within the Environment major topic code. In every single congress since the 80th Congress, members have introduced bills and committees have held hearings that involved the subtopic. The latter would add to the broadening in every congress; the former would only add to the count beginning with the 91st Congress (1969–70). The 80th Congress (1947–48) held 2,705 hearings on 160 subtopics; the 94th Congress (1975–76) held 3,333 hearings on 201 subtopics. Not only did the activity grow by 23 percent, but the scope of government grew by 26 percent. We think it is the latter that had more drastic consequences on how the American political system operates not only then, but today as well.

Due the reliability and flexibility of the coding scheme the Policy Agendas Project employs, scholars in Europe and elsewhere have developed similar projects, allowing for a comparison of agenda-setting and policy-making processes across different institutional arrangements. This collaborative effort, the Comparative Agendas Project (https://www.comparativeagendas.net/), makes the comparative study of broadening a distinct possibility.

The Legislative Hearing: A Prime Indicator of the Legitimacy Barrier

In this book, we use congressional hearings as our prime (but by no means only) measure of the scope of the policy-making agenda. If an issue is considered by a congressional committee, either in its bill referral or oversight function, that issue is clearly up for serious consideration and thus on the formal agenda. The issue has crossed Wilson's legitimacy barrier; it is no longer unacceptable for the federal government to consider it for policy action. A proposal addressing the issue may not get enacted into law; indeed, it may not even make it out of committee. Nevertheless, its probability of advancing is greatly improved once the committee devotes time to its consideration. We could use bill introductions as an indicator of crossing the legitimacy barrier, but the bar is too low. It is too easy to introduce a bill, although introductions can be important in "softening up" the system for eventually crossing the legitimacy barrier. Other measures, such as receiving a formal vote by a legislative chamber, miss the importance of getting action via informal pressure from the visibility provided by a formal legislative hearing. Moreover, as we show in chapter 3, once an issue reaches the hearings stage, it seldom drops entirely off the formal agenda. It almost always receives attention in hearings in subsequent congresses.

Unfortunately, as the political parties have taken an increasing role in recent years in controlling legislation, it is possible that this measure may not be as meaningful in the future. But it remained a vibrant indicator during the period of study addressed in this book.

The Great Broadening in the Data

After the 82nd Congress (1951–52), committees began holding hearings on a growing array of new policy areas (see fig. 2.1). Committees in the House held hearings on 114 different subtopics in the 82nd Congress (1951–52) and steadily increased up to 187 subtopics in the 94th Congress (1975–76). Since then, the number of subtopics addressed by hearings has varied between 158 and 193. The expansion of topics in Senate hearings follows a similar pattern. In the 82nd Congress, Senate committees held hearings on 97 distinct subtopics before their agenda broadened to a peak of 177 subtopics in the 96th Congress (1979–80). Following this peak, the Senate held hearings on no fewer than 152 topics in each subsequent congress. This exemplifies the plateau pattern that approximates the lock-in pattern of historical institutionalism and punctuated equilibrium.

Of 220 subtopics we analyzed, 62 appeared in at least one hearing in every congress from 1946 to 2013. These issues had become the province of the federal government by 1946, and never avoided the active purview of congressional committees during our period of study. These issues included basic defense, economic, transportation, and regulatory subtopics, many of which were established during the 1930s. Another 118 of these subtopics gained access to the policy-making agenda at one time or another during the postwar period. Around 30 came onto the agenda during the late 1940s and early 1950s;[1] these issues included many additional foreign-policy and defense issues, along with others concerning the economy, agriculture, and labor relations. The other issues in this group (90 or so) joined the agenda during the Great Broadening, and included civil rights, health care, product regulation, environmental issues, and other primarily domestic matters. Finally, 30 subtopics moved on and off the agenda, sometimes attracting congressional attention and sometimes not.

Most of the issues addressed by congressional committees in the post–World War II era have remained "stuck" on the policy-making agenda. Only a few seem to have been subject to the window of passing attention. Nevertheless, selective attention and policy prioritization are critical in understanding which of the prospective policies move from the committee stage to the floors of the House or Senate. Being subject to continuous interest does not mean that an issue has necessarily resulted in policy change.

We provide a more detailed analysis of the cumulative addition of issues in chapter 4, but this summary indicates that most issues, once seriously

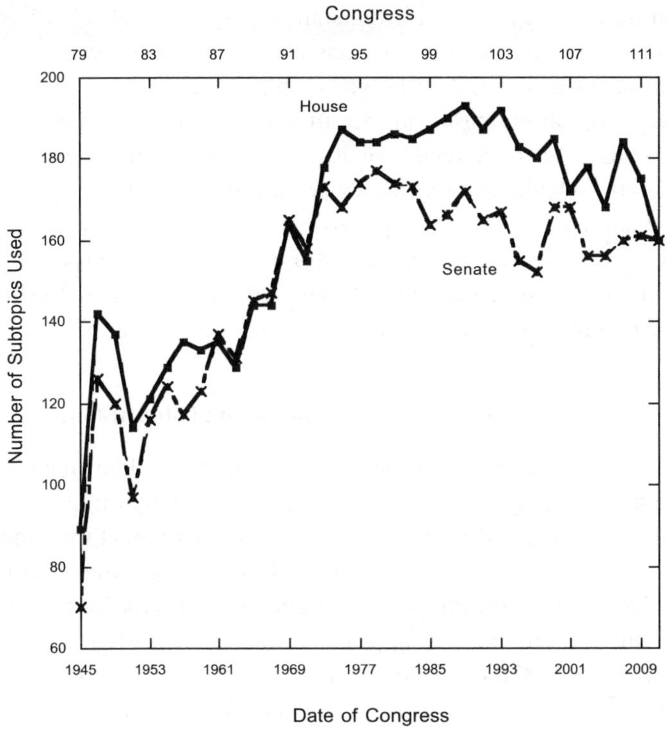

FIGURE 2.1. Count of subtopics addressed in at least one hearing, House and Senate, 80th–112th Congresses

raised in committee, do not exit the agenda; only a few issues move on and off the formal legislative agenda; and the system incorporated the new issues in rapid-fire fashion during a historically brief period of time.

How the American Politics Literature Changed as the Political System Evolved

A notion that has gained great credibility among political scientists is that a science of politics must affirm timeless generalizations. To construct generalizable theories of politics, one needs abstract laws that apply regardless of place and time. If it existed, such a science of politics would have its parallel in Newtonian physics. But if the "policy as terrain" approach is valid, then any generalization is contingent on context. Political science is more Darwinian than Newtonian.

Certainly the fundamental understanding by political scientists of the operation of the American system has changed over the years. But these observations have changed strikingly as the political system evolved, suggesting that the observations are not timeless. Rather they are historically contingent. Our selective review of some of these observations, especially those directly related to how issues get taken seriously by government, vividly illustrates our point. As government changed, theories of politics changed. Maybe theories got better or more scientific, but it is clearly possible that they changed as government changed. We characterize the literature on policy-making processes as passing through three main phases.

Phase I: The Roles of Interest Groups and Political Parties

Post–World War II political science tended to stress mechanisms that stabilized the governing system. Many political scientists had moved toward a view of democracy that downplayed citizen participation; at the time, many scholars viewed the masses as incapable of processing issues in a manner that could achieve a common good. Some scholars emphasized competition among political parties for the support of voters as the key to democratic rule (Schumpeter 1942). Others, following James Madison, stressed the role of active interest groups in a pluralistic society as critical (Truman 1951). Yale political scientist Robert Dahl (1956; 1961) provided a more complex picture by recognizing the role of the rule of law, protection of minorities, the entrepreneurial role of politicians, and elections as referenda on past performance of elites. Elites were viewed as governing because masses had authorized them to do so through elections. Because low turnout could indicate acceptance of the governing system, many political scientists were not overly troubled by low turnout elections, so long as voting laws were open and fair. Indeed, high turnout elections had characterized European nondemocratic regimes. The proponents argued that they were not pursuing normative issues; rather, they asserted that they were constructing a realistic empirical description of democracy. Nevertheless Dahl (1956) judged the United States to be close to failing the tests he established for democratic rule, so even in the very best literature of the period, scholars like Dahl harbored a nagging unease.

Phase 2: Integrating the Excluded

The 1960s brought a more radical critique of this elitist theory of democracy. Against the widespread disenfranchisement of blacks, the low general levels of electoral engagement, and the limited participation of women and the poor in political decision-making, the depictions of democracy based on the consent of the governed seemed incongruous. The obvious explanation was that disadvantaged groups lacked resources to participate at anywhere near the rates of more advantaged citizens. Moreover, change was difficult, because the institutional rules made it so difficult to assemble popular majorities and because too many citizens, particularly African-Americans, were excluded from participation by election laws. The agenda-setting perspective brought a cultural or idea-based component to the radical critique of the prevailing, more conservative model of democracy. Elites possessed advantages far beyond what a simple resource model would suggest. These included not just resource advantages, but the ability to manipulate cultural symbols to keep items off the agenda—in Wilson's terms, they could convince people that the issue was not a legitimate one for government to address.

The key to politics was the containment of conflict. If conflict could be contained to limited issues and those issues could be assigned to subsystems dominated by interests, and if a pluralism of interests were represented, then the system would be both stable and reasonably democratic. Too stable, said the critics. E. E. Schattschneider's (1957; 1960) notion of conflict expansion became the keystone. In any political conflict, losers often have the option of bringing in allies, broadening the conflict from its current confines. He saw interest groups as conflict-containing mechanisms and political parties as essential in expansion. Schattschneider warned that this strategy carried risks because the disadvantaged might be overpowered by counter-mobilization by the advantaged—a caution often ignored by both participants and analysts.

Issue expansion in the body politic involves a struggle over the prioritization of issues for public debate. In the institutional setting of American democracy, issue expansion often implies moving from a general societal discussion to a formal position on the agenda of a decision-making body such as Congress. As a consequence, the other side of conflict expansion is issue prioritization within a decision-making body. Although many authors addressed this basic idea indirectly, the first explicit use of the term *policy agenda* that we can find was in 1966 by Jack Walker in his "Critique of the Elitist Theory of Democracy" (1966). Walker referred to the "agenda of controversy, the list of questions which are recognized by the active participants in politics as legitimate subjects of attention and concern" (292).

The vigorous debate about democracy in America provided the context for the increasing interest in how formal political institutions prioritized issues for consideration. Dahl's (1961) comprehensive study of power in New

Haven was in part political theory, expanding the pluralist understanding of democracy. It recognized a key role for political leaders in prioritizing issues and actively assembling coalitions to achieve progress on those issues.

The critics of the pluralist school were dissatisfied with models of democracy that tolerated low levels of participation (Krouse 1982). Many also attacked the behavioral movement that was flowering at the time, especially its emphasis on empirical tests of ideas drawn from normative considerations. Critics thought that emphasis was too rooted in the status quo—start with observing the status quo, and one ends up justifying the prevailing rules, norms, and distribution of power normatively.

Because the critics conflated the justification of American democracy with the use of empirical methods, and sparred with behavioralists over these methods, it took quite a while for the study of agenda-setting to become established as a rigorous pursuit. Many empiricists dismissed the notion of agenda-setting because it seemed to them not capable of systematic measurement and hence unscientific.

In every society some individuals and groups are more influential in politics than others. In democracies, this division is less important than whether it is immutable. Can the less politically powerful change their situations through the democratic process? Can disadvantaged groups "break through" the cultural and institutional barriers to get their ideas taken seriously? Or do wealth and status confer such enormous advantages that the less fortunate are, for all practical purposes, shut out of the political arena?

The key insight of the scholars adopting an agenda-setting perspective was that politics had a predecisional phase. Politics occurred not only in an overt struggle over issues between parties, among groups, and within the formal branches of government, but it also happened "primordially." Peter Bachrach and Morton Baratz (1962; 1963) introduced the notion of *non-decisions* to describe those predecisional features of choice that involved a decision-maker taking into consideration factors before the actual debate took place. These aspects could involve anticipated reactions of powerful actors, but they also could involve cultural limits on what were seen generally as appropriate actions for government to take. Items viewed as not proper objects of new government policy interventions sometimes crossed over into the domain of active controversy, but most did not.

It is hard to overemphasize the radical connotation that the term *agenda-setting* had when it initially appeared in the scholarly literature. It was radical in three senses. First, many political scientists were unprepared to accept the idea that anything beyond the purview of normal, observable political interactions could be important. Certainly it seemed to run counter to the move to make political science less normative and more quantitative—two basic tenets of the behavioral movement.

Second, agenda-setting carried with it the notion that barriers to participation by new groups carrying new issues into politics were powerful and went beyond the formal barriers of friction and resistance in political systems. The democratic playing field was not fair, and it was not fair because of the abilities of political elites to structure the terms of the debate to suit their preferences. Pluralists and behavioralists were quite prepared to accept the unfairness but saw it as based in measurable aspects of the polity, such as the distribution of resources that could be marshaled in the political fight (e.g., income, wealth, knowledge, votes). But the agenda-setting perspective implied that the terms of the debate—the cultural rules of the game—were set unfairly. That proposition resisted measurement and threatened the more comforting view of democracy championed by the pluralists.

Finally, the whole notion of agenda-setting was radical because of the solutions some of its proponents proposed. Many scholars who adopted the agenda-setting perspective viewed major change as occurring through disruptions, not simply through the normal practice of politics. Parties and groups were not enough; social movements, destabilization, and even violence seemed to many agenda-setting scholars to be necessary components.

Schattschneider (1957; 1960), while noting the imbalance in the interest-group system and the defects in theories of democracy relying solely on group interactions, found an opportunity for redress within the rules of democracy. He saw an ability of the disadvantaged to expand political conflict from confined decision-making systems, such as the interactions between legislatures and interest groups, to broader venues, especially public debates involving political parties, the press, and broad groups of voters. Later, Emmette Redford (1969), although never citing Schattschneider, developed a robust institutional framework for what Schattschneider termed *conflict expansion*.

Both Schattschneider and Redford saw self-corrective mechanisms within the institutional structures of democracy. Yet a substantial group of scholars did not. Rather, they saw, in the words of sociologist William Gamson (1968) a system of "stable unrepresentation." This scholarly debate broke out into outright hostility in the arena of the study of community power. The largest firefight about democracy came from behavioral political scientists, who chose the place to fight those more critical of the extent of democracy. The behavioralists, arguing that political science should rely more on direct observation and quantitative data than it had previously, challenged the critics on both their theory of power and the methods they used for studying it (Polsby 1963). At its height, the debate, which morphed far beyond the confines of urban governance, where it began, became highly spirited and contentious (Walker 1966; Dahl 1966).[2]

The behavioralists were not wrong in their insistence on measurement and testing, nor were they wrong in noting the self-fulfilling nature of the reputational approach. Yet they underestimated the power of cultural barriers to steer the debate and even thwart access to the active political debate. Elitists, for the most part, had discredited themselves by taking on both pluralism and empiricism at once. But the pluralists risked throwing the proverbial baby out with the bathwater by dismissing the idea of nondecisions. Pluralist Raymond Wolfinger's (1971) rejection of nondecisions (incidentally the most accessible summary of the idea), though, was based on the difficulty of assessing the components of nondecisions rather than on the quality of the ideas.

Phase 3: Taming the Radical Idea of Agenda-Setting Through Measuring Issue Attention

Over time this radical idea was tamed through the work of scholars focusing on the analytical elements of the notion. Cobb and Elder (1983) developed the idea of policy agendas by collecting a set of related ideas from Schattschneider's notion of conflict containment and expansion to Bachrach and Baratz's (1963) nondecisions. They started with a good dose of the radical critique, but toned down the language, gave pluralism full credit for the power of its ideas and empiricism, and went on to develop an integrative and empirically grounded inventory of propositions relating to agenda-building (as they called it) and issue development.

In Cobb and Elder's (1983) formulation, challengers had two problems. First, they had to gain access to the "systemic agenda," which they defined as "issues that are commonly perceived by members of the political community as meriting public attention, and as involving matters within the legitimate jurisdiction of existing governmental authority" (85). That was not enough; second, challengers had to access "the formal or institutional agenda," which they defined as "the set of items explicitly up for the active and serious consideration of authoritative decision-makers" (86). That did not guarantee success, as their proposals might well not survive the normal processes of government. It did, at least, allow serious consideration by decision-makers.

Part of the agenda-setting dynamic was always based in the limited attention spans of political systems. The idea that policy-making organizations have limited abilities to focus attention on problems was central to the initial development of the agenda-setting concept. Crenson (1971) distinguished non-decision-making stemming from limited attention from that more attributable to manipulation by entrenched elites. He depicted political issues as "transitory, episodic phenomena" (178) that offered but brief openings for those who would challenge the status quo. Yet he centered much of his analysis on "offstage power to enforce political inaction" (24).

The issue-attention aspect of agenda-setting proved to be far more amenable to measurement and hence systematic analysis than other aspects of the agenda-setting problem. Cobb, Ross, and Ross (1976) detail three models of agenda-building, two of which emerge inside government and one outside; they do not dwell on the "offstage" agenda-denial component of the idea. John Kingdon's (1995) work incorporating Cohen, March, and Olson's (1972) garbage-can model viewed the key to accessing the formal agenda as a window of opportunity, as when problems, solutions, political feasibility came together in time. The key driver of the model is attention—when attention to the three metaphorical streams came together, policy change was possible. The confluence of streams occurred through the sublimely boundedly rational notion of limited but focused attention—an approach that came to be known as attention-driven choice (Jones 2001).

Agendas and Instability (Baumgartner and Jones [1993] 2009) carries some of the democratic critique inherited from Cobb and Elder and the early theorists. The book begins: "Does the American political system provide safe haven for privileged economic interests, or does it ensure competition among political ideas, constantly providing opportunities for those on the losing side of the debate to reverse their fortunes?" (1). The dynamics of the punctuated equilibrium model proposed in the book are well within the parameters of the operation of American politics, but with much more attention to the institutional structure of issue attention and policy change. *Agendas and Instability* recognized the disadvantages of minorities and other excluded groups but treated the barriers as mostly resource-based. But Baumgartner and Jones thought that in a dispersed democracy with multiple venues, such as the United States, it was difficult to stop determined political actors from finding leverage to gain access to the policy-making agenda.

Over time, as measurement strategies and analytical techniques evolved, the attention limits of policy-making institutions became increasingly dominant. The process of better measurement and tighter analysis was accompanied by a decline in the more radical elements of the initial concept. Today we stress issue attention and the nature of friction in political systems (Jones, Sulkin, and Larsen 2003; Jones and Baumgartner 2005), the institutional and resource-based components of agenda-setting.

By the mid-2000s the agenda-setting problem had become a part of a broader *issue-attention literature* (Jones and Baumgartner 2005). This focus led to important developments in the policy-process literature by allowing the initial idea of punctuation to develop into a robust theory of information-processing based in bounded rationality in the policy-making process (Jones 2001; Jones and Baumgartner 2012; Baumgartner and Jones 2015; Workman and Shafran 2015). As these theoretical developments proceeded, so did the ability of scholars to measure the ascension of issues to the formal policy-making agenda.

All of these developments rely on the conception of agenda-setting as issue attention. More critical views of the political system have not disappeared from agenda scholarship. Roger Cobb and his collaborators (Cobb and Ross 1997; Rochefort and Cobb 1994) have provided close analytical and empirical studies, particularly focusing on the "cultural denial" component of agenda-setting. Schneider and Ingram (1993) highlight the difficulty of addressing issues where the target population is generally viewed negatively—suggesting that these issues face a cultural barrier, not just resource limitations. It is hard to accept that agenda-setting is nothing more than issue-juggling, and agenda scholars may have done so because the measurement of the formal agenda has improved so dramatically. But it is more likely that the political system evolved to allow for many more issues to coexist on the agenda, with policy-makers shifting attention from one to another, and with this component occupying more and more of their time and effort.

The Tension between Political Mobilization and Institutional Resistance

The Great Broadening was the "big bang" of modern American politics, but was it unique, a historical confluence of forces not likely to be repeated? Causation in the case of a singular event in a social system with multiple interacting parts is devilishly difficult to determine, and we examine this causal complexity later. For now, we set the stage for what is to come.

We can think of agenda-setting in a somewhat different light that captures the role of institutions in a more dynamic fashion. Political institutions provide stability by requiring an orderly process for addressing issues, but by doing so they also act as a brake on change. William Riker (1980, 445) once referred to institutions as "congealed tastes" from the past.

In the American system, with its requirements for supermajorities to enact policies, this resistance is deliberately set high. This resistance, or friction (Jones and Baumgartner 2005), means that policy change can be quite difficult. The first step in that process is to get policy-makers to take an issue seriously—that is, to get it on the policy-making agenda.

Institutional resistance is not the only barrier to getting an issue on the agenda. Indeed, it is easier to get an issue considered than to get it passed, at least if we focus only on institutional resistance. But cognitive (for example, the status-quo bias most people hold most of the time) and cultural resistance can also make agenda access difficult for less-favored groups and the issues they champion.

If both cognitive and cultural resistance augment this normal institutional resistance, then the barriers to change become truly daunting. Large-scale resistance leads to long periods of limited policy change. Policy change is not inevitable, but a plausible process of *error accumulation*, in which a policy-making system falls further and further behind what might seem to be adaptive necessities. Error accumulation does not necessarily imply mistakes; it simply means that a system's responses to its environment are not in sync with environmental pressures for change.

Because of the built-in stabilizers of institutional resistance, any policy-making system responds disjointedly and episodically to adaptive pressures from its environment. This resistance is overcome not magically but through political mobilization, which can be through traditional means, such as parties, interest groups, and individual activity. It may also come through social movements, which are based on mass activity, driven by high levels of passion and commitment, and are often not connected strongly to the traditional means of political mobilization. These mobilization movements are sometimes termed grassroots movements to connote their bottom-up nature. It is not uncommon for parties to try to coopt the energy in such movements, aiming to harness it for electoral purposes.

If cognitive and cultural pressures augment institutional resistance, then mobilization must be large to overcome the resistance. Large-scale mobilization generally comes via social movements that may or may not sweep up political parties and interest groups in their cause. Large-scale mobilizations can lead to large-scale changes through the mechanisms of contagion and spillover. In such cases, it may be necessary for traditional avenues of mobilization to join the passions of the grassroots movement to overcome the structural, cognitive, and cultural barriers to agenda access and subsequent policy change.

That is what we think happened in the Great Broadening. Waves of social movements wracked the political system in quick succession—civil rights, environmentalism, women's rights, and consumer protection, with the political parties sorting through the rapidly changing policy terrain as barrier after barrier fell.

The role of mobilization uncontained by the party system and sometimes in spite of it is a natural occurrence in the American system—it is a feature, not a "bug." The high levels of resistance to change mean that at times strong levels of mobilization are necessary. Moreover, as political elites try to consolidate their gains, they can build an even more resistant system through all the mechanisms that some of the more radical theorists of the 1960s discussed. While the American political system has become more open, and hence more subject to the dynamics of issue-juggling, it is not immune to the rarer dynamics of the Great Broadening.

Agenda-Setting Today

The process of breaching the legitimacy barrier in an area is qualitatively different from the subsequent growth of government in that area. That initial action in a new policy area is a precursor to subsequent growth, and it makes that growth easier. Even more critically, the breaching process alters the very terms of the debate fundamentally—from "whether" to consider an issue to "how?" or "how much?" Moreover, after the breach, problems often emerge in the policy that *only* government can address.

Yet resistance to new ideas still exists in the system, formal checks and balances stymie action, and opponents continue to use the strategy of treating ideas as illegitimate. "Culture-induced equilibria" operate to reinforce the status quo by structuring what topics are appropriate for discussion in politics (Cobb and Ross 1997). Ironically, many of those issues are in areas that have already been breached by government action—such as gay rights, where activists have called for a reduction in government regulation. Many issues that crossed the legitimacy barrier long ago still face cultural resistance. Today, the issue of excessive police force has gained legitimacy in the wake of a seeming pattern of incidents directed at minority citizens—replacing the older meme of respecting the uniform.

Because more issues crossed the legitimacy barrier during the Great Broadening, fewer issues are viewed as beyond the pale of government action. They are already addressed by government; consequently, they are ripe for government amelioration. As Wilson (1979, 41) noted, "Once the 'legitimacy barrier' has fallen, political conflict takes a very different form. New programs need not await the advent of a crisis or an extraordinary majority, because no program is any longer 'new'—it is seen, rather, as an extension, a modification, or an enlargement of something the government is already doing."

New barriers—including the manipulation of jurisdictions for political gain, the direct influence of money in politics, and the increasing ideological polarization in national politics—have come about through the increasing inability of the system to respond after an issue reaches the systemic agenda. Less recognized is the role of the expansion of issues in limiting the ability of any particular issue to garner attention. As more and more issues cross the legitimacy barrier, the ability of serial-processing (that is, one-at-a-time) institutions to address any one issue is more constrained. Simply because issues have become legitimate fodder for government does not mean that all groups pressing issues are viewed with the same legitimacy, as Anne Schneider and Helen Ingram (1993) have so convincingly argued. The difficulty in establishing police accountability in part reflects the respect police have, as well as the lack of legitimacy of African Americans in the minds of too many Americans. But keeping issues off of the systemic agenda has become increasingly difficult because almost all issues are already on the formal agenda.

The issue expansion during the 1960s and 1970s overwhelmed the legitimacy barrier in a sudden burst, establishing a very large set of issues as legitimate for governmental action almost simultaneously. The explosion in the number of issue areas addressed during the Great Broadening had feedback effects on the conduct of politics. For example, as a consequence of the expansion of the scope of government, groups attempting to gain access to government meet much more resistance in the form of the pure limits on the attention spans of policy-makers. The expansion of the lobbying system means that any group raising an issue is more likely to meet a concerted counter-mobilization than in the past, when fewer interests were organized and active in lobbying (Baumgartner et al. 2009; Drutman 2015).

Much current analysis is premised on a bare-bones conception of politics—mass publics, a party system, an electoral structure, and a set of governing rules. But to students of public policy, this cannot be accurate; changes in the policy-making system must feed back into the very structure of government and the conduct of politics. As we show in subsequent chapters, the massive growth in the interest-group system, changes in the conduct of legislative business that pushed Congress from a lawmaking body to an oversight one, much more policy conducted through bureaucratic rule-making compared to legislation, and even the polarized nature of the party system can be linked to changes in the scope of government. It is inconceivable that the process of setting the public agenda has not changed as well.

Finally, we are witnessing a political system that has closed considerably more to new ideas and policy proposals in recent years. The capacity of government to address diverse issues, a capacity forged during the cauldron of the Great Broadening, has partially succumbed to the onslaught of partisan polarization, the flood of money into politics, and the increasing manipulation of the electoral system. We will briefly address this potential signature moment in the last chapter, but this book is primarily about the last signature moment and what we can learn from it, not the next one—if it is to come.

THREE

Arcs and Plateaus

The burst of new issues that the federal government addressed during the Great Broadening reveals itself in many different datasets. A fairly limited scope in the 1950s gave way to an explosion of attention to new issues in the 1960s and 1970s. While that pattern is consistent across the datasets, what happens to the pattern once the Great Broadening had peaked is somewhat dependent upon the dataset being examined. Our analysis shows that, upon peaking, the trends take one of two paths.

First, Mayhew's count of major laws and the scope of public policy areas that they addressed both contained a curve that describes bursts of political activity at critical junctures throughout human history. They each form an arc or horseshoe pattern, technically a *parabola*, described algebraically by a quadratic equation. The plateau, noted in chapter 2 (see fig. 2.1), is an additional signature of the Great Broadening—a curve that rises in a similar fashion as the arc and reaches a pinnacle in a similar fashion as the arc. There the similarity ends. This second curve stays elevated or falls only slightly, basically reaching a plateau. In technical terms, it is an *asymptote*.

Our analysis shows that the trend did not continue to go up as it did during the Great Broadening, although that was theoretically possible.[1] Either Congress continued to address the panoply of issues that it addressed during the Great Broadening, resulting in a plateau, or it withdrew from certain policy areas, resulting in an arc. These two signature curves indicate two distinct paths that we think are associated with any major burst of political activity. One, the arc, represents counter-reaction and reversal. The other, the plateau, represents path-dependency.

To understand these two very different paths, we explore them in detail in this chapter, examining their generality using different datasets, many of which come from the Policy Agendas Project. We show when the horseshoe pattern emerges and when the plateau holds—that is, when the broadening process is temporary and when it is permanent.

Huntington's Horseshoe and the Lawmaking Surge

In the decade after the Great Society began to wind down, Samuel Huntington (1981) noted a horseshoe-shaped arc of several indicators of political activism through the period. He wrote, "The distinctive profile of the politics from 1960 to 1976 is dramatically revealed in the horseshoe bulge that recurs during these years in a variety of important quantitative indicators of political activity" (172). Investigating such phenomena as protest activity, Huntington assumed that public policies had followed this period of creedal passion but did not investigate this relationship quantitatively.

That is our first task in this chapter. Congress is our starting point. We want to know if the level of protest and other more qualitative estimates of political activity that Huntington's horseshoe traces can be linked to trends in legislative productivity. Political scientists have developed various metrics to describe how legislative activity has increased since World War II, particularly during the Great Society. The search for sound measures of legislative productivity began with David Mayhew (1991), who was interested in examining the generalized belief that divided governments are less productive than unified governments. So that minor or irrelevant laws did not influence his analysis, Mayhew developed a method of tracing important enactments. Because he noticed an abnormal amount of activity from 1963 to 1976, he included an indicator variable for these congresses, which he refers to as "public mood," "activist mood," or "surges" throughout his analysis, so that he could examine the role of unified versus divided government in quiet periods as well as during the surge. In statistical analyses that controlled for various other explanations of congressional productivity, he finds significantly more major enactments during congresses characterized by divided government. Several other scholars have modified Mayhew's assessments of major enactments, generating similar results.

Since the publication of his book (and the publication of a second edition in 2005), Mayhew has continued to update his list.[2] He has counted 416 major enactments from 1947 to 2016 (an average of just under twelve major enactments per congress). The time trends between Mayhew's major enactment data, which we present as column data to ensure that we do not gloss over the congress-to-congress differences, and Huntington's protest data, which we present as a dashed line, are striking (see fig. 3.1). The dashed line is the amount of protest activity that Huntington finds in each Congress.

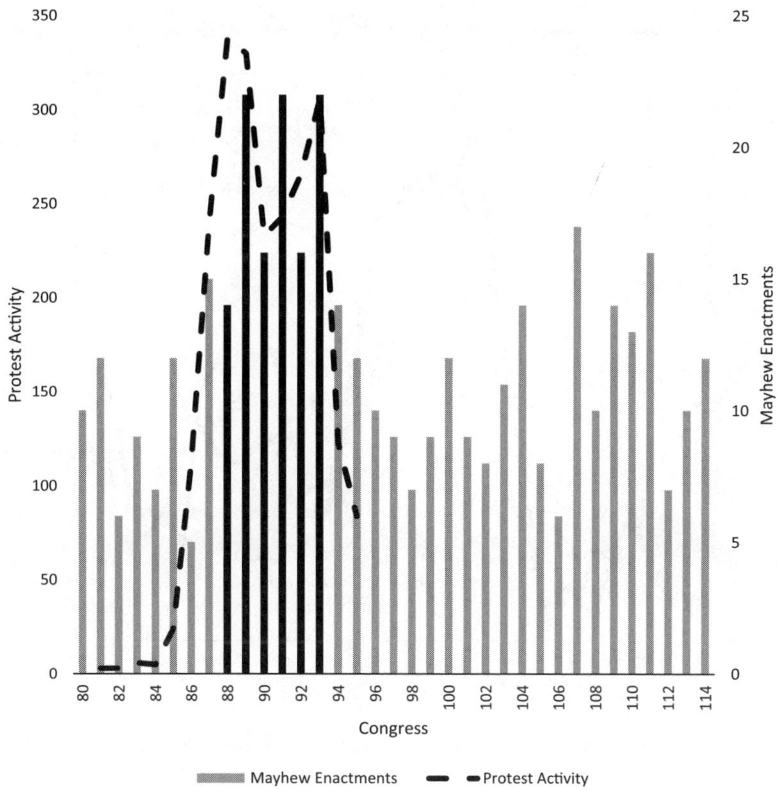

FIGURE 3.1. Huntington's horseshoe of political activity and Mayhew's major enactments by Congress, 80th–114th Congresses

The bars are the number of major enactments that Mayhew (1991; 2005) finds during each congress. The dark bars are the congresses that Mayhew includes in his "surge" (the 88th through the 94th Congresses), a period of time in which Congress was extraordinarily productive.

Although both series display considerable variability, the surge identified by Huntington and Mayhew stands out. During Mayhew's surge, an average of 18 major laws per congress were enacted; outside of this period, just 10.3 per congress. Mayhew's surge in lawmaking closely follows Huntington's arc. Note that protest activity tends to lead lawmaking during the surge, and to precede its fall during the decline from the peak.

An examination of the available datasets on landmark legislation shows a remarkable degree of agreement with Mayhew, even though the scholars employed different measurement strategies and had divergent aims in assembling

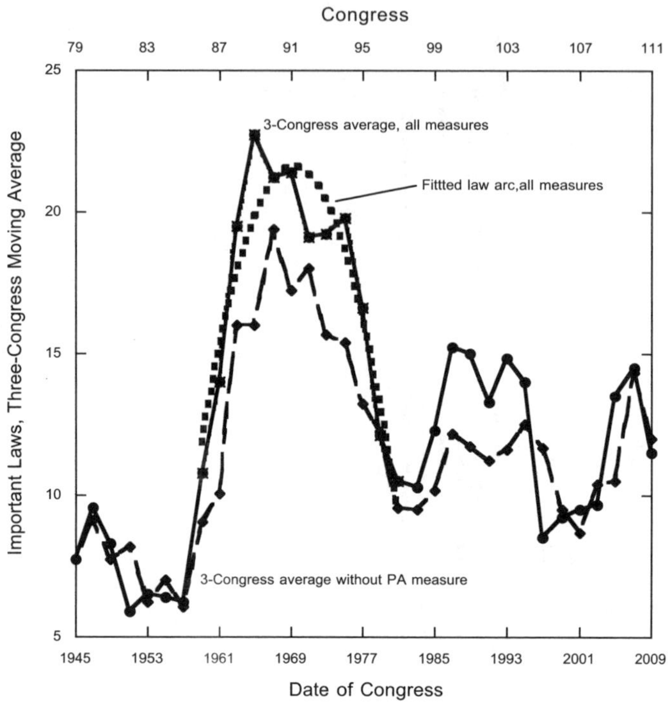

FIGURE 3.2. Important laws per congress, 79th–112th Congresses

the data. Ansolabehere, Palmer, and Schneer (2014, 8) compare three datasets of significant legislation assembled by Mayhew (1991) and Howell et al. (2000), who included two different estimates, with their own compilation. Each series begins its ascent in the late 1950s and declines in the late 1970s. The peaks of time series change a bit, but their overall shape is largely consistent. The Policy Agendas Project compiled a list based solely on coverage in the *Congressional Quarterly Almanac,* but it includes flexibility in the number of laws included. More recently, Grossmann (2014), who named Mayhew's surge "the Long Great Society," developed his own list of major enactments.

Because of the similarity between each of the data series, we average them and then take the three-congress moving average to show the over-time variation (see fig. 3.2).[3] We present the averages separately, including the Policy Agendas Measure (solid black line) and excluding it (dashed black line), because it relies on a single indicator. While that indicator seems to heighten the importance of the surge (and a secondary one around the 100th Congress), the overall trends are clear. We fit the law arc for the surge period for all measures ($r = 0.94$). Furthermore, lawmaking, which began its surge in the 86th Congress (1958–59), never returned to its initial state. Congress passed more important laws after the surge than it did before it.

The datasets depicted in figures 3.1 and 3.2 measure the same activity: the passing of law. All of them measure the amount of the activity, not necessarily the scope of activity. The amount of activity assessed in lawmaking addresses the thickening of government, but that is not the whole story. While that activity is important in understanding congressional output, it does not capture the scope of the vast changes that came about during the Great Broadening. In particular, it fails to address the agenda-setting dynamics of surmounting Wilson's legitimacy barrier as the federal government's agenda expanded. Because of the consequences the Great Broadening had for the development of the American polity, we document it in a variety of measures in the next few sections.

Measuring the Great Broadening in Congress

Political scientists and pundits have focused—almost exclusively—on the thickening of the federal government. When they say that government has grown, they tend to point to expenditure growth. Or when they say that the government does more, they count bills, hearings, or laws (or even important laws), but these speak to the amount of activity, not to the breadth of activity. We show that the government has broadened as well—it deals with new issues in areas previously left to civil society or to the states.

Utilizing the coding schemes and the datasets of the Policy Agendas Project allows us to document that increasing breadth of government action. In this section, we examine these datasets to show that in addition to doing more (thickening), the government's agenda moved into more policy areas (broadening). We can order each stage in the policy-making process (or, put more colloquially, how a bill becomes a law) according to the resistance an issue typically meets in moving from one stage to another. For example, it is relatively easy for a member to introduce a bill on an issue, but harder to get a hearing held on it, and harder still to get the bill voted on and passed into law.

Bill Introductions

Introducing a bill is the first formal step in the legislative process. From 1947 until 1956, representatives in the House introduced bills on around 170 policy subtopics (see fig. 3.3, solid line). Over the next decade,

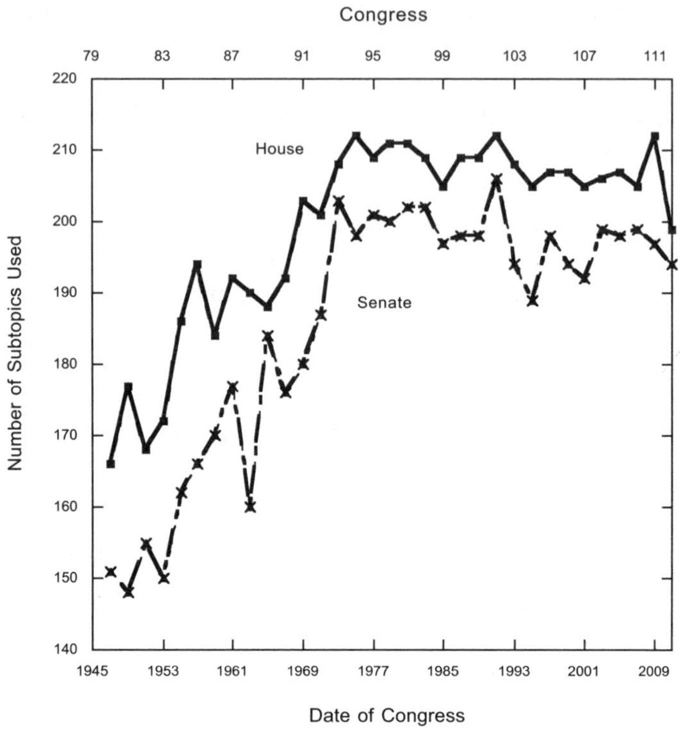

FIGURE 3.3. House and Senate bill introductions, 80th–112th Congresses

representatives introduced legislation on around 15 additional topics, and in the next decade, an additional 15 topics. In no congress before the 93rd (1973–74) did House members introduce bills on more than 200 subtopics. Since then, they have introduced bills in at least 200 subtopics each congress, with the exception of the 112th Congress (2011–12), when the bills covered 197 subtopics.

The Senate experiences almost exactly the same trend in the scope of bill introductions, though their numbers are slightly reduced from those of the House (see fig. 3.3, dashed line). Whereas the House subtopics stabilized at around 205 for each congress, the Senate's have stabilized at around 190. Both chambers' broadening ended at precisely the same time—the 93rd Congress (1973–74)—and then remarkably, reach an asymptote. After a period of vigorous growth in introducing new issues onto the congressional agenda, each series reached a saturation point when each chamber stopped adding subtopics in the bills introduced. Then each series levels off and stays more or less constant for years. The series fail to contract as Mayhew's law measure does. Bill introductions are emblematic of this second pattern of government action; once government enters a new policy area, legislation is required to adjust policies to changing demands. Some of these demands may reduce the level of government commitment while others may increase it, but the overall levels don't change in a consistent direction.

We can also tabulate bill introductions issue-by-issue (see fig. 3.4). If we do so, the overall impression is of the arc or horseshoe pattern, not the plateau that characterizes the general measure of figure 3.3.[4] The difference is due to two factors. First, while bill introductions clearly spike collectively at around the same time, a more careful examination of the graph indicates that issues do not access the agenda simultaneously. Rather, there is a rough order to the increases in the 1950s and 1960s. Transportation, agriculture, and civil rights precede welfare, the environment, and crime. Second, after an issue accesses the agenda and gets established in programs and agencies,

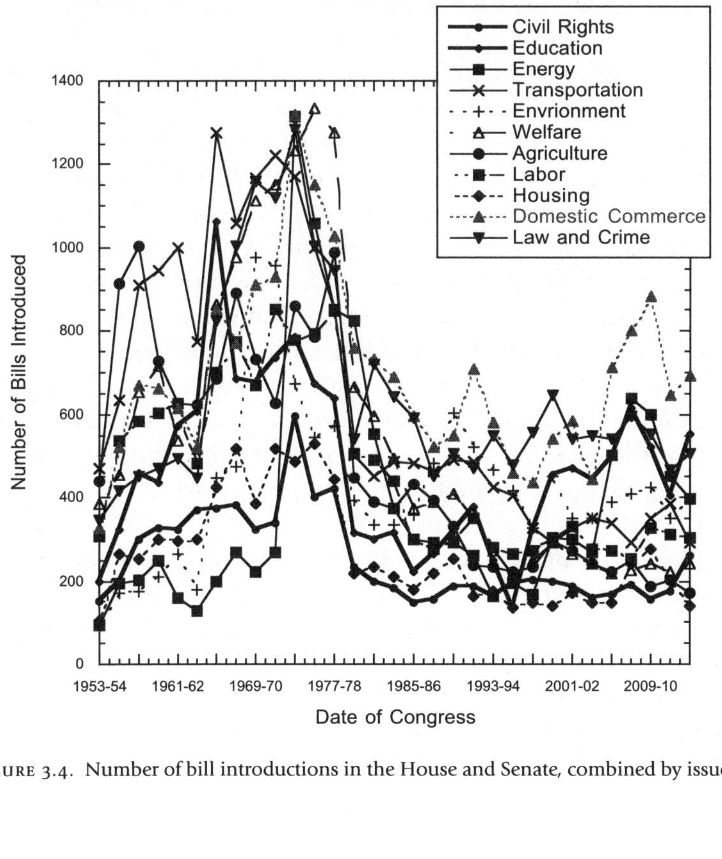

FIGURE 3.4. Number of bill introductions in the House and Senate, combined by issue area

Congress engages in what amounts to issue-shuffling. All issues are not addressed simultaneously; rather, they are addressed as adjustments are needed or as attention focuses on one rather than others.

Bill introductions constitute one of the best measures we have to assess the movement of an issue onto the formal agenda of government. The mid-1950s began a frenzied period of increasing activity in the introduction of bills across most issue areas, but the activity leveled off as members stopped introducing bills on new issues and turned to shuffling their activities among the issues already introduced. Once government begins to address an issue, it generally continues to be involved with that issue, resulting in the plateau pattern in the overall series of figure 3.3.

Roll-Call Votes

Because we measured the Great Broadening through the lens of congressional hearings in the previous chapter, we now move to the chambers' floors in our examination of broadening in the legislative process. A more difficult goal to achieve than introducing a bill or holding a hearing is met when an issue is the subject of a roll-call vote on the floor of the House or Senate. Because the process for bringing bills to the chamber floor is so different in the House than in the Senate, we conduct separate, but parallel, analyses of the respective chambers. The consistency of results across chambers indicates that the larger forces at work swamp the idiosyncratic differences between the chambers.

Particular issues, assessed empirically as subtopics, can become the subjects of roll-call votes through various avenues in the House of Representatives. First, the Rules Committee can report a rule for a bill's debate in the underlying subtopic. Second, the Rules Committee can permit an amendment concerning the subtopic on a bill addressing the same subtopic or even a different subtopic so long as it is still germane to the underlying bill. Third, the Rules Committee can provide for an open rule for a bill's debate, during which a member can offer an amendment concerning a particular subtopic (again, it can be a different subtopic so long as it is germane to the bill). A number of other paths for subtopic votes can occur through the House's legislative process (e.g., votes on a motion to recommit a bill to committee based on the substance within a subtopic or a sense of the House resolution involving the subtopic). Suffice it to say, given the restrictive nature of the House floor and the way that party leaders increasingly control it, an individual member has a harder time forcing the House floor to address an issue within a subtopic than if the member simply introduced a bill on the subtopic or convinced a committee chair to hold a hearing on it.

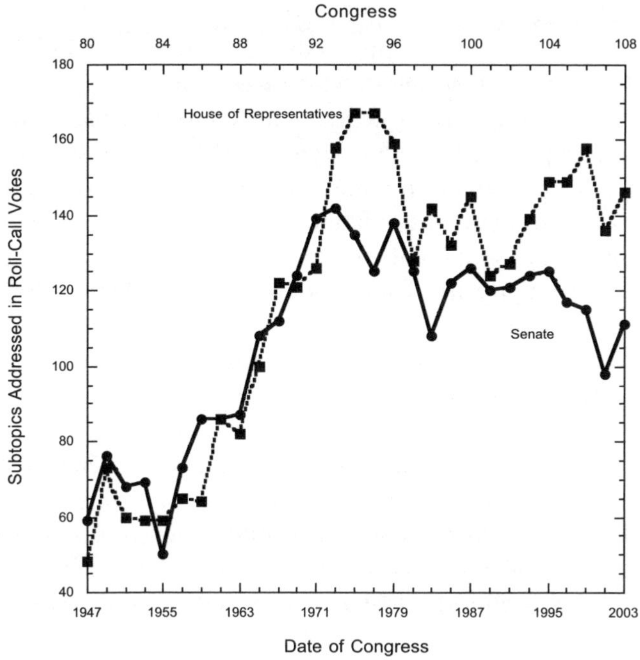

FIGURE 3.5. Number of subtopics with roll-call votes in House and Senate, 79th–112th Congresses

Not surprisingly, the number of subtopics for House roll-call votes is not as high as it is for bill introductions or hearings, but it does show a similar trend (see fig 3.5). In the 1940s and 1950s, approximately 60 subtopics (out of the total 213) were subject to roll-call votes. In the 1970s, that number increased by more than 150 percent—the congresses during which members took roll-call votes on the highest number of subtopics were the 94th (163 subtopics), 95th (162 subtopics), and 96th (155 subtopics)—exactly the same congresses in which the introductions and hearings data peaked. After the 1970s, the number of subtopics that were the subject of roll-call votes decreases, though not nearly to the low levels observed prior to the Great Broadening.

The one complicating factor in this time series is that the House used a genuine roll-call in its voting through the 92nd Congress—that is, up until 1972, when the House took a non-anonymous vote on an issue, the clerk called every single representative's name. These roll calls took as long as a half hour. Beginning in 1973, the House permitted electronic voting. Sure enough, the time series jumps from 120 subtopics in the 92nd Congress (when the House cast 649 votes), the last Congress in which electronic voting was not used, to 153 subtopics in the 93rd Congress (when the House cast 1,078 votes), the first one in which electronic voting was used. This change of 33 subtopics was the largest of the time series; bigger than the 20 additional subtopics in the 90th Congress or the 21 fewer subtopics in the 97th Congress. Quite apart from the disjoint of electronic voting, the series was increasing before the disjoint and, eventually decreased, even during the electronic voting era. So, the use of electronic voting makes the series jump, but does not play any other important role in validating the existence of the Great Broadening.

Over the entire span, the House has not taken a vote on only five subtopics—Arts and Humanities (under the Education topic), Low Income Assistance (Social Welfare), Other (Social Welfare), Research and Development (Domestic Commerce), and Other (Foreign Trade). One topic—Other (Macroeconomics)—had just one vote. The subtopics with the most votes were as follows: 1,851 votes on Branch Relations (Government Operations), 1,284 votes on General (Government Operations), 792 votes on National Budget (Macroeconomics), 515 votes on Specific Country (International Affairs), and 502 votes on General (Defense). On average (including the subtopics with no votes), the House took 99 votes on each subtopic.

In comparison to the House, the Senate is less restrictive in the topics that individual senators can bring up. Even amendments that are not germane to the underlying legislation, under normal circumstances, can be considered. Nonetheless, because the Senate floor time is still constrained, it is not as easy for a senator to demand a roll-call vote on a subtopic as it is for the senator to simply introduce a bill on the particular subtopic. Despite this difference, and even though the Senate still does not vote electronically, the pattern in the number of subtopics addressed through roll-call votes in the Senate looks similar to the House data, with a few minor differences. First, the data peak at 137 subtopics in the 93rd Congress (1973–74), which is one congress earlier than in the House. Second, the number of subtopics addressed in the Senate was lower than it was in the House, despite the fact that senators can more easily raise issues than House members. On average, senators address 10 fewer subtopics than did their House counterparts. Third, the Senate roll-call data are more reflective of hearings than they are of House introductions; that is, after peaking in the early 1970s, the number of subtopics addressed in Senate roll-call votes drops more in both percentage and in actual numbers than the House roll-call votes. The arc of the Senate roll-call votes is both a bit higher on the right-hand side and a bit more elongated, reflecting that the rate of decline after the peak is not as large as the rate of increase before the peak. These differences between the House and the Senate are relatively minor compared to their common attributes.

The Senate did not take a vote on six subtopics. The four subtopics that the House also did not take a vote on were Arts and Humanities (under the Education topic), Low Income Assistance (Social Welfare), Other (Social Welfare), and Research and Development (Domestic Commerce); the Senate also did not take a vote on the Other (Macroeconomics) or Other (Public Lands) subtopics; the House took 1 vote on the former and 13 on the latter. The only other no-vote subtopic in the House was Other (Foreign Trade), on which the Senate took 3 votes. At the top, the Senate's most-voted subtopic category was Appointments (Government Operations), on which there were 955 votes; there were 833 votes on Branch Relations (Government Operations), 775 on Tax Code (Macroeconomics), 719 on National Budget (Macroeconomics), and 677 on General (Government Operations). On average, the Senate took 101 votes in each subtopic over the entire time period we analyze.

In the roll-call vote data from both chambers, we see a tendency toward stabilization, with the count of subtopics reaching more-or-less an asymptote. Note the pattern of slow growth, then rapid growth, followed by leveling off that is characteristic of the sigmoid growth curve. Because of the differing mechanisms used to get a measure to the roll-call vote stage, a couple of substantive differences exist between the two chambers. The trends diverged after reaching the peak, with senators taking votes in fewer subtopics since the peak in the 1970s, while representatives have maintained about the same level of subtopic activity. The House carries a greater variety of issues to the floor than does the Senate, which focuses its floor activity more intensely on fewer issues in any single congress.

Laws

Successful final passage votes in both chambers, and a supportive president (or, in the absence of that, two-thirds support in both chambers), herald the passage of a new law. At the time Congress enacts them, laws mark a formal boundary between governing in theory and governing in practice. Citizens become bound by their precepts, and federal agencies are required to implement their provisions. The number of subtopics that are addressed in the laws follow the familiar arc—the trend starts low, peaks in the 95th Congress (1977–78), and ends as low as it started (see fig. 3.6; $r = 0.77$).

Each successive step in the legislative process shows the same rise but has a different reaction once the peak of the Great Broadening is reached. For bill

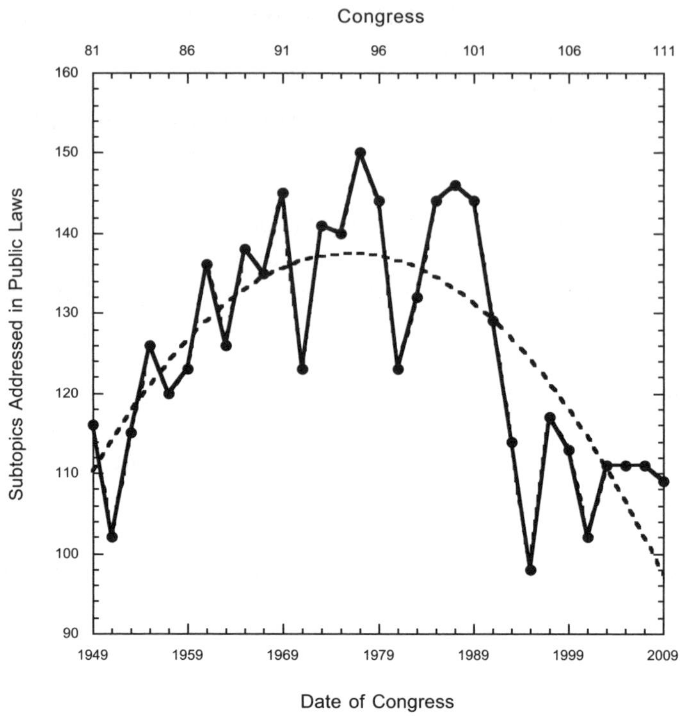

FIGURE 3.6. Number of Policy Agendas subtopics used in public laws, 80th–111th Congresses

introductions, the peak drops in the 97th Congress. The peak for congressional hearings never drops (we have more to say about that in chapter 9). For laws passed, the peak lasts longer than it does for bill introductions, but then experiences a rather precipitous drop in the 103rd Congress and has stayed relatively low ever since.

Coverage by the Congressional Quarterly

What Congress does is one thing. What gets covered may be something entirely different. Perhaps the most comprehensive observer of Congress is the *Congressional Quarterly* (*CQ*), which was established in 1945. The *CQ*, in covering the technicalities of Congress and the federal government, provides summary reports and analyses for newspapers and other media outlets. It includes detailed coverage of major legislative activity, congressional committee hearings, lobbying activities, and the individual records of congressmen.

It has become an essential part of the internal communications network of policy-makers, lobbyists, and the attentive public.

The Policy Agendas Project coded the articles in each *CQ Almanac*, which is issued annually as a summary of the year's activities. We would expect this source to expand and contract its coverage of subtopics as the federal government expanded and limited its reach across issue areas. Indeed, this is the case: *CQ* coverage of subtopics expanded in the 1960s, covering a high number of subtopics from the 87th Congress (1961–62) through the 103rd Congress (1993–94); subtopic coverage peaked in the 92nd Congress (1971–72) at 166 subtopics (see fig. 3.7). The drop in the 104th Congress occurred as Congress limited the scope of its legislative activities and cut back on the number of hearings it conducted.

As one would expect, the number of subtopics covered annually is closely associated with the number of articles in the volume (with a correlation of

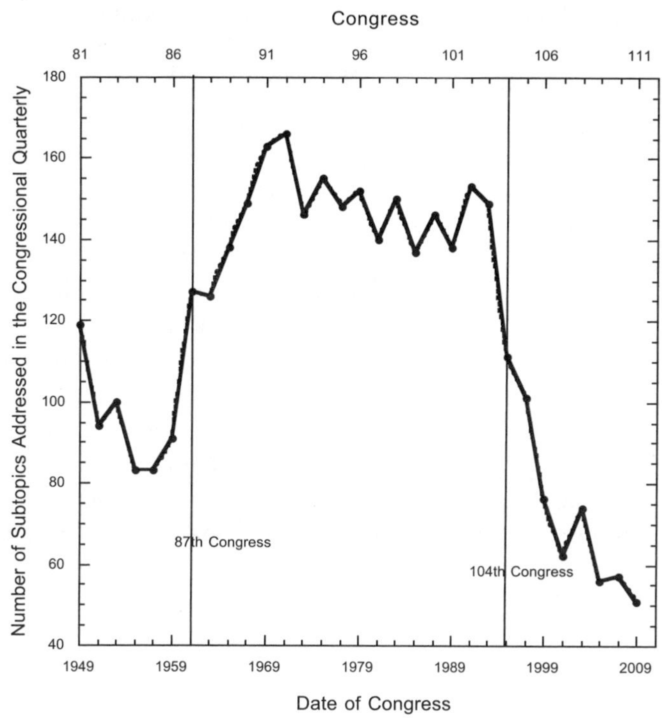

FIGURE 3.7. Number of Policy Agendas subtopics addressed in *Congressional Quarterly Almanac* articles, by Congress

0.95). Interestingly, though, the number of subtopics covered by the *CQ* has a much lower correlation—only 0.24—with congressional hearings.[5]

Measuring the Great Broadening at the Institutional Level

The previous section explored the range of policies that the House and Senate engaged in at the various stages of the legislative process. Chamber action within Congress, of course, must happen before laws are challenged and implemented. This section examines the Great Broadening in these downstream activities.

Supreme Court Cases

In cases where federal statutes may contradict or violate existing laws or the Constitution, the judicial branch is responsible for conducting statutory interpretation and judicial review. The late Justice Antonin Scalia, noting that a major role of the court is "just figuring out" what a particular law means, put it this way: "It takes about a decade to get all the kinks out of a major piece of legislation" (Cohn 2011). But "there are fewer major statutes" to consider, so this means a lighter caseload for the Court.

Given the accretion of federal law across an increasingly wide array of policy areas, the amount of legislation the court is responsible for interpreting has increased in the postwar period. Thus, we expect the broadening of Congress's agenda to be followed closely by the broadening of the Supreme Court's agenda. But as Scalia suggests, we also expect to find that the Court addresses a declining number of subtopics as its caseload declines.

We trace the number of subtopics in Supreme Court cases from 1950 to 2008 (see fig. 3.8). The Court experienced a more extended peak period, from approximately 1973 to 1989 before declining in 1993. Judicial scholars, most notably Owens and Simon (2012), have attributed this decline to ideological and contextual factors. They show that as the Supreme Court became more ideologically fractured, justices who held divergent worldviews were less likely to grant certiorari to cases, many of which would have split the Court. Additionally, Congress's decisions in the 1990s to reduce the Court's mandatory appellate jurisdiction resulted in the Court deciding fifty-four fewer cases during an average term (Owens and Simon 2012). Such changes in jurisdictional scope may account for some of the changes in the breadth of the judicial agenda. Nonetheless, the pattern most assuredly also reflects the Court's response to the same dynamics of surge and decline we observed in the lawmaking process.

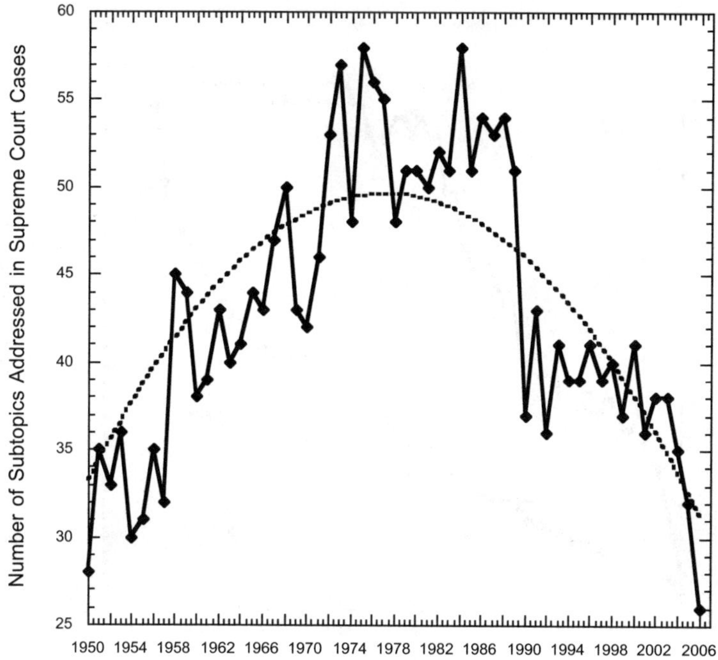

FIGURE 3.8. Number of subtopics addressed in Supreme Court cases, 1950–2008

The policy scope of the Court's decisions is closely associated with the number of cases it decides. The correlation between the number of subtopics addressed in cases and the number of cases decided is a robust 0.81. Both series follow the arc pattern. Moreover, both experience very large drops in the 1990–91 term. Whatever the particular reasons for the drop then, it is clear that by limiting the number of cases it takes, the Court also limits the policy diversity of the cases it decides. A Court taking a smaller number of cases becomes a more focused Court.

Budget Categories

One of the standard conservative complaints about government is its out-of-control growth. "Spending" and "out-of-control" are paired in a meme that is repeated seemingly endlessly in America's political dialog. An examination of federal government expenditures since World War II tells a different story (see fig, 3.9). It is true that the funding level, which we present in constant dollars since 1947, has gone up over time, but an analysis of

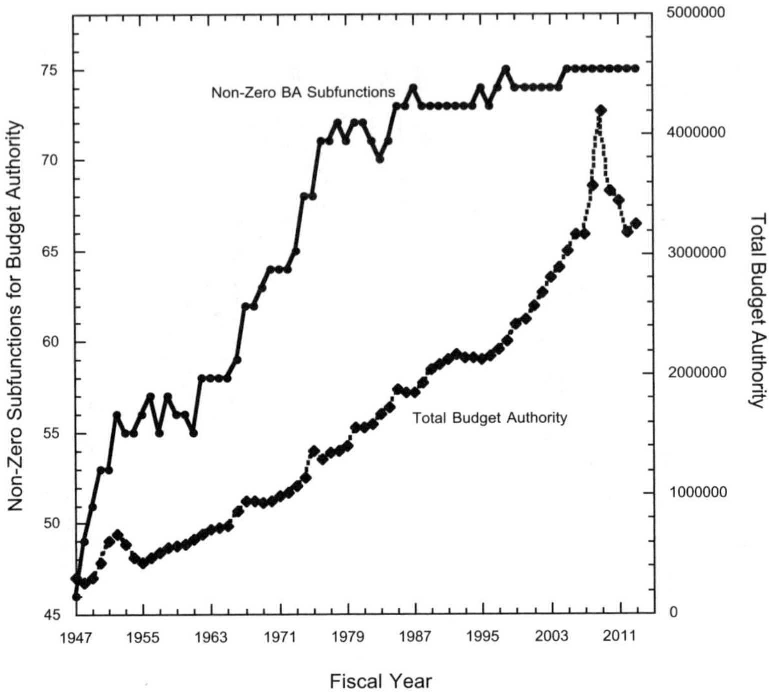

FIGURE 3.9. Total Budget Authority in constant (2009) dollars (right axis) and the count of funded subfunctions (left axis) on an annual basis

goodness of fit tests for both exponential and linear growth shows that an exponential trend line barely fits the data better than a linear trend does.[6] The trend line seems far from alarming. In comparison to economic growth, moreover, the growth in governmental expenditures is far from alarming. According to the Office of Management and Budget calculations, in 1969, the ratio of federal expenditures to GDP was 18.4; in 1979 it was 19.6; in 1997 the ratio was 18.9; in 2016 it had reached 20.6.

The Great Broadening period is quite undistinguished when viewed from the full budget authority series, which we consider a thickening of government activity. The steep spike in Fiscal Year 2010 represents the authority granted in the American Recovery and Reinvestment Act of 2009 (Obama's stimulus package). Regardless of the stimulus spike, it is clear from the graph that government actually grew faster from 2000 to 2008 than in the Kennedy-Johnson period and was slower during the G. H. W. Bush and Clinton presidencies.

A look at public budgets through a different lens yields a completely different picture. The U.S. Office of Management and Budget (OMB) reports Congressional Budget Authority divided into the government functions and subfunctions the funds are allocated to address. OMB's categories are consistent only back to 1962, but the Policy Agendas Project has adjusted the data to ensure comparability back to 1947, using the OMB's own categories rather than the Policy Agendas Project categories. The budget authority data contain lots of zeros, especially in the early years—generally because the programs that utilize these funds were created later. OMB adds budget categories as necessary to span the functions that the federal government has assumed. For example, Budget Authority for Medicare is characterized by zeros from 1947 through 1965, the year in which it was created, and then shows positive figures afterward, once it received funding. Energy Conservation includes zeros until 1976. If we count the nonzero entries per year and follow them across time, we get an idea of when the federal government added particular functions.

The subfunction view is quite different from the constant dollars view. From the late 1940s to the late 1970s, government added twenty-five subfunctions to its repertoire, fully one-third of what it does. Ten of these subfunctions were added in the early 1950s, most of which were related to military and foreign affairs. After a lull during the rest of the 1950s, the great burst came in the fifteen years between 1961 and 1976. The line representing how many Budget Authority subfunctions have funds allocated to them in each fiscal year resembles the sigmoid growth curve, with a period of rapid growth, which then reaches a plateau around FY 1976. This Great Broadening period may not have been distinguished by thickening, but it definitely was characterized by the expanding scope of federal government outlays.

Moreover, we can begin to see what is a much firmer basis for conservative complaints. Once OMB adopts a new subfunction to use in categorizing expenditures, the expenditure categories are used thereafter. Once a new program is funded, so it remains at least at some level. While some of these functions did not expand much, others did. Once government broadens, that is, expands its reach into different areas of civic life, it is more likely subsequently to thicken. The more issues government moves into, the more likely dense networks are to develop around these new policy arenas. As Aaron Wildavsky (1979, 62, 81) noted at the end of the period of the Great Broadening, "Because policy is evermore its own cause, programs depend less on the external environment than on events inside the sectors from which they come; . . . public agencies are ever more involved in making adjustments to past programs, creating new ones to overcome difficulties."

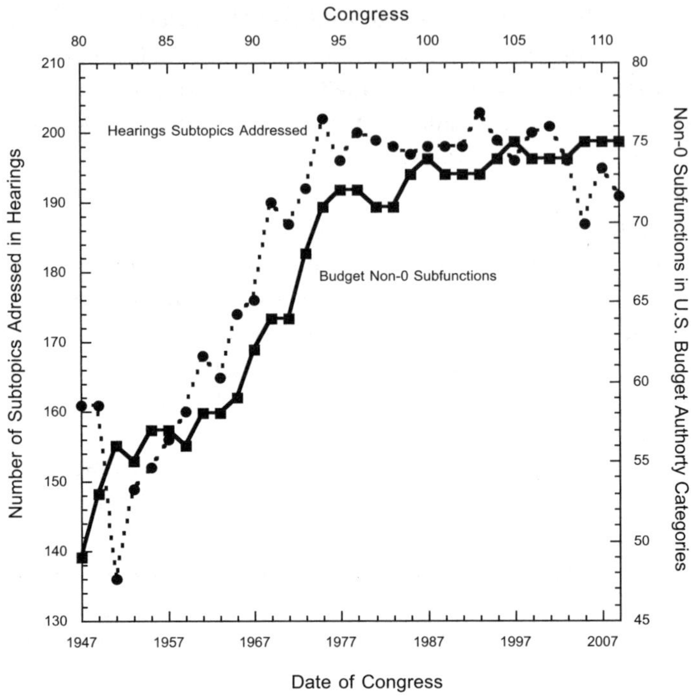

FIGURE 3.10. A comparison of budget categories with congressional hearings

What happens if we compare the budget categories added by OMB and the count of Policy Agendas subtopics in congressional hearings, congress-by-congress? We should note that these data series were constructed through completely independent data-generating processes. The OMB budget-categorization system is not only separate and distinct from the Policy Agendas content coding system; it was set up in a different time period for different purposes by a different group of researchers. The trends of these two distinct systems need not be similar—unless, of course, they are both picking up the same underlying dynamic.

Amazingly enough, the patterns traced through time are very close to identical (see fig. 3.10), and they correlate 0.91. Each grew during the same period of time, which corresponded to the peak period of the Great Broadening. Hearings peaked in the 94th Congress (1975–76) at the same time that the increase in the number of budget categories entered an era of very slow growth. It is no surprise that the hearings series leads the budget category series, because OMB adds budget categories in response to Congress's funding of new programs. What is surprising is that budget categories get funded according to the same plateau pattern as congressional hearings considering new issues. Both experience a rapid growth period in which Congress addresses new issues, adds new programs, *and* provides funds to operate these programs. Both experience a peak at about the same time, after which each reaches a plateau when neither adds new functions.

We stress the importance of the correspondence between our two measures of the scope of governmental activity applied to budget authority and Policy Agendas data. It adds considerable confidence that the findings presented in this book are not a function of reliance on a single system of measurement.

Arcs and Plateaus

Starting in the years after World War II, America experienced a gradual increase in political activity. During the 1960s and 1970s, this gradual increase was augmented by an intense burst of government policy-making, which we have termed the Great Broadening to signal that it was so much more than bigger government—it was federal government with a longer reach into civil society and state and local government. Other historical analyses of the period have made it clear that the expansion was part of a longer period when the government became much more prominent in American society and that it was perhaps part of a broader dynamic that accounts for lurches toward larger government followed by periods of consolidation (Dodd 1979; Huntington 1981; Patterson 1996; Schlesinger 1986).

Some students of historical institutionalism see major periods of change such as the Great Broadening as critical moments, leading to new society-wide equilibria. We argue, and provide empirical evidence in this chapter, that this account is only one of two general paths that change can take after a disruption. The first, and most obvious, is the signature arc, or horseshoe pattern. In it, the opponents of the rapid changes get organized and are able to reverse some or most of the gains through counter-mobilization. The conservative counter-revolution and the resurgence of the Republican Party are major parts of the story of policy-making in the latter half of the twentieth century in the United States.

But a second pattern also occurs—one more consistent with the ideas of historical institutionalism. Some of the Great Broadening additions to the scope of the federal government—what liberals view as "gains" and conservatives view as "losses"—are *built in* to government and become institutionalized in policy subsystems.[7] While they can be reversed, these patterns are very resilient.

We found that the time series in this chapter all have a common beginning—a strong surge from the late 1950s through the late 1970s. Almost without exception, all the datasets showed not only an increase in the action of the federal government, but also an expansion of what the federal government considers. After the 1970s, the series part ways, tracing two distinct paths: first, the arc, horseshoe, or parabola and, second, the plateau or the sigmoid-type growth curve, in which a series expands rapidly before reaching an asymptote, in which the series peaks but fails to fall.

Tracing out the horseshoe pattern are the following data series: protest activity, landmark laws, all public laws, *Congressional Quarterly* articles, and Supreme Court cases. The series peak at similar times, but vary in the steepness of the quadratic curve that describes such arcs.[8] In the plateau pattern, the data series reach an inflection point, but unlike the horseshoe, they do not decline. They either do not decline at all from that point, or decline only slightly, or exhibit variability. Once government addresses a function, it does not withdraw its presence; rather government continues to debate, adjust, modify, and even reform policies. This continual adjustment process shows up in budgetary subfunctions and congressional hearings. In some cases, like bill introduction, the number of topics shrinks, but not to its pre–Great Broadening level.

The data presented in this chapter show that the government grew not only during the Great Society period, but even in the period after it (thickening). More than that, the government, almost at exactly the same time, began addressing more policies in a wider range of areas (broadening). We think it was the latter of these trends that has the greater consequence on how it the American polity practices politics and enacts public policy even today. From institutional changes to congressional voting behavior, the Great Broadening is one of the most consequential trends escaping the eye of social science researchers.

FOUR

Dynamics of the Great Broadening

The data from Congress, the Supreme Court, budgets, and other activities show that the Great Broadening of the federal government's scope began in the late 1950s. In areas of public policy that had previously been the purview of civil society or state and local governments, the federal government took a much more proactive role. In the late 1970s, the activity either leveled off or in some cases declined to even its pre-Great Broadening level.

In this chapter, we examine the nuts and bolts of this process in more detail by focusing on the congressional hearings dataset, which we introduced in the second chapter. We have chosen this step of the legislative process because the literature suggests that it is the clearest indication of what issues have Congress's attention (Baumgartner and Jones 2009). Introducing a bill certainly has one member's attention, but just that, one member. At the other extreme, the roll-call voting stage of lawmaking presents a high bar for congressional attention. Many issues receive attention but fail to get a roll-call vote. We show that the addition of issues to the hearings agenda is cumulative—that is, when an issue accesses the agenda, it tends to stay there. Additionally, if it falls off the agenda, we detect a clear tendency for it to have been added later in time in a last in, first out process.

In our analysis of congressional hearings in this chapter, we do not distinguish between the House and Senate or between legislative referral hearings and oversight hearings; rather, we combine all the hearings of both chambers to come up with a composite number of hearings. In our attempt to scale up from the trees to the forest, we ignore the idiosyncrasies of the different chambers in this chapter and the different reasons for holding congressional hearings to reach a broader understanding of congressional attention. Nothing in our analysis suggests that we would have seen anything differently if we had separated the chambers, or had separated the hearings into their primary functions, or even if we had utilized different Policy Agendas datasets. While the words of the song may vary, the tune is consistent across chambers, across hearings, and even across datasets.

Cumulative Building of the Issue Space during the Great Broadening

Up until now, our focus has been on the total number of issues (assessed as Policy Agendas subtopics) per congress without regard for which particular issues were added and when. Although we have shown how the number of issues increased during the Great Broadening, we have not shown how specific issues were linked across congresses. It could be that an issue gains Congress's attention, gets resolved, and falls off the agenda, only to reappear when it again becomes a problem. Or, it could be that issues simply shuffle on and off the agenda without much rhyme or reason. Those are not the patterns we find. Rather, we see that once an issue gets on the agenda it tends to remain.

Although some issues shuffle on and off the agenda, the vast majority are either always discussed at some level, or appear on the agenda and are discussed during most subsequent congresses. Issues added later in the period have a higher probability of dropping off the agenda (although most do continue to occupy the formal congressional agenda). The issues always on the congressional hearings agenda during the period of study included taxes, agriculture crop subsidies, labor relations, energy, transportation, housing, financial regulation, and defense. Education and environmental regulation appeared on the agenda in the 1960s and stayed. Others, exemplified by alternative and renewable energy, came on to the agenda in response to technological advances, high prices of traditional sources, and climate change. Some subtopics seem to be ramifications of a broader policy area, as when Congress addressed the increasing complexity of social and governmental interactions, such as indoor hazards (part of the larger focus on the environment).

Some issues waxed and waned during the period. After displaying little interest early in the period, Congress examined minority discrimination at a relatively high level as the Great Broadening peaked, but it lost interest over time. Between the 91st and 102nd Congresses (1969–92), congressional committees held at least ten and as many as thirty-five hearings on discrimination during each congress, but after the 103rd Congress, held four or fewer, except in the 110th Congress (2007–9), when fourteen were held. This pattern of increasing and then declining interest is the most common pattern after the two dominant patterns of continuous attention throughout the full period of study and the pure cumulative pattern. Increasing and declining interest also characterizes urban development, tourism, and elderly housing. These declines can indicate that the topic has been addressed by adequate solutions (or turned out not to be the problem at first anticipated), or legislative interest waned, even as the problem continued as intensely as ever.

To analyze the nature of expansion and contraction more systematically, we have developed a graphical procedure based on an old method from psychometrics: cumulative, or Guttman, scaling. If it is true that issues on the agenda tend to stay on the agenda, we should see issues added gradually and then quite dramatically during the Great Broadening. If so, this would lead to a classic Guttman (or scalogram) pattern.

In this analysis, columns represent congresses, and rows represent Policy Agendas subtopics. If either the House or Senate held one hearing on the subtopic in a particular congress, the block representing the subtopic for that congress is shaded (see fig. 4.1). If not, it is white. The chart keeps the congresses in chronological order (Hayes and Ellickson 1990) and orders the subtopics according to the number of congresses in which the subtopic was discussed over the period of study from the 79th to the 112th Congresses (1945–2012); thus, the subtopics with the most shaded cells are at the top of the figure, and the ones with the fewest are at the bottom. When subtopics are tied, we put the one that got on to the agenda first before the one that arrived later. The small font size makes the particulars of the issue topics impossible to decipher. These specifics are less important than the overall pattern. To aid interpretation, we have divided the subtopics into three distinct blocks.

The first block represents issues always on the agenda throughout the period; it is a shaded rectangle. In the 79th Congress (1945–46), Congress held hearings on 106 different subtopics. Hearings on 63 of those subtopics were held in every single congress. These 63 subtopics make up the shaded rectangle we label as the first block. Not surprisingly, only 1, 2, or 3 of the subtopics within most Policy Agendas major topic codes are included in this list of 63. It does include 5 of the 9 subtopics within the major topic of Transportation, 7 out of 14 subtopics in Domestic Commerce, 9 out of 18 topics in Defense, 10 out of 18 topics in Government Operations, and 6 out of the 7 subtopics in Public Lands. We can think of these issues as making up the permanent congressional agenda, at least since the end of World War II.

The second block represents issues that are cumulatively added to the agenda. The cumulative pattern stands out, but the line only suggests the pattern, which contains considerable variability. More often than not, once an issue has entered the agenda, it tends to stick there, though not with as much regularity as the subtopics within the first block. Our rough approximation is that 119 subtopics make up this second block. Forty of these subtopics were on the agenda in the first congress of our analysis but fell off at some point. Almost twice as many (79) entered the agenda after this first congress. Of these 119 subtopics, all but 23 were still on the agenda in each of the last five Congresses of our analysis—from the 108th to the 112th Congress (2003–12). We can think of these issues as those that got added—most of them during the Great Broadening—and then, for the most part, remained on the agenda.

The final block, which represents issues that come on and off the agenda, is less well-defined. Of the thirty-three subtopics in the third block, only three were on the agenda in the first congress of our study and just two were on the agenda in each of the last five congresses we analyze. Four major topic codes had three subtopics in the third block (Environment, Social Welfare, Housing, and Government Operations); only one major topic—Civil Rights—had four subtopics in this last category. Only in this block do issues appear to arrive on and fall from the agenda without much rhyme or reason.

The cumulative nature of adding issues is clear; once an issue makes it on the agenda, it tends to stay on the agenda. Other issues appear less frequently, and when they do, they access the agenda more sporadically. A few issues do fall off the agenda, and those have a tendency to access the agenda later. We find almost no evidence that solved issues stay off the agenda or that the congressional agenda is random. What is clear is the cumulative addition of issues, especially during the Great Broadening. We present more evidence of the timing of these additions later in the chapter.

While the cumulative pattern of issue ascension to the agenda offers a bird's-eye view of the process, it obscures the fascinating pattern of just how Congress adds issues to its agenda. We've chosen six issues from Policy Agendas subtopics to demonstrate the dynamic of cumulative agenda construction: Taxes, Military Personnel, Higher Education, Drinking-Water Safety, Air Pollution and Climate Change, and Age Discrimination. The limited number of issues examined allows a more detailed scrutiny of the cumulative nature of the process of agenda-building in Congress. By choosing fewer subtopics, we can also indicate a distinction between less and more intense hearing activity, which we show through the shading of the cells corresponding to the congress and the subtopic. Deeper shading is reserved for subtopics on which twenty or more hearings were held, while lighter shading indicates that Congress conducted one to nineteen hearings, and,

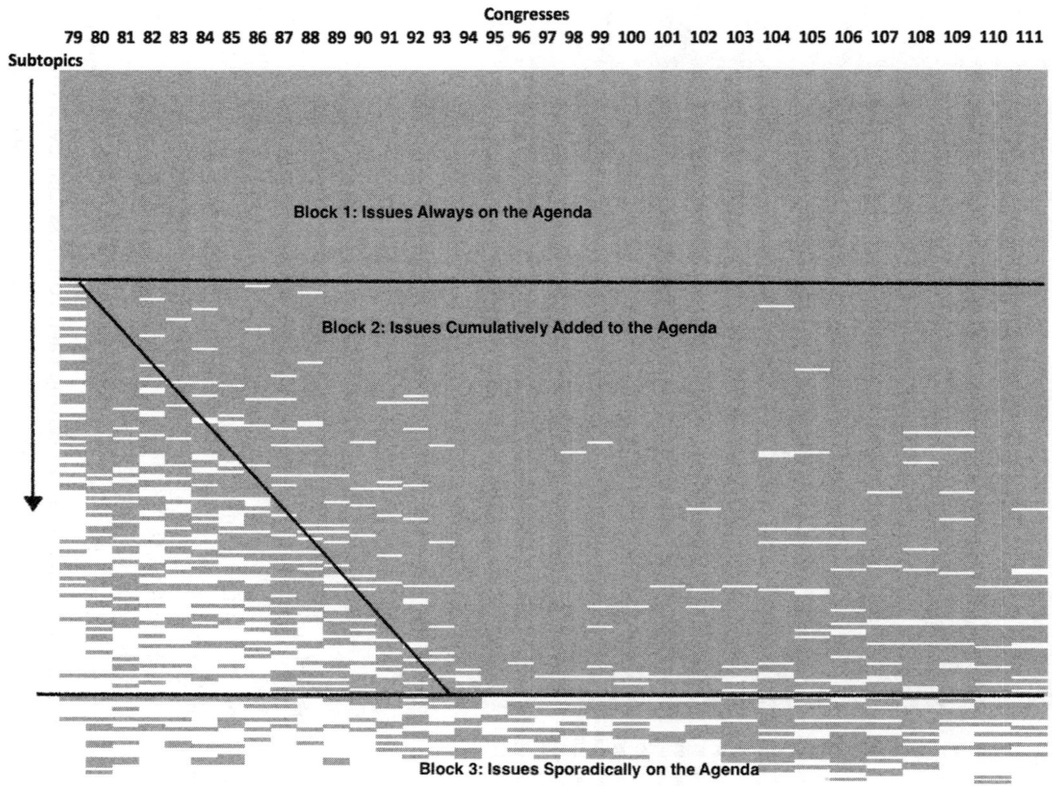

FIGURE 4.1. Cumulative scaling of issues on the formal congressional agenda

Congresses	Military Manpower	Tax Policies	Higher Education	Drinking Water Safety	Air Pollution and Climate Change	Age Discrimination
79 (1945-47)	87	6	3	0	0	0
80 (1947-49)	223	21	12	0	0	0
81 (1949-51)	150	15	6	0	0	0
82 (1951-53)	110	15	4	0	0	0
83 (1953-55)	104	15	8	0	2	0
84 (1955-57)	101	18	13	0	0	0
85 (1957-59)	60	19	5	11	0	0
86 (1959-61)	60	20	12	32	6	0
87 (1961-63)	58	26	8	32	1	0
88 (1963-65)	37	24	14	21	12	0
89 (1965-67)	57	16	16	19	1	0
90 (1967-69)	39	10	18	41	1	1
91 (1969-71)	44	34	27	27	11	1
92 (1971-73)	52	16	16	21	14	0
93 (1973-75)	47	45	30	36	5	1
94 (1975-77)	48	39	20	23	15	4
95 (1977-79)	83	69	23	29	24	8
96 (1979-81)	73	73	36	31	59	9
97 (1981-83)	70	72	34	24	41	9
98 (1983-85)	46	82	31	21	45	3
99 (1985-87)	37	83	29	33	51	6
100 (1987-89)	46	33	19	32	55	6
101 (1989-91)	50	24	18	24	44	11
102 (1991-93)	45	31	51	28	41	3
103 (1993-95)	57	27	6	29	40	1
104 (1995-97)	38	48	10	16	12	0
105 (1997-99)	56	9	34	16	16	1
106 (1999-2001)	48	24	4	13	19	0
107 (2001-2003)	45	16	17	17	19	1
108 (2003-2005)	44	33	31	21	14	1
109 (2005-2007)	76	38	19	21	32	1
110 (2007-2009)	92	27	36	19	12	0
111 (2009-2011)	85	10	23	26	18	2
112 (2011-2013)	42	24	15	27	20	1

FIGURE 4.2. Number of congressional hearings within selected topics, 79th–112th Congresses (1945–2012)

again, blank cells indicate the absence of congressional hearings and, hence, the absence of the subtopic from the congressional agenda. Additionally, we show specific numbers of hearings per congress in each Policy Agendas Project code (see fig. 4.2).

Taxes, military manpower, and higher education were in block 1 in figure 4.1, indicating that they were always on the congressional agenda, though they vary considerably in how much Congress scrutinized them. Military personnel issues received intense examination during each congress, but even then the degree of focus varied. Although congressional committees held hearings on taxes and higher education during each congress, they did so with an even higher variance of attention. Perhaps not surprisingly, during the Reagan Administration, taxes received much more examination than in earlier or later periods. Higher education, perhaps surprisingly, always preoccupied Congress, but attracted the most hearings during the 1970s and 1980s.

Drinking-water safety and air pollution joined the formal agenda during the Great Broadening and stayed, which puts both issues in block 2 of figure 4.2. Shortly after the Great Broadening ended, the intensity of inquiry into both waned, though it rebounded a bit by the end of the data series.

Age discrimination also entered the agenda during the Great Broadening, though not nearly with the gusto of drinking-water safety or air pollution and climate change. As the Great Broadening was reaching its climax, Congress was holding around ten hearings per congress on age discrimination, though this interest fell precipitously—so much so that it fell completely off the agenda in three of the last ten congresses, and in six others it had only one hearing. Such a disparate pattern places age discrimination in block 3 of figure 4.2.

The finer analysis in figure 4.2 validates our approach from figure 4.1. Once an issue accesses the congressional agenda, it almost always stays there. While on the agenda, attention to the issue can wax and wane. An increase in the number of hearings is a measure of thickening, which has garnered appreciably more research time and energy than the scope, which is both understudied and significantly more consequential in understanding the development of American politics over the last fifty years.

Agenda-Setting: Cumulative Broadening and Moving Windows

Again returning to the complete dataset of congressional hearings, we can track how congressional committees hold hearings within issues by congress (see fig. 4.3). We divide the Policy Agendas subtopics within a single congress into one of four categories: (1) issues on the *continuing agenda*, comprising issues addressed in hearings in the preceding congress as well as the current congress; (2) issues on the *new issue agenda*, comprising issues within hearings in the current congress that had not had hearings during the previous congress; (3) issues that *drop off the agenda*, comprising issues not considered in the current congress that were addressed in the preceding congress; and (4) issues *not on the agenda*, comprising issues addressed by neither the preceding nor the current congress. By and large, the data show that once congressional committees hold a hearing on an issue, they continue to do so (the solid black portion of the columns). Less frequently do committees hold hearings on issues that they didn't address in the previous congress (the darker grey portion of the columns). Even less frequently, especially earlier in the time period, do they decide not to hold a hearing on an issue that they addressed in the previous congress (the lighter grey portion of the columns).

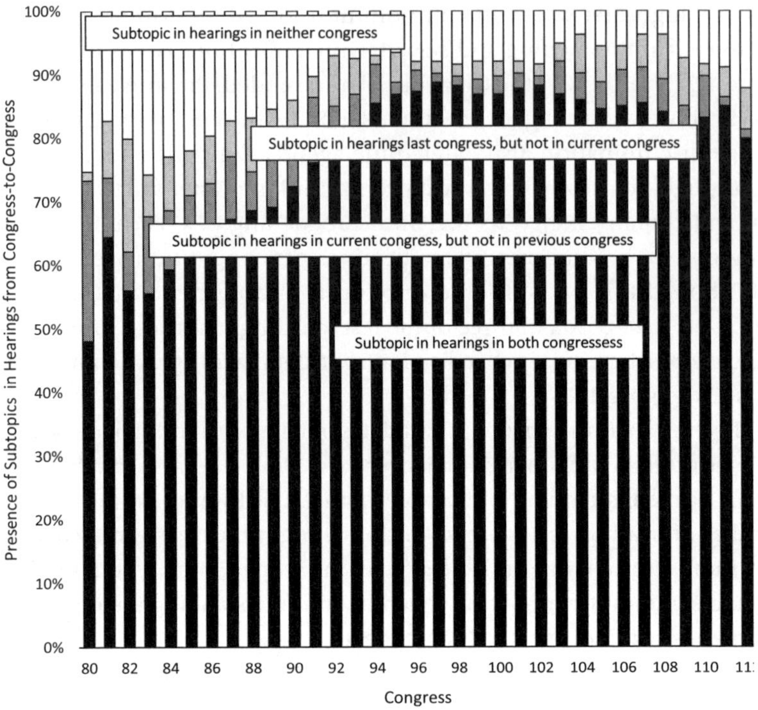

FIGURE 4.3. The congress-to-congress change in congressional hearings, by issue area

If we take a closer look at this pattern by comparing directly the issues freshly accessing the agenda in a congress with those that were dropped off the agenda in that congress (issues not addressed that were addressed in the previous congress), we find that the signature depiction of the Great Broadening stands out (see fig. 4.4). Over the eleven congresses of the Great Broadening, congressional committees hold hearings on sixteen additional issues, on average, each congress; they ignore twelve issues, on average, that they had addressed in the previous congress. As we noted earlier, the congresses directly following World War II (80th through 82nd Congresses; 1947–54) considered many issues, only to drop many of them. The issues that stayed on the agenda tended to address defense and foreign affairs, as one would expect.

The figure shows that, by the end of the Great Broadening, committees lost steam in holding hearings on new issues. Once the Great Broadening ends, the pattern becomes even starker. After the 94th Congress (1975–76), the number of new issues dropped, and the number of previously addressed

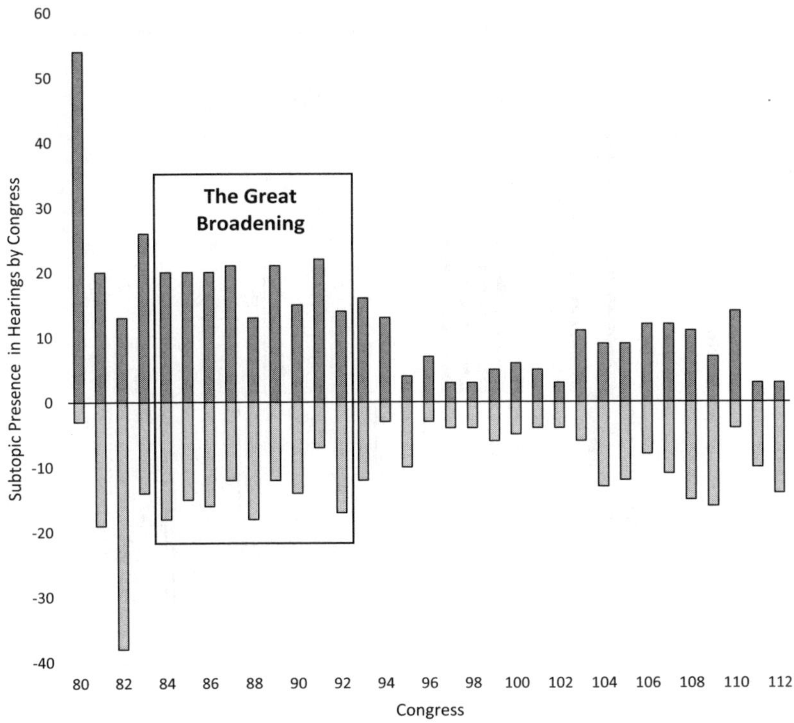

FIGURE 4.4. The number of new issues receiving a congressional hearing (dark grey bars) and the number of old issues not receiving a hearing (light grey bars)

issues increased. For every new issue that committees address, they stop holding hearings on approximately 1.3 issues.

On and Off the Congressional Agenda

The analysis of the congress-by-congress variation in how congressional committees hold hearings gives us an adequate first cut on which issues are getting attention and which aren't. We think that Congress's attention span is greater than one congress, but not much longer. We think members have some historical recall, though we expect this to fade rather rapidly. To gain additional leverage regarding what issues are on and off the agenda, we develop a more sophisticated measure.

We offer now as conjecture—and show more definitively later—that new issues operate differently than old issues. Determining what is new

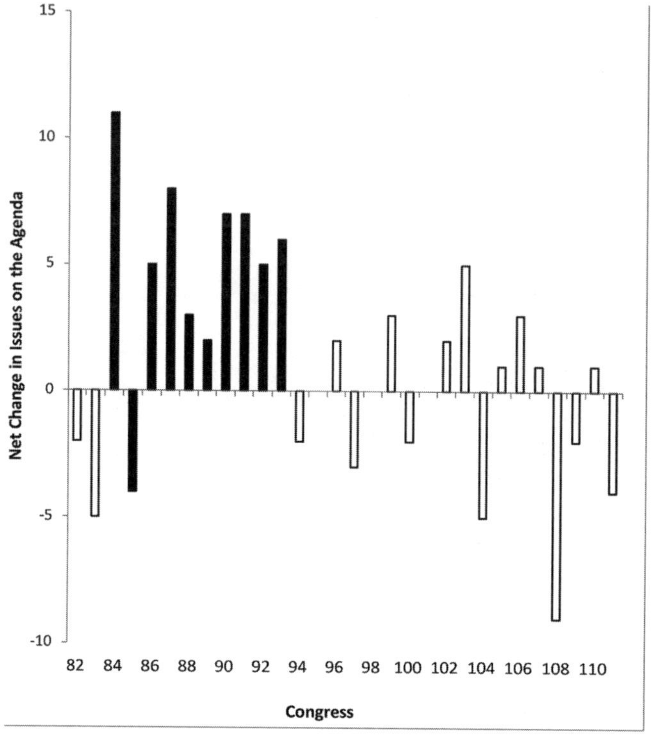

FIGURE 4.5. The net change in the number of issues on the agenda, 82nd–111th Congresses

and what is old is somewhat subjective. The measure we use for the new-old distinction is that if a subtopic had a hearing in two or three of the previous three congresses, it was an old issue. If it only had a hearing in one of the previous three congresses or none at all, it was a new issue.

Viewing the data in this manner is consistent with the broad trends presented earlier in this chapter. Again, the Great Broadening (as denoted in solid black bars) stands out (see fig. 4.5). From the 84th to the 93rd Congresses (1955–74), the agenda grew by fifty additional issues. During the brief period before and the long period afterward, the agenda shrank by sixteen issues. Throughout the remainder of this book, we use this operationalization of new and old issues to analyze the dynamics created by the Great Broadening.

While it provides an adequate picture of what happens in each individual congress, we think this figure obscures a more important trend happening over the Great Broadening. Any individual congress-to-congress change is dwarfed by the accumulation of those additions over an extended period of time. Because our measure of what is on the agenda refers to the two preceding congresses, we do not consider the first two congresses in calculating it.

Those congresses that have net gains in the number of subtopics are represented by black bars and those with net losses, as grey bars (see fig. 4.6). As examples, congressional committees held hearings in the 11 new net subtopics in the 84th Congress (1955–56), and in the following Congress, they held 3 fewer. In the 86th, they netted 4 additional subtopics, which brings the running total during the Great Broadening to 12 (11 from the 84th, minus 3 from the 85th, plus 4 from the 86th). Over the period of the Great Broadening, the agenda grew by 5.8 additional subtopics each congress. We start the accumulation of issues over with the 97th Congress, because it was then that the Great Broadening reached its peak. Afterward, the agenda shrank by 1 subtopic every two congresses. In the last four congresses of the

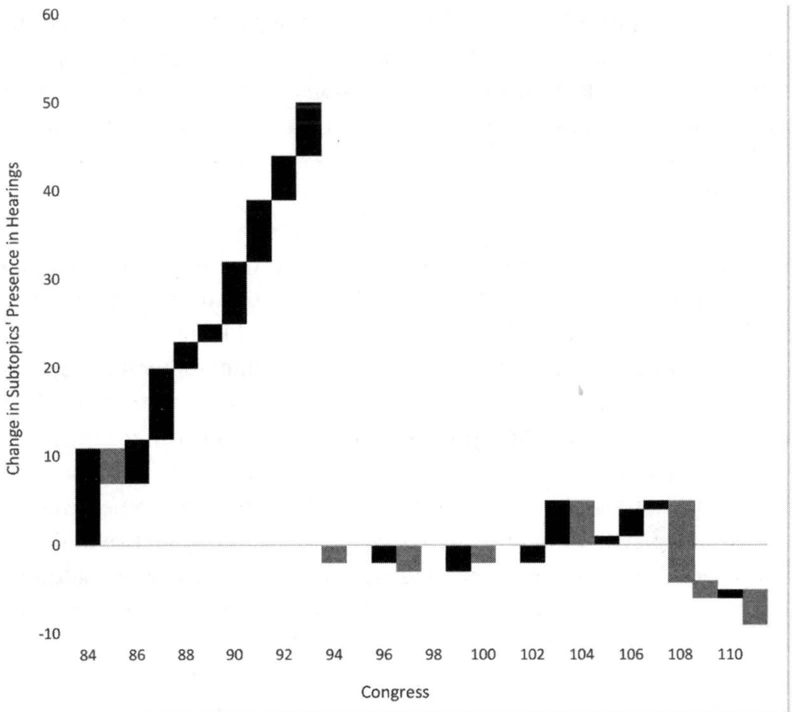

FIGURE 4.6. The cumulative adding (black bars) and subtracting (grey bars) of subtopics over time, 84th Congress to 111th Congress

time series (2003–10), the agenda lost more subtopics (6) than it gained during the Great Broadening.

Reevaluating Agenda-Setting, Policy Settlements, and Legitimacy Barriers

Congress added issues to its formal legislative agenda cumulatively. That is, if an issue appeared on it, there the issue usually remained. While Republicans succeeded in the latter part of the period in limiting the legislative agenda, they were not so successful in limiting the scope of investigatory hearings, although they certainly tried to do so. In 1995, Speaker Newt Gingrich initiated several measures to rein in the autonomy of committees, limited the resources of congressional analytical agencies—the Congressional Budget Office, the General Accountability Office, and the Congressional Research Service—and eliminated one (the Office of Technology Assessment). Moreover, committee staff resources faced severe cuts (Baumgartner and Jones 2015).

That approach has endured in the more recent Republican congresses. But, as Wilson (1979) noted, once the legitimacy barrier is breached, it is hard to "delegitimize" government's role in the area. The executive agencies created during the Great Broadening continue to issue rules and regulations and to enforce them. Congress must debate budgets and appropriations, and its oversight duties actually expand as new functions are added to the government's portfolio.

Fundamental to modern understandings of policy agenda-setting is the idea that policy-making attention is limited, and that issues shuffle in and out of a window of attention that moves through time. Initial conceptions of agenda-setting stressed the "breakthrough" nature of issue development; indeed, Cobb and Elder (1972) refer to "agenda-building" rather than "agenda-setting," which implies a long-term lodging of the issue in the portfolio of governmental priorities. We report clear support for this conception, as well as the more familiar issue-juggling understanding currently in vogue.

Up until now, we have shown that the US federal government has not expanded so greatly if we measure government spending relative to the size of the economy. But it has broadened greatly—in the sense that it addresses far more issues today than earlier—and it broadened very quickly. When government takes on new responsibilities, it generally does not drop them.

This broadening was massive and consequential. It had great policy effects as laws were enacted, budgets were both broadened and thickened, and information processing capacity grew. How could any observer doubt that this huge change failed to have subsequent political effects? Even in the data we examined here, we can detect a partisan change that affected the net subfunctions addressed in the lawmaking process, as congressional Republicans fought to limit the scope of government.

Yet far too many observers—political scientists as well as others—overlook the transformation of the American political scene wrought by the Great Broadening. We too often treat party polarization, the influence of interest groups, and money flowing to influence the conduct of public business as if they came from contemporary dynamics. Or even if we recognize the historical roots of our current political malaise, we fail to connect the current state of our politics with the policies that previous politics produced.

It matters for contemporary politics that political conflict is no longer about some things—at times, it seems that it is about all things. In the United States, as well as other Western democracies, the political debate has fundamentally shifted from what the government ought to be doing to how much it costs, what it is worth, and what level of government should do it. Our politics is driven in large part by issue-juggling—what issues we address and when—rather than what elements are legitimate for government action and what are not.

We are not claiming that internal political dynamics do not influence current politics. Clearly they do. Polarization can be self-reinforcing, as can interest-group politics (Drutman 2015). Moreover, government has used its authority in the past to reinforce *policy settlements*, as Greenstone and Peterson (1973) termed the process, to establish a status quo that has the same legitimacy as the distinction between civil and public society. Governments in the South set up a system to restrict black voters. Homosexual marriage was prohibited by law. Women could not vote. And the list goes on. These past policy settlements often disappear from the public discourse and reenter the public debate as new issues in a similar way as issues crossing the legitimacy barrier. In the United States, often the past policy settlements were forged by state governments, so the debate about ameliorative action fuses with a debate about the proper organization of policy functions in the federal system. In any case, these debates based on past policy settlements that have become accepted in law and custom, if they breach the agenda at the federal level, are indistinguishable from those issues crossing the legitimacy barrier for the first time. Data from the Policy Agendas Project and the analytical approach we use to understand the Great Broadening are such that these two processes are indistinguishable empirically.

One can make a strong case that they should be so treated. If such policy changes were part of the Great Broadening—as indeed they were—then they contributed to that broadening and were part of the same process. Indeed, the destruction of these past policy settlements was an important component of the complex set of causes that led to the broadening, as we shall see in the next chapter and in chapter 13. And these changes added to the complex set of effects that strongly influenced our current politics, as we document in the second half of the book.

PART II

Causes of the Great Broadening

The Great Broadening brought such a massive shift in how the United States was governed that the traditional ways of accounting for policy change proved inadequate to the task of explaining it. It is not that the traditional explanations of parties, groups, and institutions are irrelevant; they clearly play a critically important role. But the creedal passions of social movements seem to have been the more substantial drivers of the changes.

FIVE

Causes of the Great Broadening: Conventional Explanations

During the Great Broadening, the federal government greatly expanded its scope, co-opting policy areas that had previously been firmly within the spheres of civil society or state and local government. Having described the nuts and bolts of this encroachment, we now focus on its causes in this and the next chapter.

We test the more conventional explanations for policy change in this chapter. These conventional explanations add to our understanding of the Great Broadening, but it is clear that, even when combined, they offer an incomplete picture of its origins. The Great Broadening is no minor policy change, nor even a conventional accumulation of policy changes. Consequently, we incorporate, in the following chapter, what we think are additionally necessary components to explain this exceedingly rare transformational change in how the federal government operates and in what it is doing.

Contemporaneous Dynamics as Explanations

The analyses in this chapter are based on *contemporaneous dynamics* because the variables we evaluate occur at about the same time or just before the policy effects. Because contemporaneous dynamics must explain bursts of activity by factors that are approximately coterminous with the event, they require that large abrupt policy changes directly follow the cause. The usual suspects in which public policy change is a dependent variable are elections, party control, and such institutional features as divided government. None of these alone—or even in combination—work very well in explaining the rise of the Great Broadening or its subsequent fall.

The Problem

One of the most persistent arguments about major eruptions of policy change is the notion that political parties drive them. Political scientists may debate the manner in which incremental adjustments to policy are accomplished, but they are virtually unified in their focus on parties as engines of major policy changes. If a political party or coalition of parties unified around a common program can gain substantial majorities in Congress and control the presidency, it can achieve major programmatic change. Unfortunately this explanation does not work for major policy enactments, and we have provided evidence that it works only in a limited sense for the Great Broadening.

David Mayhew (1991) surprisingly concluded that unified governments, when a single party controls both chambers of Congress and the presidency, did not enact a higher number of important laws than divided ones. If these different regimes do not yield systematically different outcomes, political parties cannot be the keys to understanding policy change. Recall that Mayhew quantified a lawmaking surge in the 1960s and 1970s. Most subsequent studies of lawmaking have concentrated on better or different measures of congressional output rather than on understanding this surge. While an arc-shaped pattern is evident in Mayhew's surge and in the alternate output measures, subsequent researchers did not pursue a strategy directed at understanding the pattern. Rather, they continued to focus on divided government and other aspects of contemporaneous dynamics—features that were temporally associated with measures of landmark legislation or legislative productivity.

While this was a sensible strategy, it has not been particularly successful. Ansolabehere, Palmer, and Schneer's (2014) analysis of significant legislation back to 1789 encompasses the whole history of the Republic. They isolate several bursts of legislative activity beyond the Great Society period, including the 1st and 2nd Congresses; the 36th (1859–61), 51st (1889–91), and the 65th (1917–19) in the nineteenth century; and naturally the New Deal. They offer a concise assessment of the political science literature: "There are historical explanations as to why these bursts of activity occurred. The political science explanations are less convincing" (13). Our analysis of the Great Broadening is entirely consistent with this conclusion.

While we show that the standard political science explanations have serious deficiencies, they are by no means irrelevant. Indeed, they show great promise in helping to explain *changes* in the general trends, but they are not very effective in explaining the trends themselves. By addressing, in turn, elections, partisan control of Congress, and public opinion, we show clearly how the problem of policy change has been dramatically underspecified. That is, we fail as political scientists to grasp the key dependent variable—what is to be explained. We ought to focus on the broad and obvious trends in the data—here, the arc we have termed Huntington's horseshoe and the plateau of policy lock-in. Instead we have tended to concentrate our selective attention on the variables that are implicated in our theories of politics or are easier to measure, omitting those that are clearly implicated in the causal process. Here we examine some of the most obvious independent variables in explaining the patterns evident in the Great Broadening, showing where they have been successful and where they have come up short.

Mandate Elections

Theoretical studies of American institutions point to disjoint changes following shifts in partisan control driven by elections (Krehbiel 1998; Brady and Volden 1998). Elections occur, and the newly elected Congress, altered in its partisan makeup, changes the course of public policy. Yet whatever shifts might be associated with such contemporaneous political dynamics do not easily explain the now familiar trends.

One would not necessarily expect minor changes in the partisan composition of Congress to change public policy dramatically. But major electoral earthquakes should. Baumgartner and Jones (2015) examined three "mandate" elections, as described by Grossbeck, Peterson, and Stimson (2006)—1964, 1980, and 1994—focusing on the number of subtopics addressed by the laws themselves. We expand the search to include the effect of mandate elections on the number of subtopics addressed in congressional hearings. For this analysis, because it is focused on policy change rather than simply activity, we concentrate not on all congressional hearings, but only on those hearings in which the committees are considering actual legislation. These bill-referral hearings are designed to decide whether a committee should recommend a bill for action on the chamber floor. Committees also conduct nonlegislative hearings, many of which involve oversight of federal agencies.

The number of Policy Agendas subtopics addressed in lawmaking hearings follows the classic arc pattern of the Great Broadening. Moreover, this measure of the broadening agenda is closely correlated to the number of subtopics addressed in laws enacted. Both follow the arc pattern (the quadratic fit for hearings is $r = 0.86$; for laws $r = 0.77$). Even though the latter series is more variable, they correlate 0.78 (see fig. 5.1). Congressional interest in examining the scope of laws for potential enactment is closely related to the scope of laws passed.

If mandate elections are at the root of the Great Broadening, we should see major policy shifts in the scope of attention to lawmaking immediately following them in our various broadening curves. In short, we don't (see fig. 5.2). Neither a visual inspection nor a statistical one would suggest that those mandate elections affect the scope of Congress's attention any differently than the elections surrounding them. While they have no disjoint effects on the overall time series, the figure does raise the possibility that mandate elections are involved in bending the trend line; the first two elections are prominently featured around the peak of the Great Broadening. The landslide election of Lyndon Johnson in 1964 led to the legislatively productive 89th Congress (1965–66), which is not particularly distinguished in its expansion of the policy-making agenda, as assessed via congressional hearings. Ronald Reagan's election in 1980 occurred just after the peak, but it exercised no disjoint effect in the contraction of the agenda.

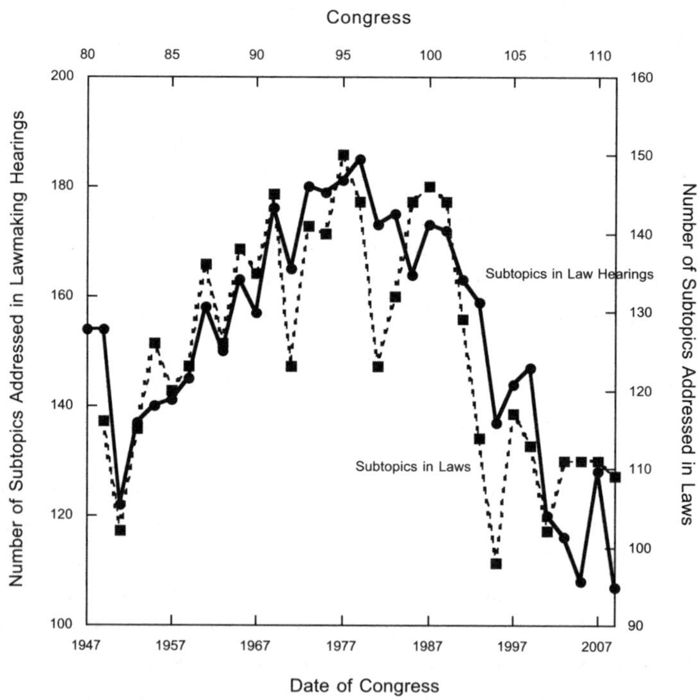

FIGURE 5.1. The scope of congressional hearings on laws and the subsequent scope of laws

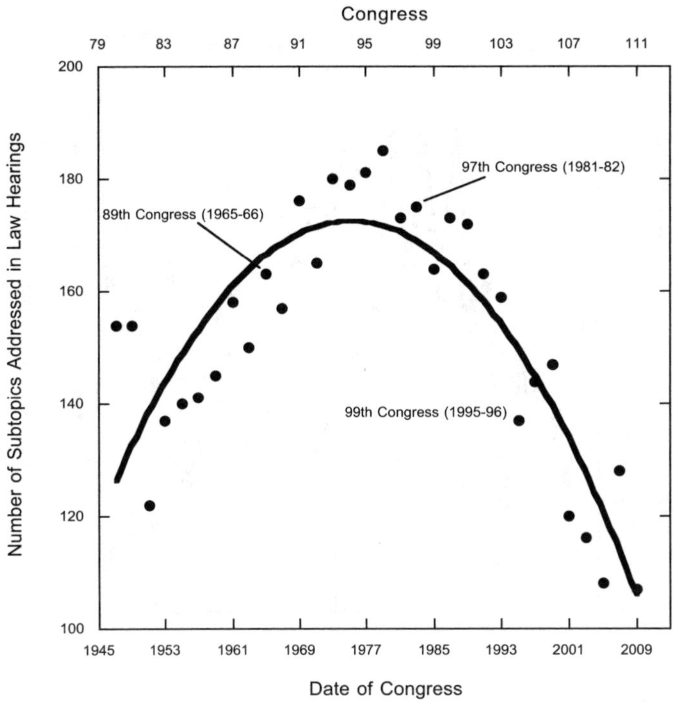

FIGURE 5.2. The arc and mandate elections

Before setting aside the importance of mandate elections to our story, it is useful to examine them in light of another measure of policy change. In chapter 1, we examined the surge of lawmaking associated with the Great Broadening using Mayhew's list of landmark statutes. Mayhew's measure of landmark laws highlights clearly and distinctly the peak period—the measure leaps upward in the 89th Congress (1965–66) and collapses in the 95th Congress (1977–78). Unlike our measures of agenda expansion, the law measure suggests quite distinct beginning and ending points for at least the critical lawmaking portion of the expansionary period (see fig. 5.3). The beginning of the period is marked by one of the landmark elections of the second half of the twentieth century—1964. But the period of most intense lawmaking ends *before* the mandate election of 1980, which means that some other mechanism than the straightforward electoral explanation is at work, or that different factors explain the lawmaking burst and lawmaking collapse.

We also display our standard measure of the broadening of lawmaking,

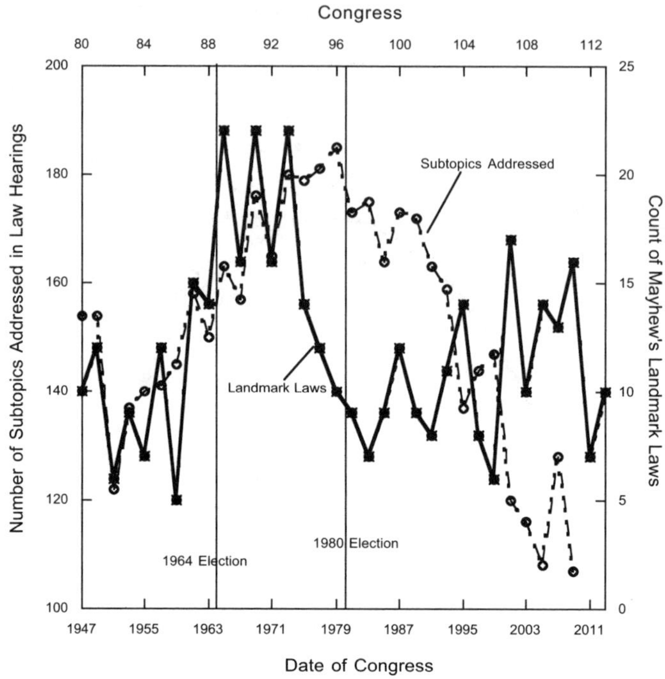

FIGURE 5.3. The Great Broadening and the number of landmark laws passed by Congress

which is the number of subtopics addressed in lawmaking hearings. Interestingly, the peak for important laws precedes the peak for law hearings. The lawmaking burst in the 89th Congress (1965–66) follows a long period of incorporating new issues into the formal congressional agenda *and* a mandate election. Moreover, the number of landmark statutes was trending upward before the 1964 election. The 1980 election occurred during the peak of agenda expansion in the 96th Congress, but well past the last peak of the Mayhew surge in the 93rd Congress (1973–74). It is possible that the broadening curve is "bent" in response to the 1980 election, which points to an asymmetry between these two critical elections in their effects on the policymaking process. It is also possible that the 1980 election reinforced a trend that had already been established—a point substantiated by the qualitative evidence (Hacker and Pierson 2010, chap. 4). Finally, the last of Grossbeck, Peterson, and Stimson's mandate elections, 1994, is in the middle of a trend of contraction in law hearings, and neither increased nor reduced landmark legislating. But surely it reinforced the contraction.

It is hard to escape the conclusion that the trend is the story, not the upheaval caused by mandate elections. Mandate elections (and hence elections generally) can bend or reinforce a prevailing trend, and the 1980 election is a classic example. In the 97th Congress, right after Reagan's election, the scope of lawmaking began to decline. The lawmaking agenda gradually become narrower, a trend that has continued to the present day. Somewhat similarly, the 1964 landslide election seems to have boosted an already-established trend toward more landmark legislation, perhaps making possible laws that otherwise would not have been able to overcome institutional and cultural resistance.

Nonetheless, serious puzzles remain. First, the number of landmark laws enacted fell during the three congresses following its last peak in the 93rd Congress (1973–74). Second, the general scope of congressional investigations (as assessed by the number of Policy Agendas subtopics addressed in all hearings) plateaued in the 94th Congress (1975–76), a Congress not associated with generalized election mandates. Interestingly, however, 1974 brought large Democratic gains as a consequence of the Watergate scandal and President Nixon's resignation.

No simple systematic connection exists between elections that can be interpreted as mandates, or even elections more generally, and the broadening of government and its subsequent narrowing. That holds regardless of whether we use agenda expansion or lawmaking activity to assess this process. Since existing models predict simple relationships between elections that result in changes in the partisan composition of Congress and policy outcomes, these models are at best wanting.

Congressional Majorities

The absence of broadening bursts in response to mandate elections does not necessarily mean that the steady accretion of political majorities (and the loss of them) likewise fails to have effects. To examine this more closely, we analyze the Great Broadening though the lens of the number of Policy Agendas subtopics addressed in congressional hearings involving potential laws and the seat share Democrats have in Congress (that is, the House and Senate summed). The latter is a crude but seemingly effective measure of Democratic power in the two chambers, although it obviously does not capture any distinction between them. Nonetheless, the result is quite striking: the curve depicting the general increase in Democratic seats from the early 1950s to 1977–78 and the decline afterward closely parallel the curve describing the Great Broadening, with the congressional party balance slightly leading the broadening (see fig. 5.4).

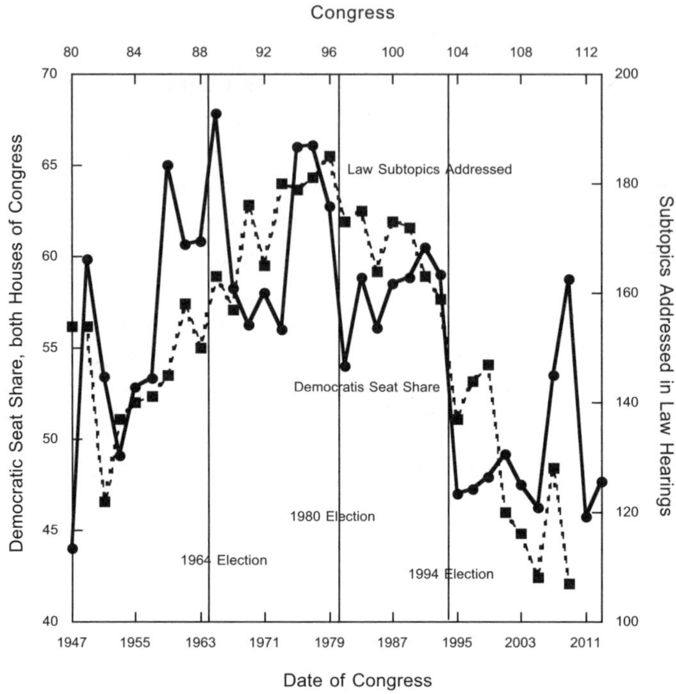

FIGURE 5.4. The Great Broadening and the Democratic seat share in Congress

It surely is not surprising that Democrats acted to broaden government, while Republicans tried to restrict it. But why did broadening in lawmaking act so systematically throughout? Why does the process seem part of a trend rather than disjoint shifts as party balances changed? Why did the broadening process decline while Democrats still had substantial majorities? Republicans did not hold majorities in both chambers of Congress until 1995. Indeed, the 104th Congress of 1995–96 experienced a big drop in the scope of law hearings, but that drop was also clearly part of the arc-shaped trend. Did the shift from Democratic to Republican control of the Senate in 1980, which lasted until 1987, affect the broadening process? The correlation between the number of lawmaking subtopics addressed in the House and the Senate is 0.93, and the curves for each trace the arc characteristic of the broadening process. Yet it is clear that Senate lawmaking hearings declined beginning in 1981, whereas House lawmaking hearings continued at about the same rate as before. So the election seems to have had an effect by attenuating the Senate's aggressiveness in considering new legislation. That was not true for the House, which the Democrats continued to hold. Yet this decline was not abrupt; rather it set in motion a downward trend that was not reversed when Democrats won control in 1976. Moreover the scope of lawmaking hearings in the House began to decline in the 102nd Congress (1991–1992) while Democrats still held that legislative chamber. Partisan majorities matter in the scope of issues considered for legislation, but they only influence the trajectories of trends; they do not cause disjoint shifts in them.

The buildup of the Great Broadening bears a similar relationship to partisan legislative majorities. The huge electoral victory of the Democrats in 1964 yielded only a slight increase in the broadening of the policy-making agenda. Furthermore, the loss of seats in 1966 yielded an increase in broadening! Why the decline in the 96th Congress, even though Democrats suffered only slightly in the 1978 election?

Another possibility exists. Perhaps the trends in lawmaking are extremely sensitive to losses or gains in partisan majorities and less sensitive to shifts in partisan control of the two chambers. If we correlate the percentage change in the seat share of Democrats with the percentage change in our subtopic measure, the correlation is zero—more accurately, –0.03. That is, any change in seat share as a result of an election has absolutely no effect on the scope of the laws being considered in the next congress. While the curvilinear trends in both broadening and in Democratic control in Congress parallel each other, incremental, year-to-year change in Democratic seats does not explain incremental changes in broadening. We conclude that incremental changes in party seat shares have no influence on the scope of issues considered for legislation and that major shifts in partisan control of the chambers influence these trends, but do not cause large disruptions in them.

In addition, changes in party control of the presidency do not seem to carry explanatory punch. Broadening increased under Republican Presidents Eisenhower, Nixon, and Ford, and decreased during Democrat Clinton's presidency. In all cases, trends dominated changes in partisan control of the presidency.

What is going on? These findings seem to indicate that political parties are in some way relevant to the Great Broadening. But it is less clear what mechanisms are at work. What does seem to be wrong is a systematic overestimation by political scientists of the immediacy of the causal connection between changes in party government and policy outcomes. Even explosive changes like the Great Broadening and the conservative revolt against it display accretion rather than sudden, disjoint change. Remember too that we study formal agenda-setting processes—the point at which government begins to examine the issue as one potentially deserving of policy action. Until now, scholars have devoted little time to this perspective, at least in part because of the lack of a systematic measure of general policy agenda change.

These processes probably operate cumulatively through a variety of mechanisms, including both elections and party control. Moreover, as we argue in the next chapter, other changes in society that are reflected in the broad mobilizations of a succession of social movements may explain the puzzle of the coterminous horseshoes. For now, we can say that our analysis shows that simple models of immediate policy change following a change in the governing party do not seem to be tenable. While the incremental changes in the seats controlled by the governing party are associated with incremental changes in the policy-making agenda, they do not seem to be causally linked.

The Public Mood

Public opinion scholars now accept the thesis that public policy and public opinion operate in dynamic equilibrium, each responding to the other. As public policy became more liberal, public opinion, responding to the excesses, became more conservative. Wlezien (1995) termed the relationship *thermostatic* because his analysis showed that the relationship was governed by a mechanism that prevented excesses. Erikson, Mackuen, and Stimson (2002) built error-correction models of the broader governing process premised on a similar understanding of the policy-opinion dynamic. The thermostat dynamic has been thoroughly researched in both the United States and comparative contexts (Soroka and Wlezien 2010; Ellis and Faricy 2011). While there remains substantial debate about whether this dynamic operates at the issue level or if it acts more broadly, studies have almost exclusively concentrated on output measures, such as expenditures (Wlezien 1995; Soroka and Wlezien 2010; Ellis and Faricy 2011) and the number of laws moving in a liberal direction (Erikson, Mackuen, and Stimson 2002).

What happens if we apply this logic to broadening?[1] We evaluate the relationship using Stimson's policy-mood measure, which analyses public opinion questions across time to derive a reliable estimate of the liberal-conservative balance in the public. It basically assesses what Free and Cantril (1967) termed *operational liberalism*, since it is based mostly on responses to particular issues facing government. We expect, on the basis of the thermostat model, to find an inverse relationship between broadening and policy

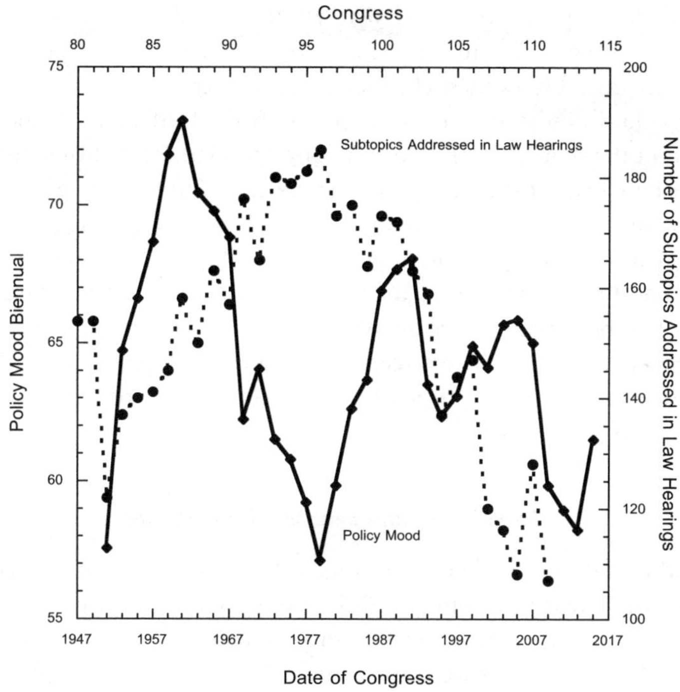

FIGURE 5.5. The Great Broadening and Policy Mood

mood. As the Great Broadening proceeded, policy mood should have become more conservative.

The actual story is considerably more complicated (see fig. 5.5). Policy mood rose throughout the 1950s, reaching its peak for the entire series in the 87th Congress (1961–62).[2] During this period, our law-hearings measure of broadening increased as well, but with a lag. As policy mood shifted direction and fell from the 97th to its nadir in the 96th Congress (1979–80), the Great Broadening as assessed by lawmaking hearings reached its peak. Then, as the scope of lawmaking decreased, policy mood increased until the early 1990s, when it fell, rose, and fell again.

The data reveal huge swings, with trends continuing for years and years and through election after election with no reversal in policy direction by the governing coalition. For more than a quarter of a century, Congress expanded the policy agenda, even though public opinion, as assessed by Stimson's policy mood measure, turned sour during the mid-1960s. A similar pattern took place after 1978, with government constricting the policy-making agenda year after year, while the public became more and more supportive of expansion. While the thermostat metaphor seems apt to describe this, it is a very sticky thermostat indeed.

The data do indicate that in the period from 1961 to 1991, the policy mood and the scope of the policy-making agenda have a strong but sticky thermostatic relationship. Policy-makers seem to ignore the signals sent by the general public, both on the upswing and the downswing periods. Before and after those periods, however, the relationship between public opinion and policy activity seems more direct. From the late 1940s to the early 1960s, both series move up. After the late 1980s, the general direction of both series is down. There seems to be a contingency in the influence of public opinion on the scope of policy-making that cries out for further examination.

The Relationships between the Variables

The traditional causes of policy change offer a mixed bag of results in explaining the Great Broadening. While the number of Democrats in Congress seems to have some connection to the federal government's agenda, considerable slippage between the series calls into doubt a simple story of elections. Furthermore, while the first two mandate elections bookend it, the Great Broadening actually ends before the second mandate election. The general downward trend in the scope of Congress's agenda seems to have been accelerated by the 1994 election but not caused by it. And, while the public's mood toward liberal policy bottoms out as the Great Broadening reaches its peak, the series shows significant stickiness, which suggests that there's much more to the story than just public mood.

These results, in isolation, cannot speak to a causal story that involves an intricate interaction between congressional majorities, policy mood, and the Great Broadening. If we examine Democratic seat share, policy mood, and broadening together, we find (as expected) that Democratic seat share operated positively on broadening and policy mood negatively (see table 5.1). Party control is more highly correlated with broadening than public opinion, at least throughout the full series. Furthermore, during the most critical period (circa 1960–94), policy mood is negatively related to broadening. We ought not to rule out the possibility that public opinion was especially crucial in this particular period, perhaps acting in tandem with party control. In any case, Democratic seat share in Congress is systematically related to broadening—the greater the number of Democratic seats in Congress, the more likely Congress is to expand the lawmaking agenda.

Table 5.1 Relationship between Broadening, Democratic Seat Share, and Policy Mood

	Democratic seat share	Policy mood
Broadening	0.57	−0.11
Democratic seat share		0.27

The scope of the federal policy agenda peaked and subsequently plateaued in the 94th Congress (1975–76). Democratic seat share reached its peak in the 95th Congress (1977–78). Policy mood reached a nadir, and lawmaking scope reached its peak in the 96th Congress (1979–80). Conservative Ronald Reagan was elected president in 1980. It is pretty difficult to conclude that the dynamic equilibrium of the thermostatic model is not in play, given figure 5.4. Four major trends in American politics shifted direction in a very short period of time. Whatever happened, the late 1970s are surely the historical key.

Much more could be done in exploring these relationships. While we do not attempt to construct a more robust statistical model here, we speculate how the intertwined factors are operating. Democratic seats in Congress are directly proportional to expanding the reach of government, although the relationship is not as strong as many would have expected. Policy mood is associated with policy broadening, as the thermostatic model would suggest. After the early 1960s, policy mood has a negative impact on broadening at first, as it declines throughout the early part of the period of our study. But the broadening continues unabated; the public signals of desire to go more slowly in the expansionary phase are ignored within the political system because the Democratic seats actually increase. Policy mood becomes more liberal after 1980 and after the peak of the Great Broadening, and increasingly supports broadening as the delayed dynamics of the policy process act to retard and then stop the expansionary trend (as we measure it).

Is not this the democratic process we would expect? Democrats act to bring new issues to the agenda and are better able to do that as they gain seats. Public opinion exerts a brake on too much expansion (or contraction), but at least during the Great Broadening it was not an effective constraint until the breaking point of 1980. The connection between the direct effect of public opinion and its indirect effect via congressional elections is probably more complex than is commonly realized, at least when it comes to changes in the size of the policy-making agenda.

Even though peaks and troughs occur in policy mood, causation between it and our broadening measure does not seem to operate instantaneously. Mood seems to be reacting to broadening rather than the other way around. It may affect broadening as well through a thermostatic relationship, but while the public's policy mood can react directly to broadening, broadening cannot react directly to public-policy predilections. That takes some translating via more focused public debates and policy proposals. As a consequence, we would expect that the public would react more quickly to government's expansion than government could react to changes in the public's mood about that expansion.

We cannot lose sight of the arc of policy change that dominates the political landscape during the second half of the twentieth century. More than anything else, it remains mysterious so long as we focus on the standard variables of contemporaneous dynamics. If we integrate the conventional understanding of policy change with the related measures of candidate arguments and specific promises, as well as the news coverage they receive, we may provide a more complete picture of the dynamics underlying the Great Broadening. Before we turn to the less-standard dynamics of social movements and "creedal passions" in chapter 6, we get a bit closer to the policy-making action within America's national institutions. Perhaps more immediate causal influences can be detected in variables in the public and partisan debates over policy rather than in the party balances in Congress or in the generalized policy predilections of the public. We turn to one way of doing this in the next section.

Policy Platforms and Partisan Debate

Students of public policy think of government as an adaptive system responding to various inputs. Yet because of the design of policy-making systems and other factors, that adaptation is not instantaneous. As a consequence, this resistance can cause errors in adaptation to cumulate, leading to policy bursts. Political systems with high friction (or resistance to change) experience more dramatic outbursts of policy change than those that have lower levels of change (Jones and Baumgartner 2005; Jones, Baumgartner, et al. 2009). The idea is based on an *error accumulation* approach, in which unaddressed problems and demands can cumulate and later burst, somewhat like the pressures in plate tectonics that lead to earthquakes.

In a similar vein, Hacker and Pierson (2010) see a major challenge in "policy drift," in which past policy solutions do not address current realities because they are not updated to account for actions taken by private actors.

The ability of groups to use the system's many veto points to stymie change is a major reason for the dominance of policy drift. Conservatives might cite a similar mechanism, in which bureaucracies on "automatic pilot" do not adjust for the dynamism of a creative economy. The mechanism is not directional. This approach has the decided advantage of integrating institutional features into the mix, but it doesn't build in the emotion and contagion that animate creedal passion and amplify calls for policy changes.

Maybe we are witnessing a combination of two factors: the lock-in and friction so characteristic of the US political system in combination with a dynamic evolution of the public debate. Public discussions and partisan debates about policy issues can change over time, but the policy responses to such changes are not instantaneous. The debate runs ahead of the policy adjustment. When this resistance is overcome through creedal passions or crises, policy adjustment occurs, but it does so through a response over several years and on an issue-by-issue basis.

It behooves us to try to measure aspects of the public debate independently of contemporaneous factors, such as party control of government. Party platforms are ideal measures of a major component of such democratic debate. While they may not bind elected party members, and in the United States they have never been intended to do so, they are excellent indicators of what issues the parties want to address.

Here we analyze two issues that relate to the party platforms. The first is whether the parties cumulate issues in a manner similar to what we found for Congress in chapter 4. That is, do the issues that parties address in their platforms enter into the public debate and stay there? Or are these issues more transient, moving in and out of the platforms as they gain and lose visibility in public attention? The second is whether parties take up issues before or after government addresses them.

The Policy Agendas Project codes the subtopics discussed in the quadrennial party platforms from the national conventions that officially select the party's nominees for the presidential elections.[3] In the weeks leading up to the conventions, party insiders wrangle over which issues are to be discussed in the platforms and how they are discussed. The manner in which these subtopic discussions are added to the parties' priorities supports the argument for issue accumulation (see fig. 5.6). To analyze the nature of expansion and contraction, we use the same Guttman scaling that we did for congressional hearings in the last chapter. If at least one of the parties included the subtopic in its platform that year, the block representing the subtopic for that year is shaded. If not, it is white. The chart keeps the platform

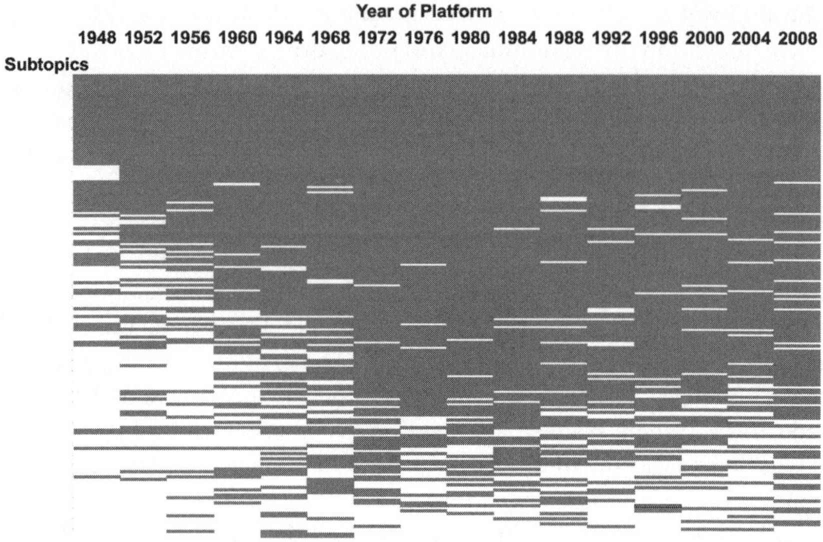

FIGURE 5.6. The addition of policy issues to the party platforms

year in chronological order (Hayes and Ellickson 1990) and orders the subtopics according to the number of subtopics discussed over the period of study (1948–2008).

The particulars of the issue topics don't show up very well in the figure, because of the reduction in size necessary to depict the overall pattern. In any case they are less important than that overall pattern. As with the congressional hearings, three distinct regions emerge, but with some ambiguity in where the actual lines should be drawn. The first is a large shaded block at the top, representing issues that at least one party raised in its platform during the full period. The second approximates a right triangle, where issues are added cumulatively. The final block displays a sporadic pattern in which issues move in and out; they are not permanent. Overall, the cumulative nature of adding issues is reasonably clear, although some subtopics appear more or less sporadically. Also, the parties dropped discussion of subtopics entirely later in the period, indicating some winnowing of issues, but this trend is dwarfed by the cumulative adding of issues. If at least one of the parties addresses an issue, that issue tends to continue to appear in the platform of one or both of the parties throughout the period.

The content of the issues that fall in each of the three sectors differs systematically. In the first block—issues discussed throughout the period—economics dominates. Five of the thirty-two issues that were discussed in one or both platforms centered on macroeconomic issues—inflation, unemployment, the federal budget, tax policies, and general economic matters. Other matters preoccupying the platform writers throughout the period were labor affairs, education, housing and community development, defense, and minority discrimination (civil rights). Two subtopics involved public lands, natural resources, and water development. If we look at the six issues not discussed in 1948, but mentioned thereafter, we find three other public lands and resource development topics, making a total of five of the thirty-seven issues discussed throughout the 1952–2008 period. These issues are, for the most part, the old, established issues that have preoccupied the federal government since the industrial revolution. Economics, labor issues, and land and resource development were the mainstays of US partisan conflict long before our platform measurement began.

The second block of issues represents the cumulative adding of new issues to the public debate. This block is a right triangle, in which issues at the top of the block have been discussed during most of the period, while the newer issues, added later, are at the bottom. Early in the development of the platforms, social welfare and health issues appear along with more civil rights subtopics. As time proceeds, environmentalism appears as a central matter for debate, health care issues broaden into more components of this complex problem, and energy becomes a focus. Crime and justice appeared as national issues in the 1970s and lodged there. Characteristic of all these issues is that once they appear on the party platforms, they tend to stay there.

The final segment of the figure, at the bottom, are those issues that appear sporadically but are not matters of continued interest. They appear on the partisan agenda at times, but at other times they disappear. Domestic commerce and science and technology are signature issues in this block.

While many issues do not entirely disappear from the agenda, it is worth noting a few of those that do. Regulating domestic commerce and antitrust enforcement were issues of great platform concern early in the period, but faded as time went on (remember, though, our measures stop in 2008). The parties targeted antigovernment activity in the 1950s and 1960s, but interest faded over time.

The second analysis we perform on platform data is whether the parties anticipated the Great Broadening through their platforms, or whether they simply addressed the issues after government already had taken them up. By combining the subtopics addressed in each party's platform for a sum of the total topics discussed, we ensure that if a topic is addressed by either party, or by both, it appears in the data. We term this measure the *party system*'s

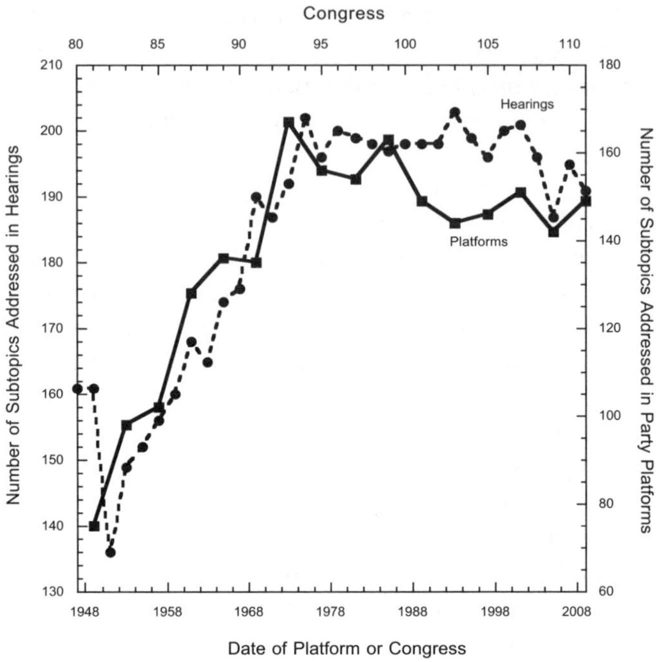

FIGURE 5.7. Broadening, according to party platforms and congressional hearings

policy agenda. Differences between the parties exist, as we will see shortly, but for now we concentrate on the totality of the party system agenda. We compare the subtopic measure for the party system's agenda to the congressional agenda measured as total hearing activity (see fig. 5.7). The two series are matched so that the hearings data for a congress match the platform data in the election the year before.

The platforms trace the agenda asymptote pattern, in which a large-scale broadening of the parties' agendas occurs. But can we say more about the relationships between the two series? Indeed, we can. The parties' broadening of the agenda occurred first, and congressional hearings followed. In each year except 1968, the number of subtopics addressed by the platforms exceeds the number of topics addressed in hearings. After 1976, however, the number of subtopics in hearings exceeds the number of subtopics in platforms. Before the peak, the parties led government in addressing issues, but after that period, party platforms became more focused, no longer raising new issues. Party platforms instead concentrate on debating the issues already on the governmental agenda in lieu of raising them for consideration by government.

Perhaps this may seem trivial—prevailing wisdom would suggest that parties lead government in establishing the policy-making agenda. But given that elections are not so clearly related to agenda-expansion, the simple platform-election-policy link that is almost conventional wisdom among political scientists and pundits as well is strained. At first platforms perform as the standard model would predict—leading the governmental discussion of new issues; but the relationship inexplicably reverses itself. Why would the pattern reverse itself after the late-1970s? Now platforms seem to trail the government's formal agenda. Platforms become more focused—in the sense of touching on fewer topics—after the peak of the Great Broadening. Hearings, at least until after the mid-1990s, do not.

The most likely answer to this quandary is the conservative countermovement, which in all likelihood was spawned in considerable part by the rapid broadening of government. We'll explore this relationship in greater detail later, so that we can now take a closer look at the role of platforms in the broadening process. It will surprise few to find that the Democratic platform addresses more issues earlier than the Republican platform (see fig. 5.8). In

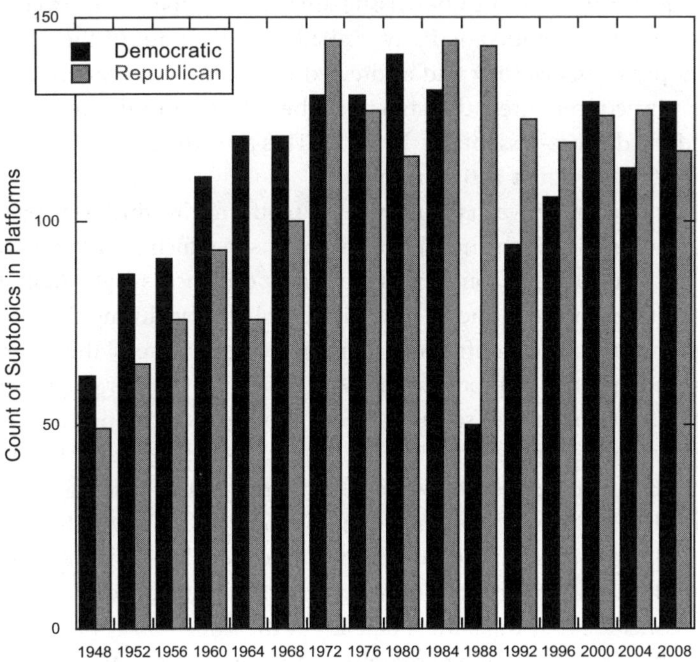

FIGURE 5.8. The scope of the party platforms, 1948–2008

every pair of platforms between 1948 and 1968, the Democrats addressed more issues than the Republicans. By 1972, both party platforms had reached the typical asymptote—and each party addressed fewer than 150 Policy Agendas subtopics throughout the rest of the period.

We can also look at each party's platform separately. The Democratic Party platform leads the Republican Party platform in addressing the Policy Agendas Project's subtopics for the first part of the period, but not thereafter. The number of subtopics addressed in the Democratic Party platform exceeds the number of subtopics addressed in the Republican Party platform until 1972. After that, the Republican platform exceeds the Democratic platform in addressing issues. Note the considerable idiosyncrasies in the Democratic Party platform, particularly in the very focused platform written in 1988.

Let us now focus on a strange divergence. We see that in figure 5.7, the total number of subtopics addressed in both platforms combined reaches a peak of around 160, yet as figure 5.8 shows, neither party addresses more than 140 subtopics in any one platform. The only probable explanation is that the parties talk about the same subtopics over time, but they do so in different platforms, which could result from Republicans criticizing the Democrats for moving into new issue-areas during the Great Broadening. But in 1988, the Democratic Party virtually dropped out of the debate on the panoply of issues they had addressed only four years earlier. Republicans continued to address the larger number of issues until the Democrats rejoined the debate—essentially by 2000. This time the debate was far more focused, topping out at 120 subtopics.

The correlation between the number of platforms in which one party discussed a subtopic with the number of platforms in which the other party did so is a moderate 0.42. In some areas the correspondence is high: Republicans discussed taxes in every one of their sixteen platforms during the 64 years, and Democrats did so in fifteen of theirs. But at other times, the divergence was just as stark. The Democrats discussed bankruptcy in thirteen platforms, while the Republicans did so but once. Republicans mentioned agricultural subsidies in thirteen platforms, but the Democrats did so in only five. On the other hand, the correlation between whether the parties raised a subtopic at any time during the period is a much more robust 0.72. Only eight subtopics out of 220 had only one party comment, while the other remained silent; an additional thirteen subtopics did not receive a comment from either party. We can conclude that the parties talk about the same issues, but not necessarily at the same time. One party raises an issue, and the other addresses it as well, but often not in contemporaneous platforms.

During the Great Broadening, party platforms raised issues before Congress scheduled them for formal debate. The Democratic platform raised more issues during that period than the Republican. In each presidential election between 1948 and 1980 (excepting only 1972), Democratic platforms raised more issues than Republican ones. But Republican platforms between 1984 and 2004 (except in 2000), raised more issues than Democratic ones, and in 1988 and 1992 the divergence was huge. For the whole period we studied, Republican platforms raised issues as aggressively as Democratic ones. These conclusions, again, suggest that dynamics above and beyond political parties need to be addressed in understanding the Great Broadening.

What Happened in the Late 1970s?

In this chapter we have discussed some of the major political science understandings of the causes of policy change, including such standard suspects as changes in party control of the legislature and electoral mandates. Standard theories of policy change based on electoral factors and party control imply disjoint changes after the election. That is not what we find; rather, expansion is not easily connected to any of the factors we examined: elections, partisan control of Congress, and public policy mood.

Or rather, the connection is not simple; perhaps further examinations of the process will lead to a set of interacting causes that combine to produce the broadening phenomenon. For example, the mandate election of 1964 occurred near the peak of the agenda-expansion process but right before the explosion of lawmaking. But the 1980 mandate election occurred after the decline of lawmaking, so it was incapable of causing the decline—although clearly the election could have accelerated it. We are working toward a holistic approach to what caused the Great Broadening, but we need to expand our explanation, which we do in the following chapter.

Nevertheless, some interesting facets of what happened during the period are unveiled by our examinations in the last few chapters. The Great Broadening peaked around 1978 and then declined. Why 1978? Electoral students have searched in vain for a great realignment to mark the shift from an electoral era dominated by the long Democratic Roosevelt coalition to something else. Surely Republicans have not dominated the period electorally, even though they have done vastly better than during the 1930s to the 1970s.

Jacob Hacker and Paul Pierson (2010, 96) had the right perspective when they advised us to quit looking at elections and to look instead at "what the government was actually doing." They point out the legislative accomplishments during the Nixon administration and the refusal of congressional Democrats to work out legislation with both Nixon and Ford on health care and welfare reform. Then they cite 1977–78 as the "great turning point in modern American political history," which "marked the rapid demise of the liberal era" (99). We have shown how this narrative can be depicted as a great arc, or horseshoe, although it misses the traces of the arc of liberal activity throughout the rest of modern US political history (the asymptote).

An amazing confluence of streams of seemingly independent activities also turned virtually on a dime in the late 1970s—in or around 1978:

- The Great Broadening, as measured by Policy Agendas subtopics and in such activities as bills introduced and hearings on laws, peaked.
- Interest groups, as measured by the *Encyclopedia of Associations*, leaped upward during this period, from an increase of 3 percent in the 95th Congress to 11 percent in the 96th Congress, in a trend that only abated in the late 1980s. The estimated number of groups increased almost 150 percent between these two periods.
- Democratic Party seats in Congress reached a peak in the 94th Congress (1975–76).
- Partisan polarization, after staying fairly constant for more two decades, began to rise sharply in the 95th Congress (1977–78).
- Newt Gingrich entered the House of Representatives and, with the Conservative Opportunity Society behind him, reoriented Republican politics on Capitol Hill away from the Bob Michel's "Go along to get along" approach toward confrontation at every stage and arena of the legislative process (Theriault 2013).
- Liberal Policy Mood, as measured by James Stimson, reached its nadir. Policy Liberalism reached its lowest point during the 96th Congress (1979–80).

Indeed, around 1978, everything changed. Government stopped broadening; the agenda expansion ended. Moreover, as we explore in more detail later, the interest-group system began to expand rapidly; the steep trend toward more and more partisan polarization began; and liberal public opinion began its recovery. Why would there be such an easily identified pivot point in modern American politics? Why is that pivot point at least partially decoupled from electoral, partisan, and public opinion dynamics? It is probable that electoral students, at least those studying government and public policy as hostage to the exogenous movements of electorates, have quite simply been looking in the wrong places.

SIX

Causes of the Great Broadening: The Role of Social Movements

Assessing the relative merit of the various potential causes of a single historic event is difficult—*overdetermined* has become the term of choice for such situations. Perhaps the Great Broadening across so many issues was a historical fluke, a confluence of forces that happened once and cannot be expected again. Indeed, some historians argue that the postwar development of government was unique. And the historical story is indeed persuasive. That is unlikely to satisfy many social scientists, who want to find generalizable causes—even of great events. Nor is it theoretically impossible to study such events more systematically—ask astrophysicists examining the creation of the universe, surely a unique event, through both theoretical and empirical lenses.

The results from the previous chapter indicate how difficult it is to pin the broadening on the important set of factors that political scientists usually turn to first. Even in combination, they offer at best a partial explanation. It is likely that the path forward involves some combination of elections, public opinion, and the issue-focus of the parties; as we argued at the end of the preceding chapter, however, these parts cannot comprise the whole story. In this chapter we combine those causes into a broader explanation that includes the role of history and the power of social movements. In so doing, we hope to provoke a broader appreciation of historical periods of great passion and emotion alternating with quieter, "normal" politics and the operation of our political system (Dodd 2012; 2015). We gain leverage on this cycle by exploiting an underappreciated element of the development of liberal social movements in the 1960s and 1970s: namely, that they were sequenced, peaking at different times during the broadening period. Yet many of the macropolitical dynamics did not change during the period—for example, large Democratic majorities in Congress and favorable public opinion. Control of the presidency changed, but not in a way that would explain the sequencing. In chapter 13 we show a similar sequencing pattern of conservative reaction as the expansion of the federal government ebbed.

A Feature, Not a Bug

Social movements in America are a feature of our politics, not a "bug." Samuel Huntington (1981, 89) wrote that "there are thus two American politics: the politics of movement and causes, of creedal passion and reform, and the politics of interests and groups, of pragmatic bargaining and compromise." By "creedal" Huntington meant that the reformers see the existing system as failing to live up to the American constitutional creed. He continues: "Creedal politics tends to be intermittent rather than continuous, passionate rather than pragmatic, idealistic rather than materialistic, reform-minded rather than status-quo oriented, and formulated in terms of right and wrong rather than more or less" (105). Throughout history these sprawling movements have shaken American politics, not infrequently transforming it. The religious Great Awakenings of the early nineteenth century, calls for democratization epitomized by Andrew Jackson, abolitionists, advocates of women's rights, agrarian populism, temperance advocates, progressives, Southern redeemers, the Ku Klux Klan in its 1920s heyday and its 1950s resurgence, labor organizations, civil rights, consumer rights, and right-to-life groups all displayed the passionate critiques of creedal commitment. These irregular outbursts are nevertheless predictable, in occurrence if not timing. It is high time that political scientists incorporate these "irregular regularities" into our understandings of the mainsprings of American democracy.

Political scientists think of political parties as representing broad interests and opinions in democratic polities, while interest groups represent narrower interests. Social movements sprawl outside the bounds of normal partisan and interest-group politics, but they tend to focus on narrower inequities and grievances than parties. As a consequence, it is not always easy to distinguish interest groups from social movements (Burstein 2002). Often social movements over time lose passion and settle into the more normal give-and-take of coalitional politics.

Why in America cannot these passionate movements be captured within the party structures? Why were they not so captured during the Great Broadening? There are both institutional and sociocultural causes. Institutionally, the "first past the post," single-member district electoral system discourages party formation and hence the representation of new and passionate interests in a changing society. Culturally, the specific promises of the founding documents—the Declaration of Independence and the Constitution itself—were not fulfilled at the founding, nor have they ever been fully realized. Indeed, the whole founding enterprise was premised on fallible humans in an always imperfect society. This condition led to Huntington's astute observation that social movements generally hark back to the founding and the failure of the political system to live up to those ideals. That is true of social movements on both the right and the left. Finally, many social movements were intertwined with religion, giving them a particular moral authority, as openness and innovation in religion spilled over into politics (Marone 2003).

Social movements are not contained by the confines of the coalition-building of political parties and interest groups, because parties and groups represent the present, and social movements conceive of a more perfect future. Adaptive parties often move to capture the passion of social movements, pushing them rapidly toward reform. The American Constitutional system, argued James Madison in *Federalist 10*, was built on restraint and friction as the founders strove to make it difficult for passionate factions "whether a majority or minority of the whole who are united and actuated by some common impulse of passion, or of interest, adverse to the rights of other citizens or to the permanent and aggregate interests of the community" to enact those passions into public policy. But the virtue of constitutional resistance to passions leads to delaying reforms. Moreover, some social passions dissipate, but others build, causing greater ruptures in policy when they occur (Jones and Baumgartner 2005).

Social Movements and the Great Broadening

Some periods in history are more wracked by social movements than others. The period of the Great Broadening was clearly one of these periods, but how did this come about? As with elections, parties, and public opinion, we do not accept social movements as a cause without testing that idea. The occurrence of street protests and heightened passions does not necessarily mean that they caused the broadening. Indeed, grassroots activity tends to be focused on single issues, whereas the Great Broadening spilled over many issues in a complex pattern across a broad sweep of policy areas and in a relatively short period of time.

By including social movements in the explanation, we attempt to fold in the outbursts of energy and action that Huntington captured with his phrase "creedal passions." In social movements, leaders channel these passions toward a set of interconnected policy aims that are generally not closely associated with the regular politics of political parties and interest groups. We show that the series of social movements was sequenced such that earlier movements affected later ones. This happened through a social learning process that unified this sequence of movements into a cascade of change—the Great Broadening.

Social movements, of course, are not the whole story. A multiplicity of interacting causes seems to be implicated in the agenda explosion of the 1960s and 1970s. To capture this broader explanation, we deploy explanations from the policy-process literature, including policy feedback and punctuated equilibrium. Policy-process theories are even more critical in explaining the Great Broadening's downstream effects, which preoccupies much of the remainder of this book.

A broader examination turns up none of the explanations most cherished by political scientists. Indeed, Mayhew's idea of periods of public activism, societal demand for activist government, Schlesinger's thinking about liberal-to-conservative cycles of history (even if the existence of cycles is highly suspect), and Huntington's periods of passionate reform probably come closer to the truth.

Again, we set out to explain a singular event: the Great Broadening. The study of a singular event is not unscientific. Yet it is historical, in that bursts of policy change may emerge from a seldom-repeated confluence of forces. So we study the Great Broadening directly, in effect returning to Huntington's initial project—understanding the horseshoe and similar bursts—in detail, using the more precise measures of the Policy Agendas Project.

Historical Causes of the Great Broadening

While studies of contemporaneous political dynamics have focused on such standard political variables as political party control and divided government, historical accounts have focused on the passions of reform movements. Huntington (1981) views American political history as consisting of two distinct phases: creedal, moralistic reform on the one hand, and the transactional politics of groups and parties on the other. He thought that the Great Broadening period was similar to a limited number of others in US history, in which reform groups became passionate and articulated a "creedal" justification for their programs. Schlesinger (1986) saw similar outbreaks of activity, interspersed with quieter periods of "liberal" (as opposed to the passionate messianic) periods of pro-government activism.

Others have addressed the period alone, without comparisons to other eras. Historian James Patterson (1996) depicts politics in post–World War II

America as a unique confluence of forces that led to world leadership and a problem-solving attitude toward domestic challenges, both of which required rapid expansion of government. Sparrow (1996) sees the development of the American state in the early postwar period in similar terms—outside forces, particularly World War II and the Cold War, propelled the growth of government during the period.

This narrative has support in the quantitative record. Studies of federal budget authority found a great deal of volatility after the World War II (Jones, True, and Baumgartner 1997; Jones, Baumgartner, and True 1998). "Contrary to popular myth, the early postwar years were remarkable for dramatic changes in spending priorities, not for a staid and dampened politics based on incrementalism" (Jones, True, and Baumgartner 1997, 1321). We called these shifts in priorities experimental, because some budget categories increased, while others decreased, unlike the upward budget punctuations of the 1960s, which were associated with the Great Broadening.

Both the budget data and the data from our study of policy topics support the historical interpretation that the US Government was experimenting to determine what new functions to adopt following the massive disruptions of the war. It is also clear that this period of experimentation led to a sustained broadening of government beginning in the 83rd Congress (1953–55), a pattern that continued unabated until 1979. It is worth noting that President Truman's "Do Nothing Congress" (80th Congress, 1947–48), when Republicans held both the House and the Senate, was just as active by our measures—hearings and laws—as the 81st Congress. If any Congress during the period was "do-nothing," it was the 82nd (1951–52).

It would be folly to think of the Great Broadening as stemming solely from an adjustment to the postwar reality of the Cold War and US leadership. It is possible that World War II set off a chain of events that led to the broadening, as happened in such areas as housing (which was not produced during the war) and education (with the GI Bill). But that would ignore the domestic side of the equation—the civil rights movement was gaining steam, the environmental movement was born, and Democrats scored a smashing victory in 1958, particularly bolstering the urban liberal wing of the party. As a consequence, the historical accounts also offer an incomplete explanation.

A major problem with the historical accounts is that they don't provide a basis for deciding which are the important periods of successful reform in the United States. Huntington (1981) finds four periods of creedal passion in American history: the Revolutionary, Jacksonian, Progressive, and the 1960s and 1970s. Huntington sees the activism of the New Deal as stemming from different forces, a frustrating tactic for political scientists trying to explain legislative outbreaks. Schlesinger's cycle theory does incorporate the New Deal, but it led him to predict a sharp change in the direction of the national mood in the 1990s. His *New York Times* reviewer thought that was likely a pipe dream, as indeed it was (Barber 1986).

Historical examinations of major outbursts of policy change have other problems. In addition to Ansolabehere, Palmer, and Schneer (2014) finding different legislative outbreaks from those cited by Huntington and Schlesinger, academics underestimate the conservative counter-reactions in American politics during these periods. This counter-reaction could have been missed because it seems to be lacking after both the Progressive and the New Deal periods, but it cannot be ignored in the aftermath of the Great Broadening. Conservatives responded to the Great Broadening passionately and effectively, and this counter-movement is an important part of its "downstream" effects.

Waves of Social Movements

Social movements are relatively broad-based but loosely organized agglomerations of people focused on large-scale changes. These movements are not generally associated with political parties but are unified around a set of coherent ideals. In the 1960s, such movements sprang up, mostly on the left, first around civil rights and then around environmentalism, antiwar demands, women's rights, and consumer protection. Each of these movements drew passionate followers and had deeply moralistic undertones, which seems fully appropriate for civil rights, women's rights, and environmentalism, but might be surprising for product safety, except that Ralph Nader and other activists framed product safety as a moral failing of corporations almost contemptuous of the well-being of their customers.

All of these movements were creedal, claimed failures in the ideals of America, had distinct ideologies and were not partisan—deliberately so for the most part. Some of these movements began finding more sympathy in one party and ended up closer to the other. That was clearly the case for the women's movement (Wolbrecht 2000) and environmentalism. Both of these movements, today associated with the Democratic Party, were much more closely affiliated with the middle-class base of the Republican Party in their early years. Labor unions were strongly suspicious of environmentalism as job-threatening, and the urban ethnics and rural Southern whites of the Democratic Party were hostile to changes in the traditional roles of women in society (1950s style). A much longer process characterized the civil rights movement, but it too spanned parties well into the 1960s (Schickler 2016; Carmines and Stimson 1989; Lee 2002).

The liberal social movements of the 1960s and 1970s were also sequenced, appearing on the formal policy-making agenda in the following order: civil rights, environmentalism, consumer safety, and women's rights. Later movements drew lessons and talent from earlier ones (Wolbrecht 2000). This interaction and spillover among movements and their rapid sequencing indicate a politics spanning the more typical politics of elections and political parties. Organizations representing these groups provided an extra voice for underrepresented groups and constructed cross-group coalitions. They continue to do so today, but there is evidence that they have become more traditional in their approaches (Strolovitch 2007).

Civil Rights, Women's Rights, and the Policy-Making Agenda

We start with an examination of the emblematic social movement of the period: civil rights. No issue represents the tension between cultural and institutional resistance, on the one hand, and political mobilization, on the other, better than civil rights. Resistance was powerful and reinforced by the ability of Southern Democrats in Congress to control the major institutional pathways to legislative success. Even more severe barriers blocked success at the state level, since in the 1940s and 1950s most African Americans lived in the South. Yet after decades of resistance and repression, change came, and when it came, it did so rapidly and repeatedly. The Historian of the House of Representatives termed the period from 1945 to 1968 "the Second Reconstruction."

Advocates knew access through legislative pathways was blocked, but they were able to gain traction through the courts and via executive actions. But more than anywhere else, success came in the streets. The House Historian's web page, History, Art, and Archives, in its series of essays on African Americans in Congress, tells visitors that the Second Reconstruction "consisted of a grass-roots civil rights movement coupled with gradual but progressive actions by the Presidents, the federal courts, and Congress to provide full political rights for African Americans and to begin to redress longstanding economic and social inequities."

The data bear out this relationship. Huntington's (1981, 185) measure of protest and the coverage of civil rights in the *New York Times* from the Policy Agendas Project share a striking resemblance (see fig. 6.1).[1] Huntington's measure covers all protest activity, and it is certainly not perfect by today's measurement standards. Moreover, civil rights articles in the *Times*

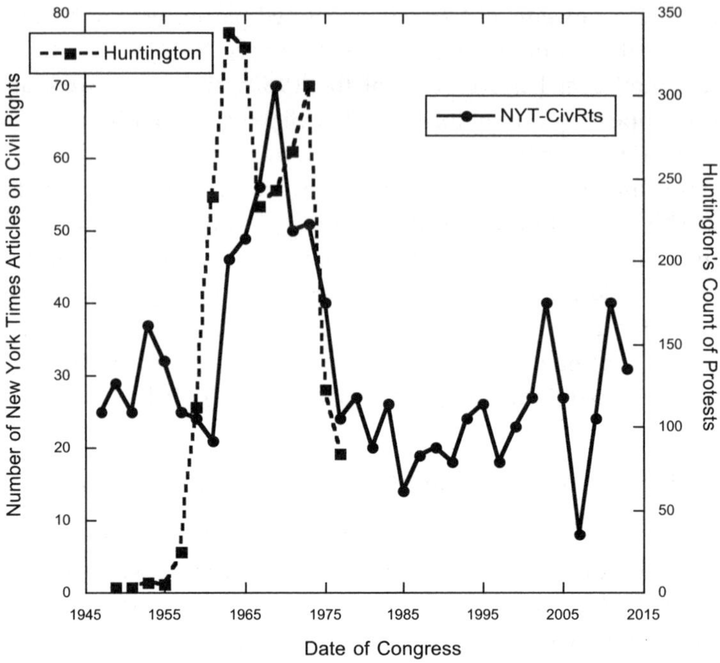

FIGURE 6.1. Number of *New York Times* articles published on civil rights and protest activity, aggregated by congress

cover much more than protests. But because we are interested in the extent to which civil rights occupied the systemic agenda, its expanse is not a disadvantage. Although they are admittedly rough measures, their trends and sequencing are highly suggestive. Beginning in the late 1950s, protest activity increased, and in 1960 newspaper coverage leaped as well. Both trace the arc pattern of surge and decline that characterizes the Great Broadening and its aftermath more generally.

Earlier work has shown that friction in institutions is generally lowest at the agenda-setting stage and increases as the difficulty of assembling enacting coalitions increases through the lawmaking process (Jones, Sulkin, and Larsen 2003). Getting on the formal agenda is easier than achieving legislative victory; getting a bill introduced on a topic meets less resistance than holding a hearing, which in turn is easier than getting a roll-call vote on the issue, and that is, of course, simpler than passing a law on the matter. Moreover, public priorities, as assessed by Gallup's Most Important Problem, are most faithfully represented in the agenda-setting stage: for example, in presidential State of the Union Addresses, congressional bill introductions, and congressional hearings (Jones, Larsen-Price, and Wilkerson 2009).[2] But if resistance is high in the earlier stages of the policy-making process, as it probably was in the case of civil rights, then different avenues may be activated.

Does the standard pattern of issue expansion through the policy-making process hold for civil rights? The Policy Agendas Project has several subtopics under its Civil Rights major topic. We have combined two of them—Minority Rights and Voting Rights—in constructing a civil rights index for congressional bill introductions and for law referral hearings (see fig. 6.2). To take account of the greater friction at the later stage in the process, we use two different scales on the graph, which allows us to focus on comparing the trends rather than on the absolute levels for the index.

It is clear that bill introductions led hearings in the early part of the series. Hearings considering proposed legislation do occur in the 1950s, but they display no trend. On the other hand, members introduced bills at an increasing rate, until the drop-off after the 1964 Civil Rights and 1965

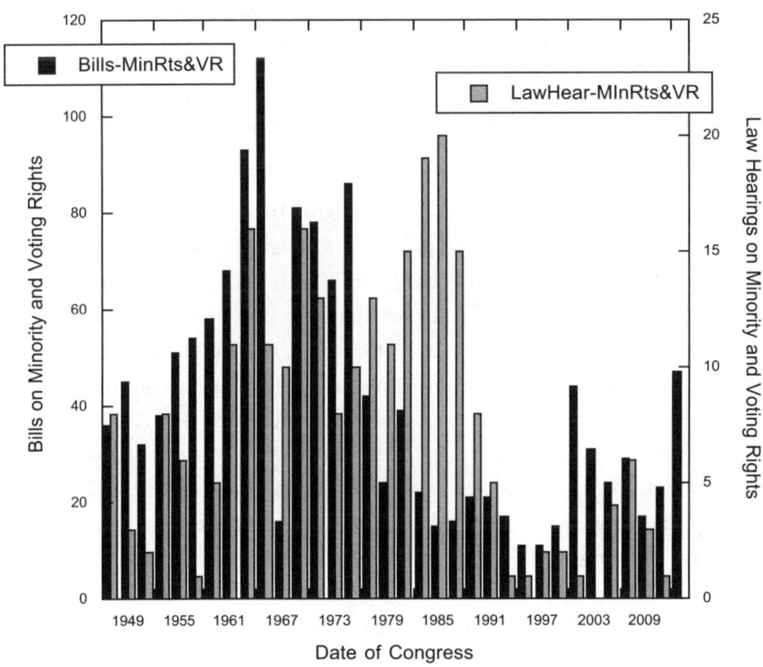

FIGURE 6.2. A comparison between bill introduction and hearings on minority and voting rights

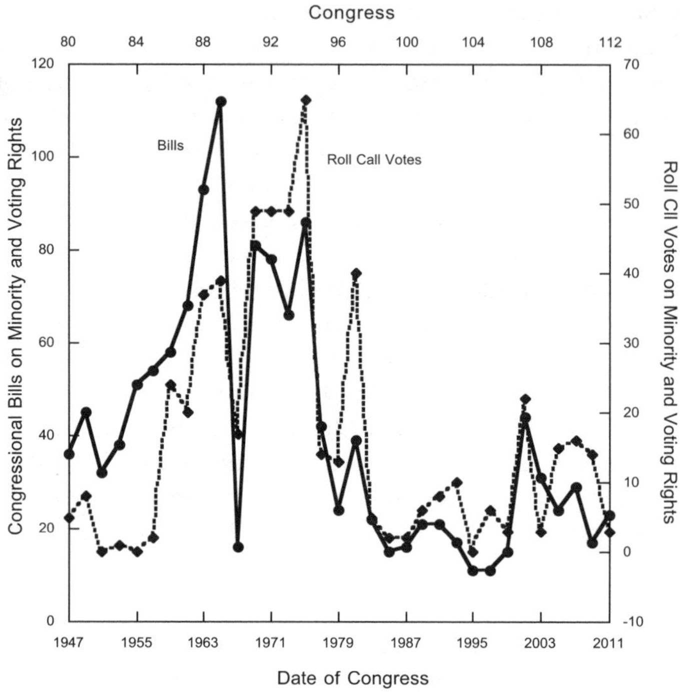

FIGURE 6.3. A comparison between bill introduction and roll-call votes on minority and voting rights

Voting Rights Acts became law. In addition, hearings involving potential laws fell off then, but rose again quickly and were regularly held throughout the 1980s. After the 99th Congress (1985–86), such hearings dropped off, never to regain favor. Somewhat surprisingly, bill introductions increased rapidly during the 84th Congress (1955–56), before either protest activity or newspaper coverage began their upward surges. Surely the increase in bill introductions, an easy activity, was a leading indicator of what was to come.

If we turn to a comparison of bill introductions and roll-call votes on minority and voting rights, we see a similar pattern (see fig. 6.3). Roll-call votes and hearings, as we would expect, lagged behind, as the process for scheduling hearings was generally controlled by committee chairs dominated by Southern Democrats in both chambers. The notion that members of Congress use bills as a way to raise issues neglected by the legislative agenda is supported by the precipitous decline in bill introductions in the 90th Congress (1967–68), after the great legislative victories for proponents of civil rights in the previous two congresses.

Exploring this pattern further by comparing law referral hearings and those not involving potential laws separately in a column graph reveals that the peak of the former precedes the peak of the later (see fig. 6.4). This pattern suggests that the civil rights laws themselves spawned hearings to oversee the acts. The 71st Congress (1969–70) considered school desegregation; the 79th Congress held hearings on business practices; the 87th Congress focused on issues from farm credit for black farmers to the status of Hispanics. Most of these hearings dealt with oversight of the Civil Rights and Voting Rights Acts, along with *Brown v. Board of Education*, the Supreme Court's 1954 landmark school desegregation case.

The figure also clearly depicts the drop-off after the 99th Congress (1985–86) in lawmaking hearings on civil rights; and it also shows a similar drop-off in non-law hearings a few congresses later. The non-law hearings continued apace until the 1990s, after which they declined and basically ended after Republicans won control of Congress in 1995. The spike in hearings beginning in the 109th Congress (2005–6) reflects the reauthorization

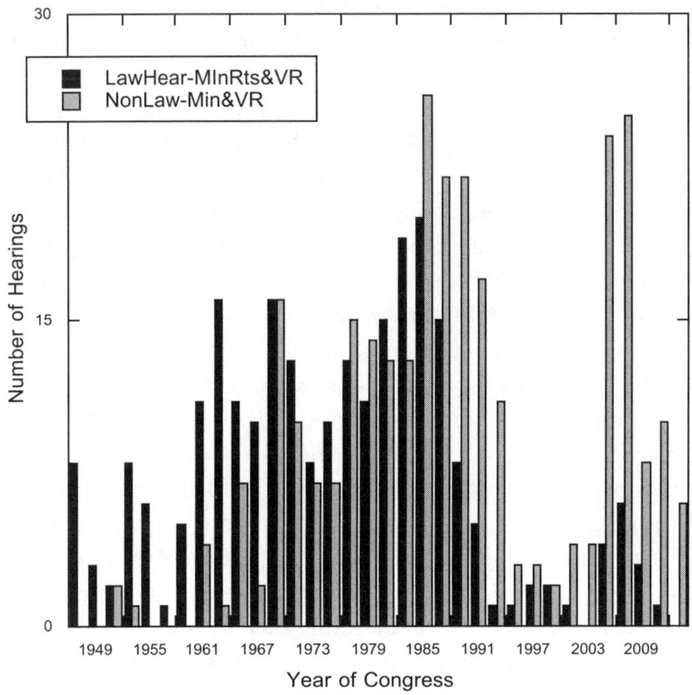

FIGURE 6.4. Law hearings and non-law hearings for minority and voting rights

of the Voting Rights Act and, in the House, an otherwise exclusive focus on voter fraud. The Senate, controlled by Democrats, held hearings exclusively focusing on the reauthorization.

The trace of hearings in the area of minority and voting rights is a record of the conservative counter-mobilization generated by the Great Broadening. Lawmaking on minority rights ceased, with the exceptions of the reauthorizations of the Voting Rights Act in 1992 and 2006. Oversight and other non-law hearings occurred only when Democrats held power.

We can see a similar pattern of activity in the area of gender discrimination (see fig. 6.5). Members of Congress introduced quite a few bills on the issue, starting as early as the late 1940s, but committees only occasionally scheduled hearings on it. Bill activity on gender discrimination peaked in the 93rd Congress (1973–74), just after Congress had submitted the Equal Rights Amendment in 1972 to the states for ratification, which required a two-thirds vote in each chamber. In the 93rd Congress, members introduced more than two hundred bills on gender discrimination. Both parties had embraced the issue by then. Congress began to schedule more hearings as bill activity rose, with hearings peaking in the 98th Congress (1983–84). While the House, where Democrats were a majority, held most of the hearings, the Senate, where Republicans were a majority, had hearings on the problems of female-led small businesses, pension inequities, and job-entry problems for low-income women.

By the mid-1980s, the conservative gender rights counter-mobilization was in full flower, as typified by Phyllis Schlafly and her Stop-ERA campaign. *Roe v Wade*, the 1973 Supreme Court decision constitutionally protecting the right to an abortion, stimulated an even fiercer reaction. Over time, the parties sorted on this issue, with Republicans in Congress becoming increasingly wary of defending the ERA and abortion rights. The last burst of activity on gender rights occurred in the early years of the Clinton presidency. After the Republicans won control of Congress in 1994, committees held few hearings on the issue. Democrats regained congressional control after the 2006 elections, and resumed more vigorous hearing activity, but that interest declined after they lost control of the House in 2010.

Examining the trace of bill introductions and hearings shows the surge in congressional interest in minority, gender, and voting rights, and the decline in legislative and oversight activity on these issues as conservatives gained political power in the federal government. Issues seen as bipartisan at the height of the Great Broadening, such as voting rights and gender discrimination, became much more partisan as the parties took sides and distinguished themselves on these issues. We pursue the counter-reaction by conservatives further in chapter 13.

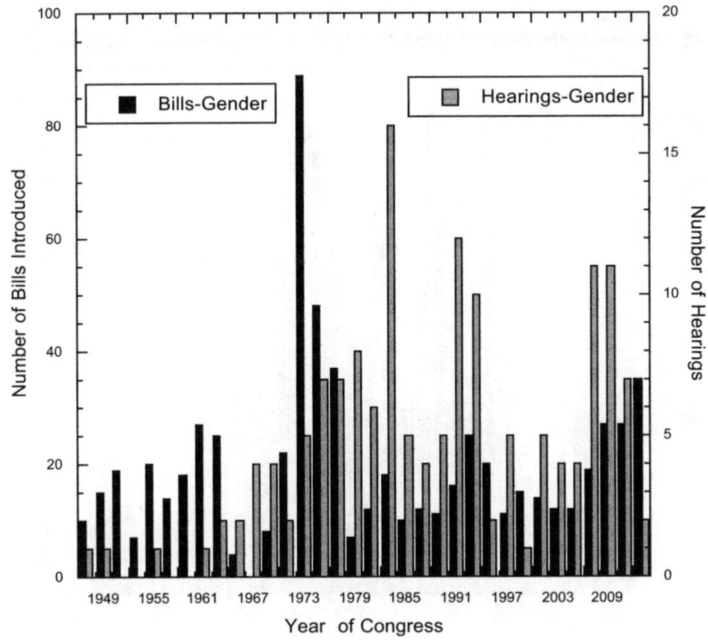

FIGURE 6.5. Bills introduced and hearings conducted on gender discrimination, by congress

Other Venues: The Supreme Court

Congress was not the only policy-making venue that civil rights activists used. The National Association of Colored People (NAACP) devised a court-based strategy after finding so little support in the democratically elected bodies, winning successes when legislative strategies failed. So one might think that attention to minority and voting rights by the Supreme Court would precede similar attention in Congress.

Surprisingly, this sequence was not the case during the Great Broadening. Rather, these issues leaped onto the agenda of both the Court and Congress at approximately the same time. Using the technique of the double-column graph to depict lawmaking hearings and Supreme Court cases on minority and voting rights shows that these two trends are distinctly similar, especially during the early stages of the Great Broadening (see fig. 6.6).

One possible explanation for this similar trend is that the Supreme Court took more cases appealed to it in the civil rights area during the period of the Great Broadening. To examine this further, we relied on a dataset constructed by Michelle Whyman (2011) of writs of certiorari that were accepted

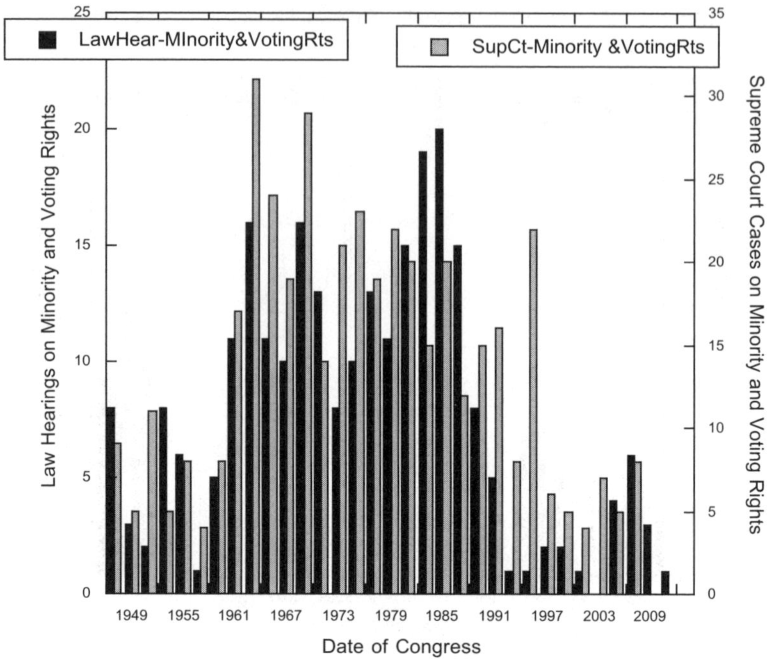

FIGURE 6.6. Supreme Court cases and congressional law hearings on minority and voting rights

and denied from 1947 to 2000, coded according to the Policy Agendas Project categories.[3] We calculated the deviations of the difference between certs accepted and certs denied for the two subtopics of Minority Rights and Voting Rights and compared it to the average for all issues. Then we graphed this variable against the number of cases decided involving these two subtopics in a scatterplot.

The two series correlate at 0.76, indicating that the higher the proportion of certs that the Court accepts, the more cases it decides (see fig. 6.7). Because the cert measure is adjusted for the average, the positive correlation indicates that the first critical decision lies in whether or not the case is accepted. This matters as much as, or perhaps even more than, the nature and direction of the decision itself. If the Court refuses to take up a case, then it can't decide on the issue one way or another. The number of cases (at least for civil rights) does not simply reflect the number of appeals; rather, the justices exercise choice across issues. The scatterplot has a selection of years noted, showing that the period from the early 1960s to the early 1970s was one in which the Court chose to hear more cases on civil rights relative to the cases appealed. The Court was more open to the issue at the height of its intensity.

We strongly suspect that this pattern of issue intrusion (Jones and Baumgartner 2005, chap. 3) is characteristic of the issue expansion process that heralds major policy change. Rather than intrude on the ongoing, relatively stable governing process sequentially, the issue spills over from venue to venue rapidly. It is likely that the Supreme Court began to accept more cases in these areas as the issue became more salient in other venues.

Civil rights, after bouncing around on the national agenda, exploded in the early 1960s, forging similar responses across diverse governing institutions. The Supreme Court and Congress seem to have responded quickly and in concert in a manner that would be missed if we employed the traditional, institution-by-institution approach of political science. What about the executive? Our Policy Agendas measures are rougher there but, as assessed by mentions in the State of the Union addresses, civil rights accessed the presidential agenda in 1953, and the issue was never off that agenda

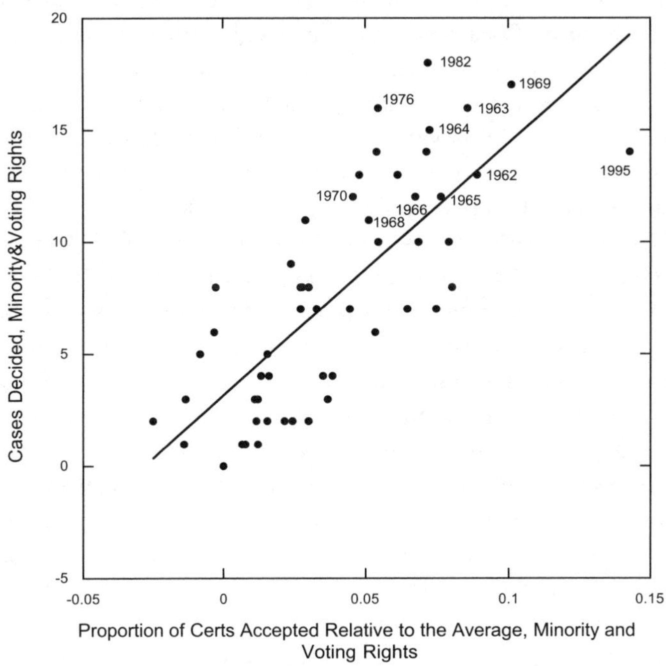

FIGURE 6.7. Proportion of certs accepted to those denied, relative to the average, versus the number of cases decided, for minority and voting rights cases

until after the major civil rights enactments of the Johnson administration. State of the Union discussions roughly approximate bill introductions in Congress: both display activity during the 1950s, both expand rapidly in the early 1960s, and both drop off in the late 1960s. Bill introductions rebound in the 1970s, whereas the speech discussions do not. Both seem to be leading indicators of what is to come, but are less related once the policy change happens.

A single issue, as important as it was (and is), does not a Great Broadening make. The central question is whether the civil rights movement spawned other social activity, and if we can document even partially and incompletely this connection. We turn to this task in the next section.

Sequencing in Social Movements

The disruption of the US political system did not end with civil rights. Rather, a sequence of movements, including environmentalism, women's rights, and consumer product safety, driven by passion and falling outside of the traditional party and interest-group system, wracked the system. While the assault was not orderly, we can detect using data from the Policy Agendas Project a sequence of peaks in activity in roughly the following order: civil rights, environmentalism, consumer safety, and women's rights. Group-to-group contagion occurred as later movements adopted the strategy and tactics successful in earlier movements; indeed, some activists pursued more than one cause. None would have been possible without the passion of reform and outrage that pervaded the entire period.

Two common components unify these movements. First, passionate commitment went far beyond the typical partisan passions (at least for the time). The deep commitment to a cause and the association of the cause with defects in the realization of American ideals—Huntington's creedal passion—were essential to the motivation that drove activists to take risks that are difficult to understand using standard cost-benefit choice models (Chong 1991). The second is a deliberate attempt on the part of activists to remain independent of standard partisan divisions, which at the time centered more on issues of economics and labor relations rather than the newly emerging issues of civil rights, women's rights, environmentalism, and consumer product safety. These issues were not nearly so partisan then as they later became (Jochim and Jones 2013).

The Policy Agendas Project codes some issues motivating social movements at the subtopic level, allowing us to trace policy activity on these issues. But these correspondences are partial. Moreover, the *New York Times*

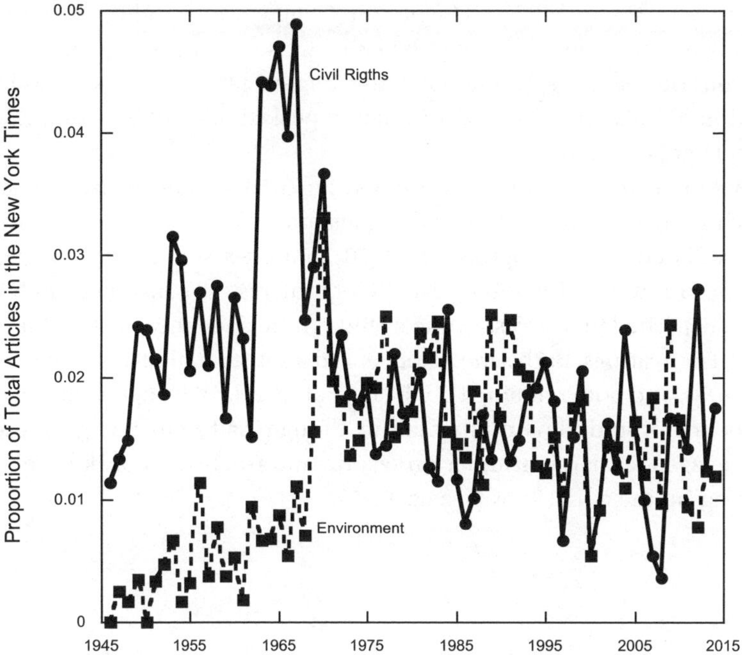

FIGURE 6.8. The proportion of *New York Times* articles published on civil rights and the environment per year

sample is coded only at the major topic level, so we cannot fully trace news coverage for the issues motivating these movements. But what we can do is illuminating. Sequencing is clear, with civil rights coverage preceding that for the environment (see fig. 6.8). From our sample, we estimate that the *New York Times* published many more stories on policy issues during the late 1960s through the early 1970s than before or afterward, and we used the proportion of stories on civil rights and the environment in figure 6.8. News coverage peaked for civil rights in 1969 and for the environment a year later.[4] Note that the proportion of newspaper space devoted to civil rights far exceeded that for the environment. While civil rights coverage had been high for years, environmentalism leaped onto the agenda in 1969 and became even more prominent in 1970 as Congress considered and enacted the Environmental Protection Act. Coverage of both civil rights and the environment declined as the 1970s proceeded.

We can't use newspaper coverage for comparisons of Gender Discrimination and Consumer Safety, as these are Policy Agendas subtopics, not major topics. But if we use bill introductions in Congress as an indicator of interest among members in addressing the issue, we see that introduction of bills on minority rights peaked in the 88th Congress (1963–64), whereas introduction of bills on gender discrimination peaked in the 93rd Congress, ten years later (see fig. 6.9).[5]

A similar trend is present for environmentalism and consumer safety, and it holds for both bill introductions and hearings. For bills, both series peak in the 91st Congress (1969–70), but interest in environmentalism had been building for some years before interest in consumer safety (see fig. 6.10). The latter accessed the agenda more suddenly in the 91st Congress. For hearings, both series experienced a substantial increase in the 91st Congress, and both remained on the formal agenda of Congress throughout the period of study. Environmentalism, though, had a much larger presence on the agenda than consumer protection and reached its peak number of hearings in the mid-1980s (see fig. 6.11).

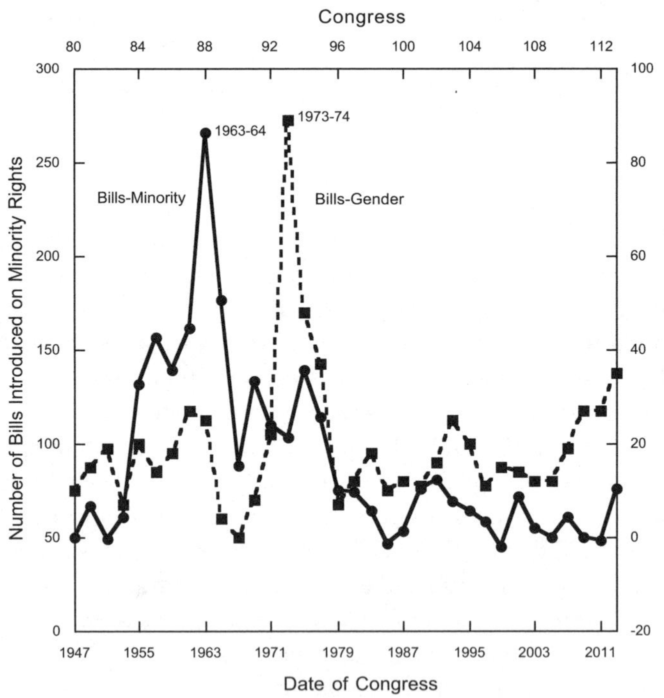

FIGURE 6.9. Number of bills introduced in Congress on minority rights and gender discrimination, by congress

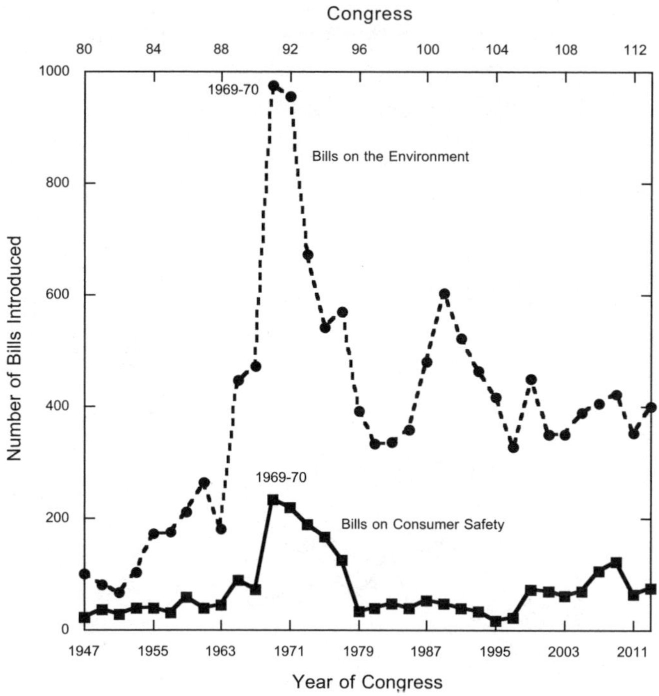

FIGURE 6.10. Number of bills introduced per congress on environmental issues and consumer safety

Because of the tendency of social movements of the 1960s and 1970s to specialize in a single or an identifiable cluster of issues, we are able to order the movements according to when the issues they championed accessed various components of the policy-making agenda. It is difficult to disentangle the initial movement from later conservative reactions to it in the data we deploy here, but the evidence clearly points to an ordering of civil rights, environmentalism, consumer safety, and women's rights.

In focusing on the importance of the process of broadening, we have deliberately neglected policies that could have influenced thickening but did not broaden the scope of government. What about social movements that could have amplified the effects of broadening but were themselves directed at policies that had long been on the governmental agenda? In the 1960s and 1970s the "elephant in the room" was the vast and intense mobilization against the US military involvement in Vietnam. Directed at limiting, not expanding, commitments in a well-established government responsibility, the Vietnam anti-war movement could not alone have broadened

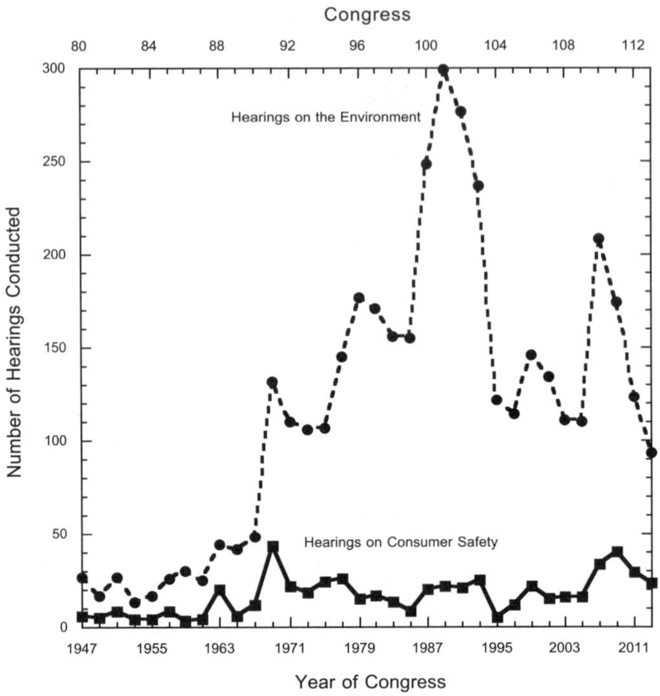

FIGURE 6.11. Hearings on the environment and consumer safety, per congress

government. But the emotion and ideas generated by the frenetic activity of the anti-war movement could have spilled over into other movements occurring simultaneously or even later.

Moreover, clearly the anti-war movement affected the party system; it split the Democratic Party in 1968, helped lead to the 1972 changes in party structure, and shifted the responsibility for continuing the war to the Republicans. This process could have indirectly led to more calls for a broadened government.

The Role of Social Movements

The traditional political science analyses using party control and public opinion do not suffice to explain many facets of the Great Broadening. As a consequence, we turned to an examination of the major social movements of the period, using a very different approach. Instead of focusing on the movements themselves, we traced their consequences within government.

These movements, creedal in nature, demanded that the federal government act to stop state governments from interfering with the constitutional rights of citizens (as in the case of civil rights for blacks), extend those rights across the gender line, and protect citizens from environmental degradation and unsafe consumer products. Because all these movements wanted positive government policies to correct the situation, the federal government's agenda necessarily had to expand. We can trace this expansion quantitatively.

The Policy Agendas Project database offers fruitful ground for studying the effects of social movements and the conservative counter-reaction to them. Most studies of social movements have focused on the groups carrying the banner for the causes, not the substantive issues within government as they expand (or fail to expand) as components of the policy-making agenda. We have only touched the surface of the possibilities here as we hasten to explore the wider phenomenon of the Great Broadening.

We cannot neglect the roles of political parties in the process, but these roles are more complex than many political scientists have suggested. More is going on than the standard party control model implies. During the most intense period of the Great Broadening, the parties acted more or less in concert to support many of the actions demanded by the leaders of these social movements. The energy of social movements influenced the reactions of political parties to these issues that were accessing the policy-making agenda with such force.

Soon counter-mobilizations, both within the parties and independent of them, exerted strong pressures on party leaders and offered enticing electoral opportunities as well. Republicans, beginning with President Richard Nixon, saw party advantages in moving to attract Southern white voters feeling cast adrift by the Democratic Party's pro–civil rights stance. A similar partisan calculation led to an increasing appeal to social conservatives. Business counter-mobilization against increased environmental, consumer product, and workplace safety regulations appealed to the business-oriented elements in the Republican Party as well.

As a consequence, over the period we studied, the two major parties increasingly sorted on these issues, with the Democrats becoming the champions of civil rights, environmentalism, consumer safety, and women's rights. Republicans became increasingly cautious on these matters, after first either being more or equally sympathetic to these causes. The party became more pro-business on environmentalism and consumer safety, more traditionalist on women's rights, and increasingly resistant on minority rights. Both parties remained diverse on all of these issues for many years, but over time party sorting across the issues increased (Jochim and Jones 2013). We speculate that this issue-sorting process led to the polarization that plagues our political system to this day. The Great Broadening, and in particular the shifts in issue politics driven by the intensity of social movements, led to polarization. They were not coterminous events, nor did polarization cause broadening. We pursue this conjecture in chapters 10 and 11.

Political parties are an essential component of the Great Broadening, and an even more essential component of the counter-reaction to that broadening. They are intertwined with social movements—both those pushing for change and those demanding reversal of those changes. Neither social movements nor political parties stand alone as explanatory factors for the broadening and its partial reversals. Yet political scientists have devoted far more time and effort to understanding the role of the party system in policy-making than the role of social movements. Given our findings here, it seems time for scholars to focus more effort on examining the interactions between parties and social movements in seeking to understand policy change.

SEVEN

Feedback Politics

In the last several chapters we explored some of the internal dynamics and potential causes of the Great Broadening. In treating causes independently and analyzing them separately, we were able to eliminate some as prime suspects. Even in other cases where we found evidence that potential causal factors may have played an important role in generating the Great Broadening, it was unclear exactly how they combined to bring about the great changes in public policy during the 1960s and 1970s. Only when the traditional explanations of partisan control and public opinion are combined with the passions of social movements can an adequate explanation be crafted.

In the chapters following this one, we examine the effects of the Great Broadening. Surely such a large and sustained burst of policy-making would have strong downstream effects. This massive policy intervention had the potential to affect not just policy development but contemporary politics as well. Hacker and Pierson (2014) have laid out the case for what they call "policy focused analysis," which examines the effects of past policy implementation on contemporary politics. In this framework, past policy can affect contemporary political dynamics by changing the political behavior of individuals (Campbell 2003; Mettler 2005; Soss 1999).

Before getting to the effects, though, we consider feedback politics, which is more important than modern public policy studies suggest. This chapter provides a critical conceptual link between the Great Broadening and its consequences for the American political system. In reviewing and extending the ideas emerging from feedback politics, we show its relevance to both the emergence and later impacts of the Great Broadening. We've shown, and will provide more evidence in future chapters, that the period of the Great Broadening was characterized by different dynamics than what came before and afterward. Lots of things happened that were highly consequential for later politics and policy-making. From a bird's eye view, the historical institutionalists' critical junctures look like straightforward turning points. But if we look inside these periods, as we do here, they are characterized by a complex dynamic process that is less structured, more chaotic, and offers more opportunities for policy entrepreneurship.

Intensity of Activity during the Great Broadening

In the early part of the book, we concentrated on measures of broadening, noting that many variables that assessed the breadth of activity intensified during the Great Broadening. Media coverage intensified, protest activity increased, the creedal passions associated with social movements buffeted the political system, and the production of important statutes surged.

Yet this is not the whole story. During the Great Broadening, most activity indicators intensified. For example, both the number of bills and the number of Supreme Court cases decided increased and then declined (see fig. 7.1).[1] The arcs fitted for the period indicate that the two series peak at

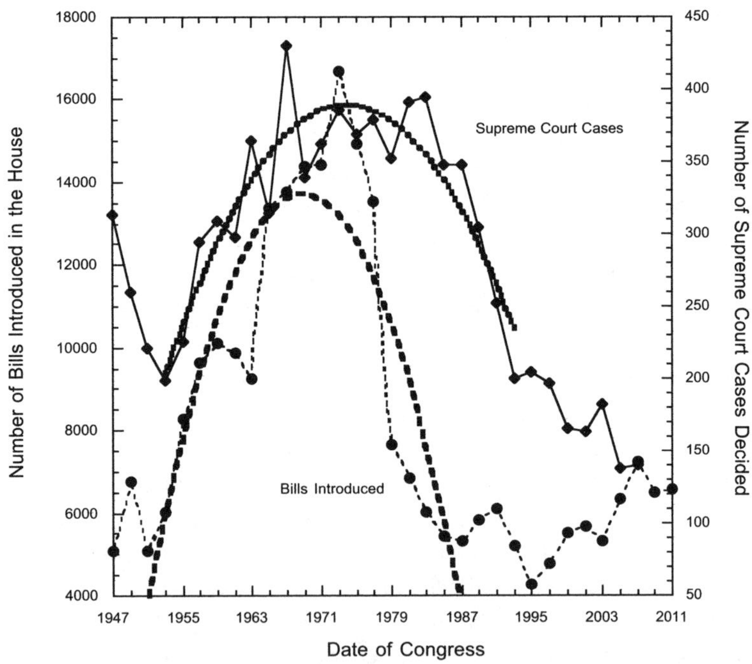

FIGURE 7.1. Number of bills introduced in the House of Representatives and the number of Supreme Court cases decided

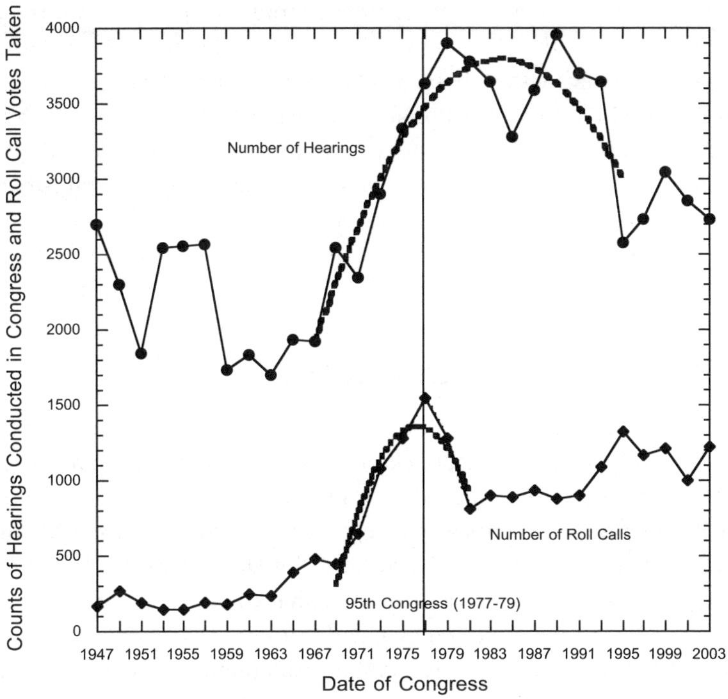

FIGURE 7.2. Counts of hearings conducted by Congress and roll-call votes taken in the House of Representatives

slightly different times, but both rise quickly and peak during the Great Broadening.

The arc pattern of activity is found in other series, such as congressional hearings and roll-call votes (see fig. 7.2).[2] The arc for hearings reaches its apogee several congresses later than the arc for roll-call votes. We use votes for the House only so that the different rules in the House and Senate for bringing a bill to the floor for a vote will not confound the comparison, but the Senate displays a similar arc pattern, with a peak one congress prior to that in the House.

The arc was not the only pattern of activity. In some cases, such as investigatory activity by congressional committees (to be addressed in chapter 9), plateaus characterize the data, and in others, such as the accumulation of law, the upward trend continued (addressed in chapter 8). We explore these patterns in detail in the coming chapters.

It would seem that action begat even more action, both within and between domains. At the same time, the intensity of political activity was increasing, and the scope of government rapidly broadened. Yet the existence of the arc and the plateau in activity and in the broadening of government policies indicate that this period of political frenzy attenuated.

How the reinforcing cycles of activity sustained themselves for so long, how the process came to an end, and the longer term effects of the Great Broadening constitute a—perhaps *the*—great puzzle of modern American politics. To gain some perspective on this, we develop and extend some of the basic ideas of the study of public-policy processes, offering a fresh look at the puzzle.

Policy Feedback

Clearly we are dealing here with an interacting set of interdependent parts characterized by complex feedback processes, a system that defied decomposition and part-by-part analysis—at least during the intense stage of the Great Broadening. The critical concept of feedback has a long history in the study of policy processes. Introduced by David Easton (1953) in his general systems approach to politics, feedback became a lynchpin of the policy-cycle heuristic developed by Charles Jones (1970) and James Anderson (1975). The basic idea was that an implemented policy changed the environment of the policy-making system, and changes in the environment fed back into the system as a fresh set of demands for adjustments relevant to the policy's effects.

Systems theory implies adaptation to an environment that itself is some function of the action of the system. General systems theory, on which Easton based his framework, in recent years has come to serve as a basis of complex systems theory (Érdi 2008). Early versions of systems theory were essentially linear models of causes and effects that linearly fed back into the system, generating future causes of system adjustment. Complex systems approaches added the possibility of variables that interact nonlinearly, such that small changes can lead to large effects.

The story of the Great Broadening and its aftermath vividly illustrates three types of feedback processes that both stabilize and destabilize policymaking. The first form, *negative feedback*, is a stabilizing form, in which policy changes generate forces in the opposite direction. Each new input into a system results in a less than equal response. The system attenuates the signal, essentially damping down its effects over time. Negative feedback leads to stable systems; an everyday example is a thermostat. Negative feedback can be seen in the relationship between public opinion and policy (Soroka and Wlezien 2010). Negative feedback is also prominent in incrementalist accounts of policy-making.

Positive feedback amplifies external changes. For any given input, the system response is stronger, stimulating further inputs from the outside. Such phenomena as arms races display positive feedback. Systems can destruct if positive feedback is not contained, as could be imagined in an unchecked arms race.

Positive feedback takes two forms, and they need to be distinguished. One is transformative and in some cases destructive, because each increase in a variable leads to an even bigger increase as the feedback processes operate. If the process does not cease or transform into negative feedback, it destroys the system. Major examples include arms races, electoral bandwagons, and social movements. Positive feedback is prominent in the theory of punctuated equilibrium, which addresses the transformation of subsystems under pressure from new emerging interests (Baumgartner and Jones 2009). Positive feedback in policy subsystems can act to bring about major policy changes, after which negative feedback stabilizes the system. This work, in hindsight, can be seen as part of the more general dynamic of the Great Broadening.

Interestingly, a policy choice can be stabilizing but lead to unstable outcomes that may require major changes in the future. A key example is budgetary incrementalism. If we build in a positive percentage increment to a budget, rather than a positive amount, the result is exponential growth in the budget: exponential incrementalism (Jones, Zalányi, and Érdi 2014). Calculated in percentages, the budget increase seems sustainable. Calculated in amounts, the budget is a case of positive feedback, in which each increment leads to a larger increment the next fiscal year.

The second form of positive feedback is better described as positive returns to scale. Born in the work of economist Brian Arthur (1994) and brought into political science by Paul Pierson (2000; 2004), the concept refers to payoffs in which each return on an investment yields a higher return. This form is similar to positive feedback, and at first it is destructive, as better products (or political philosophies) drive out competitors. The ensuing high cost of entering the market increases inefficiency, as competition is reduced. Arthur (1994) refers to this as "increasing returns to scale," because once the lock-in occurs, companies can reap benefits that are not proportional to subsequent investments.

Both markets and policy-making systems stabilize at some point and become subject to the dynamics of stabilizing negative feedback. By then, the cost of market entry for firms or political entry for new political groups may be so high as to "lock in" the prevailing system. This process is often known as "path dependence," because of the inertial tendencies of such systems to continue through time in a fundamentally unchanged manner.

These sorts of dynamics interfere with a system's ability to return to any sort of adaptive equilibrium. In *The Quark and the Jaguar*, physicist Murray Gell-Mann (1994, 295) asks "why adaptive systems seem so often to be stuck with maladaptive schemata? Why haven't they just developed better and better schemata and progressed to higher and higher fitness?" If the statement is taken as fact, numerous reasons could possibly explain it. If we limit ourselves only to social phenomena, paramount among them is the ability of human social organization to affect an environment so severely that it itself becomes artificial—a creation of human action rather than a set of independent forces tangentially influenced by human action (see Simon 1996).

In the study of policy and politics, feedback processes are frequently so powerful that the so-called independent variables in a model are themselves creations of past actions of the policy-making system. The Great Broadening was so massive that it requires a whole reordering of how we think about politics. No longer is it adequate to see policy effects as a side consequence of policy enactment, the way that Eastonian systems theory and the policy-cycle approach do. The feedback effects in modern policy systems are so powerful that they distort the entire policy-making process, in effect reversing it so the system works backward. Dependent variables become independent variables, and vice versa. Specifically, policy becomes independent, and other seemingly input variables, such as interest-group activity and partisan polarization, are at least partially dependent on the path that policy-making has taken. Such a complex formulation becomes harder to test systematically; ignoring the formulation because of its complexity renders scholarship certainly neater but at the dramatic cost of relevance.

But policy does more—much more. Hacker and Pierson (2014, 651) develop the metaphor of "policy as terrain" to capture the fundamental notion that past policy alters the very terms on which later political debate occurs. Part of this involves a shift in the "arrangements that losers must adjust to even if their side wins future elections." The entire terrain on which the "game" of politics is played is often altered by the enacted policies. It is, in effect, a new game.

As Larry Jacobs (2014) shows in regard to health policy, winners must also adjust to the new policy terrain. That happened in the case of the very regulated insurance market and cost-containment system built into the

Affordable Care Act. The policy has become a framework for the conduct of future policy-making. By "winners" and "losers," policy scholars don't mean just parties and voters; they mean organized groups, activists, and even users of the new service (or losers of the service if the policy moves in a conservative direction). Groups organize, grow, and change strategies and even goals concerning what they want from government as the policy terrain changes.

At this juncture, policy studies and studies of political processes part ways. Many studies of politics ignore this feedback, assuming that a simple adjustment of the "status quo point" can represent all that has gone before. Politics is viewed as a repetitive game, played again and again with nothing different but whether the last play of the game has pushed politics to the right or to the left. Because it focuses on causal forces on a playing field that adjusted left or right after the last round of the game, we call this approach "contemporaneous dynamics." This view precludes a role for the feedback processes so important in policy-process studies. It need not do so, however, as Anzia and Moe (2016) show. In the future, therefore, both formal and empirical models of politics may begin to incorporate the feedback process more systematically. To date, however, that is not the case.

At its best, what we have termed the contemporaneous-dynamics approach, which focuses only on contemporary causes and linear effects from the past, misleads because it misses so much of what is relevant to modern politics. At its worst, it is wrong, as it is unable to account for developments that offer new opportunities for political actors and cause a whole set of new problems—"policy as its own cause" as Wildavsky (1979, chap. 3) put it. The approach severely underestimates the complex patterns of causation generated when we allow for policy feedbacks.

Understanding Feedback Politics

It is easier to grasp the complex causation involved in the policy feedback approach if we examine one policy at a time. In an important pair of articles, Anzia and Moe study the effects of laws on collective bargaining (2016) and of public-sector pension policies in the states (2017) on subsequent politics. They introduce a new set of ideas into the "policy as terrain" approach—including the rationally strategic politicians who use these policies to adjust the terrain in the future to benefit their political parties. They write, "If policies make their own politics, then it seems straightforward that politicians would want to use policy to shape politics to their advantage" (2016, 765). Incentives facing politicians can be crosscutting: for example, constituency pressures and partisan issues sometimes conflict, which makes it difficult to pinpoint strategic actions. Nevertheless, it seems clear that political actors try to make these calculations. One lesson of this work is that using analytical methods of maximization can be fruitful if one models the incentive structure correctly by building in the policy-generated changes to those incentives.

In their study of underfunded state pensions, Anzia and Moe (2017) address changes in the nature of problems facing these plans caused by the lackluster economic growth. As the funding problems intensified, press coverage increased, and politics moved from cross-partisan support for pension increases to a system in which Republican support declined, while Democratic support remained high. While the system was more partisan, it was not polarized. While the changed policy terrain offered advantages to Republicans and disadvantages to Democrats, it is also the case that the problems objectively needed addressing. Under such conditions, the policy as terrain approach leads to more nuanced predictions than does the standard party conflict model.

These seemingly straightforward policies indicate just how complex causation is in feedback politics. First, as policies are changed, the incentives of politicians are changed, in some cases by the anticipatory actions of politicians themselves. Second, the problem space changes and alters the range of discussions of the alternatives. In growing economies, pension benefits can be increased easily, and both parties were happy to do so. Underfunded pensions offer only the dismal choices of limiting benefits or increasing taxes. Third, exogenous events may have multiple, reverberating effects on the system. The Great Recession altered the problem space, changed incentives for political actors, offered more advantages to one political party, and limited the set of reasonable solutions. The effects of such major events are not additive—they don't just add or subtract an increment to the policy status quo. They cause complex interactions that deform the policy space.

Explosive Feedback Systems

The full implications of policy feedbacks are not easily grasped through example or case study. Moreover their applicability to specific policy challenges actually underestimate the effects of such major policy bursts as the Great Broadening, which we argue was an extreme case of positive feedback. Each input generates an ever-larger output—disproportionate and multiplicative. Punctuated equilibrium (Baumgartner and Jones 2009) relies on outbreaks of positive, reinforcing feedback and a shift at some point in policy development to a self-limiting, negative feedback. Even the most apparently stable system is subject to potential destabilization in certain cases (Jones and Baumgartner 2005; 2012). In single-policy areas, this process can lead to large overinvestment in particular policy solutions—a *policy bubble*, such as occurred in crime policies during the 1980s (Jones, Thomas, and Wolfe 2014).

Punctuated equilibrium theory conceived of the US political system as a network of quasi-independent policy subsystems that were episodically disrupted by the intervention of "macropolitical" forces. The issue based in the subsystem reached the agenda of major political actors, such as the president, Congress, and political parties. This heightened, sustained attention could lead to positive feedback effects that disrupted the subsystem for a period of time. After the disruption produced new policies, more normal negative feedback processes based on limited participation of the interested reestablished themselves. Sometimes those policies resulted in the incorporation of new actors into the subsystem, as clearly happened in environmental policies when environmental activists with legal and policy skills entered the fray. These activists sparred with the more typical business interests, resulting in a competitive subsystem with two competing "advocacy coalitions" (Sabatier and Jenkins-Smith 1993).

In some cases, positive feedback can "spill over" across subsystem boundaries, as happened with the civil rights, environmentalism, and consumer safety social movements. It is likely that in most cases such movements are contained within related subsystems. In rare cases, social movements that are more or less related can affect the political system more broadly. If the associated positive feedback effects also spill over across policy arenas, a much broader destabilizing trend may result. That is what we think happened in the case of the Great Broadening.

While public-policy scholars have addressed in detail the structure of feedback and the consequences of single policies, they have failed so far to offer a more systematic assessment of the vast changes in the policy-making process that can be traced back to the Great Broadening. Agenda expansion in the 1960s and 1970s led to changes in the very nature of politics in America. Political systems evolve, and they evolve under the pressures of endogenous forces—feedback from previous policies—not just external ones, such as changes in the composition of the electorate.

We offer one striking example, which we pursue later in this book. In the 1960s and early 1970s, Congress held about one investigative (including oversight) hearing for every two referral hearings. By the 2000s, Congress held about nine investigative hearings for every referral hearing. This change does not reflect changes in the rules so much as changes in the congressional agenda. It reflects the changing challenges for the legislative branch as it copes with the broadening of American government. More agencies and programs meant more demand for oversight of them. Nevertheless, changes in rules were important, as the parties centralized the lawmaking process after 1995, transferring lawmaking from the committees to party leaders. Students of Congress tend to highlight the latter while ignoring the former. Without understanding both aspects, scholars have run the risk of misinterpreting the very nature of the legislative branch.

This broadening process has implications for many of the current political phenomena we study today, from the proliferation of interest groups in Washington to the polarization of our political parties. Most especially it affects the nature of the agenda-setting process, because the government's presence has expanded into all areas of modern life. As a consequence, the ideas that new groups raise almost always fit into a preordained conflict structure and are understandable in that structure. Oversight hearings by Congress, almost 90 percent of hearings conducted today, quite clearly fit into this predetermined conflict structure.

Downstream from the Great Broadening

We expect huge feedback effects on virtually every element of our political system from the Great Broadening. Indeed, American political history has been wracked by great intrusions that have transformed our system—wars, panics, depressions, and social and political movements, from women's demand for the vote to the Redeemer counter-reaction to Reconstruction, black empowerment, and agrarian populism. These interventions generated major changes in public policy and in most cases changed the very rules and informal norms that governed politics.

Quantitative scholars cannot fruitfully simply enter a dichotomous variable into a time series to account for the effects of these shifts. New ideas about how political change works and new methods to study policy dynamics are necessary. In the study of government budgets, regression analyses with "era" step function estimates resulted in a misleading picture. Only when Padgett (1980) introduced stochastic process approaches and punctuated equilibrium scholars (summarized in Jones and Baumgartner 2012) followed up on his lead did a more appropriate picture of budget politics appear.

While we are not prepared to offer new methods to capture emerging theories of policy dynamics, we will rely on the new ideas emerging from policy studies and from other related and even unrelated fields. We've already noted several of these: positive feedback, policy lock-in, spillovers, and interaction effects are just a few examples.

We analyze two separate kinds of effects, which can be characterized as endogenous effects, based in the internal dynamics of a system, and exogenous effects, resulting from forces that are external to the system. For our purposes, endogenous changes are those more centrally based within the Washington policy-making system, whereas exogenous changes are those that involve the broader polity. The former effects include changes in the interest-group system, the organization of Congress, the lawmaking process, the growth in regulatory and other executive branch functions, and the increased polarization of the legislative parties. The latter include political party organizations, general public opinion, and the electoral dynamics of governments at the state and local level. They also include elite opinion and the media. We cannot trace all the ramifications of the Great Broadening, but we do trace several, mostly within the governmental system, although we touch on its effects on electoral dynamics and elite opinion. Probably most consequentially, the Great Broadening generated a powerful conservative counter-revolution in both elite and mass politics.

Two New Concepts for Feedback Analysis

In this section, we introduce two new concepts that are critical for understanding both the causal processes that led to the Great Broadening and the transformational effects on the political system that followed.

Partially Decoupled Systems

In an amazingly integrative essay originally written in 1962, Herbert Simon defined a hierarchic system as "a system that is composed of interrelated subsystems, each of the latter being in turn hierarchic in structure until we reach some lowest level of elementary subsystem" (184). He called such systems "nearly decomposable" (197) and argued that such arrangements appear in both social and biological sciences due to the trial-and-error processes in both. For biology, the key mechanism was natural selection; for social science, it was the problem-solving process. In both cases, these systems "found" hierarchical organization to be efficient and hence replicated the solution in other situations.

Such decomposability allows humans to construct complex organizations, including formal bureaucracies and legislative committee systems.

Tasks that would otherwise be overwhelming can be decomposed into parts that can be addressed separately in subsystems. Information can be processed in parallel, with many subunits working on different problems or aspects of a complex problem, as legislative committees do (Jones and Baumgartner 2005). Such decomposability clearly occurs in the formation and maintenance of policy subsystems, in which executive branch agencies, congressional committees, and interest groups operate to set policies in areas in which technical expertise is necessary, and generalized policy interest is almost always low.

Many scholars have noted that the subsystem model, based on the motives of the interested, was flawed from a perspective of democratic theory. Yet the balance between democracy and expertise continued to plague scholars of public administration. Emmette Redford (1969) noted that the subsystem model did not operate in a vacuum; it was always possible that what he termed the *macropolitical actors*—Congress, the president, and the political parties—could intervene in stable subsystem politics, introducing sporadic democratic accountability into the system. This model implies that policy-making is sometimes decomposed into subsystems, but sometimes these subsystems are linked to the broader macropolitical system. We call them "partially decoupled."

While the label "partially decoupled" may not be familiar, political scientists will understand the phenomenon of partially decoupled systems. Systems may not be connected continually with the same linkages; these linkages can come and go, often in a disjoint and episodic fashion.

Theories of grounded cognition exemplify this distinction. Our thinking does not rely on continual connection to direct experience; thinking can be endogenous through such devices as imagination, imagery, and fantasies. But in sane people, thinking and experience are intermittently connected—thinking is grounded. As one student of grounded cognition puts it, "Imagery works together with memory, planning, dreaming, and projection to allow us to decouple thought from direct experience. . . . The fact that cognition can become partially decoupled through imagery should not be construed as meaning that it is fully decoupled" (MacWhinney 2005, 201). Our thinking processes are partially decoupled from what we observe.

Another way of stating this is that the process of cognition is partially endogenous and partially exogenous, and those states are time-dependent. That is, sometimes systems are coupled, and sometimes they are decoupled. Sometimes causation is exogenous, and sometimes endogenous.

In conflict-expansion theories of policy-making, partially decoupled systems are a core concept, even if they are not labeled that way. These include the "garbage can" approach to policy change (Cohen, March and Olsen 1972; Kingdon 1995), in which "streams" of inputs combine via the mechanism of attention, producing policy change; the Redford (1969) dynamic of the sporadic intervention of macropolitical institutions into policy subsystems; and the punctuated equilibrium dynamic of shifting attention among policy areas (Baumgartner and Jones 2009). In each case, connections between partially decoupled systems of action are sporadic, driven by attention and mobilization. Systems act independently until connections are activated.

The idea of partially decoupled systems can be used to help understand what is wrong with what we have termed the "contemporary dynamics problem." How are the external factors of public opinion, elections, and ideas connected to the internal workings of our policy-making systems? Clearly, it is not a continuous feed from citizens to politicians. We saw in chapter 5 how difficult it is to connect public opinion, party divisions, and elections to the Great Broadening. But it would be both empirically and normatively disturbing if we had to report that the dynamics within government were entirely driven by interactions among policy-making elites.[3] Indeed, the entire debate, which seems to recur, over whether business elites "run things" or have disproportionate influence, or whether the system is highly sensitive to public opinion, could benefit from incorporating the notion of partial decoupling.

In chapter 13, we examine a prime example of partial decoupling. In response to declining prices during the Great Depression, the federal government regulated a sizable portion of the economy, particularly in transportation. Congress created agencies to conduct price and safety regulation, and these evolved into independent policy subsystems. During the 1960s, a confluence of forces attacked these arrangements. Economists argued the benefits of competitive market systems, public administration scholars raised governance issues critical of the undemocratic nature of the subsystem arrangements, and consumer advocates argued that organized interests were damaging diffuse consumer interests. These forces coalesced into a deregulatory movement, ultimately destroying or significantly weakening many of the regulatory subsystems.

Partial Decoupling and the Great Broadening

We've shown two underlying patterns in the period following the Great Broadening. Some measures show an arc in which political dynamics somehow "bend the curve" from growth to decline. Others show a plateau, or asymptote, and a leveling off; growth is stanched but not lowered. Our working hypothesis is that much of the dynamics of broadening is endogenous, but it takes external factors to "bend the curve" via episodic interventions. We offered at least a plausible electoral story for the bend in the broadening curve, especially for the mandate elections of 1980 and 1994, in chapter 5. Elections may affect the internal processes of government only occasionally, and then the effects are not often disjoint; rather, they have more of a curve-bending quality. We might say that the two systems—electoral and policy-making—are partially decoupled (or maybe we should say "partially coupled") through time.

What is true of election dynamics is also true of the politics of ideas. Conservatives such as William Buckley recognized in the 1950s that they did not have a powerful set of ideas comparable to the liberal ideas generated in the wake of the Great Depression. Nor did the right have magazines comparable to the *New Republic* and others on the left to carry those ideas to a broader public. Buckley founded the *National Review* in 1955, and he and other conservative opinion writers began to promote conservative interpretations of policy and politics. For the most part, these developments did not influence policy-making, but they carried on in an independent stream quite separate from the Republican politicians who might be attracted to the ideas.

We argue below that the "crossover" came through the Great Broadening, which swiftly engulfed the entire issue space. Neoconservatives, former liberals who had become alarmed at the reach of government during the period, saw this as destroying the whole distinction between public and civil spaces (Wilson 1979). Indeed, the recruitment of neoconservatives and respected academics and journalists such as James Q. Wilson and Irving Kristol was an important broadening in the conservative intellectual base and helped to integrate intellectual conservatism into practical, governing conservatism.

The conservative ideas, developed in literary elite circles, crossed into practical governance through the Great Broadening explosion. Some were quite bluntly expressed: founding father, William Buckley clearly took a conservative view of social issues in the pages of the *National Review*. In opposing the civil rights movement, he wrote a famous editorial in 1957 titled, "Why the South Must Prevail," justifying legal segregation and the right of Southern whites to subjugate blacks, even "in areas in which it does not dominate numerically. . . . The White community is so entitled because, for the time being, it is the advanced race." Intellectual conservatism under the banner of the *National Review* had become a set of ideas that by the late 1950s integrated economic liberty and limited government with Southern racism. In opposing the 1957 Civil Rights Act, Buckley was opposing conservative Republicans who were progressive on civil rights, including President Eisenhower's attorney general, Herbert Brownell, who proposed the act; Senate Minority Leader William Knowland, who cosponsored it; and Vice President Richard Nixon, who strongly supported it (Feltzenberg 2017). In this form, intellectual conservatism was an ideal vehicle for the Republican "Southern strategy" that followed the major civil rights initiatives during the 1960s.

The first test of these ideas came in the form of Barry Goldwater, whose campaign was based on a strong economic and military ideological conservatism. He also supported "states rights" in the areas of open accommodations and voting rights, which made him the darling of the Deep South. The national electorate repudiated his views; the Great Broadening was just getting started. Goldwater, however, aided the crossover of ideological, journalistic conservatism to practical electoral politics. And he clearly had an appeal based on his conservative approach to race relations, at least in the Deep South; he carried his home state of Arizona, plus South Carolina, Georgia, Alabama, Mississippi, and Louisiana.

No study directly links agenda expansion to conservative intellectual resurgence. Hans Noel (2013) does show that ideology in elite publications on both right and left became ideological before either Congress or the public did (and it is easy to show that the legislature polarized before the public). Elite publications began to become more ideological in the Progressive era, and experienced a jump between 1930 and 1950, but then clearly slackened between 1950 and 1970, the time period of the Great Broadening (Noel 2013, 79).

Jochim and Jones (2013) show that polarization did not happen all at once in Congress but was incorporated into the party structure over time, issue-by-issue, supporting Noel's contention that party polarization followed issue polarization. While Noel does not study the broadening of the agenda, his data imply that broadening. As we show in the chapters to come, issue expansion occurred before polarization and hence cannot have been a consequence of increasing ideological differences between left and right. The opposite, however, is quite likely.

The above discussion suggests that one could trace a rough causal chain from the development of conservative ideology in elite circles to the development of conservative ideas among practical politicians activated by the Great Broadening, and then to the general public in the last stage of the diffusion of conservative ideology from intellectual elites to party elites to mass publics. No feedback system can occur in a vacuum; it must be transmitted through networks of human actors. Moreover, feedback that spills over into different policy arenas must connect actors in those arenas by spanning subsystems. Grossmann (2014), in an analysis of case studies of major policy changes in several major issues in the United States, reports that, in most areas, change was a result of interacting networks among policy-making elites. Indeed, many of these networks seemed to have formed during the Great Society period, and they spanned issue areas.

While Grossmann addresses a different question than either the ideological basis of policy-making that Noel addresses or the agenda broadening that we study here, we have examined his measure of important, legislatively centered policy change and find that it follows the horseshoe pattern that we have documented regarding broadening.[4] Moreover, Grossmann shows how networks of actors are critical to change, and that may be the lasting impact of his work. Such networks likely provided the transmission devices that became transformational during the Great Broadening. We revisit this connection below.

Networks such as Grossmann describes are intimately involved in the dynamics of partial decoupling. They are not always activated, but when they do become active, they have the potential of linking disparate subsystems. Partial decoupling applies to issue-based networks like those Grossmann studies, but it also applies to connections linking the internal dynamics of policy-making within government and factors exogenous to policy-making.

Social Autocatalysis

The second critical notion in the study of policy feedback is *autocatalysis*. The idea was developed in chemistry, and it describes a form of positive feedback in which new elements emerge from the interactions of existing elements. As complexity theorist Péter Érdi (2008, 9) puts it, "Autocatalytic reactions have a specific property: n components generate $n + m$ components, $m > 0$." Autocatalysis can be simple (linear), in which one component (molecule) "produces two molecules by using some other component, *A* [the catalyst]." Or it can be more complex, in which existing elements are transformed into multiples of new elements.

Padgett and Powell (2012, 2) brought the notion into social science, focusing on innovation in organizations to provide "an analytical framework for specifying with some precision the social science problem of emergence." The authors were thinking of complex forms of autocatalysis and refer to *autocatalytic sets*, which can account for the emergence—in politics, as elsewhere—of new patterns of organization that can displace the old. Biochemists use the concept to account for the emergence of life, an impossibility under standard linear-style models (chap. 2).

"Positive feedback loops or cycles of self-reinforcing transformations lie at the core of autocatalytic sets" (Padgett and Powell 2012, 8). The key to the authors' theory of organizational change is the network, but it is a special kind of network: "networks of transformation, not networks of mere transmission" (9). Under such dynamics, large bursts of activity can occur, as intense punctuated equilibria in one domain spill over into others via the network structure connecting them. It is entirely possible that these types of networks are what Grossmann describes.

The authors distinguish between innovations, which are activities, conceptions, and purposes that improve on existing ways of doing things, and inventions, which change the ways these things are done. It is, of course, difficult to distinguish invention from innovation, but the authors note that "invention, if and when it does break through, can appear as rapid 'punctuated equilibria,' with unintended consequences for organizations in collateral domains" (Padgett and Powell 2012, 9).

At some point, networks of transformation must settle down into networks of transmission; positive feedback loops of transformation cannot last for long. Having disrupted or even destroyed the system, networks operate to stabilize the new reality. But they may stimulate counter-reactions in other partially linked systems that can exhibit their own versions of autocatalysis.

Understanding the Great Broadening and Beyond

The two patterns we isolated in the first part of this book—the arc (or horseshoe) and the plateau (or asymptote)—may be explained by differing feedback dynamics. From Grossmann's work, we can infer that the Great Broadening involved the intense linkage of previously decoupled networks, basically unifying them across previously autonomous policy subsystems. A rapid series of policy punctuations ensued, altering the scope of government, which resulted in a large-scale transformative event with two distinct sets of effects: the familiar horseshoe and asymptote patterns. For horseshoes, the conservative counter-reaction to the Great Broadening is critical. Conservatives mobilized ideologically first, developing a network of like-minded people via the *National Review* and other conservatively oriented media. That alone was not enough; it was a self-sustaining network of actors transmitting information but having marginal effects on policy-making. Republicans were in the minority and seemed more interested in deflecting what they saw as the worst elements of Democratic big government and incremental gains, such as shifting from grants-in-aid to block grants in implementing Great Society programs. Then the Great Broadening provided the window of opportunity—a catalytic effect, if you will, activating policy-making elites and ultimately affecting electoral dynamics.

Plateaus represent parts of the policy-making system that were either beyond the reach of the conservative counter-mobilization or were not contested by it. Friction in the policy-making system meant that most laws enacting Great Society programs could not easily be reversed. Conservatives saw little reason to spend a great deal of time and energy on such proposals, but they were able to stop Democrats from enacting even more policies and programs aimed at broadening the scope of government. Democrats recognized that the intense lawmaking period had generated an ungovernable morass of new programs and agencies, and they reasoned that sound oversight, in part through a vigorous subcommittee system and professional analytical agencies, could help rationalize the system.

Arcs in policy-making data are likely the consequence of counter-mobilization, in which positive feedback sustains demands for change across networks. Plateaus are consequences of transformative networks settling down into transmission networks, in Padgett and Powell's terms. In the process, dependent variables became independent ones, as policy outputs altered the terrain of politics, transforming and then stabilizing the system.

This framework involving partial decoupling and social autocatalysis is an aid to understanding the Great Broadening and its consequences. But whether or not one is skeptical of our approach to grasping the nature of the broadening process, the data we use to support our contentions cannot be dismissed out of hand. It is high time that we integrated complex feedback effects into our understanding of policy and politics.

PART III

Consequences of the Great Broadening

The Great Broadening transformed American politics and policy-making in ways large and small. Some of these are obvious. If there is a burst of policy activity, surely bureaucracies grow, and the corpus of law expands. But less obvious are such facets as the expansion of the interest-group system, the transformation of the size of particular laws, the shift of Congress from primarily a lawmaking body to one overseeing its earlier creations, and the polarization of the party system. We show strong evidence that each of these trends has its roots in the Great Broadening.

Finally, the conservative counter-reaction to what liberals had wrought was energetic and at some points effective, but in other ways conservatives adopted the ways of big government, expanding crime and military policy and fighting over the mechanisms of policy delivery.

EIGHT

Transformation of US Law: Broadening and Then Thickening

During the Great Broadening, social functions and policy areas that were once reserved to the states or civil society became the subject of federal laws. These new programs, which included such issues as housing assistance for low-and moderate-income families, rural housing assistance, medical liability and malpractice, energy and environmental conservation, youth employment, and child abuse, were woven into a dense collage of policies that formed the newly broadened federal government's agenda and eventually its legal corpus. In this chapter, we show that the last stage of the burst of expansion in the federal government involved the country's legal corpus—the totality of statutory law passed. Its scope eventually broadened in just the way that it had with bill introductions, hearings, and roll-call votes, and then thickened in the policy areas added during the broadening period.

The Great Broadening triggered two dramatic changes in the laws that reverberate even today. First, Congress passed increasingly complex bills. After the Great Broadening, each law, on average, contained more titles, was longer, and cut across more major topics and subtopics than those passed before it. Second, the legal corpus greatly expanded after the Great Broadening. As with so much else in this book, the sequencing of these things is very important and helps shed light on the appropriate causes. The scope of the government did not change because Congress was considering more complex or longer bills. Rather the scope of government caused the laws to become larger and more complex. This chapter lays out this sequencing of the expansion of the federal government's scope, the increased complexity of laws, and the growth in the legal corpus.

Measuring Statutory Broadening and Thickening

Because we are interested in documenting the broadening and thickening of the US legal corpus, we need a measure of legislative output that can be accurately coded by policy content and length.[1] For a first cut of our description of the Great Broadening, we used Mayhew's count of landmark legislation, which began a cottage industry of how to measure and explain congressional productivity (Howell et al. 2000; Krutz 2000; Jones 2001; Jones and Baumgartner 2004; Clinton and Lapinski 2006; Grant and Kelly 2008; Dodd and Schraufnagel 2009; Adler and Wilkerson 2012; Ansolabehere, Palmer, and Schneer 2014). This subsequent research built on and refined Mayhew's classification of significant laws, while preserving the idea that productivity hinges on the number of laws Congress enacts. Furthermore, these refinements were concerned only with the count of the laws and not with their underlying substance.

Despite their prevalence, count-based conceptions of productivity—even those measures that distinguish important laws from trivial laws—have two important drawbacks. First, counts of laws do not measure the volume of law added by each Congress. Quite simply, the laws enacted prior to the Great Broadening are much shorter than those enacted after it. During the 1950s, a bill's average length was 1,383 lines; by the 2000s, it had almost tripled to 3,738 lines.

Second, law counts cannot speak to the scope not only of the overall federal government's attention, but also the scope contained within each individual law. Just as they have grown over time, laws have become more internally complex. Existing measures of congressional productivity are incapable of capturing this complexity because they do not investigate the substance of laws, let alone the diversity of substance within any given law. Much as relying on counts of whole laws underestimates the volume of new law Congress accretes onto the legal corpus, relying on counts of whole laws, even if they are coded for substance, may not be nuanced enough to pick up the diversity of topics within any given bill that Congress has considered over time. Because our goal is to measure the broadening of statutory scope and its subsequent thickening, we require a measure of congressional policy output that takes into account the internal complexity of legislation. If constructed properly, this measure produces a more accurate count of the thickening of the legal corpus and the accretion of law within each policy area. It is to that task that we now turn.

To account for both the increase in length and potential complexity, we continue to focus on laws, but not as a unit of observation in and of themselves. Rather, we examine the policy content within the laws. As they wrote longer bills, members of Congress began using titles to organize the various components within the legislation.[2] Modern laws often contain titles that were originally conceived as stand-alone bills. Sometimes these disparate titles are not even related. Much as a short story does not require the separate chapters of a novel, so it is that longer laws have distinct titles that are not necessarily required for shorter laws.

Because not all public laws, even in the modern era, contain titles, we treat small laws, which address a single topic area, and titles as equivalent units of law for the analysis in this chapter.[3] As a result, our final dataset is a mix of titles (16,012) and small public laws (17,646). This dataset contains 33,658 distinct units of law, which, for the sake of simplicity, we refer to as "titles," even though roughly half of them are laws unto themselves and thus do not have any titles per se. Of the 19,913 laws enacted between 1948 and 2011, 2,282 contained one or more titles. The most complex law in our dataset is a consolidated 2008 appropriations act (Pub. L. 110–161), which contains 130 titles. Among the most compact units of law in our dataset is a single sentence that amended the Federal Perkins Loans Program in the College Cost Reduction and Access Act (Pub. L. 110–84).

Once we break the law down into its core components, we can more easily and accurately code the content into both major topics and subtopics. We can also measure its length to get at the total volume of new law enacted in each policy area by each Congress. To do so, we use the *US Statutes at Large*, which chronologically compiles all federal law. Within its volumes, every law that meets the formal requirements for enactment laid out in the presentment clause of the Constitution is published in the order in which the president signs it. As such, it contains in a uniform manner the complete record of statutory law for the United States. We recorded the length of each new law enacted between 1948 and 2011 to the nearest quarter-page increment. Such a fine-tuned measure gives us an estimate of how and where the legal corpus has thickened.

Our analysis rests on the assumption that titles and small laws are roughly comparable units of measurement. For the most part, we find this to be true. Small laws and titles are, on average, more similar in length than are small laws and omnibus laws, which may contain many titles. Just as laws vary in length, so to do titles, but to a lesser extent than the omnibus laws from which they emanate. After the 97th Congress (1981–82), titles doubled in length on average from 4.4 to 10 pages (see fig. 8.1), whereas laws tripled in size over the same period. Over the entire postwar era, the average title per congress has varied between 3 and 15.5 pages, with a mean

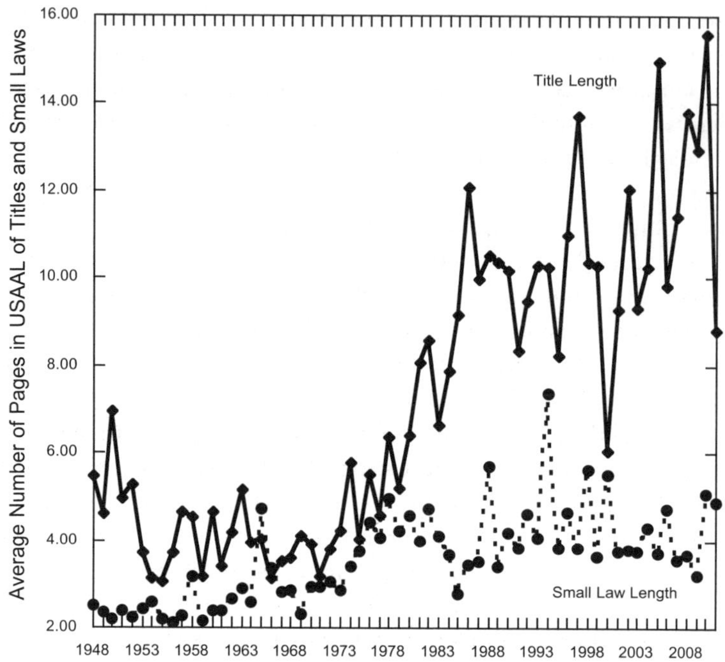

FIGURE 8.1. Average length of titles and small laws, by year

of 7.2 pages. The longest title in our dataset spanned 394.5 pages and dealt with amendments to the Elementary and Secondary Education Act of 1965. The shortest title spanned a mere quarter of a page. Small laws per congress vary between 2.1 and 7.3 pages, with a mean of 3.6 pages. While titles enacted after the early 1980s tend to be longer than small laws on average, they are still more comparable to each other than either are to omnibus laws, whose average length per congress has varied between 4.3 and 343.5 pages, with a mean of 83.7 pages.

The Broadening of the Law

Before focusing on how the law has broadened and then thickened, we first discuss how the number of titles has changed over time (see the dashed line in fig. 8.2). While Mayhew's measure of important legislation shows a surge between the 88th and 94th Congresses (1963–76), our measure shows that the number of titles enacted into law exploded between the 99th and the 102nd Congresses (1985–92), which include President Reagan's second term and the entirety of President George H. W. Bush's presidency. In the thirty-five years before that time period, which include Mayhew's surge, the number of titles fluctuated between 110 and 130 with a slightly negative time trend. The difference between Mayhew's surge and the explosion of titles in the 1980s under Republican presidents casts even more doubt on the conventional explanations of elections and political parties as the drivers of legislative output. Congress passed many landmark laws that contained few titles. The number of titles passed probably measures complexity rather than importance, but complex laws may make it more difficult to engineer important laws.

We showed in chapter 3 that the number of subtopics addressed per congress followed the characteristic broadening arc. Here we use the policy content of titles rather than entire laws to gain a more accurate assessment of statutory broadening. Aggregating these subtopics by congress reveals the well-recognized Great Broadening arc for both laws and the titles within them (fig. 8.3; the correlation between the quadratic curve and the actual data are 0.81 for titles and 0.77 for laws).

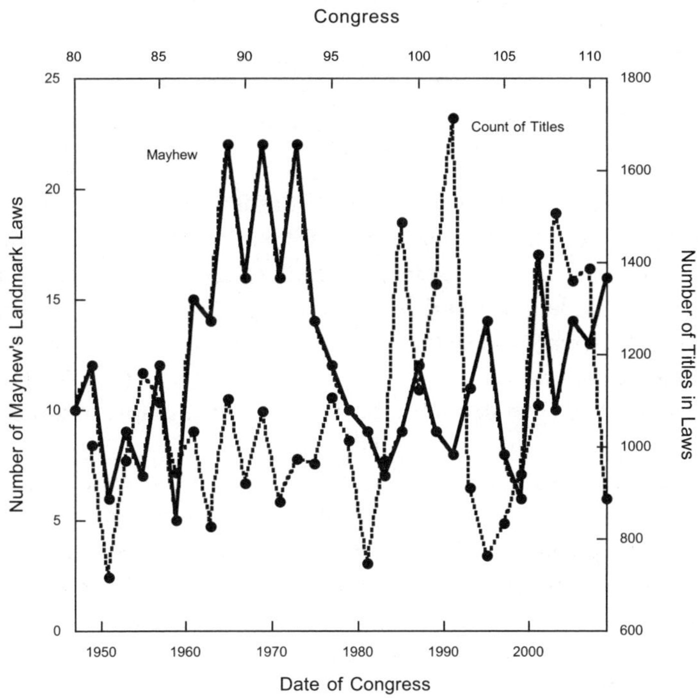

FIGURE 8.2. Number of titles in laws and the number of landmark laws enacted per Congress, 80th–111th Congresses

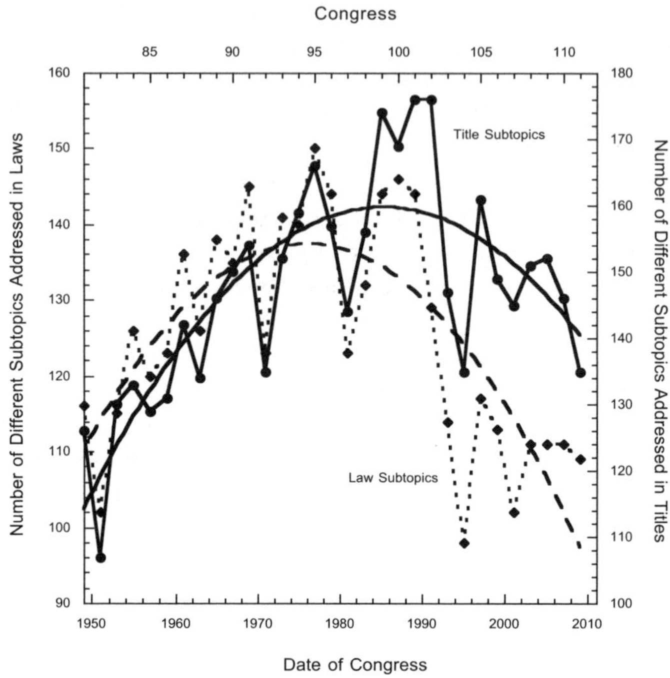

FIGURE 8.3. Number of Policy Agendas subtopics addressed in titles and in laws enacted per Congress, 80th–111th Congresses

The time series for both the number of subtopics in statutes passed during a congress and the number in the titles that comprise those statutes by congress differ in the predicted manner. Both series display the signature arc of the Great Broadening, but they trace different patterns through time. We detect three differences. First, the increase in subtopics is faster for titles. Second, the peak for laws occurs earlier—the 95th Congress (1977–78) versus the 101st (1989–90). And, finally, the decline in the number of subtopics in laws is much steeper than the number in titles.

The increase in subtopics addressed in titles for a considerable period of time beyond those addressed in laws indicates a continuing expansion of the statutory agenda until the late 1980s. As laws got longer, they included more issues, something that the title measure assesses but the law measure simply cannot. The increasing length of laws obscured this trend, but our study of titles reveals it. The likely explanation for the divergence in laws and titles is that the proliferation of titles was caused by increases in the diversity of the policy-making agenda.

Consistent with the chapter 3 figures, the peak of the broadening in Congress's statutory scope lags peaks for earlier stages of the policy process by roughly a decade. As in earlier stages of the policy process, the number of topics addressed in law titles begins its expansion in the mid-1950s. Unlike earlier stages of the policy process, the public law titles series reaches its peak in the late-1980s and declines thereafter. Laws moved from involving 130 subtopics during the 83nd Congress (1951–53) to a peak of 176 in the 101st Congress (1989–90) and back to 135 by the 111th Congress (2009–10). We expect some lags between these series because they represent different stages of lawmaking. A new subtopic must first reach the legislative agenda through the text of an introduced bill or in hearings before Congress takes a vote on it or enacts it into law. In this case, the federal government's legislative intrusion into a variety of new issue areas in the 1970s and 1980s follows congressional attention to those issues in the form of bill introductions and hearings roughly ten to twelve years earlier. Nonetheless, the federal government's persistent congress-by-congress encroachment on new policy areas is present. Following an extended peak, both the scope of topics addressed by titles within laws and the scope of the statutory agenda overall begin to contract.

The scope of laws is critical in assessing the power of the counter-reaction to the broadening of government, for two reasons. First, conservative opponents of government growth have a motive to stop the spread of government via law enactments because, once enacted, they are hard to change. Second, broadening via laws is easier to stop than discussions of issues on the formal government agenda. Discussions, alone, do not expand the reach of the federal government; laws can and frequently do. And in a system of divided powers with multiple veto points, laws are much easier to stop than bill introductions, hearings, or votes.

Broadening as measured by the policy content of titles reached its peak in the 101st Congress, after which it declined dramatically even before the 104th Congress (1995–96), which initiated a period of Republican control of Congress. It is likely that the Republican successes in 1994 and after "bent the broadening curve," but the expansionary period in the scope of laws had peaked for three congresses (101st through 103rd) before the Republican electoral successes. Everything did not happen at once, even with an electoral earthquake such as 1994. The arcs of both laws and titles indicate the strength of the counter-reaction and suggest that simple notions of transformative critical junctures are less useful as descriptions of political change than they might seem at first glance. The decline in the number of subtopics addressed continues well into the twenty-first century, indicating that the Great Broadening is not locked in as tightly as the critical-juncture–path-dependence approach suggests.

We have shown that when a topic enters the public debate, it tends to stay there. One major reason is the stickiness of laws. By incorporating an issue into a law, it becomes necessary to repeal that law explicitly in order to constrict the scope of government; generally, amending the law merely entrenches it. As such, the extent of statutory spread is strongly path-dependent. Policies, such as those regulating asbestos or providing funding for rural housing assistance, that had been the subject of committee debate in the 1950s became the subject of federal laws in the 1960s. While Congress may stop having asbestos hearings, which would reduce its scope at the committee-hearing level, the law remains. By the late 1980s, lawmakers were passing legislation across a wider spectrum of policy areas than ever before. The 102nd Congress (1991–92) represented a peak not only in the diversity of Congress's legislative agenda, but also in the cumulative number of distinct policy areas it addressed (see fig. 8.4). It is the classic representation of the asymptote, which is associated with path-dependency.

To examine more closely the relationship between the scope of the fed-

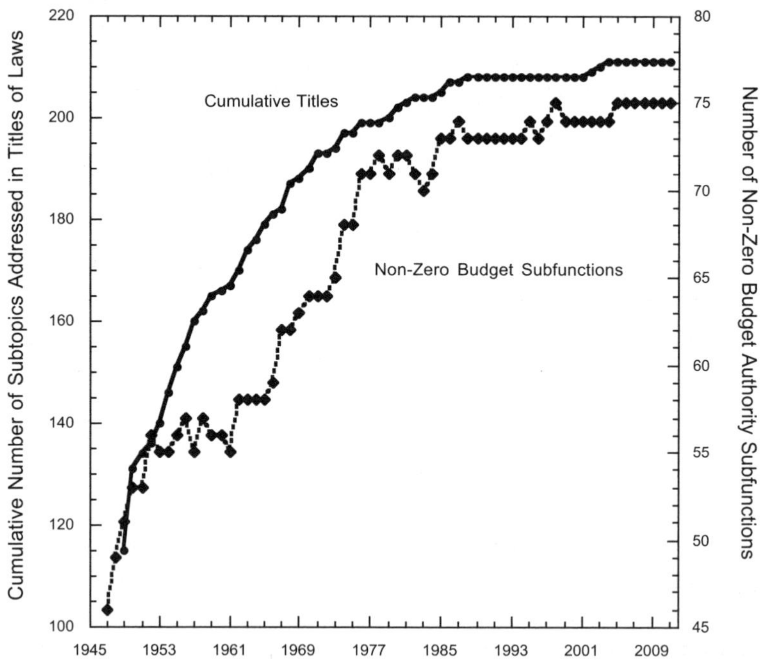

FIGURE 8.4. Cumulative count of subtopics added by Congress in public law titles and number of budget subfunctions, 81st–111th Congresses (1949–2011)

eral government's lawmaking and the scope of its funding practices, we also graph the number of Office of Management and Budget subfunctions used in categorizing what policy topics attract budget allocations. It too displays this plateau. Note the close correspondence between these two series ($r = 0.986$). The number of policy subtopics in titles increases first and then budget categories. Budget allocations clearly follow law creation. By the height of the peak, Congress had enacted laws addressing all but three of the unique Policy Agendas Project subtopics. After the peak, Congress took an additional twenty-one years before passing legislation addressing the residual topic areas of computers, prescription drug coverage, and research and development programs associated with education. Except for the comparatively late adoption of legislation addressing these three topics, Congress had fully embraced a broadened legal corpus and all the new federal functions it entailed by the 101st Congress (1989–90). Budget subfunctions reached a plateau in about the same period as the titles.

The consequences of the federal government's initial foray into a broader range of policy areas are ill-understood. We do know that the consequences of legislators talking about policy change or even voting on policy change are, at a minimum, different from the results of actually enacting policy change. Policies debated in earlier stages of the policy process, such as committee hearings, are policies in theory, not policies in practice. They may fall onto or off the agenda with little fanfare or cost to the government. But once policies are solidified in statutory law, Congress has a much more difficult time extricating itself from them.

Over time, Congress added new policies to its statutory repertoire. Unlike the scope of congressional hearings, the new policies endure in the legal corpus, even after legislators stop discussing them. Even if individual provisions dealing with a newly infiltrated policy area are repealed—and they sometimes are—enough provisions remain within that policy area that it is never fully extracted from the statutory corpus (Whyman 2014). In thinking about the consequences of the Great Broadening, it is important to remember that while the scope of Congress's statutes peaked in the late 1980s, these functions were built one-by-one into the legal corpus prior to its peak. While a conservative counter-revolution against the excesses of a broadened federal government may have been successful in causing Congress to stop holding hearings on particular topics, it has not proven successful in causing Congress to withdraw entirely from its statutory involvement with these topics. In the following two sections, we investigate two potential consequences of new functions being built into Congress's statutory agenda: the internal complexity of lawmaking and the thickening of statutory law across Congress's newly broadened agenda.

The Internal Complexity of Legislation

Current lawmaking bears little resemblance to the lawmaking of sixty years ago. It bears even less resemblance to lawmaking at the turn of the twentieth century and still less to that which was practiced following the founding of the nation. Compared to their World War II predecessors, today's members of Congress are more ideologically polarized, operate within a denser network of lobbying organizations, are far more dependent on fund-raising appeals, and have come to rely on unorthodox techniques to garner legislative successes needed to secure reelection (Matthews 1959; Polsby 1968; Sinclair 2011; McCarty, Poole, and Rosenthal 2006; Mann and Ornstein 2006; Theriault 2008). Despite knowing quite a bit about how lawmaking has changed in the last half-century, we know very little about how the Great Broadening may have influenced these developments.

As World War II ended, the public relied on the federal government for a comparatively limited menu of services, including conducting military and foreign operations, negotiating trade deals, regulating the financial industry, managing a national social security program, and operating a postal system. Contrast that with the list of services for which the American public came to rely on the federal government after the Great Broadening: housing and welfare assistance, recycling programs, youth employment programs, and protections against age and gender discrimination. E. E. Schattschneider (1935, 288), in reaction to the earlier New Deal era, provided an important insight into how this new scope would disrupt the equilibrium that existed prior to the Great Broadening: "New policies create new politics." The new policies implemented during the Great Broadening created new demands on government. Citizens across the country now had reason to believe that the federal government could and, in many cases, should provide solutions to problems that had previously been addressed by state or local governments or relegated to the private sphere. This demand on the federal government grew as citizens became the beneficiaries of new programs and defended these programs against retrenchment (Patashnik 2008). The limits that federalism set on the reach of the federal government dissolved under the weight of malapportionment, the under-representation of booming diverse urban populations, and the public's desire to retain the benefits and protections these new programs provided. Yet the same public remained both skeptical ideologically of a big and remote federal government and resistant to increases in taxes. Consequently, the job of a modern member of Congress often now includes the maintenance or expansion of existing programs. Many times, when these programs are debated, the subject of the debate is what mechanism to use—usually some form of privatization.

To maintain or expand the programs Congress created during the Great Broadening, lawmakers needed to pass laws or delegate authority to bureaucratic agencies to pass rules. Given that polarization between Republicans and Democrats has been steadily increasing since the 1980s, the job of passing policy has become harder but no less pressing for lawmakers. Democratic theory suggests that legislators' electoral fortunes hinge on their ability to convince their constituents that they are actively representing their interests. If lawmakers are unable to pass policy across the wide range of functions demanded by citizens, they run the risk of losing the support of their constituents and, consequently, their bids for reelection.

To retain their seats, members of Congress needed a solution that would, first, enable them to attract large enough enacting coalitions to overcome the hurdle of polarization and, second, help them to enact provisions across the broad spectrum of policies their constituents demanded. It is plausible that lawmakers adopted the use of omnibus legislation because it killed both birds with one stone. Omnibus is derived from the Latin, "for everything," and has become the preferred term-of-art to describe bills that contain separable policies that manifest as huge titles or divisions of a law that originally were, or could be, conceived as stand-alone laws in their own right (Krutz 2001).

In an era of polarization and partisan strife, party leaders have increasingly turned to omnibus legislation to pass their agenda for three reasons. First, by combining multiple different areas of law, party leaders try to forge an enacting coalition comprised of the supporters of each of the individual policy supporters (Krutz 2001; Theriault and Weingast 2002). Second, members of Congress have gotten increasingly adept at attaching their favored policy changes to must-pass legislation. Finally, as laws broadened, it became increasingly difficult for a law passed in one policy area (e.g., agriculture) not to affect another (e.g., the environment). So passing an agriculture law might mean including an environmental provision as well (perhaps incorporated into a title). So long as omnibus bills do not also forge a coalition of opponents or their add-ons do not act as poison pills, we would expect legislation in the aftermath of the Great Broadening to contain more disparate policies than the legislation that preceded it (Sinclair 2011).

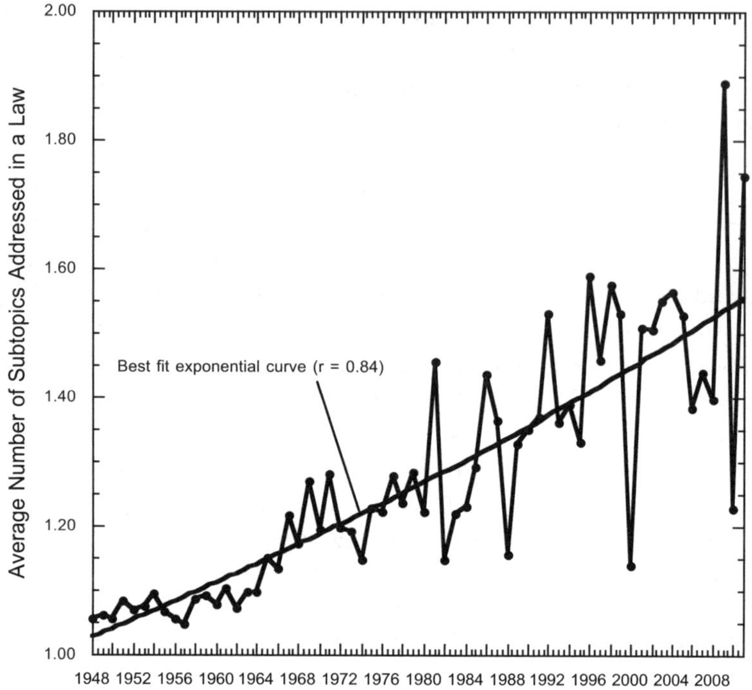

FIGURE 8.5. Changes in the internal complexity of public laws: Average number of Policy Agendas Subtopics addressed in a law, by year, 1948–2011

Lawmakers began piecing together disparate policies under one bill after the peak of the Great Broadening, adding to the complexity of laws, not just their size (see fig. 8.5). Until the early 1960s, most laws addressed a single topic, and usually only a single subtopic. As the Great Broadening proceeded, the number of subtopics addressed within a single law increased somewhat until the mid-1980s and then grew more rapidly. As the complexity of laws increased, the variance of their complexity also increased.

Over time, laws not only contained more titles, but they also included more topics and subtopics than in previous years. Beginning in the early 1960s, and intensifying in earnest after the Great Broadening was well underway, the average number of policy areas addressed in public laws increased. Whereas before the broadening, most laws addressed a single major topic area, public laws, on average, addressed 1.5 major topic areas and contained more than 2.5 titles afterward.

The Thickening of the Law

This increase in the length and complexity of legislation has profound consequences for the thickening of the federal legal corpus. Scholars can no longer treat modern laws as if each addresses a single topic. Omnibus bills allow congressional leaders to pass a high volume of pages of law across a wide spectrum of policy areas. Every page of law that Congress passes results in the statutory corpus expanding by an approximately equivalent amount. Given that Congress increasingly relies on omnibus legislation to pass policy, more recent final passage votes have resulted in more dramatic changes to the statutory corpus across a wider range of policy areas than did earlier votes. By conceiving of productivity at a granular level, we expose congressional activity in policy areas that might have remained hidden had we only examined whole laws.

Having used the policy content of titles in the previous section, we use their length in this section. In aggregating the title lengths by congress, we can determine the volume of new law that each Congress passes. A comparison of a more conventional measure of lawmaking productivity, the count of laws passed, and a count of the total length of the laws passed, reveals a striking difference (see fig. 8.6). Measuring the number of total statutes passed since the 81st Congress (1949–50) suggests decreasing productivity, whereas measuring the total pages passed suggests sustained and even increasing productivity in the modern era. On average, with each passing Congress, lawmakers enact fifteen fewer laws, but 176 more pages of law. In the 81st Congress, they enacted 846 laws spread over 3,104 pages. By the 111th Congress, they enacted 383 laws spread over 8,372 pages.

By combining the Policy Agendas code of a title's policy with its length, we can accurately measure the volume of topics Congress passes into law and its depth of involvement in each topic area. The combination produces a more accurate assessment of Congress's statutory spread than has previously been possible (see fig. 8.7). Some policy areas have thickened at much higher rates than others. Congress has passed many more pages of law on defense than on housing, for example. And a great deal of thickening occurred in government operations, which captures the routines of government including management issues, contracting, and civil service issues. With program thickening comes organizational thickening.

To illustrate the differences between coding whole laws versus individual titles, we compare the proportion of pages of Policy Agendas Project public laws coded by major topic area with the proportion of pages of titles coded

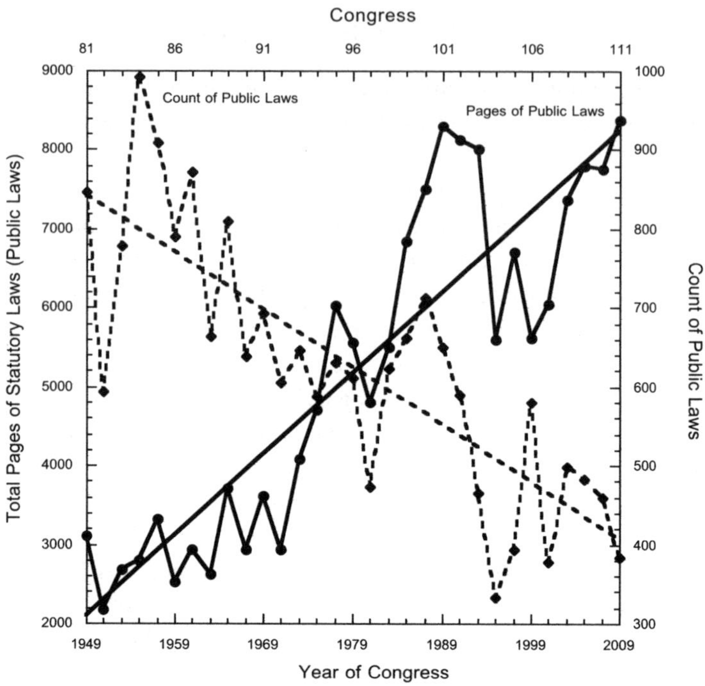

FIGURE 8.6. Measuring statutory thickening by counting the pages versus number of public laws, 81st–111th Congresses

by major topic area for the postwar period (see fig. 8.8). If we measure legislative output using the policy codes assigned to whole laws, Government Operations appears to be the largest category, followed closely by Public Lands and Water Management. These categories, along with Defense, dwarf all others and give the impression that Congress's output is highly skewed toward these functions. Coding whole laws artificially inflates our count of the pages that deal with these topic areas. If, instead, we assign topic codes to individual titles, a very different picture emerges. We find that Congress's legislative output as measured by individual titles instead of whole laws is far more balanced between the twenty major topics. Most notably, the number of pages classified as dealing with health, education, energy, community development and housing, and labor and employment, increases when subsections of law are the focus of our analysis.

Once the national government legislates in a new policy area, it rarely extricates itself from it. In fact, lawmakers have incentives to increase their

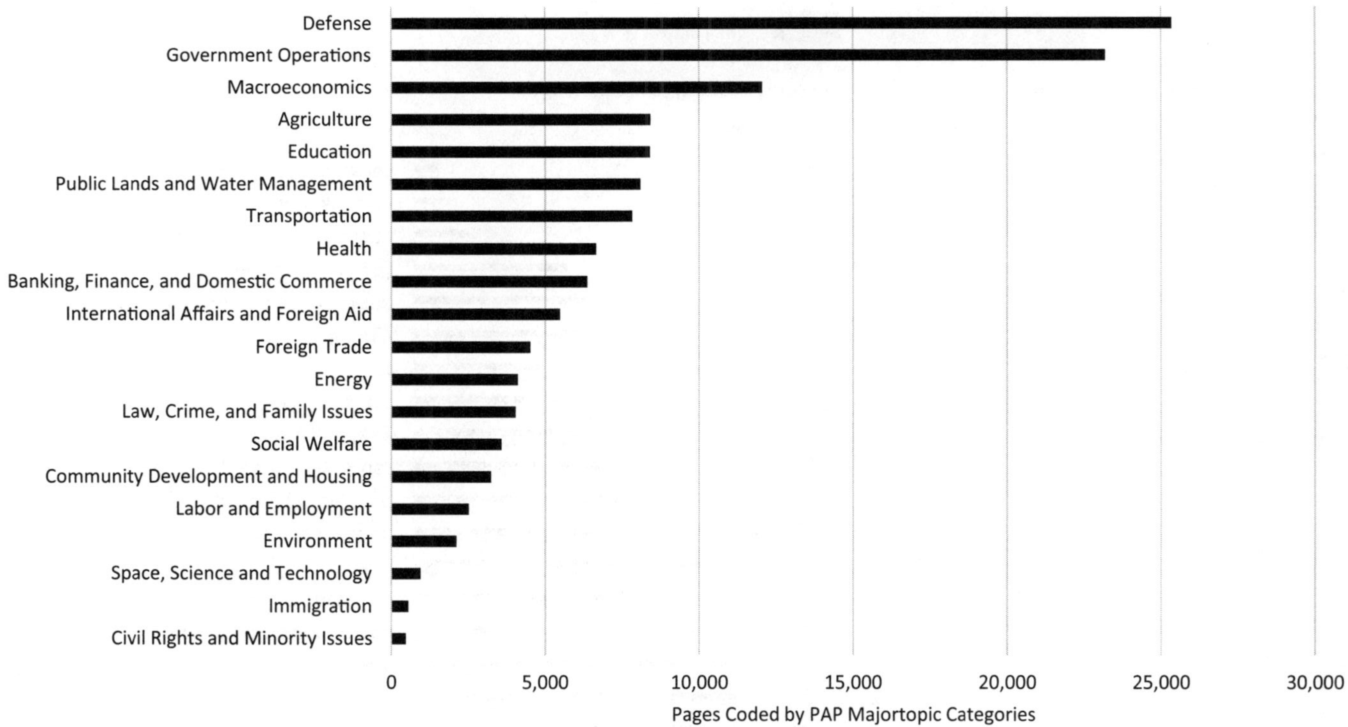

FIGURE 8.7. Length of statutory law within major topic codes

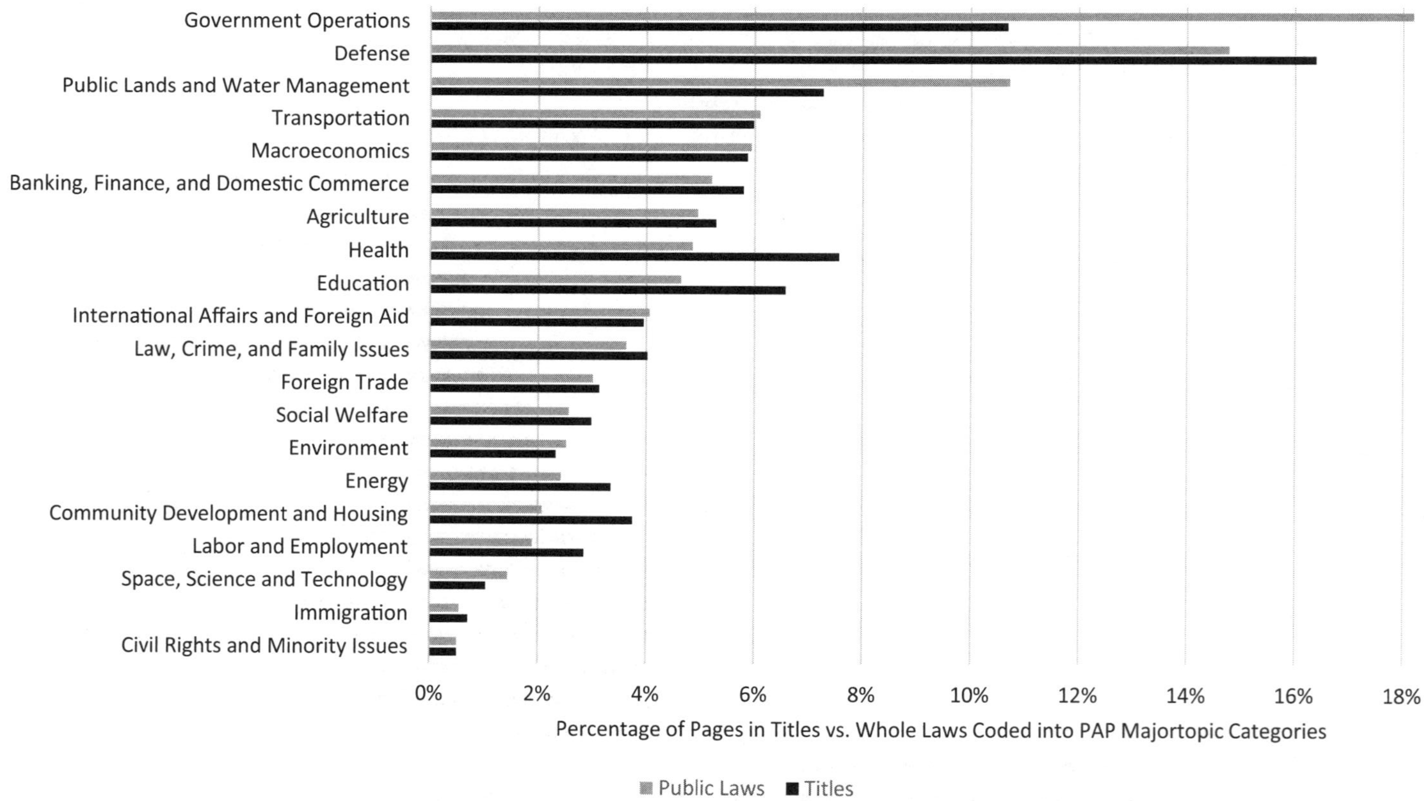

FIGURE 8.8. Comparison between public laws and titles coded according to PAP major topics, 1948–2011

involvement in a policy area following their first engagement within it. To assess the degree to which the Great Broadening precipitated the thickening of government, we determined the number of pages enacted into each Policy Agendas major topic area from the 80th to the 110th Congresses (see fig. 8.8). The figure allows us to visualize the evolution of the legal corpus over time and provides a complete record of the accreted statutory output of the United States since World War II. Gradient shades of grey represent different major topics relative to the age with which each was brought onto the agenda. The darkest shades represent the oldest functions of government, while the lightest shades represent the newest functions of the federal government. The height of each grey section on the *y*-axis represents the total volume of pages enacted by each Congress, which is noted on the *x*-axis. This figure is unique because it shows both the broadening of Congress's statutory scope (the number of topics on its agenda) and its subsequent thickening (the number of pages enacted in each topic area).

Before Lyndon Johnson ascended to the presidency in 1963, fewer laws were passed, and they primarily concentrated in policy domains like government operations, defense, transportation and infrastructure, crime, and public lands. With the passage of Johnson's Great Society programs, Congress addressed policy areas relatively new to the federal government, including specific sub-areas within health, social welfare, community development and housing, education, labor, and energy. Congress's initial foray into these policy areas was usually minimal, because it wasn't until the 1980s that the thickening of law happened. The legal corpus didn't thicken at the same time as it broadened; rather, the latter happened first and then the former.

When the Republicans became a majority in the House in 1995—and then held it for the next twelve years—the number of pages of enacted law experienced a significant decline. During this period, Congress passed fewer pages of law across most policy areas, excepting defense, government operations, and transportation, although the pattern broke down during the last four of those years they controlled Congress. After the 107th Congress, lawmakers have experienced a sustained resurgence in productivity, culminating in a greater number of pages enacted than at any other time in US history. The passage of these pages represents the greatest thickening of the federal government to date, and it is across a broad spectrum of policies.

Congress addressed virtually no new issues in this later period, but it added a plethora of adjustments to the existing set of issues addressed in the corpus of law (see fig. 8.9). The greatest cumulative growth in pages of federal law occurs after this peak, during which Congress doubles down on

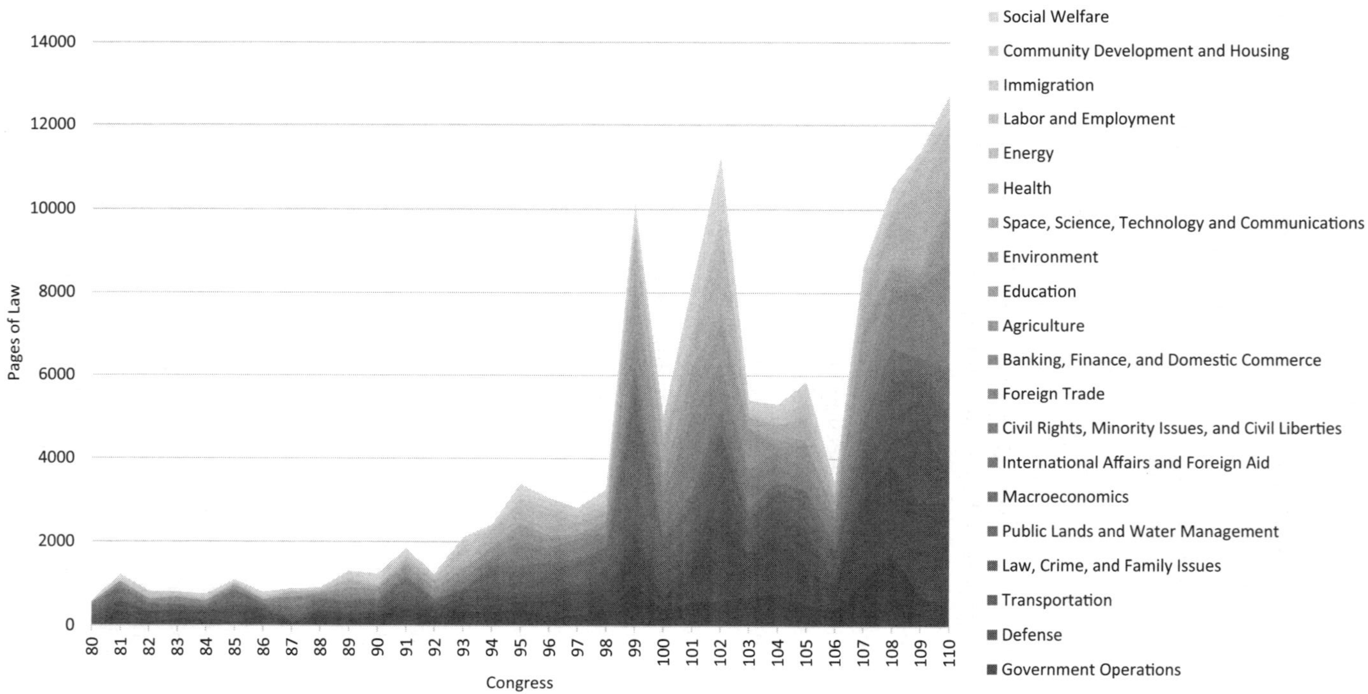

FIGURE 8.9. Stacked area chart of pages of law enacted by policy area, 80th–110th Congress

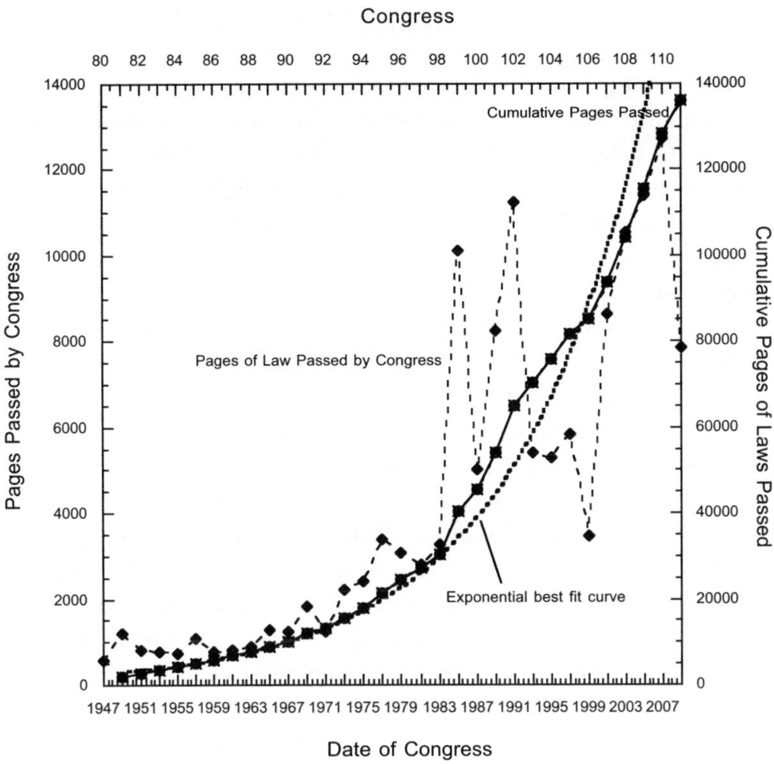

FIGURE 8.10. Numbers of pages of law passed by each Congress and cumulatively, 81st–111th Congress (1949–2011)

issues it has already addressed by passing more pages of law in those areas. Almost all the activity depicted in figures 8.9 and 8.10 involves making law denser in the areas that already had the attention of the federal government. The cumulative number of pages of law passed per congress is best fit by an exponential growth curve of 6.8 percent per year over the full series ($r = 0.98$). Some periods were characterized by faster growth in law than 6.8 percent; indeed, during most of the period from the beginning until the mid-1990s, law grew faster. Since then it has grown slower, but with great congress-to-congress variability (see fig. 8.10).

Laws become dense because of Wildavsky's insight that "policy is its own cause." Law thickens because new problems and opportunities emerge from these laws. This classic, self-reinforcing dynamic does not need some external cause to explain it. While Congress may slow this growth rate in the future, and did so beginning in the mid 1990s, it is not clear that the growth trend can be reversed permanently without offering great latitude to administrative agencies to handle the increasing complexity.

Beyond multiplying the number of laws citizens are required to follow, increasing the density of statutory law may have important downstream political effects, including mobilizing private litigants and the courts to share the burden of enforcing statutes (Farhang 2008). Relying on historical data from 1887 to 2004, Farhang finds that interbranch conflict between Congress and the executive incentivizes lawmakers to rely on court cases brought by private litigants to interpret and enforce statutes. Given the congruence between the broadening and thickening of statutory law and the coincident growth of the role of litigation and the courts in the implementation of policy, we believe that a complementary explanation is that the thickening of statutory law incentivized Congress and the president to delegate their respective functions to the judicial branch.

As statutory law becomes denser and more complex, Congress and the executive branch are faced with the choice to expend resources to craft and carefully implement law or to delegate the problem of sorting out implementation and enforcement to actors within the judicial branch. The desire to delegate is especially acute for members of Congress, who are often rewarded for passing new laws but rarely rewarded for having carefully crafted specific statutory language for their detailed implementation and enforcement. It costs Congress fewer resources to delegate the particulars of complex policies to downstream political actors, often bureaucrats, but sometimes the legal system. Private litigants and the courts can relieve the pressure Congress faces to fully articulate public policies by acting as ex post facto interpreters of the law. Similarly, litigants and the courts can relieve the pressure on the executive branch by acting as enforcers of the law. While we do not rigorously test this possibility, it is highly plausible that the expansion of the litigation state is an additional downstream consequence of the earlier expansion of statutory law.

Law and the Expanding Policy Agenda

This chapter presents a trend that is repeated in the next few chapters. We present new evidence that measures more precisely the sequencing of when things happened, along with a powerful underlying logic to explain it. What we lack in a "smoking gun," we hope to make up for in a more thorough investigation that leaves no clue undiscovered. Indeed, it is the overwhelming number of clues and the consistency among them that lead us to the conclusion that the Great Broadening radically transformed what the federal government does and how it does it.

Consistent with using hearings, votes, and statements in party platforms, we show how the government's agenda expanded into areas of law that only a generation ago would have been unthinkable. Rather than measuring this change at the "law" level, we do so at the "title" level, which shows that Congress is passing larger and more complex laws in lieu of passing more—or even the same number—of laws. Interestingly, though, the total amount of law does not grow at the same time as the agenda is expanding. Rather, it grows later. Indeed, the camel does not enter the tent all at once. The data show that the camel's nose is first, then its head, and, in time, it's entire body. This system is self-sustaining, always growing exponentially, albeit sometimes at lower rates than at other times.

Statutory law was not the only legal corpus affected by the Great Broadening. The federal government's intrusion into new issue areas in the 1960s and 1970s triggered the broadening of policy agendas across all policy-making stages, including agency rules. In the next chapter, we explore the consequences of the Great Broadening for agency rule-making and congressional oversight of the federal bureaucracy.

NINE

The Administrative State and Its Legislative Oversight

In chapter 8, we examined the vast impact that the frenetic policy activity during the Great Broadening had on the structure of law. Here we turn to three other aspects of American government that were transformed by this activity: the capacity of Congress to analyze the structure and effects of policy action, the breadth of executive branch bureaucratic policy-making, and the transformation of Congress from a body primarily concerned with passing bills to a body primarily concerned with conducting oversight.

Demand from the fast pace of policy enactment caused the increases in institutional capacity to conduct policy analysis, not the other way around. During the same period that Congress expanded its statutory scope, lawmakers delegated more rule-making authority to executive agencies. In response, federal agencies issued a diverse array of rules, regulations, and enforcement orders to match Congress's broadened statutory agenda. Both the enactment of so many policies in new areas and the construction of administrative capacity to administer them led directly to the legislative branch moving toward more oversight of the policy implementation process constructed by new laws.

Simultaneously the conservative reaction to the Great Broadening slowed the enactment of new statutes, leading to fewer referral hearings and more oversight hearings. In the wake of the broadening, today's committees spend more time overseeing federal agencies' implementation of the expansive and thick legal corpus than they do trying to pass new legislation.

Congressional Capacity Follows Broadening

In the Legislative Reform Act of 1946, Congress enacted the most comprehensive reorganization in its history. Many committees, most of which existed only on paper, were disbanded, and others were combined and given explicit jurisdictions. The committee system established in 1946 is the basis for the committee system still used today. The Policy Agendas Project data start around the time of this very important institutional change. Students of American political development have analyzed the vigorous period of state-building that occurred after the disruption of the Depression and World War II, showing the development of the federal government as the Cold War proceeded (Sparrow 1996). Much experimentation and a focus on international relations characterized the first part of this period; not surprisingly, most of the new functions added then correspond to these issues. The Great Broadening that followed was much more comprehensive.

As the broadening of the policy-making agenda continued throughout the period, Congress responded by building the capacity to handle multiple issues in parallel. State-building meant an increased capacity to address the great addition of functions to the postwar federal government simultaneously. This involved the legislative branch as well as the executive branch.

As issues bombarded the legislative agenda, the capacity of Congress to process those issues became stressed, and terms like *overloaded government* became common. Following Richard Rose, Howard (1984, 332) defined overloaded government as "the idea that the range of economic and social problems that government is expected to solve has increased, while its capacity to deal with them has decreased." In the heady days of the early 1970s, the range of issues that government was expected to address expanded much faster than its capacity to process them (Baumgartner and Jones 2015).

The demands stemming from the political mobilizations of the 1960s caused considerable stress in the legislative system. The result was an expanded organizational capacity brought about by the growth and importance of the subcommittees fostered by the Subcommittee Bill of Rights and by the expansion of Congress's analytical bureaucracies in the early 1970s. At the height of the Great Broadening, Congress added analytical capacity in amendments to the Legislative Reorganization Act and in the Congressional Budget Control and Impoundment Act of 1974. Simultaneously Comptroller General Elmer Staats was moving the General Accounting Office (GAO) from a focus on auditing to one centering more on the emerging field of policy analysis. By 1974, Congress had expanded the capacity of the GAO, the Congressional Research Service, the Congressional Budget Office, and the Office of Technology Assessment. The productivity of these support organizations grew rapidly. As an example, the GAO in 1966 produced 37 reports; by 1973, it produced 1,600 (Baumgartner and Jones 2015, 72).

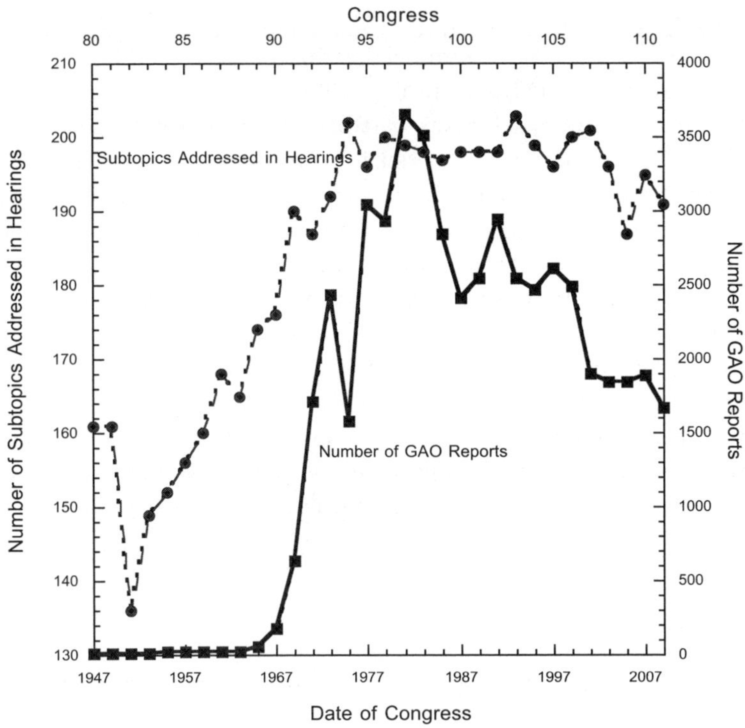

FIGURE 9.1. Capacity follows issue expansion: The number of policy agendas subtopics with at least one hearing and the number of GAO reports issued, by Congress

Congressional capacity for processing information clearly followed a broadened agenda. The existence of the capacity to analyze issues did not develop first, with the issues coming later. Rather capacity trailed broadening. For example, the number of GAO reports increased rapidly after the mid-1960s, but this increase trailed by a few years the number of Policy Agendas subtopics addressed in congressional hearings (see fig. 9.1).

Note the decline in GAO reports after the peak in 1981 (during the 97th Congress). Moreover, the agency's staff reached its peak in 1978, declining until 1983, when it stabilized until 1992 and then began a precipitous drop that accelerated with the Republican congressional electoral victories in 1994 (Drutman and Teles 2015). Indeed, this pattern was general, as the capacity of the legislative branch to analyze policy issues declined soon after the peak of the Great Broadening (Drutman and Teles 2015). GAO, House and Senate committee staff, and the Congressional Research Service all experienced substantial declines in resources during the period, with most of the drop occurring in 1995. That year Congress also eliminated the Office of Technology Assessment. Committee hearings, however, declined throughout our period of study from a peak in 1978.

This decline in capacity was part of the push-back by conservatives against the liberal initiatives undertaken during the Great Broadening. Some conservatives thought, in a kind of Say's Law of issue development, that providing capacity simply encouraged government to find more problems, which would subsequently lead to larger government as a solution. Republicans, in this later time period, explicitly attacked the left's encroachment on civil society's turf.

We examine the capacity of the government with one more data series: whether the hearing involves the creation of a new agency or a new program in the executive branch, as assessed by the Policy Agendas Project. The graph of the number of hearings focusing on creating these new agencies or programs across congresses reveals the familiar arc pattern (see fig. 9.2).

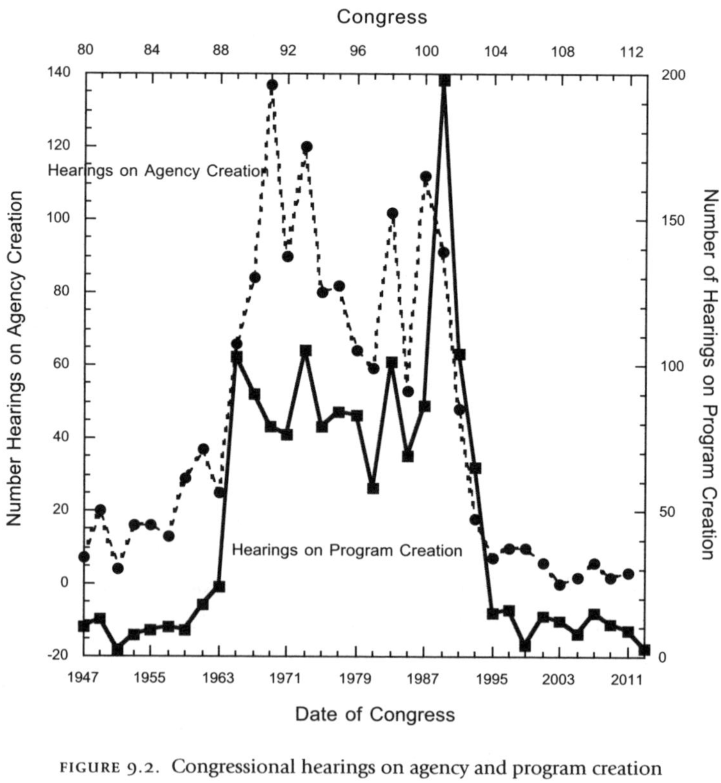

FIGURE 9.2. Congressional hearings on agency and program creation

Hearings concerning the possibility of creating a new executive branch agency rose in the 89th through 91st Congresses (1965–70) and continued at a relatively high level, albeit with considerable variability, until the 100th Congress (1987–88). Beginning in the 101st Congress (1989–90), hearings on agency creation fell, and did so until reaching a nadir in the 104th Congress (1995–96), the first unified Republican Congress in fifty years. Note, however, that the extended decline in hearings on agency creation began several congresses before the dramatic shift in political fortunes of congressional Republicans. The Republican tsunami of 1994 did not create a disjoint shift in congressional discussions of agency creation. As with our examination of important elections earlier, the analysis shows that the 1994 election was part of a trend rather than a cause of it.

Hearings about program creation follow a similar trajectory, but with a very strong peak in the 101st Congress. The decline occurred over the next three congresses, reaching a nadir in the 104th Congress. Neither series has ever recovered, even though Democrats controlled Congress from 2007 to 2011.

Is there a relationship between increases in the number and diversity of issues that Congress addressed during the Great Broadening and the addition of administrative capacity in the executive branch? Indeed, the correlation between the count of subtopics subject to one or more referral hearings in Congress and hearings on agency creation is a strong 0.81 (see fig. 9.3). The relationship may be curvilinear, such that at times of high diversity in the issue agenda, Congress holds a particularly large number of hearings on agency creation.[1] Subtopics considered in hearings and agency creation both peaked during the height of the Great Broadening. Generally, congressional consideration of executive capacity goes hand-in-glove with the expanding legislative policy-making agenda. But not always; the top of the scale contains considerable variability. When Congress considers lots of issues simultaneously, sometimes this leads to lots of hearings on agency creation and sometimes to fewer. As the Great Broadening waned, Congress considered lots of issues but lost interest in creating agencies.

Expansion of the Bureaucracy

To assess the degree to which the federal government's bureaucratic agenda has both broadened and subsequently thickened, we examine several different indicators, all of which are imperfect, but together give a good overview of the changes in Congress stemming from the Great Broadening and the

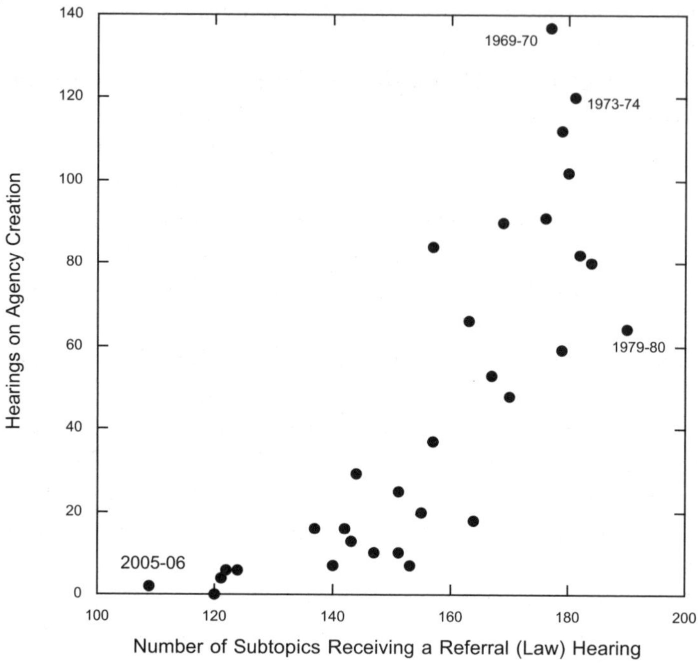

FIGURE 9.3. Scatterplot of Congress's lawmaking agenda and hearings on agency creation

ensuing thickening of law. The data we present in the following sections tell the story of a legislative branch whose role in the American political system has been transformed by its own design. After broadening the functions of the federal government, Congress and federal agencies deepened the government's involvement in these functions, requiring Congress to act less as the legislature and more as an oversight body.

The United States is governed by a mix of statutory, regulatory, and common law, each distinguished by the authority that promulgates it. Statutory laws are enacted by Congress, regulatory laws by executive branch agencies, pursuant to a delegation of rule-making authority by Congress, and common laws are the rules and norms for action (i.e., precedence) culled from reported court decisions. Although all three branches share in making law, the bureaucracy, through regulatory law, has begun to push aside statutory law in scope and importance, much as statutes once pushed aside the common law (Calabresi 1982). This process has led Jonathan Turley (2013) to suggest, "Today, the vast majority of 'laws' governing the United States are not passed by Congress but are issued as regulations, crafted largely by thousands of unnamed, unreachable bureaucrats."

Before the New Deal, extensive delegation of legislative authority to the executive was largely unknown in the United States. In the shadow of the Great Depression, President Franklin Delano Roosevelt convinced Congress to enact legislation that gave the federal government sweeping authority over the economy. Most notably, the National Industrial Recovery Act (NIRA) of 1933 required that companies comply with industry-wide codes of fair competition and abide by fixed wages and prices. The law created the National Recovery Administration to promote compliance with these industry codes. The NIRA was declared unconstitutional when the Supreme Court, led by Chief Justice Hughes, ruled that "Congress is not permitted to abdicate or to transfer to others the essential legislative functions with which it is thus vested" (*A.L.A. Schecter Poultry Corp. v. United States*, 295 U.S. 495).

Partially in response to the Court's articulation of the nondelegation doctrine in this landmark decision, Congress passed the Administrative Procedure Act (APA) in 1946. The law provided a legal framework for Congress to delegate authority to the bureaucracy and outlined the process federal agencies must follow to promulgate rules (Workman 2015). Senator Pat McCarran summarized the purpose of the act during the floor debate on its adoption:

> We have set up a fourth order in the tripartite plan of Government which was initiated by the founding fathers of our democracy. They set up the executive, the legislative, and the judicial branches; but since that time we have set up a fourth dimension, if I may so term it, which is now popularly known as administrative in nature. So we have the legislative, the executive, the judicial, and the administrative; . . . perhaps there are reasons for that arrangement. We found that the legislative branch, although it might enact law, could not very well administer it. So the legislative branch enunciated the legal precepts and ordained that commissions or groups should be established by the executive branch with power to promulgate rules and regulations. These rules and regulations are the very things that impinge upon, curb, or permit a citizen who is touched by the law, as every citizen of this democracy is (*Congressional Record* of March 12, 1946).

Since the passage of the APA, when Congress wants to do something that requires technical expertise or close oversight, it confers upon an administrative agency the power to make rules. The agency can then propose rules, regulations, and enforcement orders that regulate the conduct of citizens, so long as these do not exceed the authority granted to the agency by the delegating legislation. For example, the Clean Air Act of 1970, along with its recent amendments, authorized the Environmental Protection Agency to establish National Ambient Air Quality Standards, which included precise limits on the number of particles of sulfur dioxide, nitrogen dioxide, carbon monoxide, and lead that can be in the air anywhere in the United States.

Administrative policy-makers must announce their intentions to change policy in the *Federal Register* (*FR*). Before a proposed rule assumes the force of law, it is published in the *FR* and made available for a public comment period, so members of the public can consider it and send comments to the agency. The proposed regulation is then revised in accordance with these comments before being published as a final rule and reprinted in the *FR*. Once a regulation is completed and has been printed in the *FR* as a final rule, it is codified in the *Code of Federal Regulations* (*CFR*). The *CFR* is the codification of the general and permanent rules published in the *Federal Register* by the departments and agencies in the federal government. It is organized by subject area and roughly parallels the structure and content of the United States Code, which is the organized aggregation of all federal provisions of law enacted by Congress. Editors at the Office of the *Federal Register* are responsible for reprinting in the *CFR*, rules, and regulations, exactly as they appeared in the *Federal Register*.

The Thickening of the Regulatory Agenda

The *Federal Register* indexes bureaucratic rule-making activity. It includes a mix of newly proposed rules, final rules, and executive orders. An analogous publication for Congress might include a mix of bills that received a hearing in Congress and enacted laws. As such, the annual number of pages in the *Federal Register* provides a sense of the flow of rule-making across all federal agencies, as well as a measure of the potential regulatory burden with which citizens may be required to comply. A cumulative annual count of the number of pages in the *CFR*, on the other hand, shows the volume of existing final rules with which American businesses, workers, and consumers must comply (see fig. 9.4).

Up until the 1990s, the largest bulge in proposed and published rules generally coincides with the later stages of the Great Broadening. During this period (1975–83), federal agencies proposed a greater number of rules and regulations in response to Congress's increased legislative activity. This volume of proposed and final rules abated until 1991; the volume of rule-making has steadily increased since then. Regulatory activity before the Great Broadening averaged 11,000 pages per year in the 1950s, reached a peak of 87,012 pages in 1980, and has averaged 80,000 pages in recent years.

Unlike the accumulation of law, the accumulation of rules published in the *CFR* generally grows linearly, with an average annual increase of 2,772 pages ($r = 0.99$). A more fine-grained look at the generally linear trend reveals a period of slower growth from the mid-1950s to the late 1960s, then a surge period from the late 1970s to the mid-1990s, followed by a period of growth very close to the trend line. Importantly, this linear growth in the *CFR* indicates no self-sustaining growth, and the surge resulting from the Great Broadening seems to have been a one-time occurrence. We suspect that this controlled growth is a result of the Administrative Procedure Act, which is a classic brake on the promulgation of bureaucratic rules.

The number of pages tells us something about the degree to which federal regulations have accumulated over time, but it does not tell us in which policy areas this activity occurred. It demonstrates the thickening of the federal bureaucracy but not necessarily its broadening. In the next section, we use the policy content of Congress's oversight agenda as a proxy for the broadening of the bureaucratic agenda.

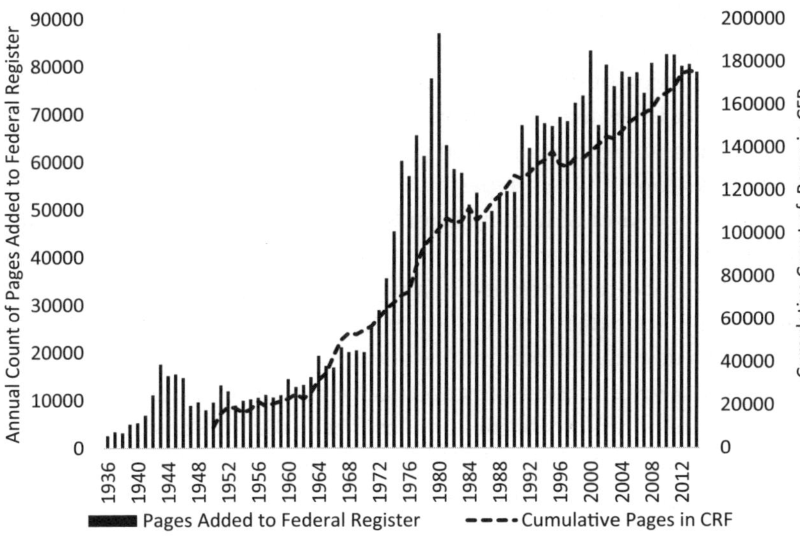

FIGURE 9.4. Pages added to the *Federal Register* and published in the *Code of Federal Regulations* (1936–2014)

The Broadening of the Oversight Agenda

The bureaucratic agenda has broadened as a consequence of congressional delegation. It has also broadened as government has become more complex because of the vast number of issues on the agenda is simply impossible to monitor in an orderly, top-down fashion. "Especially with regard to low salience issues, bureaucracy serves a representative function as a substitute, or backstop, for a lack of attention in the elected institutions of government" (Workman 2015, 27). In its role in problem monitoring, bureaucracies both propose new rules and regulations and alert Congress to fomenting issues in the country. Congress not only delegates to the bureaucracy rule-making authority, it also delegates surveillance. The process of rule-making is both self-sustaining and feeds back into the lawmaking process.

The ideal way to measure the broadening of the bureaucratic agenda would be to assign subtopic codes to individual regulations, just as we assign codes to individual titles of statutory law. Workman (2015) has done this for Policy Agendas major topics for entries in the Unified Agenda, published in the *Federal Register*. But that resource has been published only since 1983, and no single source traces regulatory activity back further in time. Yet that early period is critical for our analysis. As an alternative, we use policy codes applied to Congress's oversight agenda to estimate the broadening of the bureaucratic agenda.

As the bureaucratic agenda expands, so should oversight activity in Congress. Cobb and Elder (1972) and Baumgartner and Jones (2009) call hearings the most reliable indicator of the formal or institutional policy agenda, because they entail the attention of more than a single member, necessarily involve a trade-off with other issues that could have received the committee's attention, and consume much more time and effort of both members and professional staff.

Congress conducts two types of hearings. The first is the conventionally understood kind of hearing from Schoolhouse Rock's "Bill on Capitol Hill," where members gain information about nascent laws. The other type includes those hearings not tied to a particular piece of legislation. In this chapter, we make a distinction between lawmaking hearings, involving the creation of a new statute, program, or agency, and non-lawmaking hearings, involving the investigation of problems for future action associated with new government responsibilities or oversight of the implementation of existing laws. We use the distinction between lawmaking and non-lawmaking hearings as a proxy for the focus of congressional committee activity.

We think of lawmaking hearings as evidence of Congress' nascent statutory agenda. After a bill has attracted members' attention, getting a hearing in a congressional committee is the next step in the legislative process.

Given that the Policy Agendas Project's tabulation of non-lawmaking hearings incorporates both Congress's oversight function and its attention to unaddressed problems not ripe for lawmaking, we think of non-lawmaking hearings as a proxy for Congress' oversight agenda. The frequency of non-lawmaking hearings relative to lawmaking hearings reveals how Congress's attention has shifted from making policy to overseeing the implementation of policy and the examination of new problems.

Lawmaking Hearings: The Emerging Legislative Agenda

The number of topics addressed in House and Senate lawmaking or referral hearings manifests in the familiar arc pattern (see fig. 9.5). In the 79th Congress, both chambers considered enacting new legislation in relatively few policy areas. Following a localized increase and decline in the consideration of new topics in lawmaking hearings between the 80th and 82nd Congresses (1947–52), Congress began gradually adding more and more new topics to its lawmaking agenda. By the 91st Congress (1969–70), the House held lawmaking hearings on 155 subtopics. Four years later, the Senate reached its peak when it held lawmaking hearings on 166 topics in the 93rd Congress (1973–74).

Between the 91st and 99th Congresses (1969–87), both chambers held lawmaking hearings on a wide array of different topics, but the scope of the agenda had clearly stabilized and had begun to decline—especially in the Senate. Following the 1994 midterm elections, the newly minted Republican majority in both chambers severely restricted the lawmaking agenda. Conservative Republicans in the House, who were then led by Speaker Newt Gingrich, were adamant about not expanding government activity further into new policy areas. The House passed a series of reforms designed to promote accountability, centralize policy-making, and limit the ability of committees to expand the policy-making agenda. The shift in partisan control clearly resulted in a sharp fall in the scope of lawmaking hearings.

This shift in party control, though, is not the whole story, because both chambers had already begun the process of retrenchment. The sharp decline in the scope of the lawmaking agenda accelerated a trend already in place. We fit quadratic curves to the data to display the trends more clearly: although both data series fit the quadratic extremely well, the Senate series ($r = 0.86$) fits it slightly better than that of the House ($r = 0.80$).

In the intervening years, the number of policy areas addressed in the referral hearings that Congress holds has not rebounded and has, in fact, remained even lower than before the Great Broadening. As we discussed in the prior chapter, the statutes that Congress enacted during the height

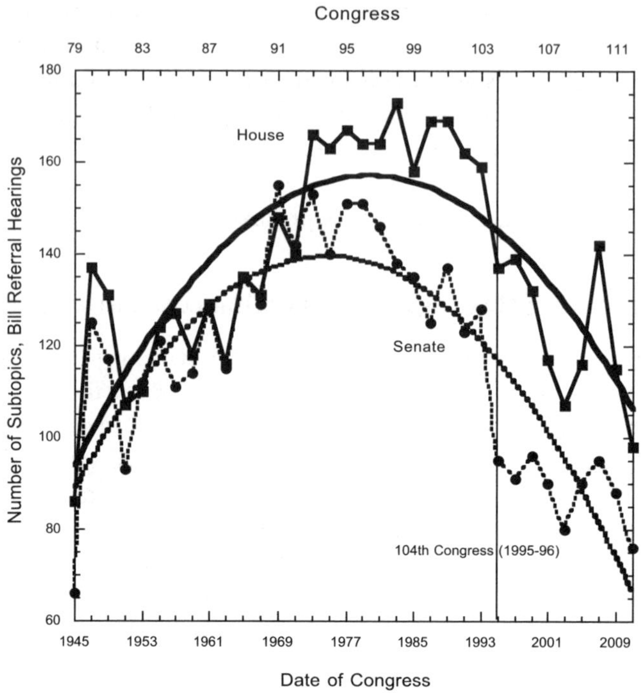

FIGURE 9.5. The emerging lawmaking agenda: Referral hearings, 79th–112th Congresses

of the Great Broadening have mostly endured. Although the conservative counter-revolution was able to "bend the curve" regarding the breadth of issues considered in lawmaking hearings, it has not been successful in constricting the scope of statutory law that had already been enacted. Congress may stop discussing a policy in hearings, but the statutory mark of the Great Broadening endures. This narrowing of the lawmaking agenda in hearings was partially a function of a sustained conservative counter-revolution and partially the result of the transformation of Congress from primarily a lawmaking body to what today is mostly an oversight body, at least based on the percentage of lawmaking hearings to overall hearings.

Non-Lawmaking Hearings: Congressional Capacity and the Shift toward Oversight

As Lewallen (2017) has emphasized, non-legislative hearings involve both a demand function, created by the growth of executive branch programs and agencies and a supply function, the capacity of committees to conduct oversight and the incentives to pursue oversight. As Congress has become more centralized, which includes the drafting of legislation, and laws have increased in size, the incentives of individual committee chairs to draft legislation has diminished. Lewallen's empirical work indicates that both demand and supply drive the relative frequencies of both legislative and non-legislative hearings.

We expect that in the years leading up to the peak of the Great Broadening, federal agencies added new issues to their repertoires, manifesting in a steady increase in the number of subtopics Congress addressed in non-lawmaking hearings. Following the peak of the broadening in the late 1970s, we expect the number of subtopics to level off as these new functions are integrated into the government. The pattern is clear and striking. The number of subtopics addressed in non-lawmaking hearings reaches a general plateau in the mid-1970s and drifts sideways thereafter with some congress-to-congress variability (see fig. 9.6).

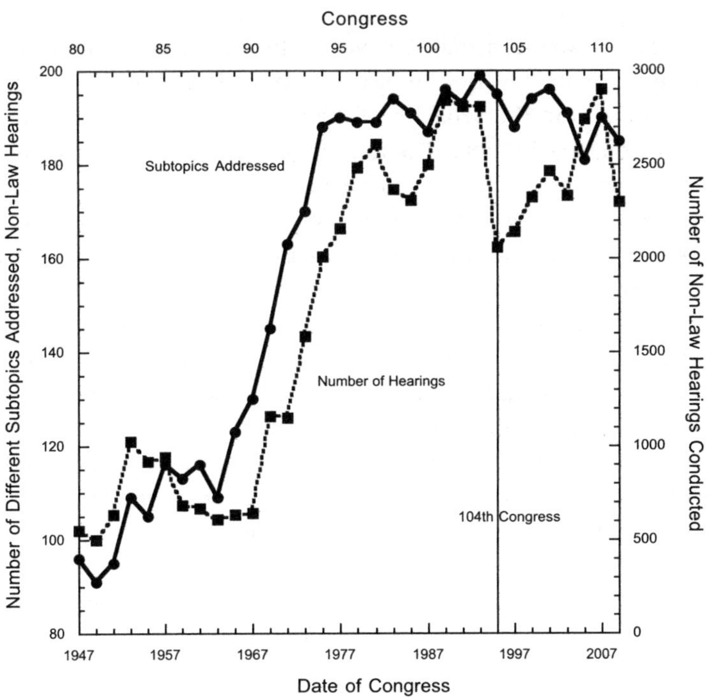

FIGURE 9.6. The broadening of Congress's oversight and investigative agendas.

After World War II, in the 79th Congress (1945–46), non-lawmaking hearings addressed 76 unique subtopics. By the 89th Congress (1965–66), this number had climbed to 106 subtopics and would continue to ascend rapidly to a local peak of 181 subtopics by the 95th Congress (1977–78). For the next seventeen congresses, the series takes the shape of a plateau, with the number of subtopics that Congress addresses in non-lawmaking hearings never moving below 173 or above 191.

We can think of the number of hearings held as an indication of congressional capacity for information-processing, while the number of subtopics addressed is a measure of the demand for added capacity. As a consequence, it is worth comparing the subtopics addressed to the number of hearings conducted. After leading until the 85th Congress (1957–58), the number of hearings drops behind the number of subtopics addressed (relative to the average of each series). After that, it lags the number of subtopics addressed in those hearings. In the 90th Congress (1967–68), the number of issues addressed in non-lawmaking hearings takes a big leap forward, but the number of hearings that committees used to study those topics did not change. Then in the 91st Congress, the number of non-lawmaking hearings takes a big leap and follows the subtopic series up to the asymptote.

Our basic contention that it is very difficult for government to drop consideration of an issue once it has crossed the legitimacy barrier receives strong support from the behavior of the two series after Republicans won control of Congress in 1994. The number of subtopics addressed remains approximately constant, but the number of hearings experiences a steep decline in the 104th Congress (1995–96). While Republicans cut the capacity of its committees, they were seemingly unable to control the scope of issues that committees addressed.

Congress could have added capacity to meet the increasing demand, as committees investigated more and more issues during the Great Broadening. Or the capacity could have been added because of other factors, such as the entry of so many more liberal Democrats during the period. The added capacity allowed liberal members moving into the subcommittee and committee chairmanships to address many of the issues being raised by social movement leaders and other policy entrepreneurs. The institutional story of the expansion of capacity veers toward that explanation.

The sequencing suggests that demand caused the supply rather than added capacity causing increases in the opportunity for the committees to investigate new areas of policy activity. In other words, the broadening (entry into new areas or subtopics) causes the thickening (adding capacity). This sequencing does not undermine the prevailing institutional story, but it does complicate it. Capacity does not emerge without politics. The new members demanded new roles through such features as increasing the scope of subcommittees (Rohde 1974), perhaps because they desired visibility to enhance electoral viability in the future, or perhaps because they wanted to become involved in the cauldron of policy-making that occurred during the time. At about the same time, subcommittees gain their own jurisdictions and their own staffs, independent of and apart from the full committees, which previously had full control over the subcommittees. We see these new members as opportunists using the increasing demand for intervention in new policy activities as a vehicle to gain increased capacity.

In sum, our analysis shows a complex connection between capacity (thickening) and the scope of congressional action. As government broadened, Congress added capacity to address the new issues accessing the agenda and to monitor the agencies charged with implementing them. While one might expect that congressional capacity would increase the tendency to add issues to the agenda, that seems to have been limited. Then, when congressional Republicans attempted to control the scope of the agenda by limiting capacity, they were not particularly successful.

Regulatory Thickening Follows the Broadening of Oversight

If we compare the broadening of the legislative agenda using the number of different subtopics addressed in referral hearings with the thickening of federal regulatory activity, we find similar peak periods. As one would expect, increases in legislative broadening happen earlier, but when regulatory thickening begins, it does so in dramatic fashion (see fig. 9.7). In particular, the rate of increase in the size of the *Federal Register* shifts into overdrive in 1971 and surges upward for a decade, peaking in 1980. As congressional lawmaking activity declines, federal regulatory activity first declines and then begins a more moderate increase. While Congress ceased the frenetic lawmaking activity that characterized the Great Broadening, federal bureaucratic activity continued apace.

Nevertheless, federal regulatory activity seems to begin a period of consolidation after 1980, generally resembling the plateau that we have found in so many of the other time series we study. Indeed, the correlation between subtopics addressed in non-lawmaking hearings and pages added in the *Federal Register* is 0.92. Rapid growth in regulatory activity and in subtopics addressed in non-legislative hearings correspond as well, with the increase in growth rate of non-legislative broadening occurring a few years earlier than for the *Federal Register*. The former occurs in the late 1960s, while the latter occurs in the early 1970s (see fig. 9.8).

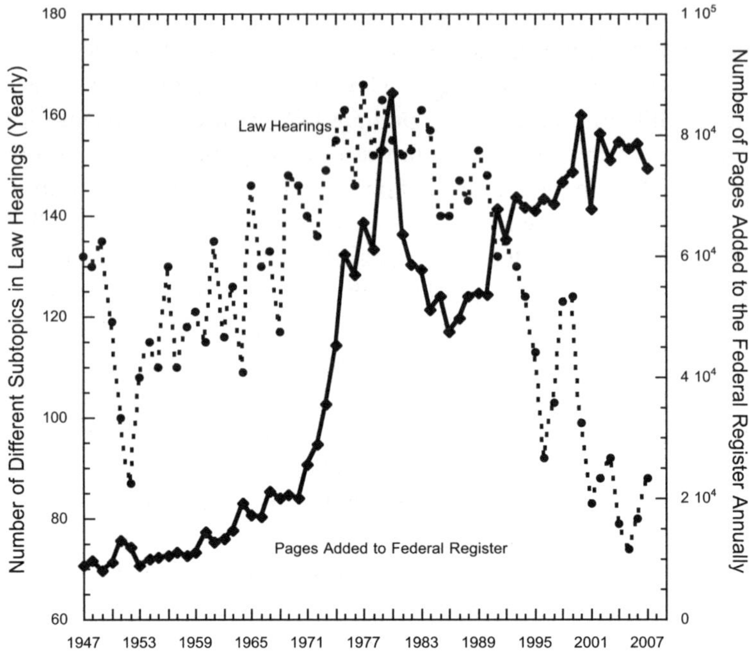

FIGURE 9.7. Pages added to the *Federal Register* and the number of different subtopics addressed in law hearings, yearly data

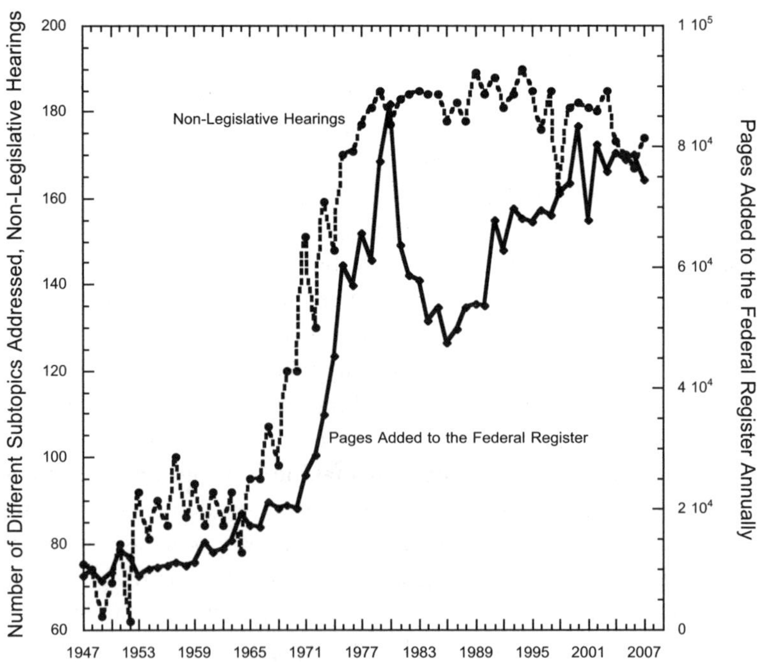

FIGURE 9.8. Pages added to the *Federal Register* annually and the number of subtopics addressed in non-legislative hearings

Lawmaking and Non-lawmaking Hearings Compared

The Great Broadening and its aftermath are reflected in two distinct curves through time, the arc and the plateau. If we graph law and non-law hearings summed for both chambers of Congress, we get both of these signature curves (see fig. 9.9). Our subtopic measure for law hearings traces a quadratic whose fit is excellent; the correlation between the curve and the data points for law hearings is 0.96.

The curve for non-law hearings traces a more complex pattern. It resembles a *sigmoid growth curve*, an S-shaped curve used to study the growth of the density of an organism introduced into an environment where it was not previously present (Allaby 2014). It is also commonly used to study innovation and diffusion among public policies across political jurisdictions. The curve depicts a pattern of slow growth at first, then very rapid growth, reaching an asymptote at the saturation point. Boushey (2010) finds that, for some policies, diffusion proceeds faster than the standard sigmoid curve, and for some more slowly. The key for us is the general shape of the curve and that it reaches a plateau rather than continuing to grow. For non-law congressional hearings, that is the point at which no more new topics are being addressed.

Unlike the various manifestations of Congress's lawmaking agenda (lawmaking hearings, laws, and substantive roll-call votes), the broadening of the bureaucratic agenda is "locked-in" after 1978 and does not narrow. Once federal agencies began implementing laws in a new subtopic, Congress was compelled to conduct oversight in that area over the long term. As polarization made enacting law even more difficult, the desires of committee chairs to realize their policy goals through oversight increased. In the beginning of the time series, the lawmaking and non-lawmaking hearings trace a similar upward path, but the former leads the latter. Congress first has hearings within a subtopic on proposed legislation and only later follows up with oversight hearings within the subtopic.

As both series reach their peak at the end of the Great Broadening, the lines cross, and the number of subtopics subject to non-lawmaking hearings is greater than the number of subtopics in lawmaking hearings. After the series cross one another, the subtopics discussed in lawmaking hearings drops precipitously: the number of hearings at the end of the series is among the lowest of the entire series. Non-lawmaking hearings, on the other hand, stay at around the same peak level.

Why does one curve rise and decline, but the other reaches an asymptote and continues at about that same level throughout the period? It would seem we are observing two different facets of what historical institutionalists

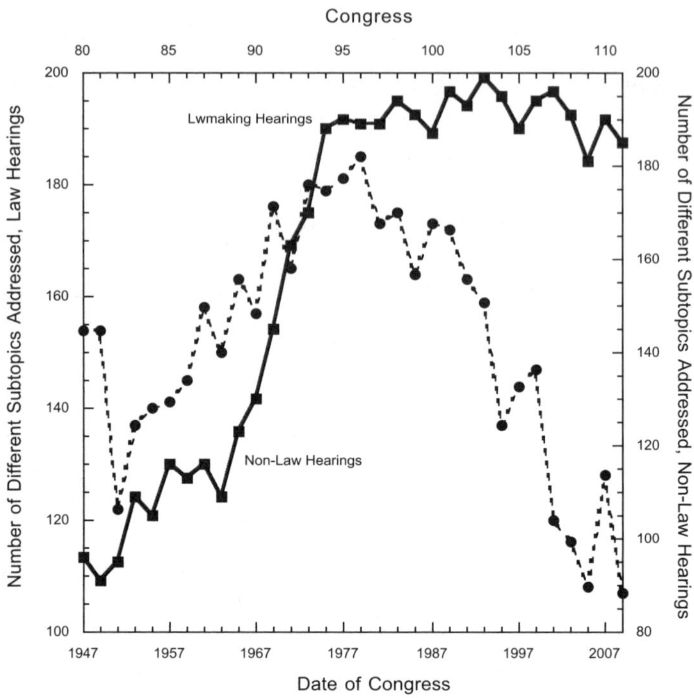

FIGURE 9.9. The two characteristic curves of the Great Broadening

would term a *critical juncture*. The arc—or quadratic—represents a pattern of reversal, in which conservative counter-mobilization pushes back against the prevailing winds of change. The plateau of the sigmoid growth curve represents a new equilibrium, sometimes referred to as path-dependency (Pierson 2000). It also takes the form of a punctuated equilibrium (Baumgartner and Jones 2009), although that approach applies only to a single subsystem. The two curves are linked. It is no accident that the quadratic reaches its peak in the same time period in which the sigmoid growth curve reaches its asymptote.

In showing the frequencies, the figure does not indicate the relationship of subtopics between the two types of hearings. To assess the extent to which similar Policy Agendas subtopics preoccupied both the non-lawmaking and lawmaking hearings during the same congress, we correlated the number of subtopics with the presence of a hearing across the two types of hearings. If Congress held both lawmaking and non-lawmaking hearings on exactly the same set of subtopics, then the correspondence would be reflected in a correlation of 1.0. By calculating correlations on the matches, we can see if lawmaking and non-lawmaking/oversight hearings focus on the same issues. Between 1946 and the late 1980s, we found that Congress addressed roughly the same policy areas in their lawmaking hearings as in their non-lawmaking hearings. After the late 1980s, however, the two series diverge, and lawmaking hearings address different topics than non-lawmaking ones. Lawmaking hearings not only address fewer issues, but they also address a different portfolio of issues from oversight hearings, as evidenced by the low correlations we found between the two venues after around 1990. Lawmaking hearings became increasingly focused, while non-lawmaking hearings remained diverse, causing the correlation between the two to decline.

The Transformation of Congress

Congress changed immensely from the 1950s to the 1970s, and it has changed just as much from the 1970s to today. Many of these changes are directly attributable to what we've been calling contemporary political dynamics. More homogenous electoral districts, a changed media environment, and a host of other factors have doubtless led to a more polarized and centralized Congress. With the notable exception of Larry Dodd (2012), few scholars have addressed these transformations outside the confines of the contemporaneous dynamics perspective. Although several have seen the transformations as at least partially endogenous (Sinclair 1989; Rohde 1991; Theriault 2008), few made the link back to the huge shifts in the course of public policy since the Great Broadening. It did not go entirely unnoticed among congressional scholars; Sinclair (1989, 51) writes, "The combination of the expansion of the issue agenda, the explosive growth of interest groups, and the increased role of the media produced a new policy community, one that rewards Senators differently than did the old policy system." Yet it is fair to say that the full nature of the manner in which the huge shifts in the policy terrain have contributed to the institution we see today has not been fully appreciated.

Most of us think of Congress as a lawmaking body, and it is still standard fare in civics texts to discuss how laws are made. During every congress, the media reports on Congress's general lack of productivity (almost always defined as the number of laws passed). But in many ways the function of Congress has changed, from primarily lawmaking to primarily oversight and problem detection. This transformation is perhaps best visualized in the frequency of both types of hearings over time (see fig. 9.10).

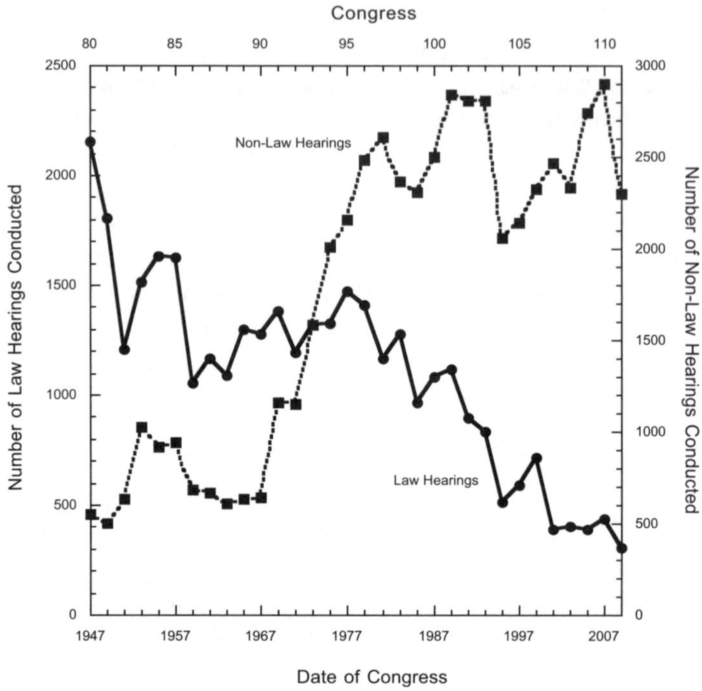

FIGURE 9.10. The transformation of Congress from lawmaking to oversight

If, as so many observers since Woodrow Wilson have noted, congressional business is handled in committees, then the business of today is oversight. Note the virtual explosion of non-lawmaking hearings beginning in the 90th Congress (1967–68), reaching a turning point in the late 1970s, after which the number of non-lawmaking hearings fluctuates around 2,500 total hearings. Lawmaking hearings began a steady decline around the time of the peak of non-lawmaking hearings, until today such hearings occupy only around 10 percent of all committee hearings. In the 1960s and early 1970s, Congress held about one investigative (including oversight) hearing for every two hearings on potential laws. By the 2000s, Congress held about nine investigative hearings for every lawmaking hearing. Note that no disjoint changes associated with contemporary political dynamics occurred—this cannot be explained by the changes in the partisan composition of Congress, for example. While the number of hearings has declined, that has not been as dramatic as the shift from lawmaking to oversight: the total number of hearings has declined from a peak of almost 4,000 during the 100th Congress (1987–88) to 3,338 during the 110th Congress.

While we will not dwell on this aspect of the changing balance of the major functions of Congress, it is true that the nature of hearings has changed. They call fewer witnesses, have become more one-sided, and are less focused on developing solutions to policy problems (Lewallen, Theriault, and Jones, 2016; In press).

The large expansion of oversight hearings happened during and after the Great Broadening. Such hearings were made much more salient by the need for the legislative branch to examine its creations—the many laws and new agencies and programs that had expanded into areas previously beyond the reach of the federal government. Parallel to this development is an institutional story having to do with reform efforts by liberal Democrats in the House of Representatives, leading to a far more decentralized Congress, with increasing power in subcommittees (Rohde 1974; Baumgartner and Jones 2015). Over the years (especially after 1994), this trend was reversed, as legislative parties grew more centralized and ideologically polarized, all while subcommittees lost power (Lewallen 2014). While committees' reduced stature may have affected the number of lawmaking hearings, it did not affect oversight hearings, the number of which remained amazingly steady after the mid-1980s.

How Policy Creates Institutions

This chapter has examined evidence that the very structure of government is caused in large part by prior policy-making. Bureaucratic rule-making, policy analytic capacity, and congressional oversight all expanded to meet the broad and dense policy environment created during the Great Broadening. The modern Congress operates in a dense statutory and regulatory structure of its own design. What began as a congressional foray into policy domains once reserved for civil society in statutory law became the foundation for the intrusion of the administrative state into many aspects of citizens' lives. Some have described this web of ever-growing bureaucrats, rules, regulations, and enforcement mechanisms as the "fourth branch of government." In Turley's (2013) estimation, the rise of this fourth branch "represents perhaps the single greatest change in our system of government since the founding." Just as we claim that the Great Broadening caused much of the thickening of the statutory corpus, so we argue that it is implicated in the rise of the administrative state. Had Congress not broadened its policy menu, federal agencies would not have been given authority to promulgate rules or implement policy in these new domains. As a result of the increased volume, scope, and impact of bureaucratic regulations, the modern Congress is compelled to spend more time engaging in oversight than lawmaking.[2] In essence, Congress has been captured by its own creation and has been required to act less like a legislative branch and more like an oversight body.

Even that is not the whole story. As Workman (2015) documents, the bureaucracy, stereotyped as a cumbersome, rule-bound obstacle to democratic governance, actually provides a reasonably nimble source of information for policy-making in both the rule-making and lawmaking processes. It is a more adaptive system than many critics give it credit for. Congressional oversight involves receiving information and integrating it into ongoing policy. Oversight, in this expanded sense, is increasingly critical—and not because Congress has shirked its responsibility in lawmaking.

These effects are part of the changes wrought by the Great Broadening—vast consequences that alter the terrain on which future political battles will be fought. Indicators of this form of path-dependency follow the asymptote pattern; non-lawmaking hearings are emblematic. It is not that these aspects cannot be changed; they can. But here resistance is not futile.

TEN

Polarization in Congress: A Macro-Level Analysis

Throughout this book we have used the sequencing of trends in data to dispel some generally strongly held beliefs about the connection between trends where causal data are particularly difficult to ascertain. And so it is in this chapter. Most pundits and political scientists treat party polarization in the US Congress as caused in large part by exogenous changes in the American electorate. They are not wrong, but exogenous changes cannot be the whole story. For starters, polarization in the electorate lagged polarization in Congress (Hetherington 2001; Pew Research Center 2014).

In this chapter and the next, we develop the argument that the Great Broadening played a critical role in the party polarization that pervades Congress. Conservative elites organized themselves in the 1950s but gained little traction until the Great Broadening, which seemed to have brought on their greatest nightmares. Republicans began to find electoral traction with their traditional anti–big government messages, and, as a result, their prominence among members of Congress grew. While final victory was not achieved for a number of years, party polarization surrounding the broadening process was fairly quick in developing. In this chapter we examine the sequencing of those broad trends. In the following chapter, we take a closer look at the dynamics within Congress to substantiate our argument.

The Macro Story of Party Polarization in Congress

Political pundits are quick to point to isolated and specific events as *the* cause of party polarization in Congress, such as when the Democrats "stole" a 1984 House election in Indiana, Robert Bork's failed nomination to the US Supreme Court in 1987, the partisan fallout from congressional malfeasance in the Abscam scandal in the early 1980s, or the House banking scandal in the early 1990s.

Political scientists have offered more systematic explanations, ranging from redistricting to political sorting, the capture of political parties by ideological extremists, and changes in the legislative process itself. One of us has been a party to that debate. Theriault (2008; 2013) suggests that all of the aforementioned contribute to polarization, but that, importantly, the process of polarizing fed back on itself when leaders generated incentives to pursue purely partisan strategies that led to even more polarization. The dynamics surrounding the Great Broadening suggests that the story on party polarization is even more complicated. The way that the federal government's agenda—specifically, the congressional agenda—expanded into more areas of the law fundamentally changed the relationship between the two parties. Not strongly polarized during the Great Broadening, they became so afterward. Once the agenda had expanded, the relationship changed even more, setting off the reinforcing arms race of polarization we observe even to this day. The reinforcing dynamic that is critical to Theriault's analysis of polarization is part of our larger theme.

We find not only that the Great Broadening preceded the dramatic rise in polarization, but also that it had reached its peak *before* the intense increase in polarization began. We use the now-standard measure developed by Poole and Rosenthal (1997) using congressional roll-call votes. The measure involves calculating the party mean differences by congress on the primary ideological dimension extracted from a metric scaling process. Indeed, the correspondence of the start of the increase in polarization and the peak of the Great Broadening is uncanny (see fig. 10.1). The Great Broadening was well underway in the mid-1960s and continued until reaching its peak in the mid-to-late 1970s. On the other hand, polarization, as measured by the party mean differences on DW-NOMINATE's first dimension in the House, drifts lazily up until the agenda has almost completely expanded, and then its great and sustained rise begins. The Great Broadening, as measured by Policy Agendas subtopics addressed in hearings, reached its apogee in the 94th Congress (1975–76), plateauing afterward. Party polarization, as measured by mean party differences on DW-NOMINATE's first dimension, begins its rise in the 96th Congress (1979–80).

Because polarization followed the Great Broadening, it cannot possibly be a cause of it. But, the reverse is not necessarily true. Nothing in the figure suggests that the Great Broadening caused party polarization; it merely shows that the Great Broadening came before the parties began their spectacular race toward the opposite ends of the ideological continuum. Before

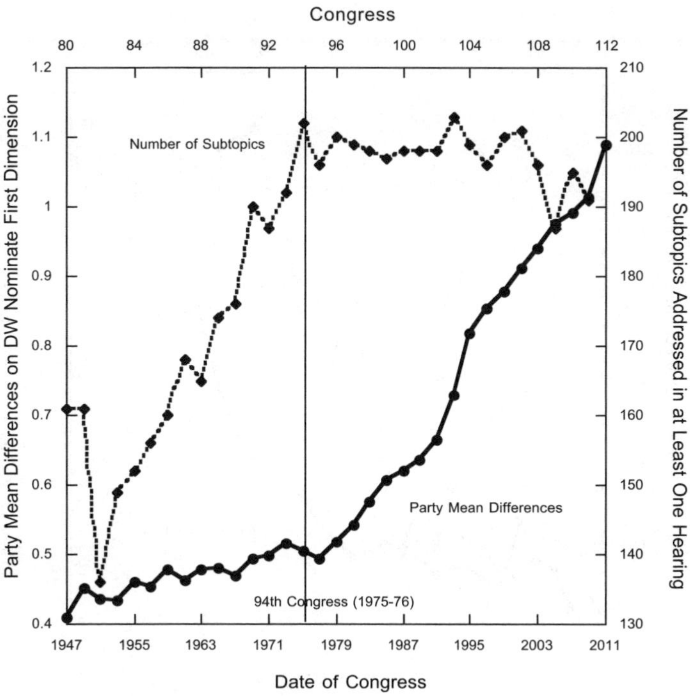

FIGURE 10.1. The relationship between party polarization in Congress and the Great Broadening

we offer evidence that more explicitly ties the Great Broadening to party polarization, we examine the relationship of polarization to additional Policy Agendas Project datasets.

Polarization and Length of Laws

The contemporaneous dynamics approach would see lawmaking as complicated by political polarization. Laws ought to be harder to pass in that context, and they ought to be longer, as simple compromises on legislative action became harder. We show in this section that this explanation is too simple. While it is true that laws grew longer during the postwar period, our analysis indicates that the Great Broadening was implicated in the process.

The argument hinges on the sequencing of these two series. After a period of relative stability, the average number of lines in the laws passed in any given year began growing rapidly in the 93rd Congress (1973–74),

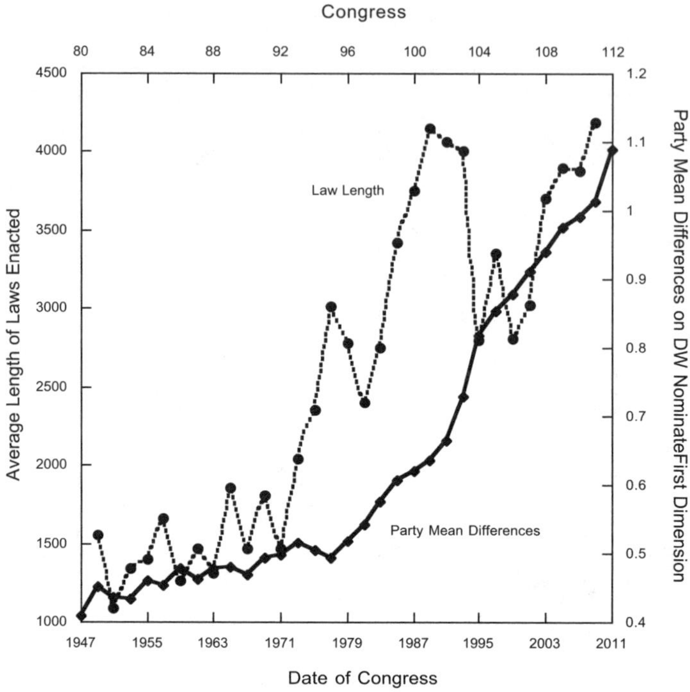

FIGURE 10.2. Law length and partisan polarization in Congress

during the later stages of the Great Broadening. This rise occurred as the total number of laws was declining. Laws increasingly reflected the complexity of the new issue spaces created during the Great Broadening.

Polarization between the parties has a complex relationship with the growing complexity of the laws Congress passed. Between World War II and the early 1970s, law length and partisan polarization both drifted lazily upward (see fig. 10.2). Then the size of laws passed in any given congress leaped upward, and the two series diverged. Even while law length rose rapidly in the early 1970s, polarization continued its lazy upward drift. Indeed, laws got larger for approximately three congresses, six full years (93rd through 95th) before the great increases in polarization began.

One might think that increasing polarization may have caused declines in the abilities of the parties to compromise, causing laws to grow as side bargains were incorporated into them to put together enacting coalitions. That is definitely not the whole story. Because the laws' robust increases in length occurred before the strong rise in party polarization began, party polarization cannot have caused the growth in the size of the typical law enacted. It may be true that once the growth in the size of laws began, polarization sustained the rise, which would be consistent with Theriault's self-sustaining polarization thesis. The story of self-sustaining processes (polarization) feeding back into initial causes (increases in the scope of lawmaking) is a common general theme in complex systems such as policy-making.

Why did laws increase in length? One reason is almost certainly that laws reflected the complexity of the new issue spaces created during the Great Broadening. But they are also longer because the body of law passed previously is more complex, with many cross-policy implications (Whyman and Jones 2012). It is hard to think of a modern law that is confined to its primary policy area. Any new law has implications not only for the previous law's primary area, but also for laws in other policy areas. The policy space became more complex and intertwined with other policy spaces as government grew in scope.

The sequencing from broadening to law length to polarization suggests that the only plausible causal story among the three has the increasing scope of the federal government's agenda at its core. While law length fell after Republicans gained control of Congress after the 1994 elections, the effect seems to have been only temporary.

Today it very well may be that laws are longer in part because of the difficulties in making compromises across polarizing parties. If so, then contemporaneous dynamics (particularly polarization) interacts with the policy terrain (the existing body of law) to make new laws longer. Lawmaking is more difficult now than in the past, and that difficulty stems from the complex structure of the corpus of statutory law. This complexity is independent from the issues inherent in political coalition building.

Polarization in an Era of Thick Government

Law is, by its very nature, cumulative. Citizens live not only under the laws enacted by the current Congress, but also all those enacted by prior Congresses. It is common practice among conservative observers of the federal bureaucracy to visualize annual cumulative counts of federal regulations to demonstrate the volume of bureaucratic rules that companies and individuals are obliged to obey. It is somewhat less common to visualize federal law in the same way, although a similar logic applies. To examine this further, we developed a cumulative measure of the buildup of law over time. We use the biannual cumulative count of titles within larger laws or laws themselves if they do not include titles (see fig. 10.3).

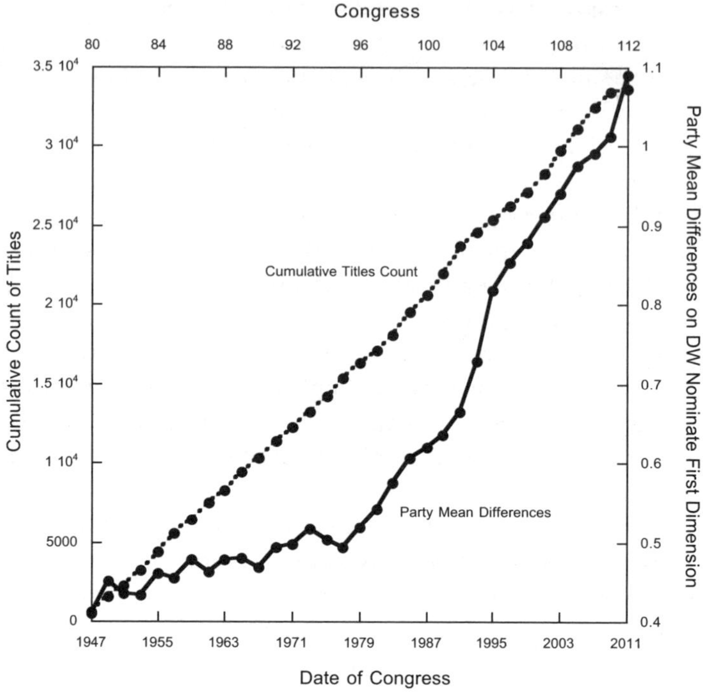

FIGURE 10.3. Cumulative number of titles and small laws and partisan polarization by congress, 80th–112th Congresses (1947–2012)

If we compare this cumulative measure to Poole and Rosenthal's measure for polarization on the first dimension of DW-NOMINATE, we find a remarkable break in the relationship. Before the Great Broadening peaks, polarization, which was drifting upward, is correlated with total volume of law substantially, because both series are moving up ($r = 0.91$). Afterward, however, polarization begins a steady rise that correlates considerably more robustly with our cumulative measure for the biannual size of the legal corpus ($r = 0.98$). More importantly, the slope of cumulative titles is constant throughout, but for polarization it shifts from shallow to steep at the inflection point of the 96th Congress. Before the bend, party mean differences on the DW-NOMINATE first dimension increased 0.03 units per Congress. Afterward, it increased 0.18 units per Congress (and with a more precise fit).[1] From the peak of the broadening, the legal corpus and congressional polarization have grown in tandem. As Congress enacts more law, which thickens the body of existing law, parties are demonstrating intense disagreement over the content of potential enactments. Despite rising levels of polarization, Congress has continued to thicken the legal corpus, which requires a corresponding large national bureaucracy to implement public policy.

Polarization and the Transformation of Congress from Lawmaking to Oversight

If it is true that the growing scope in public policy caused polarization, by what mechanisms did that occur? Different paths led to increased polarization; some external to the policy process, some within the process itself. Here we assess the separate effects of three indicators, all of which are internal to the policy process, on increases in polarization. Specifically we examine the effect of the shift from lawmaking to oversight in the hearings process, along with indicators for the broadening of the lawmaking agenda and the broadening of budget subfunctions.

The first measure addresses the degree to which the modern Congress has transformed from a lawmaking body to what is primarily an oversight body. As we noted in chapter 9, before the late 1970s, congressional hearings were primarily geared toward the consideration of bills that had the potential of becoming new laws. Following the late 1970s, Congress began holding more hearings on non-lawmaking issues, many of which consisted of oversight of the executive branch's expansion, which itself was due to the accretion of laws over time. Our specific indicator of this change is the ratio of non-lawmaking to lawmaking hearings over the post–World War II period.

Following substantial increases in the broadening of government, Congress began holding more non-lawmaking hearings than lawmaking hearings. The cumulative count of new subtopics within lawmaking crests in the late 1970s at 204 subtopics, following a period of incremental growth before leveling off and very gradually climbing to a total of 217 subtopics (see fig. 10.4).

Budgetary broadening is assessed as the number of budget categories employed by the Office of Management and Budget (OMB). The OMB adds budget categories only when government adds new functions (it broadens); thickened government simply increases the sizes of previously established categories.

We expect both the transformation of Congress from lawmaking to oversight and the associated growth of the federal bureaucracy to be positively associated with increases in polarization. As Congress passes more laws that

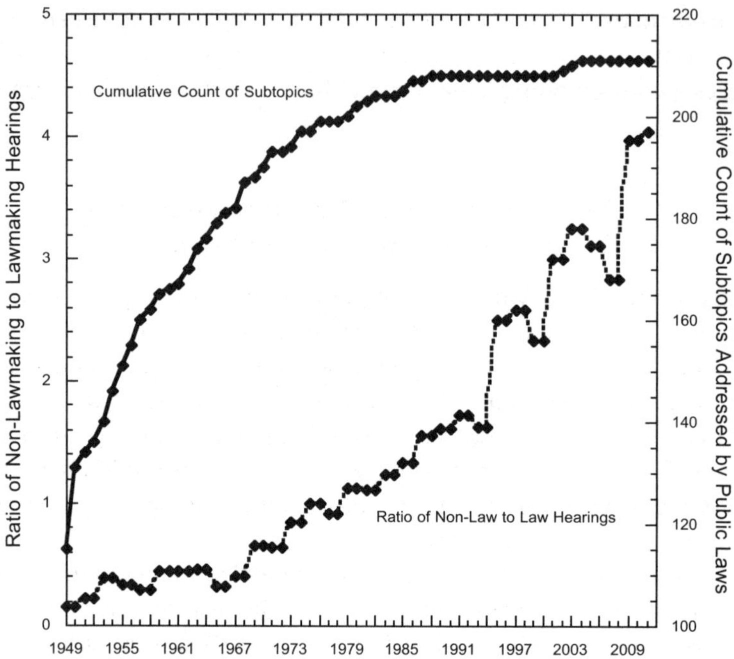

FIGURE 10.4. Legal broadening and the transformation of governance (1948–2011)

intrude into new issue areas and require a larger and more engaged bureaucracy to implement them, proponents of limited government react to this intrusion by refusing to be part of any further attempts to expand. This "digging in" results in divergent voting patterns that become manifest as polarization between the parties in Congress (we have more to say about that in the next chapter).

We likewise expect the legal and budgetary broadening of government to have positive effects on polarization. As Congress intrudes into new issue areas that were once reserved for the private sector or the states and localities by providing funding for these new functions, we expect conservatives to resist these intrusions. Substantial increases in the broadening of government, as measured by new subtopics addressed by legislation, preceded polarization increases, which did not begin in earnest until after 1978. Similarly, the annual number of budget subfunctions receiving funding clearly preceded major increases in polarization.

Assessing the effects of broadening on polarization is problematic in a traditional modeling scheme because the majority of the broadening of the lawmaking and budgetary agendas occurs well before increases in polarization, making it difficult to quantify the impact on the dependent variable without at least a thirty-year lag of our lawmaking-broadening indicator and a somewhat shorter lag of the indicator for budgetary broadening. The trends show that the lawmaking agenda had already experienced the majority of its broadening by the time polarization began to increase in 1979 (see fig. 10.5).

Similarly, the number of funded budget subfunctions gradually increases, starting in 1948 and jumping up in 1976, two years before polarization starts to increase in earnest (see fig. 10.6). Both of these figures show an increase in polarization just after large-scale increases in the broadening measures.

This brief examination of three variables implicated in polarization shows that both the broadening scope of laws and the broadening of funded OMB subfunctions lead polarization, and both plausibly get wrapped up into the vortex of polarization (a Granger causality test, presented in the appendix to this chapter, confirms this dynamic). We do not know whether these variables are linked in a causal chain, or whether both contribute

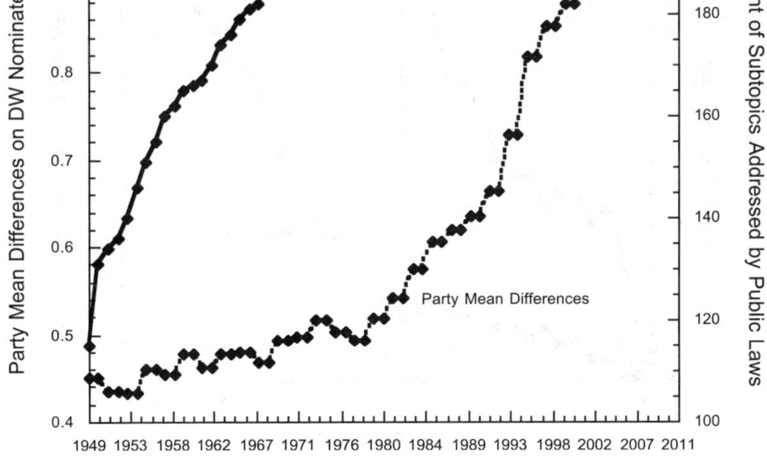

FIGURE 10.5. Divergent paths of polarization and legal broadening (1948–2011)

separately to polarization, but both lead polarization. Thus, they cannot possibly have been caused by it.

Before we leave the topic of lawmaking and polarization, we examine the relationship between changes in the structure of congressional hearings from lawmaking to oversight and problem detection, on the one hand, and party polarization on the other. These two variables are closely related to each other (see fig. 10.7). The two best-fit curves are of similar form, and they move in parallel.[2] As Congress shifted its focus from making laws to overseeing them, polarization increased. Most probably, as the political fight shifted from what government should do to how much it should do within the areas it staked out (that is, moved from broadening to thickening), partisan rancor increased.

We've covered a great deal of ground here, but we've really only scratched the surface. One possibility for examining the causal connections between these variables and polarization is to study more sophisticated models, although the limited number of years in the study hurts the statistical inferences that can be drawn, which are obviously exacerbated by the lags that

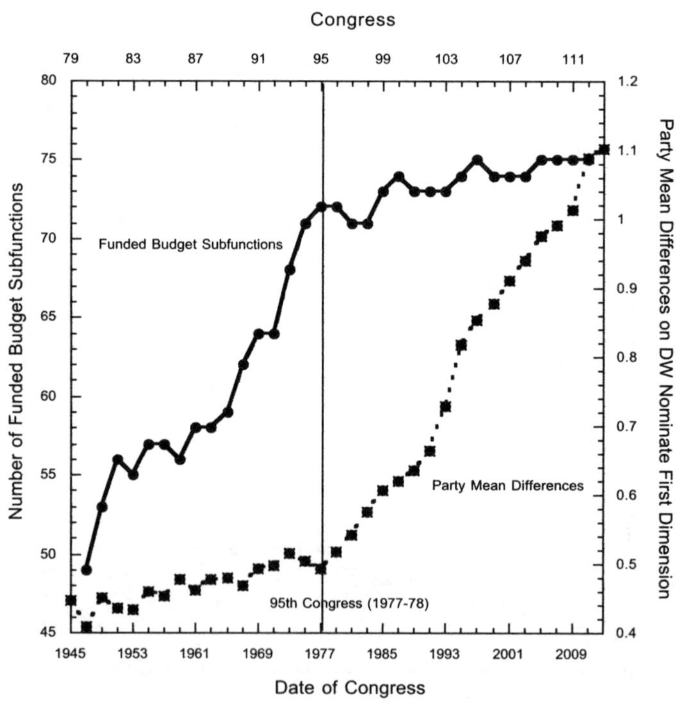

FIGURE 10.6. Polarization and funded budget subfunctions (1948–2011)

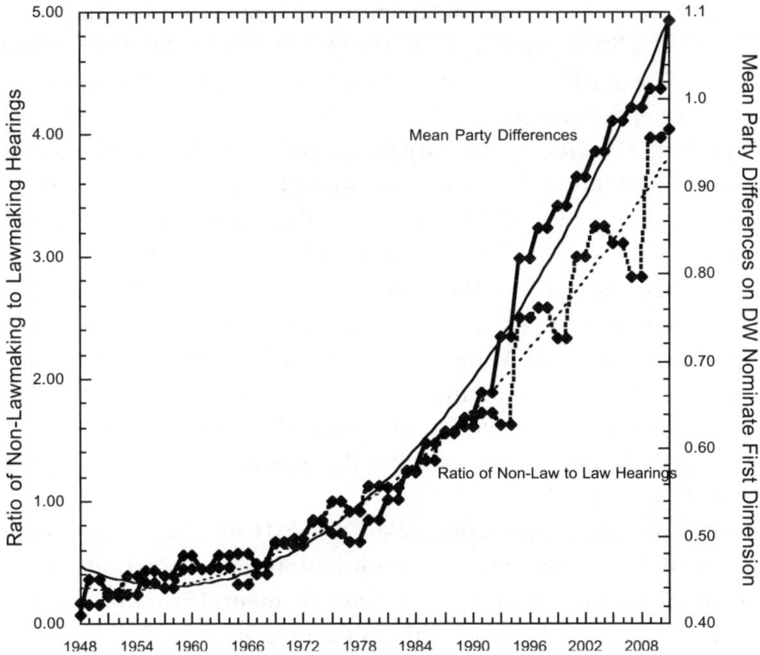

FIGURE 10.7. Partisan polarization and the shift from lawmaking to oversight in Congress

would have to be incorporated. Instead, we choose a second way to proceed: we examine causal processes within the period of the Great Broadening to see what we can learn, presenting the results in chapter 11. Before we do this, we turn to a brief examination of the relative roles of the Great Broadening, on the one hand, and changes in the electorate, particularly the southern move toward the Republican Party, on the other.

Southern Republicans and Polarization

We've stated the overall case for incorporating endogenous, policy-focused variables into partisan polarization using institutional-level measures. In the next chapter, we detail a case based on internal legislative dynamics and the behavior of individual members of Congress. Yet it seems clear that exogenous events such as the shift of the Republican Party's base to the South must also be involved. Here we take a brief look at the role of the increase in the proportion of Southern representatives comprising the House Republican Party. Can we attribute increases in polarization to changes in the geographic composition of the party? Did southerners bring a more conservative political philosophy to the House, leading to increases in polarization? The quick answer is that this is not at all likely, at least not in the initial stages of the process.

In the 84th Congress (1955–56), the proportion of Southern representatives in the Republican Party began drifting upward,[3] a trend that became more pronounced in the early 1960s. Early Republican wins came in "silk stocking" districts in places like Houston and Dallas, which elected George H. W. Bush to the House in 1960. The trend accelerated in the 1962 election and again in 1964, after Congress enacted the Civil Rights Act of 1964 and had begun contemplating the Voting Rights Acts of 1965 (in the 88th and 89th Congresses, respectively). Southerners still comprised only 15 percent of the House Republican Conference in the 90th Congress (1967–68). The proportion drifted upward throughout the twentieth and early twenty-first centuries (see fig. 10.8).

Party mean differences on the DW-NOMINATE first dimension are correlated, with both measures moving upward throughout the period ($r = 0.93$). Yet there are significant differences between them. Partisan polarization changed very little as the first Southern Republicans joined the conference (they were too small a group to cause a change). Even as the proportion of southerners increased, partisan polarization changed very little, at least until the 96th Congress (1979–80). The sustained rise in polarization began in earnest then, and continued until the present time. The turning point in the 96th Congress was not associated with increases in the proportion of Southern Republicans, however, which moved from 21 percent in the 94th and 95th Congresses to 22 percent in the 96th and 97th Congresses. There seems to have been no massive "southernization" of the Republican House Conference propelling polarization upward.

If we examine the best-fit curves for the two series, we find that the proportion of southerners among Republicans grows linearly, with a brief surge in the 1960s ($r = 0.99$). Growth in polarization, however, is nonlinear. The best-fitting curve is an upward-opening parabola, or quadratic, implying slower growth that speeds up as time proceeds ($r = 0.99$). The nonlinear fit for polarization and the straightforward linear trend in the geographic base of the Republican legislative party offer further evidence, if indirect, in support of Theriault's positive-feedback approach to polarization.

It is hard to square these figures with a solely exogenous explanation of polarization. It is possible that the Great Broadening interacted with shifts in the geographic distribution of Republicans to intensify polarization. If

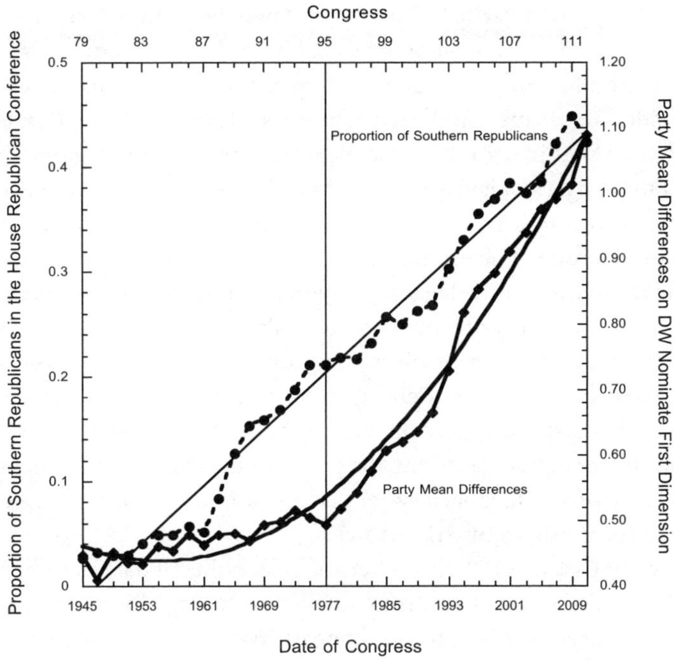

FIGURE 10.8. Political polarization and the proportion of Southern representatives in the House Republican Conference

that happened, then causal processes during the Great Broadening should deviate from those that drove the system afterward. We turn to an examination of this possibility in chapter 11.

Did Policy Cause Polarization?

In this chapter we have demonstrated that congressional polarization began in earnest after the federal government's agenda, as measured by hearings, broadened. We have also analyzed the relationship between polarization and the enacting of longer laws. We show that trends of these relationships happened in a very specific sequence: first broadening, then longer laws, then congressional party polarization. Finally, we have examined the increase in polarization as a function of the transformation of Congress from a lawmaking to an oversight body. Each of these partial pictures when combined suggest a set of interlocking causal mechanisms, which we explicate in a number of steps.

First, just as polarization began to rise, lawmakers turned to omnibus legislation to enact laws that were not only longer, but also more complex. Ten years after the hearings agenda broadened, the legal corpus fully reflected this broadening, as the number of subtopics addressed by small public laws and the titles within omnibus laws peaked in the 101st Congress. Congress enacted more pages of law across this broad policy agenda, thereby thickening the legal corpus and, correspondingly, the regulatory corpus.

The broadening of government, lawmaker's reliance on omnibus legislation, the thickening of the legal and regulatory framework, and polarization form a complex positive-feedback system. By examining the timing of these developments and the incentives they provided for lawmakers, we demonstrate that the Great Broadening is a key antecedent that helped set the wheels of this system in motion. Given the complexity of this system, lots of parts are moving, so gathering the pieces of the evidence together to paint a full picture of this feedback system is not simple. Nevertheless, we lay out the contours of our argument below.

In the 1960s and 1970s, members of both political parties facilitated the expansion of the scope of government by introducing bills in new policy domains (evidence for this behavior appears in the next chapter, covering the micro-foundations of the Great Broadening). After this expansion reached its peak in the late 1970s, Republicans resisted additional forays into most new policy domains by voting against such measures. Whereas Republicans and Democrats in Congress initially worked together to expand the scope of the government, while disagreeing on the mechanisms for implementing the new policies, they now began to work at cross-purposes. Republicans began to see electoral advantages in moving right, and the resistance became a full counter-mobilization by conservatives, which was a major factor in ending the broadening by constraining the consideration of new laws and movements into new policy areas. But it also caused an increase in the oversight agenda, which became a permanent feature of congressional policymaking. With Democrats still interested in expanding government to solve problems and Republicans becoming increasingly resistant, Congress began to register heightened levels of interparty conflict. Polarization became entrenched in Congress after the boundaries of what is politically tenable were set by the end of the Great Broadening, and disagreement over the appropriate role of government was relegated to established policy domains.

This overview is a fully endogenous explanation of polarization. It is therefore obviously incomplete because it fails to address clear changes in the partisan inclinations of the electorate. But so is any explanation that relies wholly on electoral changes as exogenous factors in shifting the character of US legislative policy-making. Partisan polarization is in large part due to the great expansion in the scope of government; no explanation can be complete without grasping this transformational understanding of the expanse of issues that Congress is debating.

Increasing polarization made it harder for members of Congress to compromise on the contours of public policy in these established domains; thus, lawmakers adopted the use of omnibus legislation to enact policies that otherwise would not have drawn enough support to be enacted on their own merits. Legislating through omnibus bills has proven an effective strategy for bypassing gridlock, enabling leaders in Congress to enact a large volume of law without compromising with their opposition. By adopting omnibus legislation as their preferred means of law enactment, the more recent congresses look more productive than most earlier congresses in terms of the number of pages of law enacted. This productivity is not lost on conservative members, many of whom have responded by "digging in," resisting the thickening of government, and thus contributing to ever higher levels of polarization. Lawmakers will likely continue to rely on omnibus legislation to "get things done" so long as polarization remains high and constituents remain oblivious to, or apathetic about, the use of this unorthodox procedure. This type of process has certainly characterized the appropriations bills passed in the 115th Congress.

This positive feedback system, ignited by the Great Broadening, continues in relative obscurity: polarization leads to the use of omnibus legislation, which leads to the thickening of government, which leads to increased polarization and heated debate over the role of the federal government in civil society.[4] The Great Broadening created the policy terrain on which battles over the role of the federal government are now fought.

TEN

Appendix Granger Causality

A Granger causality test accounts for the simple reality that time does not run backward. Because causes must precede their effects, changes in independent variables must precede changes in the dependent variable. We adopted two lags at both two and five years (see table 10.1). If the *p*-value exceeds 0.05, we cannot reject the null hypothesis listed in the left column.

For both the two- and five-year lags, we cannot reject the null hypotheses that polarization does not cause the number of new public law subtopics, nor does it cause the number of new budget subfunctions. This result means that it is more likely that the broadening of government causes polarization, rather than polarization causing the broadening of government. In only one case—a five-year lag on the number of budget functions—is the causal ordering unclear, as either variable could be causing the other.

Table 10.1. The Granger causality test

Null hypotheses, two-year lag	*p*-Value
Number of New Public Law Subtopics does not cause Polarization	0.046
Polarization does not cause Number of New Public Law Subtopics	0.819
Number of Budget Subfunctions does not cause Polarization	0.003
Polarization does not cause Number of Budget Subfunctions	0.717
Null hypotheses, Five-year lag	
Number of New Public Law Subtopics does not cause Polarization	0.004
Polarization does not cause Number of New Public Law Subtopics	0.427
Number of Budget Subfunctions does not cause Polarization	0.000
Polarization does not cause Number of Budget Subfunctions	0.002

ELEVEN

Microstory of Polarization in Congress

With a broad brush, in the last chapter, we painted a picture of the interaction between the Great Broadening and party polarization. The analysis shows that the expansion of the agenda happens before the growth in party polarization. While it is plausible, both conceptually and empirically, that the vast expansion of the scope of government in the 1960s and 1970s was a major causal factor in subsequent partisan polarization, we have not yet demonstrated the specific relationship between broadening and polarization. It is to that task that we turn in this chapter, which rests upon the same plausibility analysis that we have sketched throughout this book.

While no single result ties the Great Broadening indisputably to party polarization, we offer a series of findings that suggest that the broad trends that link the two phenomena, documented in the previous chapter, affect the microlevel actions regularly taken by members of Congress, who are increasingly wearing the uniforms of the parties to which they belong. Instead of remaining at the macrolevel, we delve deeply into the microbehavior to illuminate the changing nature of the relationship between Democratic and Republican members in Congress.

The Standard Story of Congressional Change

Most explanations of congressional change in the second half of the twentieth century involve a mix of electoral and institutional factors. We do not dispute the received wisdom, which we briefly recount in this section before we offer an additional wrinkle—a quite substantial wrinkle—to that story.

The polarization between the parties in Congress involves a complex blend of small changes in the electorate that reverberated and changed the rules, standard operating procedures, and institutions of Congress

(Theriault 2008). This explanation of party polarization is predicated upon a larger story of American political development in the twentieth century. The Great Depression, World War II, and the Cold War changed both what the American people (and the world) expected from the Congress and how the parties interacted within Congress (Shepsle 1989). In 1958, the American voters swept into Congress a new wave of liberal Democrats. Two years later, John Kennedy won the White House by incorporating some of those same themes of that election, though he presented them in a more pragmatic way. In the wake of these two strong, liberal endorsements by the voters, the long-standing edifice that kept civil rights off the agenda began to fissure. The electoral consequences of the 1958 midterm election and the 1960 election of John Kennedy started, in earnest, the legislative process by which the Civil Rights Act of 1964 and the Voting Rights Act of 1965 would become the law of the land. Certainly the expansion of the Rules Committee, Kennedy's assassination, and the ascension of Lyndon Johnson into the Oval Office played important roles in explaining the triumph of not only civil rights but also other liberal priorities that, in effect, expanded the scope of the federal government. Institutional rule-changes, events, and elections all hastened these legislative accomplishments.

The Subcommittee Bill of Rights adopted by the House Democratic Caucus in 1973 and the election of the "Watergate Babies" in 1974 are another election-institution combination that profoundly changed how Congress operated (Rohde 1991), as did the 1994 Republican electoral tsunami and the institutional changes that the Republicans implemented, including the cutting of congressional staff and the banning of proxy voting (Evans and Oleszek 1997).

We do not dispute that understanding congressional development requires both an appreciation for elections and institutional changes. We made this case in chapters 5 and 6 for the causes of the Great Broadening. Yet most accounts of congressional change fail to appreciate the role of policy itself in the future development of the institution. Beyond the civil rights legislation in the 1960s, congressional scholars fail to appreciate how major changes in public policy alter the stakes of the electoral and institutional game. The burdens placed on the government after World War II and during the Cold War required policy change—not just more policy, but policy in different areas. This expansion required institutional change, which not only helped bring about the expansion of the federal government's agenda, but also helped lock it in. In this chapter we want to add the policy part of this story, not as an alternative, but as an addition to the current understanding of congressional development.

If the Great Broadening stimulated polarization, then we expect the parties to behave differently during the broadening period than afterward on a variety of indicators. We expect more collaborative parties during the period, when both Democrats and Republicans are caught up in the zeitgeist, than afterward, when Republicans woke to the activist criticism and electoral dangers of partnering with the Democrats to expand the scope of government. Below we examine several indicators, most from the Policy Agendas Project, but others from congressional datasets as well, that support this thesis.

The Politics of Bill Introductions

We begin our microlevel analysis at the first formal stage of the legislative process: bill introduction. Members introduce legislation for a variety of reasons, only some of which have to do with actually trying to change the laws of the United States. Some legislation is introduced merely to send a message, while other bills are introduced at the behest of the president, constituents, or interest groups.

In the normal course of how Congress operates, we would not expect Democratic members to appreciably differ from their Republican colleagues in the motivations that lead to writing and introducing bills, because of their heavier reliance on the government to solve problems, though Democrats might introduce more legislation. Indeed, over the time span of this study, Democrats on average do introduce more bills (see fig, 11.1). In the figure, the bars represent the proportion of bills that members from the respective parties introduced. A bar crossing the 50 percent line indicates that the members from that party introduced more legislation per capita than the members of the other party.

From the 80th to the 113th Congress (1947–2014), Democratic members introduce on average 19.3 percent more bills per capita than Republicans (this figure adjusts for the number of members from each party in each congress). The Republican per capita bar only crosses the 50 percent line in seven congresses (80th, 83rd, 104th, 105th, 106th, 107th, and 109th), in all of which they comprised a majority. In fact, it was only in the 113th Congress that the majority party introduced less legislation per capita than the minority party. When the Republicans serve in the majority (even including the 113th Congress), they introduce 8.8 percent more bills per capita than the Democrats. Incidentally, when the Democrats are in the majority, they introduce 26.6 percent more bills per capita than the Republicans. From the outset, these data suggest that Democrats and majority parties introduce more legislation than Republicans and minority parties.

With the evidence that bill introductions follow a systematic pattern, we feel more certain in using them to analyze microlevel member behavior in the House of Representatives. Indeed, bill introductions form the first piece

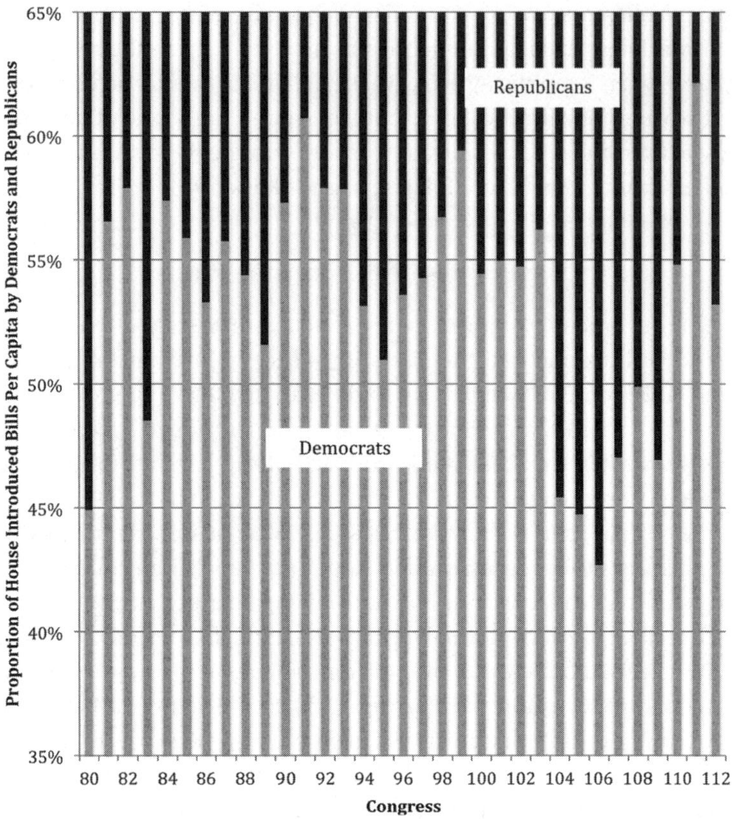

FIGURE 11.1. Proportion of House bills introduced, per capita, by political party (80th–112th Congresses)

of the microlevel data we use to justify our argument that the Great Broadening helped drive—perhaps even cause—party polarization in Congress. Using the logic of Democratic-Republican and majority-minority differences in the bill-introduction data analysis, we can draw one additional inference. If Republicans are generally less likely to introduce bills because they do not turn to the government to solve problems as often as the Democrats, we would expect that Republicans would be exceedingly hesitant to offer bills in issue areas that are not yet part of the government's agenda. In chapter 4, our distinction between new and old issues was based on whether the issue had been addressed by Congress, and we continue to use this distinction here.[1] We would expect this hesitancy to be even stronger when the Republicans are in the minority. What incentive would Republicans, while serving in the minority party, have to introduce bills into the House that encroach on new areas of public policy? Beyond the message politics that now pervades the system, we think they would have virtually none.

We test this introduction strategy by developing a proportion of bills introduced in Policy Agendas subtopics that are new to the agenda relative to old subtopics already on the agenda. If the Republicans introduced the same proportion of new to old bills as the Democrats, the measure is zero. If Republicans focused on new agenda items more than the Democrats, the measure is positive, and if they focused more on old agenda items, the measure is negative. While the number is indeed negative, which we would expect, it is even more negative when the Republicans are in the majority, which we would not expect. In fact, the number is four times as negative when the Republicans are in the majority (–7.2 compared to –1.8). These results suggest that the Republicans are more likely to address new issues than Democrats when they have almost no control over the House agenda than when they have almost complete control of it. Indeed, a puzzling result.

Once the Great Broadening is taken into consideration, the data series makes more sense (see fig. 11.2).[2] The comparison of the Republicans when they are in the majority and when they are in the minority shrinks in half (–7.2 percent to –3.6 percent) outside of the period of the Great Broadening.[3] During the Great Broadening, the Republicans were even more likely than Democrats to introduce bills in new areas of policy. The difference in the gap between the parties is 1.9 percent, meaning that during the Great Broadening, the Republicans were even more focused on newer agenda items than the Democrats, at least in the bills they introduced.[4]

These results indicate that the Republicans acted differently during the Great Broadening than they did afterward. The individual-level data comport with what we would expect from the party dynamics during the Great Broadening. If the parties chose to expand the reach of the federal government rather than fight about the issues that were already on the agenda, we would expect to see the agenda expand in all sorts of different directions to satisfy the parties' various constituencies. Republicans disproportionately expanded it into recycling and tobacco abuse, treatment, and education, while Democrats disproportionately expanded the agenda into youth employment, youth job corps programs, child labor, long-term care, home health, the terminally ill, and rehabilitation services. In other areas, the parties together entered new areas, such as general environment and vocational education.

Aggregating the subtopic codes into their major categories strengthens our argument here (see table 11.1). Unsurprisingly, the Democrats were more focused on new agenda items in labor, banking, and public lands. A value of –0.32 in labor indicates that Democrats' proportion of new agenda items was 0.32 higher than that of Republicans; a value of 0.09 for government operations indicates that Republicans had a higher proportion of off-agenda bill introductions than Democrats. The Republicans were disproportionately focused on new policies in government operations, health, and education. The parties marched into new areas in energy, social welfare, law, crime, and family issues at about the same rate as they introduced bills concerning policies that were already on the agenda. It is important to read these results in light of the politics of the 1960s rather than the politics of today.

The time-trend data in figure 11.2 convincingly show that the dynamics of bill introduction were radically different during the Great Broadening than they were afterward. Republicans were willing to allow the Democrats to expand into new areas, so long as they, too, could expand in the areas they favored. Rather than digging in their respective heels and fighting about old issues, the parties—together—decided to expand the agenda by introducing bills in new subtopic categories. The parties may have differed

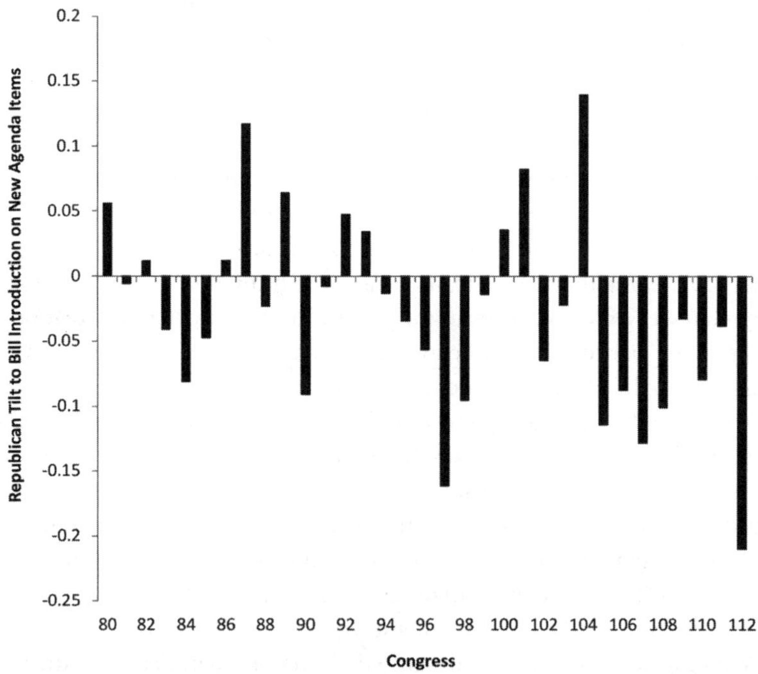

FIGURE 11.2. Proportional advantage to Republicans of bill introductions on new agenda items relative to old agenda items, 80th–112th Congresses

Table 11.1. Republican advantage over Democrats in new major topic areas relative to old topic areas

Republican preference for new agenda items	Major topic code
-0.32	Labor
-0.17	Banking
-0.16	Public Lands
-0.09	Economics
-0.04	Agriculture
-0.03	Transportation
-0.02	Defense
-0.02	Environment
-0.01	Trade
-0.01	Housing
-0.01	Social Welfare
-0.01	Energy
0.01	Law
0.01	Civil Rights
0.02	International Relations
0.04	Space
0.06	Education
0.08	Health
0.09	Government Operations

in the mechanisms deployed in their proposed legislation, but they agreed on the expansion. Once that expansion peaked, the dynamics between the parties changed. Republicans became much less willing to encroach in new policy areas, even when they were in the majority (except for the 104th Congress, the first congress after Republicans won control of Congress). The next section considers whether the dynamics of the Great Broadening reverberated in systematic behavior further downstream in the legislative process—congressional hearings.

Broaching New Subtopics: Congressional Hearings

If a bill is a target for additional action—and usually it is not—the next stage takes place in the standing committees of Congress. Of course, many hearings are not directed at examining bills, but are directed at oversight or investigating problems. In either case, if it is true that the parties—either implicitly or explicitly—agreed to grow the federal government's agenda during the Great Broadening, we would expect that the committees would engage in a bipartisan pursuit to learn as much as they could about the new issue areas. If so, we would expect them to seek expertise from a wide variety of different voices. If instead, the parties were looking to score political

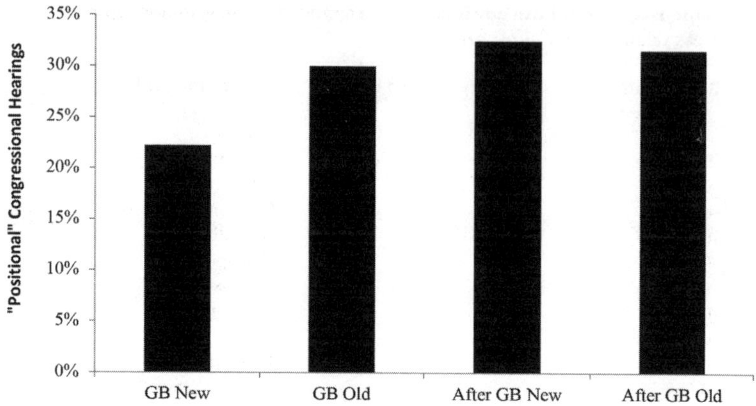

FIGURE 11.3. Percentage of congressional hearings that were "positional"

points in the committee hearings rather than learn as much as they could about policies, we would expect the committee hearings to hear from only one side of the issue.

Lewallen, Theriault, and Jones (2016) code 21,830 congressional committee hearings—roughly a third of all congressional hearings—exactly along this dimension. Each hearing is coded as either "exploratory," indicating that the hearing witnesses represented a diversity of viewpoints, or "positional," indicating that the committee only heard from witnesses on one side of the issue. If the Great Broadening was indeed a period in which both parties agreed to encroach on a wider scope of issues, we should see differences between new and old issues and differences between the period of the Great Broadening and the period afterward.

Both of our expectations are borne out, though, again, care should be exercised in interpreting the results. The number of congressional hearings included in the dataset for issues not yet on the agenda is exceedingly low, both during the Great Broadening (only twenty-seven hearings) and afterward (only forty hearings). Nonetheless, the frequencies are in the direction of our expectations (see fig. 11.3). During the Great Broadening, new topics were less likely to be positional (22.2 percent) than hearings on old topics (30.0 percent).[5] After the Great Broadening, the gap flips: new topics were more likely to be positional (32.5 percent) than old topics (31.6 percent). As with bill introductions, the gap between new issues (28.4 percent positional) and old issues (31.1 percent positional) appears to be relatively minor over the entire time series—new issues are only 8.7 percent less positional than old issues. Once the Great Broadening is taken into consideration, however, the gap becomes pronounced.

These data suggest that the parties considered broaching new issues during the Great Broadening in a fundamentally different way than they did afterward. Hearings on new issues during the Great Broadening were almost one-third less likely to hear from witnesses on only one side of the issue than hearings on new issues after the Great Broadening. During and after the Great Broadening, old issues had about the same percentage of "positional" hearings as new issues after the Great Broadening—the shift from less to more open-minded hearings and back again occurred only for new issues and only during the Great Broadening.

Roll-Call Votes and Party Polarization within Subtopics

We have now presented evidence at the bill-introduction and committee-hearing stages that the parties handled new issues during the Great Broadening differently than they did old issues during the Great Broadening and new issues in the era after the Great Broadening. The next stage of the legislative process is floor deliberation and voting. Admittedly, few datasets have been more meticulously mined among congressional scholars than roll-call votes. This voluminous literature, including Koger and Lebo (2017), Harbridge (2015), Crespin, Rohde, and Vander Wielen (2013), and Lee (2016), already provides some keen insights into the relationship between the parties over time. In particular, Jochim and Jones (2013) find that not all issues in Congress are equally divisive. Furthermore, they show that some issues polarize at different times, while other issues do not polarize at all. Additionally, Lee (2009) and Theriault (2008) show that the composition of issues that are subject to roll-call votes influences how polarized the parties appear to be in Congress. For example, Lee (2009) shows that economic issues are more divisive than social issues, and Theriault (2008) shows that procedural votes are more divisive than final passage votes. So, the more economic votes and the more procedural votes Congress takes, the more divided the parties appear to be. Beyond social issues and final passage votes, we find another set of issues that is less divisive—those issues that are new to the congressional agenda; their consensual nature exists only until the issue becomes entrenched on the legislative agenda.

We construct this argument in three steps. First, we show that party difference scores are a legitimate way to analyze party polarization. Second, we show how the new issues are less divisive than the old issues, especially during the Great Broadening. We end this analysis by speculating on why new issues during this period are less divisive.

Political scientists, including us up to this point in the book, usually measure party polarization in Congress by analyzing the difference between Democrats' and Republicans' DW-NOMINATE scores on the first, most important, dimension in a metric multidimensional scaling procedure (Poole and Rosenthal 1997). The advantage that these scores have over many of the other scores that are highly correlated with them is that DW-NOMINATE scores are comparable over time so long as the comparisons are made within the same party systems. By analyzing members with long careers in Congress and comparing their voting records to those of their colleagues, Poole and Rosenthal argue that the scores in one congress can be compared to those in the congresses surrounding it. This nice feature takes into account the underlying congress-to-congress changes in the voting agenda.

The computation of these scores has been tremendously helpful in understanding congressional dynamics. Nonetheless, of course, these scores are not perfect in all situations. First, and most importantly for us, the scaling procedure makes it impossible to detect polarization differences among issues. While Jones and Jochim scaled roll calls within Policy Agendas major topics, they could not apply the technique to subtopics by year, because of the small number of cases. More generally, Poole and Rosenthal's algorithm for calculating these scores requires a certain number of votes—different standards of how many are "enough" have been adopted by different scholars, though between ten and twenty votes seems to be the industry standard. Calculating an individual member's DW-NOMINATE score for a particular Congress when she has voted more than five hundred times is not a problem. When the whole set of votes is divided into separate subsets, though, determining a DW-NOMINATE score becomes impossible. This difficulty becomes paralyzing when the votes need to be analyzed at the subtopic level—in 85 percent of the cases where the House has taken a vote in a subtopic, they have taken fewer than ten votes in that subtopic in any one Congress; in an additional 10 percent of the cases, they took between eleven and twenty votes. As a result, in only 5 percent of our cases could we calculate subtopic-specific DW-NOMINATE scores with any degree of certainty (and this 5 percent assumes that sufficient division among the members exists so that all of the votes can be utilized in the DW-NOMINATE algorithm).[6]

Here we compare party polarization on old and new issues. In lieu of using DW-NOMINATE scores, we analyze party-difference scores, which is another method of analyzing party polarization, though, admittedly, not as widely used (see Rohde 1991 and Theriault 2008 as examples that use party-difference scores). The party-difference score is the absolute value of the difference between the percentage of Democrats who vote in a particular

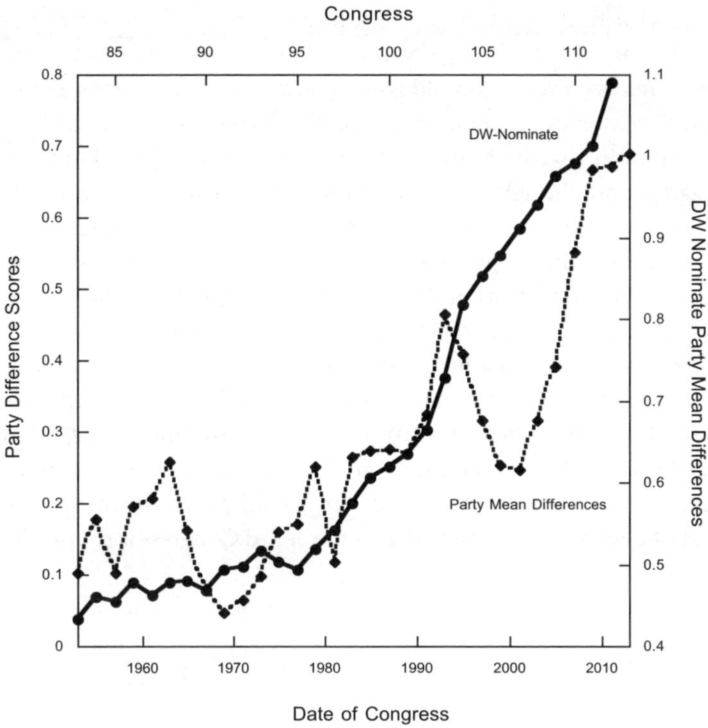

FIGURE 11.4. Polarization as measured by DW-NOMINATE and party-difference scores, 83rd–114th Congresses

direction on a vote minus the percentage of Republicans who vote in the same direction on the same vote. So, if all members voted for final passage of a bill, the party-difference score would be zero. Alternatively, if every Democrat voted for it and every Republican voted against it (or vice versa), the party-difference score would be one. Because they take advantage of the information contained in all votes, and because they can be analyzed even when there is just one vote in a subtopic, we use party-difference scores throughout the remainder of this chapter.

Although DW-NOMINATE and party-difference scores use different votes and different algorithms, they reveal similar polarization trends (see fig. 11.4). From the 1940s to the late 1960s, party polarization decreases, stays relatively flat during the 1970s, and then increases again, starting in the 1980s. The correlation between the two House datasets is 0.83.

Much as with the pattern of bill introductions and committee hearings, roll-call voting analysis aggregated across time does not show an appreciable difference between voting on old issues and voting on new ones. Policy areas that have been on the agenda (with a party-difference score of 0.37) are only 12 percent more divisive than issues new to the agenda (0.33) in the House. This aggregation, though, masks an important time trend present within the congress-by-congress variation (see fig. 11.5). It is exactly when many new issues are getting on the agenda that new issues are particularly less divisive relative to old issues. During the Great Broadening (solid black bars in the figure), new issues (0.22) are 36 percent less divisive than old issues (0.30). In the time period before the voting agenda began to expand rapidly and after the expansion has occurred, new issues are barely more conciliatory than old issues (0.38 compared to 0.40). The period beginning in the 103rd Congress (1993–94) also shows a spike in the consensual nature of new issues, but these data should be interpreted very carefully for two reasons. First, the number of new issues during and after the 103rd Congress is proportionately

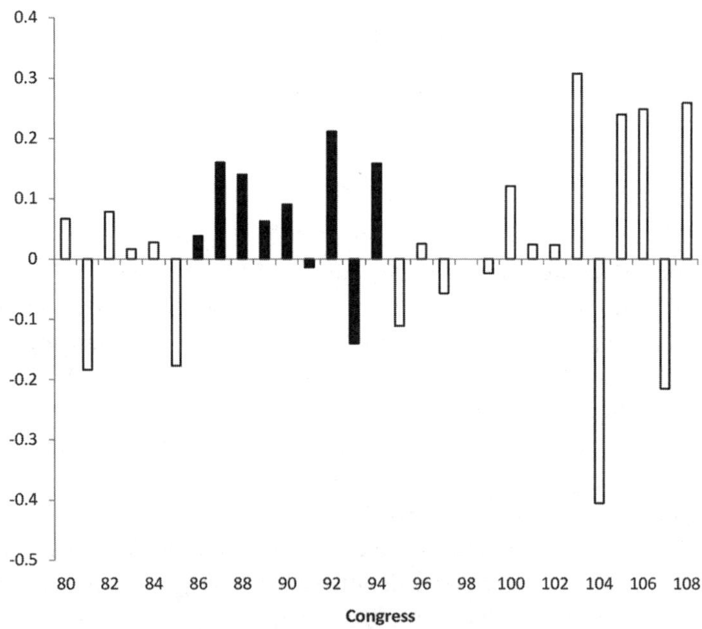

FIGURE 11.5. The relative consensus of off-agenda items to on-agenda items, 80th–108th Congresses

lower (0.6 percent of the votes in the latter period compared to 2.0 percent of the votes during the Great Broadening). And, perhaps even more important, half of the total number of new votes in the latter period were taken during the 104th Congress, when new issues were 0.4 more divisive—in fact, over the six congresses from the 103rd to the 108th (1993–2004), new issues aggregately were more divisive than old issues.

With bill introductions, committee hearings, and roll-call votes in the House of Representatives, the broad sweep of history obscures important interparty dynamics that existed during the Great Broadening. In combination, these trends and their congress-to-congress variation suggest that Republicans and Democrats agreed—perhaps only implicitly—that the government would address issues that had previously been left to civil society or the states. Once both parties independently and jointly put these new issues on the agenda, they were subject to abnormally consensual votes. In the period after the Great Broadening, partisan politics began in earnest and then rose dramatically. The final piece of the polarization puzzle that we present in the next section sets the policy subtopics aside to understand the overall voting dynamics on the House floor.

Roll-Call Votes and Party Polarization on Final Passage Votes

In this section, we show that the party dynamics on roll-call votes have changed—and in a pretty dramatic way—over the last sixty years. Because this book is concerned with the substance of legislation, we make one additional judgment about our analysis in this section: we restrict it to final passage votes, though we certainly appreciate the linkage between the procedures used to schedule substantive votes.[7] The increasing differences in how the two parties in Congress vote, of course, is not a new finding; indeed, few congressional trends have been as discussed among the public punditry and academics. Theriault (2008) and Jessee and Theriault (2014), who build on the work of Roberts and Smith (2003), show that final passage votes elicit fundamentally different party dynamics than procedural and amendment votes—a distinction that has grown over time (see also Rohde 1991; Cox and McCubbins 1993 and 2005; Snyder and Groseclose 2000; Ansolabehere, Snyder, and Stewart 2001; Cox and Poole 2002; and Jenkins, Crespin, and Carson 2005). Because of their control over the House floor (Rohde 1991; Cox and McCubbins 1993, 2005), we expect the majority party to have a higher proportion of "yea" final passage votes than the minority party. Sure enough, when aggregated across time, 89 percent of majority party members voted "yea" on final passage votes; only 60 percent of minority party members voted similarly.

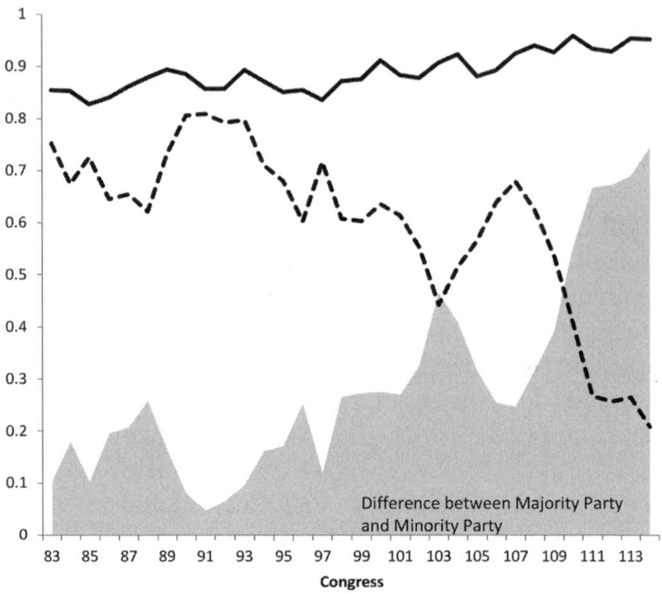

FIGURE 11.6. Majority party and minority party voting patterns on final passage votes, 83rd–114th Congresses

As with so many other trends we have documented, the congress-to-congress variation reveals an interesting pattern—and an especially interesting pattern during the Great Broadening (see fig. 11.6). The differences between the parties during the Great Broadening was relatively small—87 percent for the majority party and 73 percent for the minority party. From the 88th to the 91st Congresses (1963–70), the difference between the parties got smaller with each succeeding Congress. As the agenda stopped expanding, the differences between the parties grew. From the 92nd Congress (1971–72) until the Republicans became a House majority in the 104th Congress (1971–96), the differences between how the parties voted on final passage votes increased every Congress, with two exceptions (the 97th and 101st Congresses). The average party difference grew each congress by an average of 3.4 percent during this period. In the 104th Congress (1995–96), when the Democrats became a legislative minority, a position they hadn't held since the 1950s, they voted "yea" on more final passage votes than the Republican minorities in the preceding congresses, but they quickly acted like the Republican minority before them. Since the 108th Congress (2003–04), the party-difference scores have grown every year at an average increase of 7.1 percent each congress. At that rate, the minority party would be in negative territory (obviously impossible) by the 117th Congress (2021–22)!

The Micropolitics of Polarization

Polarization is a complex phenomenon, and it is unlikely that any simple causal argument can capture its antecedents. Congressional scholars have mostly focused on factors external to the legislative process, particularly the Southern realignment, in explaining this. We have shown in the previous chapter and this one that the policy terrain itself is critical as well, affecting both macro-level trends and the individual actions of congressmen. Surely we ought to find it inconceivable that the Great Broadening was not a major factor in the process, given how large it was and how much of the public debate focused on its ramifications.

The data analysis that we provide in this chapter is consistently supports our claim that the Republican Party condoned—perhaps even encouraged—the Democratic Party's expansion of the federal government in the 1960s under the condition that it, too, got to expand it in the directions favored by its constituents. We show how the Democrats expanded the agenda in some directions, the Republicans expanded it in other directions, and the parties together expanded it in more than a few policy areas. But for the time period during the Great Broadening, the Republican members of Congress were less willing to introduce bills dealing with policy areas that were not yet on the agenda than bills dealing with areas already on the agenda. We take this result as a sign that the Republicans were willing to go along with the Democrats in filling out the agenda, but only at that particular period in time.

We have further evidence that the parties reached some consensus on expanding the federal government's agenda. Again, except for the time period of the Great Broadening, new issues were not dealt with any differently than old issues. During the Great Broadening, members of Congress were much more likely to hear from a diverse set of witnesses on new issues relative to old issues during the Great Broadening, and new issues after the Great Broadening.

When new issues became the subject matter of roll-call votes, again a distinction in their party-difference scores emerges during and only during the Great Broadening. The parties showed much more consensus on their roll-call votes on issues not yet on the agenda during the Great Broadening. Afterward, once the agenda had expanded, new issues were no more consensual than old issues.

The final piece of evidence we offer to build our microstory of how the Great Broadening caused party polarization comes from an examination of final passage roll-call votes. We can think of these votes as the most substance-based votes that members cast. During the Great Broadening, the minority party supported final passage at rates not all that much lower than those of the majority party. Once the agenda expanded, the minority party—especially the Republicans, but eventually the Democrats too—began casting an increasingly larger proportion of "nay" final passage votes.

The Great Broadening at first caused consensus between the parties; or, to put it more actively, the parties were acting in concert to ignite and carry out the Great Broadening. In time, though, the consensus would break, and the divergence between the parties would grow to historic levels, a trend that has continued without abatement. Leaving aside an understanding of how the agenda expanded and its aftermath leaves aside an important piece of the party polarization puzzle.

TWELVE

The Interest-Group System

Most observers of American political processes view interest groups as prime movers in policy change. We make the case in this chapter that this view is misleading at best and, at worst, mostly wrong. Input from interest groups is not exclusively an independent variable, because we find that interest groups respond to policy-making activities as much as they cause them.

The proliferation of interest groups is another way in which the Great Broadening transformed the US political system in ways neither easily foreseeable at the time nor well-understood in hindsight. The broadening itself was not a consequence of interest-group activities, at least as we generally conceive of that activity. It was a consequence of the intersection of powerful forces, including mobilized and networked social movements that learned from one another, starting with the civil rights movement. But this interest-group activity was not typically depicted. It was special—interest-group activity on steroids, and it has not been repeated in the ensuing half-century.

Simply put, government transformed the interest-group system, not the other way around. Policies acted as independent variables, and interest groups as dependent ones. From the traditional (Eastonian) systems perspective, in which group activity acts on government to produce public-policy outputs, causation ran backward, at least for a time. In this chapter, we detail the process.

The Interest-Group System

The interest-group system and its involvement in the policy process through lobbying have both evolved over time, and the Great Broadening contributed in critical ways to this evolutionary process. Both the size and the composition of interest-group representation in Washington have changed; the system is larger now than in the past, and its presence in Washington is much more visible. As political scientists grasped the importance of these changes, they set about measuring them. Robert Salisbury (1984) estimated that about 628 groups were active in lobbying in Washington in 1942; by 1981, this had grown to more than 7,000 organizations.

The composition of the system of interest representation in Washington also evolved over time. The system today is much more complex than it was. Before the Great Broadening, peak trade associations did much of the lobbying on behalf of their corporate members. For example, the American Automobile Association represented the "Big Four"—General Motors, Ford, Chrysler, and American Motors—and the corporations themselves did little lobbying on their own. After the Great Broadening, this simple structure was partially supplanted by independent lobbying by corporations, specialty lobbying law firms, think tanks, other governmental units, and ad hoc coalitions of organizations pushing particular issues. The composition has varied in a second even more fundamental sense: different sectors of the system have grown at differential rates over time—a point emphasized by Jack Walker (1983). Based on a survey he conducted in 1979, Walker found that citizen groups blossomed beginning in the 1960s, and that the ratio of profit to nonprofit groups fell as a consequence. Baumgartner and Jones (2009, fig. 9.2, 181) updated their data using a second survey that Walker conducted in 1985, completed before his untimely death, showing that the ratio of profit to nonprofit groups continued to decline through the early 1980s. At that time, the interest-group system in Washington was more balanced between citizens' groups and groups representing for-profit entities than at any time before.[1]

This balanced system did not last. While we do not have data comparable to the Walker surveys of the 1980s, evidence suggests a resurgence of corporate, for-profit lobbying. The number of trade associations in the United States has increased, a trend that began in the mid-1970s and steeply increased during the 1980s (Baumgartner and Jones 2009, fig. 9.1, 178). Baumgartner, Berry, et al. (2009) report that about a quarter of the advocates on a selection of policy issues from 1998 to 2002 were citizens' groups, seemingly down from the one-third estimated by Baumgartner and Jones from Walker's 1985 survey.[2] Drutman (2015, fig. 3.2, 67) documents a vast increase in the lobbying presence of corporations in Washington, beginning in the late 1980s. So both the number of trade associations and the extent of corporate lobbying increased after the broadening period. Indeed, Drutman's overall impression from his data is that some corporate lobbying created more corporate lobbying in a positive feedback interchange resembling a multi-actor arms race, which has had the effect of crowding out the voices of citizens' groups.

We should not assume that such increases necessarily lead to the dominance of business in the policy-making process. For one thing, businesses often divide on issues, because business interests do not cohere across all policy issues. One current conspicuous example recently before the Federal Communications Commission (FCC) was the net neutrality debate, which has divided internet providers, such as AT&T and Time-Warner, and content providers, such as Netflix, Amazon, and Google. Plenty of citizens' groups have lobbied the FCC on the side of net neutrality regarding content providers, but it would be a mistake to view the debate as citizens versus corporations.

Lobbying is primarily defensive—that is, activated by a threat. Hojnacki et al. (2015), in their study of ninety-eight policy issues, found that most business initiatives are met with opposition from other types of interests, including citizen interests, which are more likely to achieve their aims. The overall study shows that most initiatives fail, with the status quo prevailing. From this and other research, one gets a picture of lobbying as primarily an activity designed to protect interests rather than gain advantage, punctuated by occasional successful forays.

Most of these initiatives come from somewhere else. Grossmann's (2014) study of major policy changes implicates networks of policy entrepreneurs, politicians, and experts in proposing, developing, and achieving policy initiatives. Of course, such initiatives can involve interest groups, but they do not act alone in these cases.

Perhaps, then, interest groups, long seen as part of the input stream into the policy-making process, are more appropriately viewed as outputs of that process. A strong and convincing line of research supports the notion that interests come to Washington as a consequence of policy action more often than they organize to cause change (Baumgartner and Leech 1998; Leech et al. 2005; Baumgartner, Berry, et.al. 2009). As Leech, et.al (2005, 28) write, "Government activity acts as a magnet, pulling groups of all kinds to become active." Moreover these scholars find that the spread of the policy agenda (that is, broadening) is more important than federal spending (that is, thickening) across the policy categories of the Policy Agendas Project in drawing new interests to Washington.

The Great Broadening Transformed the Interest-Group System

All of this is played out on a historical canvas. Interest-group dynamics certainly may be abstracted from ongoing processes and subjected to a systematic study of causes and effects. But interest groups may act differently in one historical period than in others—in particular, before and after the Great

Broadening. In this chapter we provide that historical canvas by showing just how much the Great Broadening influenced interest-group dynamics. Our narrative is simple, because the interest-group story provides the simplest and most direct connections between the broadening process and its downstream effects. We lay out the sequence in stages.

After World War II, but before the Great Broadening, the interest-group system was stable, characterized by a relatively large presence of business groups and a relatively small citizen-group presence; the ratio of profit to nonprofit groups was three to one. (Baumgartner and Jones 2009, 181). During this period, scholars of public administration detected a considerable amount of capture of independent regulatory agencies by the regulated interests (Bernstein 1955).

The second stage was the advent of the Great Broadening, which developed mostly independently of the interest-group system in the macropolitical arena (Redford 1969). Social movements and networks of activists, politicians, and policy professionals were, for a brief moment, brought together to produce a quick series of landmark policy changes. The internal dynamics of the broadening process involved a series of punctuated equilibria in which prevailing policy monopolies conducted within the confines of subsystems were vastly altered or destroyed (Jones, Baumgartner, and Talbert 1993). As a consequence, the policy-making system was rapidly opened up to new groups and interests, and the ratio of profit to nonprofit groups involved in lobbying quickly fell.

As the broadening continued, Congress created a multitude of new programs and agencies in an amazing environment in which the parties contended with proposals from two strong presidents—Lyndon Johnson and Richard Nixon—but did so in a nonpolarized fashion. In chapter 11, we demonstrated how this collaboration operated at the microlevel in Congress. The key was a rough, cross-party consensus on problem priorities, if not on the specific solutions. During the period, conservatives founded the American Enterprise Institute to serve as a mechanism for offering market-based solutions to the problems that almost everyone admitted existed. Democrats argued for program centralization and strong funding for the new programs created, while Republicans fought for lower funding and decentralization through such mechanisms as general revenue sharing, block grants to the states, and state-based regulatory agencies (such as the federalized arrangement incorporated into the Environmental Protection Act of 1970). The intense disagreements on whether or not to fund housing initiatives or regulate pollution characterize later periods, but were not sources of passionate confrontation at their outsets.

American business first reacted passively to the rapid increase in regulatory activity that affected companies in so many policy areas—environmental, occupational, consumer product, and the civil rights regulations happened so quickly that business was caught flat-footed. Big government had run way beyond the lobbying infrastructure that business had in place. Hacker and Pierson (2010, 117) write, "Before the political winds shifted in the 1960s, business had seen little need to mobilize anything more than a network of trade organizations." Even worse for business interests, citizen groups out-organized business and made up for their relative lack of resources with energy and broad support.

In the third stage, business initiated a counter-mobilization. David Vogel (1989) examined the string of political defeats that business experienced in the late 1960s and early 1970s, and he argued that the mobilization of business was a *consequence* of the policy activity during the period. A now-classic 1971 memo by a lawyer for the Chamber of Commerce, Lewis Powell, who was later to become a Supreme Court Justice, focused the effort. Powell's memo, entitled "Attack on the Private Enterprise System," made the cause of business a much more unified one than the sparse network of trade associations that existed at the time (Drutman 2015; Hacker and Pierson 2016).

From this, we postulate two general hypotheses. First, if the stages of development we discern in the historical record are correct, then the Great Broadening should have stimulated a great expansion in the interest-group system, not the other way around. Second, the growth of associations representing business interests should lag behind the growth of the interest system generally, lagging the broadening process as well.

To assess changes in the interest-group system, we use the system of reporting in the *Encyclopedia of Associations*, a tabulation of membership organizations in the United States, to gain a rough gauge of the size of that system (Baumgartner and Leech 1998; Bevan et al. 2013).[3] The interest-group system grew robustly from 1961 through the late 1980s, when growth slowed (see fig. 12.1).[4] The system experienced another spurt in 2005 through 2007, before leveling off. Looking more closely at the series, one can see a clear break in the rate of growth in the late 1970s. From 1961 through 1978, the interest-group system added an average of 340 groups each year. From 1979 to 1987, the system added an average of 846 groups per year.[5] And after 1987 until the growth spurt in 2005, the growth nearly stopped. Most important in this data series is that the shift in growth in interest groups happened *after* the peak of the Great Broadening. While we cannot say that the Great Broadening caused the growth of the interest-group system, we can

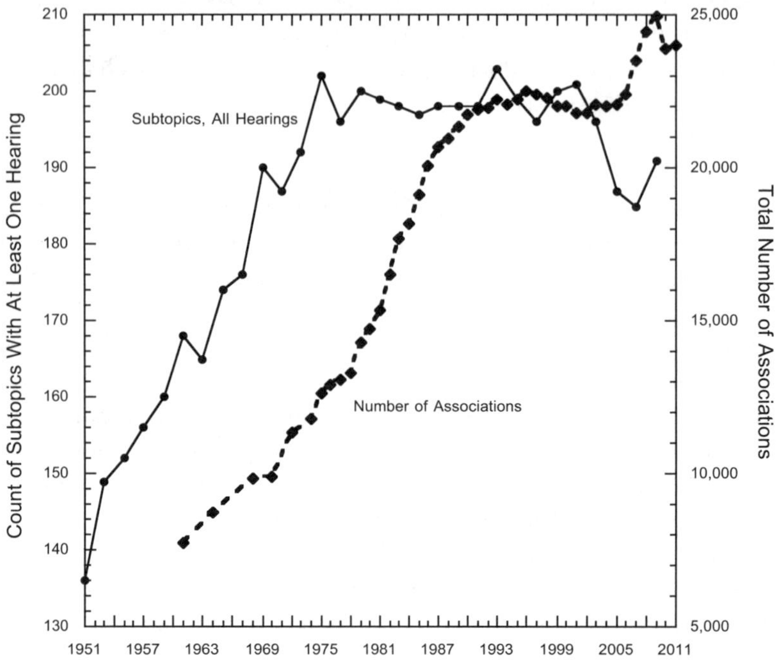

FIGURE 12.1. Growth of the interest-group system and the broadening of government

say with certainty that interest groups did not cause the Great Broadening. It defies logic to claim that B caused A when B happened after A.

Many types of groups grew during this period. The most prominent growth occurred among those the *Encyclopedia* classified as public affairs organizations—the very kind of association that could very well become active as a consequence of a broader, more intrusive (and potentially more lucrative) government (Baumgartner 2005). The scope of government attention grew, and then interest groups formed.

As with congressional action, the interest groups are also coded according to the Policy Agendas Project's policy content codes. That allows us not only to analyze the total number of interest groups, but also the number of groups by issue area. If the business counter-mobilization hypothesis is correct, the Policy Agendas codes for regulatory activity in the areas of finance and domestic commerce should increase, and they should do so after the Great Broadening got started. And that is exactly the case (see fig. 12.2). The business counter-mobilization began in the early to mid-1970s, as the Great Broadening was peaking, and was over by the mid-1980s. Compared to the growth of the full interest-group system, business interests grew more slowly in the 1960s and early 1970s. But the pattern literally turns on a dime, displaying explosive growth after 1975. Between 1975 and 1985, the number of business groups increased by a third, from around 2,200 to 2,900. Then the number of groups in the area of finance and domestic commerce leveled off. Because the *Encyclopedia* database ends in 2001, we cannot trace the business group structure further, but other evidence shows that corporate presence in lobbying increased beginning in the 1990s (Drutman 2015).

We can bore down into the business counter-mobilization by comparing our measure of it to the mobilizations that stimulated it. In chapter 6, we showed how civil rights mobilization led the waves of social movements that helped to broaden government during the 1960s and 1970s. If we compare the first of those waves, which centered on civil rights, we see that the business counter-mobilization clearly followed. By 1966, when our measurement from the *Encyclopedia* starts, environmental organizations were growing briskly, but business organizations actually drifted downward for

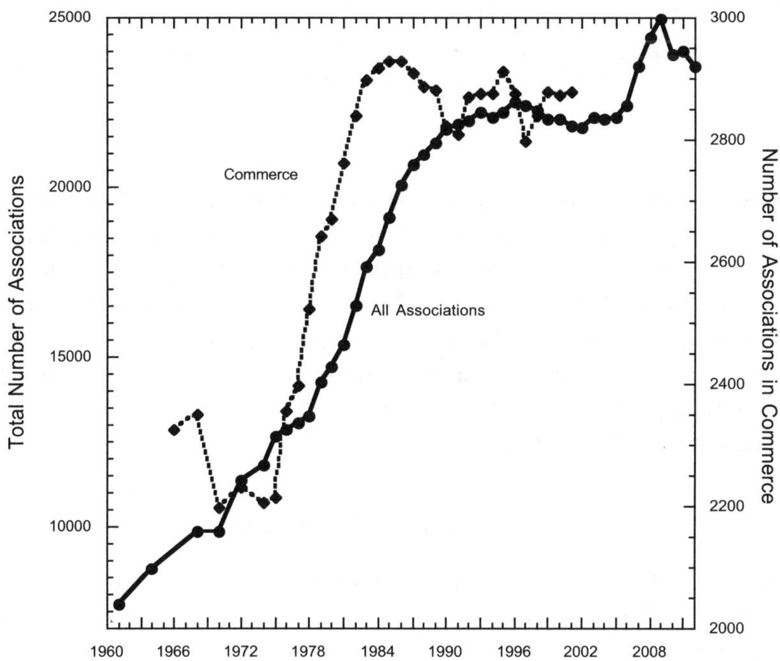

FIGURE 12.2. Counter-mobilization by business: all associations and associations involved in domestic commerce

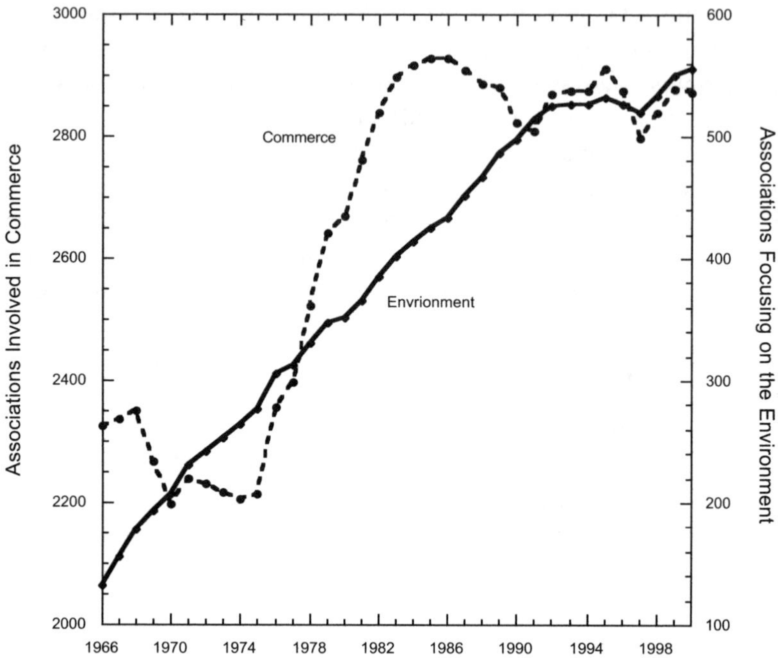

FIGURE 12.3. Counter-mobilization by business: associations involved in domestic commerce and those focusing on the environment

almost ten years (see fig. 12.3). Note that the axes are on a different scale, so we can compare growth rates, not group levels. Civil rights groups display a similar pattern of growth. We cannot say that the civil rights movement or the environmental movement caused business mobilization, which started in the mid-1970s. But the figure does suggest that business mobilization took place in response to the succession of social movements, and the resulting policy enactments that we documented in chapter 6 proliferated during the Great Broadening.

A More Systematic Approach

While it is clear that broadening led interest-group formation, it is not clear exactly what about increases in the scope of government led to the growth in the number of interest groups. We've explored the connection between adding issues to the agenda and growth in the interest-group system. But what if the connection has more to do with the funding made available by government? Surely more funds available would lead to more activity on the part of groups to capture part of the largess. Put another way, was it broadening or thickening that led to the great expansion of the interest-group system? To explore this possibility further, we examined the connection between the interest-group system and the number of OMB budget subfunctions funded, by year (see fig. 12.4). The funding came first, and groups grew afterward early in the series. When funding plateaued in the late 1970s, the interest-group system continued to grow, but plateaued a few years later. But in the mid 2000s, the system began to expand again, this time without the stimulation of added budget functions.

The stages of interest-group and social movement mobilization are clear graphically, but two possibilities could be causally related to that growth. One is the expansion of the policy-making agenda, causing groups to mobilize both to take advantage of the new policies and to defend against regulations. The other is the increased availability of funds that draw groups to

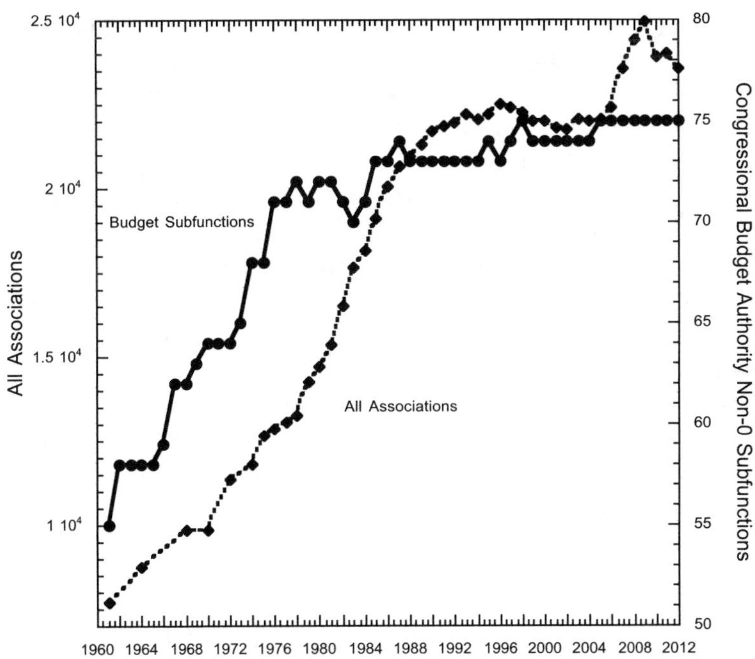

FIGURE 12.4. Congressional Budget Authority subfunctions that were funded and the number of associations included in the *Encyclopedia of Associations*

Washington to increase benefits for their constituents or to provide services for a more complex government.

Given the obvious temporal succession of these mobilizations, it should be possible to analyze the process more systematically through statistical means, which provides a comparison between the impacts of the two potential causes. So we modeled the proliferation of interest-group associations as a function of both the broadening of the lawmaking agenda and the increase in the number of budget subfunctions recorded in the US Congressional Budget Authority. We used as our measure for the broadening of the lawmaking agenda the cumulative annual count of the number of new subtopics addressed in laws between 1948 and 2011. We can think of this as an integrated measure of the persistent and growing legal environment in which interest groups have been operating since World War II.

The broadening of the lawmaking and budget agendas has individual and separable effects on the proliferation of interest-group associations. Laws are the legal commitment of government to particular functions and the framework for possible spending. Budget outlays are the monetary commitment of government to particular functions. Both laws and budgets provide opportunities for entrepreneurial associations seeking gains from policy commitments by government, but the mechanisms by which this occurs may not be the same. Perhaps adding policy subtopics causes groups to form to try to define the specifics of the policy in the implementation stage, while adding budget subfunctions stimulates groups to organize to take advantage of the new source of funds. In any case, this surely needs further investigation. An increase in the breadth of either laws or budgets seems to encourage the formation of new interest groups. Our analysis, presented in the chapter appendix, indicates that they have roughly similar effects.

The expansion of government assessed separately as legal broadening (new topics addressed by laws) and fiscal broadening (additional budget functions funded) results in increases in the number of interest groups lobbying Washington policy-makers. The broadening of law and the broadening of budgets have independent and significant effects on changes in the interest-group system. We present the specifics of the analysis in an appendix to this chapter.

Lobbying Thickens after the Burst

The data show that the steep growth in lobbying occurred in response to the Great Broadening in the 1960s and 1970s. As government broadened, the interest-group system also broadened, adding groups in areas previously sparsely occupied—or even unoccupied. The magnet of the broadening Washington policy agenda transformed the lobbying system, but the system did not simply stabilize at a constant level. It thickened.

One consequence of the failure to recognize the cumulative effect of past policy-making on present political activities is that we don't always see the processes of political mobilization and subsequent activity as distinct. They should be thought of that way. In the case of interest groups, it is both necessary and easy to detect. As Lee Drutman (2015, 7) has put it, current theories of lobbying "are all primarily explanations for why political interests mobilize. They do not explore the long-term consequences following mobilization."

We might assess public-policy thickening by such measures as increases in budgets within subfunctions or the increases in executive actions, such as rule-making in those areas. For lobbying, we could count groups as a rough start. Scholars who have done this find that groups have not been added to issue areas proportionately.

The *Encyclopedia of Associations* indicates a secondary increase in the size of the interest-group system in the mid-2000s. Using data from lobbying disclosure forms made possible by the Lobbying Disclosure Act of 1995 and from *Washington Representatives*, a lobbying directory, Drutman reports a surge in corporate lobbying between 2000 and 2010. It is possible that the surge in business expenditure was in part responsible for the increase in the size of the interest-group system, with more business groups created during the period, but we do not have the necessary data for this period to assess this claim. Nonetheless, it is clearly well beyond the burst in interest-group growth that is the main focus of this chapter, both in total and for groups involved in business and commerce.

It does not seem that the new lobbying environment created by the Great Broadening issued in some sort of new equilibrium. Rather, the new environment fostered stability in some sectors and explosive growth in other sectors of the lobbying enterprise. Drutman (2015, 6) describes business lobbying as a positive-feedback process that "has its own momentum," and he asserts that "lobbying begets lobbying." He calculates the ratio of business lobbying expenditures to diffuse interest-group and labor union expenditures, finding an increase in the ratio of about two-thirds between 1998 and 2012.

During the Great Broadening, businesses' advantage in the interest-group system was nearly offset by citizen groups. Indeed, the broadening period brought both growth in the interest-group system and an increase in diversity in it. Baumgartner and Jones 2009, 179) write, "Virtually without exception, growth in the number of groups has led to increasing diversity of views within previously homogenous policy subsystems." Baumgartner and Jones provided a more detailed examination of environmental groups, finding a pattern similar to the more general growth of citizen interest groups. They found that growth in the environmental movement involved both more environmental associations and growth and professionalization of existing groups.

Yet shortly after those words were written, the interest-group system stabilized. Groups involved in domestic commerce had enjoyed explosive growth between 1975 and 1980, as environmental group growth continued at about the same pace. Group growth in both areas slowed to a crawl, but environmental groups grew more steadily and for a longer period than business groups (measured by their involvement in domestic commerce). According to estimates from the Policy Agendas Project, the ratio of environmental groups to groups engaged in domestic commerce in 1966 was 0.056; in 1991 it was 0.183; and by 2001 it was 0.196. That is, as the Great Broadening began to accelerate, the environmental interest-group network was about 6 percent as large as the domestic commerce network. By the early 1990s, it was approaching 20 percent as large.

Data on group formation is somewhat misleading. During the broadening period, few corporations had in-house lobbyists; today many have public affairs divisions that, as Drutman (2015) suggests, tend to lobby to sustain their activities within the firm as well as lobbying government on behalf of firm interests. Both citizen groups and business groups have professionalized and spent more on lobbying, but it is likely that business has invested relatively more into this part of the enterprise.

The growth in business advantage over other groups does not easily translate into business wins in politics for several reasons. In many cases, businesses are arrayed against one another, jockeying for advantage. In the energy field, solar, wind, and natural gas interests can ally against coal, for example. Clean power rules offer an advantage to companies providing cleaner energy sources over those dependent on less environmentally friendly sources. Most environmental groups could side with the clean energy companies, but these groups are more likely to be unified on these issues than corporations. As a consequence, on this issue the relative advantage of business versus citizen groups would be misleading; the correct ratio would assess environmentally friendly lobbying in a single coalition.

Examples of such intra-business squabbles are replete over the contours of public policy during both legislative and executive branch deliberations. We noted above that the current skirmish over net neutrality involves a network of content providers, from giants Google and Netflix to mom-and-pop websites arrayed against internet service providers. Indeed, much business lobbying is directed at gaining advantage over competitors for the same market niche.

Nevertheless, sometimes business interests are united. Where business is more united, it tends to draw diverse opposition from other interests, and that makes business interests less likely to prevail (Smith 2000; Hojnacki et al. 2015). On the other hand, when business interests do not stir up opposition, they have a much better track record (Hojnacki et al. 2015).

The picture we paint of interest-group change is one of surge, countersurge, and a new reality. Before the Great Broadening, business lobbying was sparse and not particularly well-organized. For the most part, business operated within different spheres. During the broadening period, more diffuse citizen interests, often organized along movement rather than neat organizational lines, began to grow; along with that growth came an antibusiness attitude from environmental, consumer, and even civil rights groups that made doing business in America more cumbersome than it had been in the past. Environmental and other citizens groups grew and prospered for years before business interests mounted a counter-mobilization.

When business acted, it was powerful and led to a new "pervasive position" in the lobbying system (Drutman 2015). That pervasive position was due to positive-feedback systems, in which business lobbying generated even more business lobbying as firms competed, and the public affairs divisions within corporations vied to outdo one another in the lobbying realm. The interest-group system had become partially decoupled and hence partially independent from the forces that transformed it. Today internal dynamics within the system are more critical than external forces.

Polarization Follows Interest-Group Formation

The data in this chapter in combination with our findings from congressional polarization (discussed in chapters 10 and 11) allow us to make a bold claim linking the two. Again, sequencing is critical. The Great Broadening preceded the expansion in the number of interest groups (fig. 12.1), and the expansion of the interest-group system preceded the onset of polarization in Congress (fig. 12.4). As the interest-group system began to expand, polarization drifted sideways until the mid-1970s, when it began its steady climb, a climb that thereafter paralleled the growth in the interest-group system. This sequencing does not *prove* that broadening caused interest-group growth, which in turn caused polarization. The causes of polarization in

Congress are much more complex than that. Theriault (2008) argues that congressional polarization has its roots in both exogenous factors, such as changes in party identifications in the electorate, as well as endogenous ones, such as changes in the rules and the relationship between the members themselves. To this latter category, we can add interest-group growth and the broadening of government.

So long as both parties benefited from the growth in the scope of the federal government, the parties did not significantly diverge in how their members voted. Indeed, most final passage votes in the House and Senate during this period enjoyed overwhelming and bipartisan support. Once the government expanded and the business interests organized, that natural constituency for the Republican Party pushed to put the brakes on the Great Broadening. In combination, conservative Republicans and business interests were able to stop the broadening in some cases and were actually able to scale it back in other cases. Those scholars interested in single causes or undisputed regression equations and asterisked coefficients may not be satisfied with the evidence that we marshal, but the broad data could hardly speak more clearly.

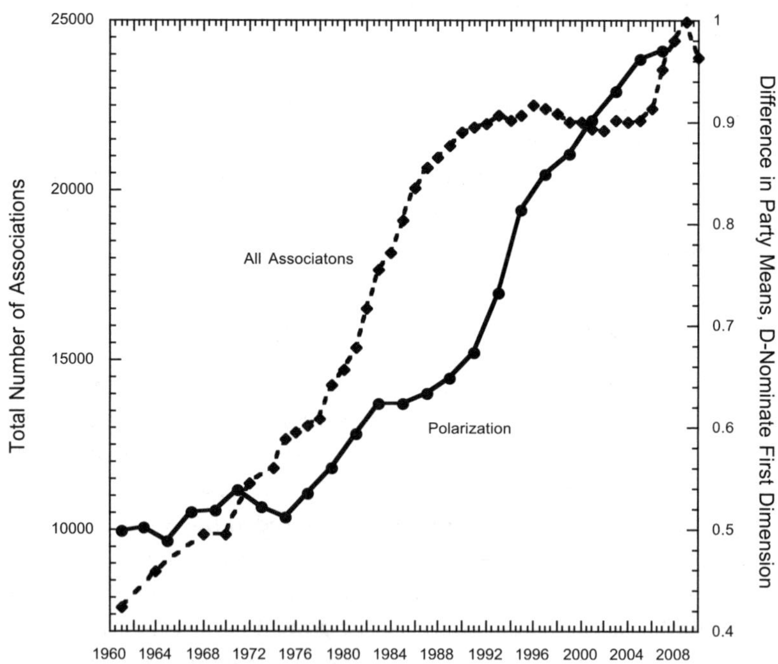

FIGURE 12.5. Growth of the interest-group system and partisan polarization in Congress

There can be no dispute over our finding that polarization in Congress did not cause the growth in interest groups any more than it caused the broadening of the government. In both cases, the trends show that polarization came afterward. A bigger, broader, macro approach, while not pinning down the one cause, can certainly point to a direction in which political scientists should focus their search.

Interest Groups as Dependent on Policy Development

The Great Broadening transformed the interest-group system. The clear sequencing of processes, the supporting literature from interest-group scholars, and the lack of clear alternate hypotheses all point to the Great Broadening as the leading suspect in the large changes in the interest-group system. Moreover, the internal dynamics of the interest-group system support this argument. The interests most closely associated with the social movements that were intimately involved in the expansion were the first movers, with business associations responding after a lag. Finally, and critically, polarization in Congress came after the businesses mobilized.

While the sequencing of processes is crystal clear in this case, it does not imply that the system reached some new equilibrium. The Great Broadening was an event of such great magnitude that it caused a variety of responses, including transformations, countercurrents, and downstream eddies. Such complex changes explain why the historical institutionalist notions of critical junctures and new institutional equilibria are oversimplifications. The metaphor of "policy as terrain" is surely instructive here, as each new dynamic process plays out on a new policy terrain.

The post-broadening terrain is much more complex than the pre-broadening terrain. Business groups once lobbied government when they perceived a threat. Lobbying was reactive, oriented at limiting government's reach into what was viewed as private enterprise. Limited government and business interests were seen as virtually similar.

Today businesses lobby on two fronts. Sometimes they lobby to obstruct government policies they view as interfering with corporate interests. In such cases, one set of business interests not infrequently oppose other business interests as well as broader, more diffuse citizen interest groups. At other times, business lobbies for government benefits for its industry; many businesses want a "piece of the action" of traditional governmental services, such as education. Once business lobbied government to "stay out of its business" and drew tight lines around what was appropriate for civil society or the states to handle and what was appropriate for the national government to address. Now it is more likely that business lobbies the federal government to take over some functions that were formerly viewed as solidly within the purview of the public sector.

We have shown how government became involved in issues previously reserved for civil society or the states quite rapidly. Yet as the relationships between business and government have evolved, business has become increasingly comfortable with "poaching" on public turf. Government may raise the revenue, but private businesses often spend the money. To date, we don't have reliable figures on how much money is raised by government but spent by private companies presumably pursuing public aims—or rather both public aims and private profits. But clearly it is enormous, and it has expanded across policy domains as government expanded into those domains. One of the under-analyzed aspects of broadened government is the business opportunities it provides, and the extent to which businesses pursuing those opportunities have caused government thickening.

The point is not to push this argument too far, but to raise it to illustrate how much the political system has become a strange corporatist mix, in which private business interests get drawn in to the system, often making it more costly than it would be otherwise. Conservative ideologues may decry the size of government, but reducing that size would paradoxically reduce the flow of public funds to private enterprise. That is how much the Great Broadening transformed government-business relations, at least according to the trends in the number and range of organized interests in the United States. And we have neither a public philosophy to guide this strange breed nor any practical descriptions of it from political scientists or other scholars.

TWELVE

Appendix

We used a negative binomial regression because the dependent variable is a count of the annual number of interest groups lobbying in Washington, DC Negative binomial regression models are a generalization of the Poisson regression and have an extra parameter to model overdispersion.[1] We also include a temporal counter, which is an indicator for unobserved trends unfolding over the passage of time.

To interpret the coefficient estimates (displayed in the second column of table 12.1) we use an incident rate ratio (displayed in the third column), which is essentially the antilog of the coefficient. This conversion allows for a direct comparison among the variables. Adding new subtopics addressed in laws and the funding of additional budget subfunctions has nearly identical effects on the proliferation of interest groups; when Congress passes legislation dealing with a new topic area, the rate of the growth of interest groups increases by a factor of 1.02, and when Congress funds an additional budget function in the prior year, the rate of growth of interest groups also increases by a factor of 1.02. We also compute marginal effects at the means for both indicators. If all other variables are held at their means, moving from the minimum number of subtopics addressed on Congress's lawmaking agenda (93) up to the mean number of subtopics addressed on Congress's lawmaking agenda (206) adds 315 new interest groups. Similarly, moving from the minimum number of funded budget subfunctions (46) up to the mean number of budget functions (61) adds 417 new interest groups.

Table 12.1. Causes of the proliferation of interest-group associations (1966–2001; negative binomial regression results)

	Coefficient	Incident rate ratio	Standard error
Number of new public law subtopics	0.02***	1.02***	0.00
Number of budget functions (lagged by one year)	0.02***	1.02***	0.00
Time counter	0.01***	1.01***	0.00
Pseudo-R^2	0.18		

*Statistical significance at 0.1 level;
**statistical significance at 0.05 level;
***statistical significance at 0.001 level.

THIRTEEN

Politics of Conservative Reaction

Throughout this book, we've made the implicit claim that the conservatives had a strong reaction to the Great Broadening. Initially, Republicans broadened the agenda in the areas that most concerned their interests, just as the Democrats had done among the issues in their areas of concern. When the full weight of the issue-by-issue expansion occurred year after year, the magnitude of the federal government's full scope in the late 1970s triggered a more concerted effort among conservatives to blunt the Great Broadening's full impact. In this chapter, we explore more explicitly the conservatives' counteraction through the lens of the three most successful domestic policies for which they advocated: deregulation, crime control, and tax reductions.

The three policies had very different characteristics. Two (deregulation and crime control) enjoyed a great deal of support across the political spectrum. The third (tax cutting) was highly contested. Deregulation benefited from a strong intellectual foundation in economic theory and was by far the most successful conservative policy initiative. It clearly reduced the control that the federal government had over businesses. It attracted great support from consumer advocates, most of whom were on the left end of the ideological spectrum. Crime control also enjoyed great support from across the political spectrum, but it increased the role of government and caused severe social dislocation and large long-term costs to taxpayers. Crime control had a basis in research, but many of the key points from criminological research were ignored as a positive-feedback cycle set in motion a bidding war over increased crime penalties. Of the three, tax policy was the most contentious. The "stagflationary" era of the late 1970s made the conditions ripe for rethinking the tax policy that had flourished throughout the Great Broadening period. During the early Reagan years, tax policy underwent substantial revision, causing persistently large deficits without generating the amount of economic growth promised by its proponents.

The three policies had different effects on government involvement in American society. Deregulation definitely constrained broadening and reduced subsequent thickening. Although it became a federal responsibility in the Johnson Administration, crime control greatly thickened government as the newly enacted policies became increasingly punitive. Tax cuts, paradoxically, also caused government thickening to increase as the previous general consensus on limiting deficit spending collapsed. The "something for nothing" claims of supply-side advocates created tax policy carve-outs that neither reduced the size of the tax code nor made it simpler.

Deregulation

By the mid-twentieth century, the American economy had evolved into a mixture of highly regulated industries and less regulated, much more competitive ones. Regulations emerged for a variety of reasons, but the major two were to curb the price and quality abuses of monopolistic industries—especially where these industries were "natural monopolies," such as utilities and railroads—and to establish price and quality stability in industries damaged by extreme competition. The agencies established to oversee these industries also issued regulations to protect the safety of the public, especially in transportation. Analysts used the terms *economic* and *social* regulation to distinguish these two forms.

This net of regulations and associated agencies formed subsystems that were by all accounts extremely powerful. Industries, unions, executive agencies, and congressional committees together regulated railroads, trucking, airlines, telephones, banks, stock trading, and oil and gas extraction. This configuration of power, economic and political, seemed to be unchallengeable. Yet between 1975 and 1980, Congress passed, and two different presidents signed, a flurry of pro-competitive legislation deregulating major aspects of air travel, trucking transportation of freight, communications, railroads, and natural gas pricing.

What happened? Derthick and Quirk (1985), in their study of airlines, trucking, and telephone deregulation, point to a configuration of forces, none of which alone brought about deregulation. These included academic analyses, economic conditions (especially the "stagflation" of the period), and political factors, particularly presidential leadership and policy entrepreneurship in Congress. These factors speak specifically to the particular timing of this deregulation. They do not speak to the overall conditions that made these factors so ripe. We cannot ignore the admittedly quixotic role of the Great Broadening, which itself was sustained by a general desire to correct social ills, whether they were caused by private actions or government itself. Particularly important was the consumer movement, which supported deregulation to protect consumers. Government could be the answer when companies produced unsafe cars, but a competitive market could be used when government conspired with industry to exploit consumers.

The Roots of Deregulation

In the 1950s, a small band of economists began to critique the regulatory structures established to govern many industries on the grounds that they interfered with the mechanisms of a free economy (Derthick and Quirk 1985, 19). The system, the economists contended, interfered with competition that, in the case of the heavily regulated transportation sector, could lead to more freight-hauling options and lower costs for them. At the same time, political scientists and students of public administration were critiquing the regulatory system as undemocratic. First came Huntington's (1952) stinging critique of the Interstate Commerce Commission (ICC); instead of the enlightened regulators of public administration lore, Huntington found a system beholden to interest groups—in particular the regulated railroads (Novak 2014). Bernstein (1955) extended Huntington's capture theory to other regulatory agencies, producing an indictment of the entire business regulatory structure, based not on economic competition but on the failure of the regulators to be responsive to a broader public interest.

Deregulation thus had an intellectual foundation, and it spanned disciplines: economics, public administration, political science, and law (Novak 2014). The deregulatory fever spread far beyond academia. Two presidents of opposing parties, Gerald Ford and Jimmy Carter, included deregulation as a major component in their programs. Ralph Nader and his consumer protection advocates backed deregulation on the grounds that the existing network of regulations protected industries in vast swaths of the economy at the expense of the consuming public. Under pressure from Presidents Ford and Carter, the regulatory agencies themselves donned the mantle of deregulation. In Congress, a plethora of overlapping committee jurisdictions allowed policy entrepreneurs such as Ted Kennedy to use subcommittee investigatory and oversight functions to disrupt the prevailing configurations of subsystem policy-making.

During the brief period of most intense pro-competitive deregulation, numerous policy subsystems were destroyed or greatly changed. Crandall (2008) found that those sectors of the economy that were regulated in 1975, including oil and gas extraction, railroads, trucking, air transport, pipelines, electricity, telecommunications, radio and television, banks, and insurance, comprised 11.5 percent of GDP. By 2001, only about 3 percent of GDP was regulated, with oil and gas extraction, railroads, trucking, air transport, and banks completely deregulated, and telecommunications, radio, and television partially deregulated.

Trucking

Acting on the combined interests of trucking, railroads, and the regulators (Moore 1993), the federal government created the regulatory structure for trucking in the Motor Carrier Act of 1935, which brought highway freight haulers under the purview of the Interstate Commerce Commission (ICC), which Congress created in 1887 to regulate the railroad industry. Over time, the trucking regulatory system settled into a comfortable and stable system in which the regulated industry, the Teamsters' Union of drivers, the ICC, and the regulatory committees in Congress all acted to protect the profits of industry, the pay of drivers, and the routes to smaller towns and rural regions—a classic regulatory subsystem, or "iron triangle." When trucking deregulation came, "Most certainly, the regulated industries . . . did not ask to be deregulated" (Derthick and Quirk 1985, 21). Indeed, the trucking companies and their Teamsters' Union allies mounted a vigorous defense of the existing system to thwart the pro-competitive reform advocates.

The Deregulation Coalition

We noted in chapter 5 the "sticky thermostat" of decreasing public support for liberal policies that aided the conservative reaction to the Great Broadening. Liberal opinion reached a nadir in 1980 as the election approached. Democratic President Jimmy Carter pursued an agenda that included broader macroeconomic policies, including supporting Federal Reserve policies that raised interest rates to deal with "stagflation," and he firmly supported pro-competitive economic deregulation. But unlike Republican Gerald Ford before him, Carter strongly supported social regulation.

Public opinion was surely reacting to the Great Broadening and Republican efforts to stem the tide of increasing government intrusion into civil society. The reaction, however, had little to do with the regulatory regimes of transportation and telecommunications that were deregulated (Derthick and Quirk 1985). Public reaction to them cannot have been thermostatic, because they were not established during the increase in the "temperature" of government intervention. These systems were put in place in the 1930s and occupied but a small part of the "excessive government regulation" that was the focus of conservatives and Republicans complaints. As Derthick and Quirk (1985, 132) put it, "Airline and trucking deregulation, neither recently created nor considered onerous by the regulated industries, were little noticed by the general public." While public opinion played a part in transportation deregulation, it was not causal. The combined thrust of a pro-competitive coalition of academics, think tanks such as Brookings and the American Enterprise Institute, the regulatory agencies themselves, entrepreneurial members of Congress, and presidential support forced deregulation on the government's agenda. Yet the generalized public reaction to the Great Broadening certainly allowed pro-competitive reformers to operate in a favorable environment in which members were increasingly happy to take credit for reducing excessive government regulation.

The number of congressional hearings on price and route regulation of trucking speaks to its place on the agenda.[1] Congress held few formal hearings on economic regulation until well into the 1970s, as pro-competitive regulatory forces began to achieve successes with the support of President Ford and the regulatory agencies themselves (see fig. 13.1). Hearings intensified as President Carter continued the deregulatory push, and entrepreneurs in Congress, including Senator Ted Kennedy of Massachusetts, adopted the issue. As the chair of the Subcommittee on Administrative Practice and Procedure of the Judiciary Committee, Kennedy held a highly professional set of hearings on airline regulation, hearings organized by the committee's general counsel (and later Supreme Court Justice), Stephen G. Breyer (Derthick and Quirk 1985, 40–45). Kennedy was likely responding more to consumerism than pro-competitive reform, and in any case his subcommittee and even the Judiciary Committee itself had no jurisdiction in the area. Nevertheless his hearings added momentum to the pro-competitive reform movement, resulting in the Airline Deregulation Act of 1978, which deregulated the industry rapidly, with the Civil Aeronautics Bureau (CAB) ceasing operations in 1984.

Airline deregulation was easier, with more public awareness and a weaker configuration of industry interests than trucking. Yet the successes in airline deregulation added momentum to trucking deregulation, resulting in the Motor Carrier Act of 1980, which began the process of trucking deregulation. Congress continued to hold hearings on trucking deregulation for many years afterward and passed several acts extending the deregulatory process. The ICC Elimination Act of 1995 completed the process under the newly elected Republican Congress, but the more important Trucking Industry Regulatory Reform Act of 1994 was passed under unified Democratic government.

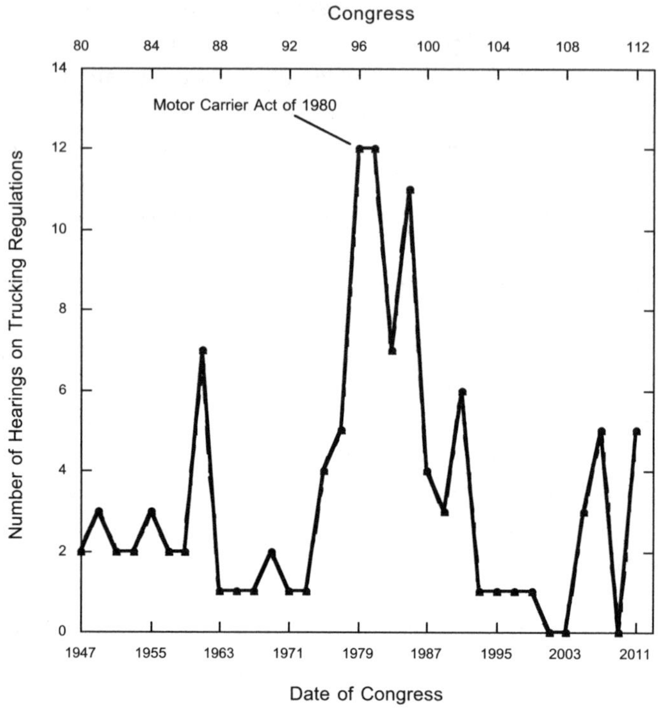

FIGURE 13.1. Number of congressional hearings on trucking regulatory actions on rates and routes

Although the arc-like pattern of trucking deregulation hearings, a conservative priority, mirrors the general arc of the Great Broadening, it is a bit offset—rising later, peaking later, and falling later. Because transportation regulation was established in the 1930s, it crossed the legitimacy barrier much earlier and had become an established function of government by World War II. Despite its earlier addition to the federal government's purview, trucking was deregulated in a manner that follows the general pattern of the Great Broadening.

Safety Regulation

While the hearings on the economic deregulation of surface transportation show the characteristic arc pattern, hearings on vehicle safety show the classic plateau pattern of the Great Broadening that is indicative of the lodging of new functions in government. We have used a logarithmic scale for the *Y*-axis of the number of hearings to smooth out the variability in these latter hearings (see fig. 13.2). When government moved into vehicle safety regulation, it did not move out, continuing to adjust regulations and oversee agencies throughout the period. This pattern was characteristic of regulatory activity directed at air and water pollution, occupational safety, and civil rights.

How it came to occupy the agenda is not the only reason that deregulation politics are better understood in light of the Great Broadening. The final congressional votes on deregulation clearly indicate the bipartisan nature of problem-solving in the intense era of the Great Broadening. Between 1976 and 1995, Congress passed nine major bills that deregulated surface transportation and one additional bill that deregulated the airlines.[2] Despite being conservative priorities, these bills enjoyed a tremendous amount of support in both parties. A majority of Republicans and Democrats in both chambers supported all seventeen of their final passage votes. On average, these votes were 42 percent less divisive than the other final passage votes taken during their respective congresses. If anything, this cross-party

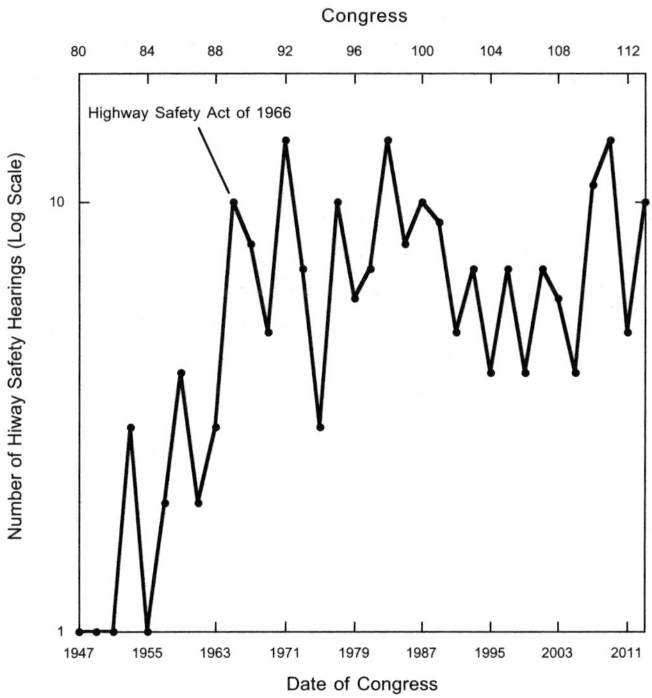

FIGURE 13.2. Number of highway safety hearings by Congress, log scale

consensus on price deregulation was even greater, because an additional ten deregulation final passage votes occurred as voice votes, where those opposed were so few that they did not even ask that their opposition be recorded.

Economic Deregulation as the First Conservative Success

The first solid conservative success in the reaction to the Great Broadening came in the move to deregulate industries that had come increasingly under the purview of government scrutiny during the Great Broadening. Businesses were also concerned with the increasing web of regulatory actions taken in what was called at the time "social" regulation—environmental pollution, occupational hazards, product safety, civil rights, and other cross-industry regulations that businesses resented and that could be quite costly. Political fights over these social regulations continue today, because no bipartisan consensus exists on them. How Congress dealt with these social regulations could not be more different from how Congress dealt with economic regulation.

Today the pro-competitive economic reforms in transportation and telecommunications are, for all practical purposes, settled law; price-regulation policies live only in limited areas, such as dairy pricing. Price issues do occasionally become politically relevant when competition fails and antitrust policies come into play. Exemplary is the case of telecommunications antitrust actions. In the cases of the airlines, trucking, and railroads, government established price regulations to offset the cutthroat competition within multifirm industries. Deregulation in the 1970s and 1980s was pro-competitive. On the other hand, prices can also be fixed without government in highly concentrated industries. For example, a single monopoly supplier, American Telephone and Telegraph, dominated telecommunications services for much of the early and middle twentieth century. The Antitrust Division of the Justice Department sued AT&T, winning divestiture of the subsidiary companies responsible for service delivery (regional Bell companies) from the company producing equipment (Western Electric) in 1982.

Antitrust approaches are pro-competitive, but today the Justice Department and the Federal Trade Commission show little interest in forcing industry de-concentration. The pro-competitive urge within the Republican Party has waned, and pro-consumer Democrats are but a weak shadow of Naderism during the waning days of the Great Broadening. And today no one clamors for price-setting by government regulatory agencies even in an increasingly concentrated economy.

The major forces in bringing about the success stories in transportation deregulation are pretty straightforward. First, the policies themselves were just not working that well and hence were vulnerable. Second, the US federal government was at the tail end of an innovative, experimental period that involved lots of new policy choices. It seemed natural to expand this innovation to the removal of unneeded federal policies. Third, pro-competitive reform included two strong ideational components that had both academic support and popular appeal. Economists increasingly pushed for increased competition in the regulated economy, and students of public administration and political science focused on the concentrated power of business and government in the subsystem politics that characterized economic regulation. Perhaps even more importantly, consumer advocates adopted pro-competitive reform as a remedy for the high prices consumers paid for transportation.

Fourth, Congress itself was increasingly organized to address policy problems and generate solutions by a flexible committee jurisdictional structure and a professional staff that was particularly adept at policy analysis. Ted Kennedy's use of his investigatory powers as the chair of a minor subcommittee illustrates the power of this organizational structure to attack the issue monopolies that had developed in the area of price regulation and elsewhere (Jones, Baumgartner, and Talbert 1993). Finally, three presidents—two Republicans and a Democrat—pushed for regulatory reform. Gerald Ford advocated general regulation but settled for economic regulation as achievable. Carter was in favor of deregulation when it came to prices and routes, but was firmly pro-regulatory when it came to safety and social regulation more generally. As the business lobby gained strength, Reagan, who was supportive of economic deregulation generally, began pushing for social deregulation, where he was far less successful.

The first conservative success came at the tail end of liberal successes, but it marked an important turning point. The next two major conservative policy success stories, in crime policy and tax reduction, lacked the academic underpinning of economic deregulation, but both focused on real problems sensed by citizens. What they both lacked were solutions that were not themselves fraught with severe problems.

Tax Policies

In the late 1970s, the US economy experienced, for the first time in combination, both stagnation and inflation, a phenomenon that became known as "stagflation." The best monetary policy to deploy in such a novel circumstance was a little unclear, but it seemed to most economists that inflation was the more immediate problem. As a consequence, the Federal Reserve began to increase what were already historically high interest rates.

This condition fueled a wave of economic discontent that propelled Ronald Reagan's presidential win in 1980. The Federal Reserve under Chairman Paul Volker, had set in place a monetary policy that centered on damping the inflationary spiral through increases in interest rates. This policy led to two recessions, a brief one in 1980, and a more severe one in 1981–82. The result was a rise in unemployment and stubbornly high interest rates.

But what about fiscal policy? Some professional economists were advocating large tax cuts, especially for higher income brackets, to stimulate more savings and investment under the label of "supply-side economics." This approach made sense when investment was lacking and underlying demand was strong. Extrapolating far beyond the basic economic theory, two policy entrepreneurs, economist Arthur Laffer and *Wall Street Journal* editor Jude Wanniski developed what Jones and Williams (2008, 32–36) termed the "miracle supply-side" theory. The proponents of the miracle theory claimed that tax cuts would "pay for themselves" by generating enough economic growth to off-set the costs to the taxpayer and would do so quite rapidly. Few professional economists thought that was possible, because the losses to the treasury would be too great.

Reagan came into office advocating for smaller government and tax cuts. He faced a recessionary period, one seemingly calling for economic stimulation. Classical Keynesian economics called for government spending increases and tax cuts under such circumstances. Reagan, becoming convinced of the miracle of Laffer and Wanniski's supply-side approach, engineered the Economic Recovery Act of 1981, a massive across-the-board cut of individual tax rates lowering the top rate from 70 percent to 50 percent along with large cuts for corporations.

The result was not pretty. The federal deficit ballooned, causing a sharp spike in interest rates and triggering the second phase of the "double-dip recession." Congress struggled with deficits, spending, and tax rates throughout the rest of the Reagan era and beyond. Commensurately, the number of congressional hearings on tax cuts rose significantly during Reagan's first term (see fig. 13.3). Afterward, Congress paid about as much attention to taxes as it had before, even while Republican politicians continued to claim that the miracle supply-side approach was valid, and both Presidents Bush and Trump used the rhetoric of tax cut miracles to justify their tax cuts. The Reagan tax cuts as well as those that came later led invariably to budget deficits, as surely as increases in spending did. The economic growth generated by tax cuts simply never offset the costs.

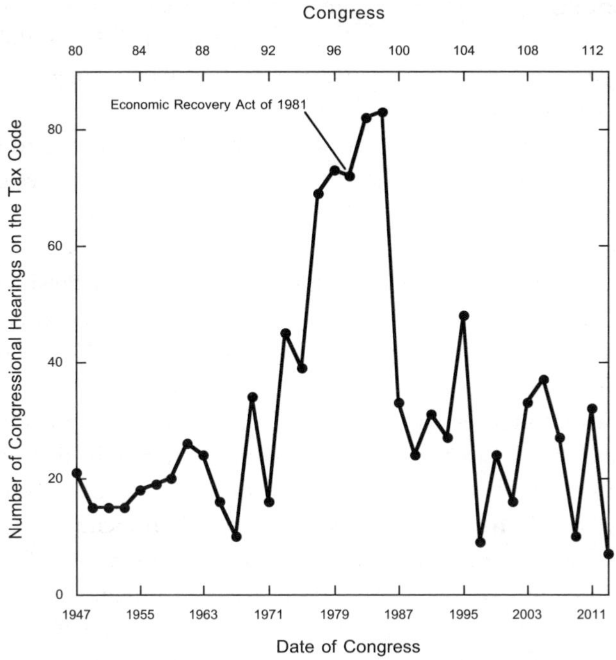

FIGURE 13.3. Congressional hearings on the tax code

In the case of deregulation, a real problem existed. An intellectual rationale for an appropriate solution developed. That rationale had support from both the right and the left, from both free enterprise economists and consumer advocates. Supporters of the existing policies proved to be weak politically—much weaker than the analyses of public administration scholars suggested. The resulting policies did have unintended consequences, as airlines consolidated, and trucking companies cut salaries and benefits by contracting with "independent" drivers, but they yielded clear consumer benefits. So the new system endured. When conservatives moved to deregulate social regulations, however, they were far less successful; those political battles continue in the regulatory trenches and in macropolitical dynamics to this day.

The Reagan tax cuts in 1981 enjoyed broad bipartisan support; the difference between the parties' final passage votes was 0.45 in the House (where 99 percent of Republicans and 54 percent of Democrats voted in favor of them) and 0.19 in the Senate (where 98 percent of Republicans and 79 percent of Democrats voted in favor of them). In Reagan's second term, the data accumulated showing that the promised nirvana of both tax cuts and balanced budgets was not being realized. In 1986, Congress, again with broad bipartisan support, enacted an important corrective to the 1981 tax cuts. The party-difference scores were even lower than they were in 1981 (0.05 in the House and 0.06 in the Senate).

Despite the bloated deficits caused by the 1981 tax cuts and the reigning bipartisan consensus on the 1986 tax reform, conservatives continued to push massive tax cuts. While the problem—slow growth and taxes that citizens saw as too high—was real, the bipartisan consensus was obliterated by the tax cut plans that Congress adopted under both Presidents G. W. Bush and Trump. The party-difference scores in the Bush tax cuts were 0.96 in the House and 0.90 in the Senate; the Trump tax cuts divided the parties at similar levels (0.95 in the House and 0.98 in the Senate).

As the additional tax cut proposals faced increasing opposition, some conservatives turned to a more cynical version of supply-side economics, initially offered by Nobelist Milton Freidman, to "starve the beast." Friedman argued that if the revenue stream were cut, then spending must follow. Californians tested this proposition in their own laboratory of democracy. In the years leading up to 1979, California's government spending had increased dramatically. In an attempt to starve the beast, thereby limiting further growth, Californians voted by a nearly two to one margin in favor of adopting Proposition 13, which reduced property tax rates by roughly 57%. This approach seemed logical and was reproduced, in spirit, with tax cuts at the federal level. In both cases, government growth was curtailed, but not enough to offset tax cuts. Benefits proved more durable than the "starve the beast" advocates imagined.

In any case, tax policies and budget politics continue to dominate our politics in a manner that would have been unimaginable during the Great Broadening. The economy was growing faster during much of that earlier period, and, just as important, a rough political consensus was reached that federal budgets ought not to get too far out of balance. The "pay-as-you-go" rules followed by Congress during the G. H. W. Bush and Clinton years attempted to reestablish this consensus, but President G. W. Bush announced that he would not abide by the arrangement and by doing so tacitly admitted that his tax cuts would not "pay for themselves."

Tax cuts lacked a serious intellectual rationale that did not also involve serious benefit cuts, and tax cuts alone had such negative side effects that they were bound to be problematic. That conservatives would continue to advocate for either the "miracle supply-side" or the "starve the beast" rationales implied that they knew they would be unable to achieve a political consensus even roughly similar to the deregulatory policy settlement. Finally, tax cuts never addressed in any meaningful sense the issue of government size. We have argued that size consists of both broadening and thickening, yet the increasingly complex tax code not addressed by the tax cut mantras actually made government broader, adding transaction costs to conducting business. Although the 1986 tax reform act did simplify the code, it was soon undermined by the tendency of both conservatives and liberals to incorporate substantive policies into the code—so-called "tax expenditures" (Faricy 2015; Mettler 2011).

In the end, Republican tax-cutting policies failed to pay for themselves, destroyed the interparty consensus on budget control, and failed to cut spending enough to offset their budgetary impacts. They did provide a new policy terrain on which new politics have been mapped—a future of large and likely unsustainable deficits and increasing inequality (this due to the structure of the Republican tax cut bills).

Crime Policies

The third and last area we examine where conservatives successfully pushed back against the liberalism of the Great Broadening is in crime policy. While crime-policy changes such as stronger punishments for drug-related crimes and mandatory minimum sentences were mostly state initiatives, the federal government certainly changed its approach to criminal justice in the 1980s. The conservative "win" on crime, however, dramatically increased the size of government—in the sense that it thickened an already involved federal government. It added to the corpus of laws on crime, it increased expenditures on crime control, and it resulted in such a huge increase in the prison population that scholars of criminal justice referred to the results as the "carceral state" (Simon 2007).

The initial broadening of the federal involvement in crime policy, traditionally mostly left to the states, occurred in the 1960s, following a period of civil disorder centering on racial injustice. These initiatives were mostly limited to grants-in-aid to states and localities to improve law enforcement capacity.

The investment in crime control addressed a serious problem. Crime in the United States began a steady rise in the 1960s. The property crime rate peaked in 1980, declined somewhat, and displayed a less prominent peak in 1991. Violent crimes peaked in 1991 as well. The rise began abruptly, rose steadily, and peaked clearly. Peaks are sharp, well-defined and unmistakable in the data series, and the declines are as steady as the rises, continuing to the present day.[3]

As the crime rate rose steadily throughout the 1970s, both Congress and state governments increased their scrutiny and policy actions in the area. The number of congressional hearings and the violent crime rate as reported by the Federal Bureau of Investigation's Uniform Crime Reporting System (2018a) are strikingly similar (see fig. 13.4). As the crime rate rose, hearings did as well, on virtually a proportional basis (the increase in hearings in the 2000s represents a focus on homeland security following the terrorist attacks on 9/11/2001).

The emergence of the crime problem did not solely account for government attention, nor did it explain the particulars of later policy action. Simultaneously, criminologists and other social scientists were in the process of rethinking the standard rehabilitative models of crime control. Substantial evidence at the time suggested that this model was not effective (Lipton, Martinson, and Wilkes 1975; IResearchNet 2018). Political scientist James Q. Wilson (1975) provided a key contribution to this process by conceiving of potential criminals as calculating the costs and benefits of engaging in

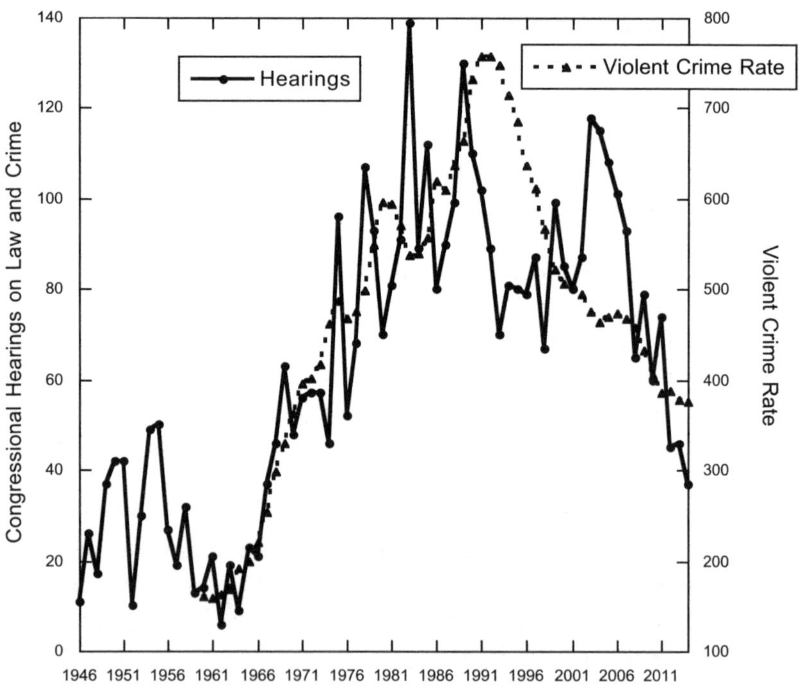

FIGURE 13.4. Congressional hearings on crime and the violent crime rate

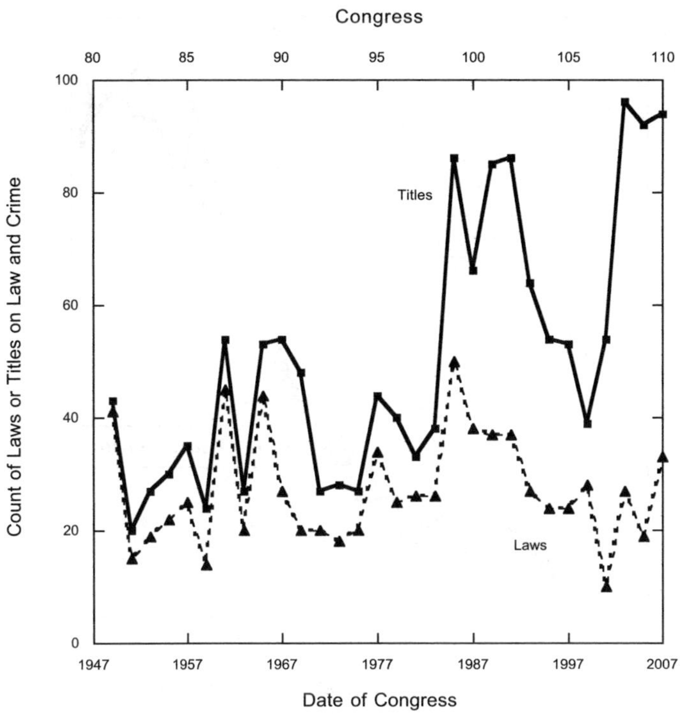

FIGURE 13.5. Public laws and titles within those laws devoted to law and crime

criminal action—calculations that were affected by social conditions. As a consequence, a number of criminologists argued, it made sense to change sentencing from a system based on reforming the criminal to emphasizing the punishment part of the criminal's cost-benefit calculations.

This intense scrutiny led to important policy action (see fig. 13.5). The major act of the period was the Comprehensive Crime Control Act of 1984, which achieved some level of support in both parties (party difference score of 0.63 in the House).[4] The act implemented the laudable goal of making federal sentences more uniform across judges and jurisdictions. By establishing the US Sentencing Commission, the act eliminated federal parole. In time, Congress enacted mandatory minimum sentences for many drug crimes and some other crimes as well.

This action, also taken up by state governments, increased the prison population greatly in a very short period of time (see fig. 13.6).[5] The Congressional Budget Authority for justice administration grew exponentially,

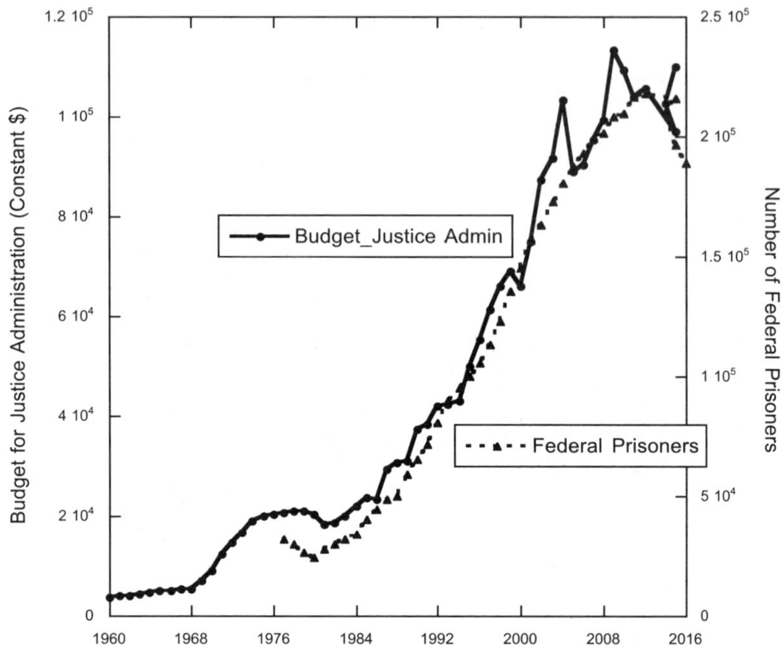

FIGURE 13.6. Congressional Budget Authority for justice administration and the number of federal prisoners

as did the federal prison population. The correlation of the two series is 0.99, and fitting an exponential curve to each series from 1960 to 2008 yields goodness of fit correlations at more than 0.98 for each variable. The "tough on crime" policies enacted in the early 1980s generated a much more intrusive federal government, thickening what was a weak involvement into a much more intensive role in the US criminal justice system. Budget commitments skyrocketed; the budget for justice administration increased 4.5 times from 1986 to 2004.

Much of the increase was due to Congress's intense interest in illegal drugs. Hearings on illicit drugs spiked from the mid-1980s to the late 1980s (see fig. 13.7). This scrutiny led to major changes in sentencing for drug-related offenses, as Congress increased the severity of punishment for possession and distribution of illegal drugs. Most of the mandatory minimum sentences that Congress imposed were for drug-related crimes.

One of the major justifications for the imposition of harsh sentences for drug crimes was that drug use led to more severe crimes. And indeed the

Bureau of Justice Statistics (1994) reported during the period that drug users were more likely to commit crimes than non–drug users. Yet arresting drug users because they have a higher probability of committing more severe crimes took the focus off violent crime and placed it on illegal drug users, who may not ever have gone on to commit other crimes. As late as 2012, 52 percent of federal prisoners were incarcerated for drug offenses; by 2018 more than 46 percent still were (Bureau of Justice Statistics 2015; Federal Bureau of Prisons 2018). Most of the prisoners incarcerated for drug crimes were convicted of trafficking (Bureau of Justice Statistics 2015), a serious crime in itself, but the questionable use of mandatory sentences meant that a high proportion of federal prisoners were serving such severe sentences with no possibility of parole. A study by the Pew Charitable Trusts (2015) reported that the average prison sentence for federal prisoners more than doubled between 1988 and 2012. Because mandatory minimums so severely affected drug crimes, sentences for inmates convicted of those crimes jumped from less than two years to more than five.

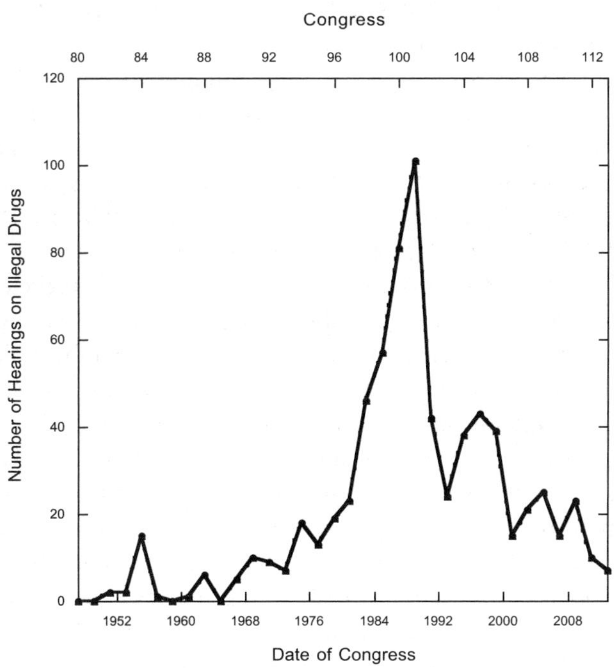

FIGURE 13.7. Congressional hearings centering on illegal drugs

The general consensus among criminologists is that, while punishment does have a deterrent effect, certainty of punishment is more important than severity. "Criminological research over several decades and in various nations generally concludes that enhancing the certainty of punishment produces a stronger deterrent effect than increasing the severity of punishment" (Wright 2010, 4). Severe sentences, which add greatly to the economic costs, have not been shown to reduce recidivism.

The governmental response to the increase in crime in the United States is a classic *policy bubble,* in which a real problem receives a disproportionate response by government, leading to a vast overinvestment in the policy (Jones, Thomas, and Wolfe 2014). Unlike economic bubbles, policy bubbles tend to be much stickier, with self-sustaining policy investment continuing far beyond the peak period of the problem. Property crimes peaked in the United States in 1980; violent crimes in 1991. Both rates have steadily declined since. Yet the number of federal prisoners did not decline until 2014, and the United States today incarcerates a higher proportion of its population than any other nation in the world (Wamsley 2016; Sentencing Project 2018).

In sum, federal crime policy shifted from a rehabilitation frame to a deterrence frame as a serious rise in the crime rate took place. This shift was in great part led by social scientists, such as James Q. Wilson, along with various advocacy groups and conservative think tanks. In the 1980s, conservatives succeeded in imposing a severe punishment system centering on both detection (more criminals were sent to prison after 1988) and severity (prison sentences increased due to mandatory minimums and the elimination of parole). Both parties saw the problem similarly, and Democrats joined Republicans in the "tough on crime" rhetoric.

The result was paradoxical. Expenditures on prisons skyrocketed at both state and federal levels. As the number of prisoners increased, the number of innocents in prison increased (even if the proportion of mistakes stayed constant). Government grew much thicker through both annual budgets and through the establishment of new correctional facilities. It became more intrusive in the lives of citizens by increasing police presence and extending prison sentences. These policies fell much more heavily on minority and poor communities, and this is particularly true for drug use policies. While blacks are slightly less likely than whites to use marijuana, they suffer arrest rates that are three to four times higher (Edwards, Bunting, and Garcia 2013). This is a picture-perfect example of Wildavsky's (1979) notion of policy causing further policy problems, leading to calls for addressing the new problems through policy action.

Conservative Successes and the New Policy Terrain

We have examined three conservative success stories in the reaction to the Great Broadening. They reveal three distinct patterns. The first, deregulation, was characterized by a strong intellectual foundation offered by both economists promoting price deregulation and political scientists promoting governance reforms. Congressional Democrats joined Republicans in the deregulatory effort, regulators adopted a pro-competitive stance, and Presidents Ford and Carter strongly advocated the deregulatory case. The result was a grand political coalition that destroyed the policy monopolies supported by regulated industries and their unions (Jones, Baumgartner, and Talbert 1993). The deregulation of prices was not only successful during the period just following the peak of the Great Broadening, but the trend continued far beyond. In the 2008 election campaign, Brookings Institution's Robert Crandall (2008) issued a position paper assessing price deregulation and advocating further deregulatory action.

Yet there were unrecognized consequences to these actions. Great turbulence in the airline industry, in particular, led to airline consolidation. Price-fixing agreements among the airlines and barriers to entry for new airlines limited competition and acted to raise consumer prices (General Accounting Office 1996). Transportation unions, particularly the once-powerful Teamsters, lost leverage relative to trucking companies, leading to severe declines in the wages of truck drivers and other workers in the transportation industry.

The movement did not succeed completely. Republicans advocated further deregulation in the spheres of environmental and product safety, but they were far less successful. Democrats opposed this type of deregulation, and such "social" regulation, as it was termed at the time, remains a matter of great political contention to this day.

The second conservative success story was tax cuts. The Reagan tax cuts and the later ones by G. W. Bush and Trump, were premised on faulty intellectual foundations. They never "paid for themselves," as miracle supply-siders claimed they would, nor did they force the entitlement reforms dreamed of by those who would "starve the beast." Nor is it certain that these cuts led to the claimed increments in growth envisioned by the more serious supply-side advocates.

The results were devastating to the country's balance sheet. With the continual tax cuts and the repeated failures to bring expenditures in line with the cuts, structural deficits increased. This issue still plagues the federal government today, as the Congressional Budget Office recently projected trillion-dollar deficits as a consequence of the Republicans' Tax Cut and Jobs Act of 2017 and the 2018 Consolidated Appropriations Act, which increased both domestic and military spending.

Finally, most of the tax bills passed during the Reagan, G. W. Bush, and Trump administrations have broadened the reach of government by adding increased complexity to the tax code. The clear exception to this increased complexity of the tax code was the Tax Reform Act of 1986, a model of bipartisan cooperation that failed to hold as partisan polarization increased.

The last conservative success, the crime-control movement of the Reagan and subsequent administrations boasted strong scholarly support for policies that emphasized deterrence. It addressed a problem that the public thought was real, and it resulted in strong congressional action. Republicans led, but Democrats, in control of Congress when the major act of the period was passed, enthusiastically joined the fray, with but a few dissenting voices. The result was a vast overinvestment in a set of overly severe crime policies that had devastating effects on lives and communities. Only today is this policy bubble being slowly reduced, as a bipartisan consensus has emerged to address the overspending and unwarranted consequences.

Conservative successes, whether they limited government (as in the case of deregulation) or thickened it (as in the case of crime policies) constructed a new policy terrain on which political contests occur. Conservative political actors often fall into the comfortable language of "big intrusive government," while liberals defend government as promoting fairness to the less fortunate. Yet this language is obsolete, and has been since the waning of the Great Broadening. Liberals demand less government in many cases, including the regulation of gay marriage, abortions, and spending on the military. Conservatives gleefully increase government's role in policing and in enforcing morality.

More subtly, the conservative counter-reaction led to a shift in the terms of the political debate. In their quest to "starve the beast," conservatives also moved the arena of political disagreement away from both broadening and thickening by opening a new front: whether government should perform public functions or whether private contractors should do so. Conservatives advocating such devices have, in effect, thrown in the towel on debates about the size of government and moved to get a piece of the action. Mostly the contracting and privatization initiatives have yielded, at best, mixed results, with no clear benefits to taxpayers or consumers of services. Both indicate surrenders on government intrusion, moving rather to arguments about how to deliver services, not whether those services should be delivered.

The result has been a complex and confusing system of delivery with high transaction costs but a number of adaptive elements. To take a major case, health care, occupying a sixth of the economic product of the United States, is a mixed public-private system of provision, and delivery is well-established and continues to be modified. It generates great inequalities in care, a panoply of rules and regulations on the government finance side, and massive costs relative to other developed countries. Privatization has not led to less government, but it does cause a different form to emerge—one based on government payments and accompanying rules, regulations, and complex financial arrangements.

FOURTEEN

Extreme Events, Feedback Policy-Making, and American Politics

From roughly the 1960s through the 1970s, the federal government began addressing public-policy issues that had previously been confined to civil society or state and local governments. This intense burst in the scope of activity, which we have called the Great Broadening, cannot convincingly be explained by the typical dynamics of politics, such as elections or party control of Congress. Social movements had an outsized influence on the nature and sequencing of the public debate that led to the Great Broadening. During the period, causal processes worked differently than they had previously done or would do afterward. Within this period, feedback effects intensified, a series of rapid punctuated equilibria in policy subsystems occurred, and the legislative parties forged more cooperative arrangements than before or afterward.

Whether we view this period as part of an ongoing political process or a single large-scale event, it transformed how the government operated. Not only did the Great Broadening change the manner in which Congress wrote, debated, and passed legislation, but it also changed Congress's basic function from legislating to conducting oversight. The sequencing of these events points to party polarization and a concentrated interest-group environment as consequences of the Great Broadening rather than as causes of it. As time proceeded, some of the effects of the Great Broadening waned as more contemporary factors gained relative importance in the causal stream. Yet even these effects did not completely disappear; they continue to affect our politics by setting the terrain for future political action.

In this conclusion we first suggest that the chain of causation from the Great Broadening extends to mass politics. Clearly, elites polarized before masses; in particular, our legislative parties polarized as a consequence of the rapid expansion in the scope of the federal government's policy portfolio.

This pattern of elite interaction was transmitted over time to mass publics. Then we summarize the major findings of the book, putting them in a perspective in which they can illuminate how our current politics are practiced. Finally, we offer some reasoned inferences about whether similar processes affected other Western democracies and about the extent of the influence of the Great Broadening on today's politics.

Inside Out? Electoral Connections

The late Nelson Polsby, an astute observer of the American political system—and of American political science—once recounted the following anecdote to one of the authors. At an American Political Science Association panel at the very height of the visibility of the National Election Studies (NES) surveys, Warren Miller was making a presentation on some of NES's recent findings. Miller was a giant in the field, not only as a scholar but also a masterful academic entrepreneur. He offered new findings on the nature of opinions and attitudes in the mass public, doubtless commenting on changes in partisan identification and other such matters. Then came a question from the audience—E. E. Schattschneider asked Miller, "Warren, why do you want to focus on the audience when the action is on the stage?"

That was classic Schattschneider, who saw politics as a contest among elites who only occasionally expanded the conflict to new groups of participants in an effort to score political victories. Communication for the most part was a one-way street from elites to the masses that was only trod when the latter was needed to resolve a political disagreement. Today, those viewing politics from a conflict-expansion perspective are more likely to see a system in which the masses are for the most part drawn in by elites, but admit a more direct role as well.

In all political systems, political elites—those holding formal governmental positions, along with activists, lobbyists, and political party leaders—are actors on the stage, and mass publics are the audience. Democracies are distinguished by their institutional and informal connections between the masses and elites, and the connections go both ways. That is, mass publics can exert influence on political leaders in a variety of ways, both through elections, which act to select office-holding elites, and during inter-election periods through various informal and formal devices—organizing, communicating directly to elites, and protesting in the streets, to name but a few.

But causation can go the other way as well. Elites communicate to masses, and that action can be very powerful. And mass publics can observe the activities of elites and tailor their political actions accordingly. These simple, dyadic relationships obviously underestimate the network of variables that affect electoral alignment, but it emphasizes the point that how government operates affects the electorate, and it does so beyond the effects of policy alone.

It is clear that polarization in the electorate did not cause polarization in Congress. Studies reported by the Pew Research Center (2014) show that as late as 2004 the American public was not particularly polarized, which was measured as the percentage of party identifiers "who expressed consistently liberal or conservative opinions." Congress was polarized long before then (Theriault 2008). Congress surely polarized because of electoral changes that moved many southerners toward the Republican Party, but, according to Pew, the masses did not polarize in any dramatic way until well into the 2000s. The sequencing of these trends, according to our analysis in chapters 10, 11, and 13, suggests that the legislative polarization process was influenced by the conservative counter-reaction to the Great Broadening.

That means that elite polarization did not immediately cause polarization in the electorate. As a consequence, it is difficult to show definitively that policy broadening was a cause of polarization in the electorate. Nevertheless, it is well within the realm of possibilities that electoral tribalism today had its roots in elite polarization that itself came about because of the Great Broadening and the conservative counter-mobilization against it.

While this inference includes a considerable speculative argument, the sequential ordering of events supports it. Moreover, various pieces of suggestive evidence are available. US political parties are still locked in arguments about the "size" of government. As we've shown, this fight is most likely related to broadening rather than spending or even thickening, and the argument follows the contours established forty years ago. Had the Great Broadening either been incorporated fully into the political system or vanquished by its conservative opponents, these terms of debate would have disappeared. Even stranger, the debate about the size of government has become divorced from the older debates about the proper roles of civil and civic societies. We see no trace of the attempts to forge proper yet distinct roles for government and civil society that were so common before the Great Broadening. The size of the public sphere is mostly debated without reference to civil society, and it is deeply influenced by the tendency of government today to do much of its business through contracts and grants to service providers.

As we move from effects of even a large-scale event such as the Great Broadening, causal connections become weaker, as they are mediated by intervening processes and by the addition of other factors that influence the present state of affairs. Nevertheless they remain visible through the fog of intervening time and indeed continue to influence the terms of today's political debates.

General Effects of the Great Broadening

Today's political contests are fought on a landscape essentially constructed during the Great Broadening. Without federal intervention in education, could citizens even fight about federal support for charter schools? With no civil rights revolution, would gay rights be a federal issue? How much would climate change be debated if the environmental programs of the Nixon Administration had not been established? Would highway safety be a government function without the consumer rights movement? We, of course, cannot rewind the clock to compare trends with and without the Great Broadening, but the vast number of issues crossing the legitimacy barrier certainly set the stage for the later thickening of the federal government. This fundamental but virtually overlooked facet of today's politics warps current understandings of politics and even the very methodologies we use to study it. We struggle to grasp what goes on right now without appreciating how current dynamics reflect past policy settlements.

In this book, we make the plausible claim that the agenda expansion of the 1960s and 1970s had powerful but generally unrecognized effects on politics then and, perhaps even more so, on politics today. The growth in the size of government was not particularly impressive compared to the heated rhetoric about it; furthermore, the intensity of the vitriolic rhetoric is not commensurate with the rather modest increase in its size. Instead, if we assess the growth of government as the number of issues into which government moved into during this period, then the effect is both vast and in some respects permanent. While government did thicken, it broadened so much more.

We found two likely effects of this expansion. The first includes direct consequences of the Great Broadening, on the terrain of which future political battles are to be fought (Hacker and Pierson 2014). Changes in the interest-group system, particularly its startling growth following the Great Broadening; the shift of Congress from a lawmaking to an oversight body, and the dramatic increase in the average length of laws involve transformations of the American political system that affect future political contests. Moreover, it is difficult to construct an account of these changes that does *not* incorporate the Great Broadening—the standard contemporary political forces of parties, elections, and media cannot do the job by themselves. Yet the limited room for lawmaking surely has changed incentives for members of Congress, especially for committee chairs and ranking members (Lewallen 2017). Interest groups, once major forces for change (Grossmann 2014), have become so dense in Washington that they are mostly involved in preventing action (Baumgartner et al. 2014; Drutman 2015).

The second effect is a counteracting one. The conservative movement surely was energized by what many saw as the excesses of the 1960s and 1970s. And surely the increases in polarization are not completely exogenous to these changes. Indeed we show that during the early period of partisan realignment, Southern Republicans did not differ markedly in ideology from their Northern counterparts. Realignment can proceed without polarization and did so throughout most of the 1970s. The major increases in polarization happened after the end of the Great Broadening—though contemporary dynamics did play a dominant role as the increases in polarization became self-sustaining.

Skeptics will doubtless object that the claim that the Great Broadening caused all these downstream effects is overblown and that contemporary dynamics, such as unified government, changes in the partisan alignments of Southern constituencies, and the media environment all contributed to these effects. And we answer "of course"—our primary aim is not to eliminate consideration of these matters, but to highlight the obvious but ignored feedback effects of agenda expansion on contemporary policy-making. The effects of agenda expansion must certainly be filtered through these variables. Moreover, contemporary policy-making is built on the Great Broadening, basically altering the terrain as politics proceeds.

Politics and policy-making are dynamic, complex systems with interlocking, nonlinear relations among variables and the multiple feedback loops. A major implication of this perspective is that any change can become autocatalytic—self-reinforcing without the intervention of outside forces—and hence disconnected from the immediate cause of the change (Padgett and Powell 2012), which surely happened in the case of the conservative reaction to the Great Broadening. We have little doubt that without the Great Broadening, the conservative mobilization would have been much harder to kick off and sustain itself. Yet certainly the movement's momentum today is considerably disconnected from the initial cause, as electoral primary systems and the partisan media fuel the passions of the movement.

Arcs and Plateaus

The Great Broadening was an enormous burst of energy directed at government, resulting in increases in numerous relevant variables assessing policy activity. Some of those variables reached a plateau and continued along the top of the plateau with some variation until the end of our measurement. The rest of our indicators of policy activity resemble an arc. Activity reached the same peak, remained there only briefly, and subsequently declined—sometimes quite dramatically.

The plateau pattern is a trace that indicates a punctuated equilibrium resulting in path-dependency in which the current path of policy activity is difficult to change. Actors incur high costs in doing so, constrained by new rules and the anticipated reactions of other actors, but limited adjustments are clearly possible. The arc represents the surge and decline expected when opposing forces counter-mobilize before the plateau pattern of path-dependency can emerge. We cannot conclude with certainty that the characteristic arc that we observed in so many different circumstances was a result of the conservative counter-reaction. But we have assembled considerable qualitative and some quantitative evidence that the arc was more than just a waning of interest on the part of mobilized supporters. It involved counter-mobilization on the part of conservatives.

Conservatives were successful in stopping the self-reinforcing dynamic of the Great Broadening, but at the cost of accepting many of its effects, or at least being unable to change them. These new programs required massive increases in government agencies to implement the various aspects of the Great Broadening and, subsequently, fostered new constituencies who benefitted from them. Both the agencies and the constituencies then organized for political action or to defend the status quo against reformers hoping to dial back these programs. This new political reality led to later transformations of our governing mechanisms, including Congress and our political parties (the subjects of chapters 8, 9, and 10), the regulatory state (discussed in chapter 11), the interest-group system (covered in chapter 12), and the very nature of electoral politics (noted above).

The counter-mobilization of opponents of change may be underestimated in the historical institutionalist perspective. The emphasis in those accounts has tended toward a focus on the plateau pattern, with a burst of change resulting in a new equilibrium in the whole political system. On the other hand, cycle theories of political change have stressed the petering-out of reform movements and a counter-mobilization by the forces supporting the status quo, ignoring the plateau pattern that signifies path dependency.

Methodology

To verify our claims, we employed a new approach, which we termed *plausibility analysis*. That term implies that we are able to ascertain the causal sequencing of events, but we cannot definitively nail down causation. In some circles, this deficiency is viewed as a terrible failing. We demur. The most stringent forms of causal analyses require completely isolated systems that are decoupled completely from the context in which they occur. This decoupling can be accomplished through careful experimentation, which is not possible under most circumstances in political science and historical studies. An alternative is complete modeling of an embedded system. That can be extraordinarily difficult when variables interact in complex systems and when those systems can vary across time. A premiere example of this is the different characters of causal processes during and after the Great Broadening.

Such difficulty does not mean that, as social scientists, we should either surrender to solely anecdotal evidence or confine our analyses to those parts of a complex system that are amenable to precise causal analysis. But we need to move to a higher level of empirical rigor in historical studies. So in addition to establishing causal ordering, we add other constraints—robustness tests of what we claim. First, we require a historical narrative consistent with the causal ordering we ascertain. That allows a somewhat stronger inference, but it falls short of today's causal inference perspective. Second, we show similar patterns across different time series. The more we can show that the data series follow one or the other of the two fundamental patterns, the stronger our belief in the causal mechanisms we postulate.

This latter process requires consistent and reliable measurement of policy trends across extended periods of time. Here the Policy Agendas Project was invaluable. We believe that our study represents the full flowering of that project. The data today span some seventy years, enough to trace the Great Broadening from its modest beginnings through its intense peak and to its decline. The data from that project also allow us to follow the long-run historical traces of the Great Broadening on the American political system. Because of the nature of our enterprise, we use graphical and visual approaches, relying less on statistical model-building and testing. There is surely a place for these more sophisticated models, but not until the overall terrain is mapped.

Cumulative Addition of Issues

Our analyses show that the federal government added issues to the policy-making agenda cumulatively during the Great Broadening. Issues were not shuffled on and off as attention to them waxed and waned; rather, they continued to occupy the time and energy of policy-makers as they adjusted governmental responses to those issues. Party platforms displayed a similar cumulative pattern of addressing issues. As the broadening waned, some issues where pushed off the agenda on a last-in, first-out basis. We cannot determine with any precision how policy-makers addressed issues across time, because we were not able to assess the directionality of the issues. It may be that issues were sequenced, such that each new policy decision aggregated in one direction (Segal 2016; Shpaizman 2014; 2017), most likely because of the subsequent thickening of statutes and budgets in the issues that had been raised and debated during the broadening period. Nevertheless, it is possible that the policy measures debated by Congress sometimes reduced government commitment to the policy. From the overall patterns we detected, both occurred, depending on the issue and the political circumstances, but the dominant force was toward more government, but with reduced fervor as time proceeded. In any case, few issues moved in and out of the purview of government. Once they breached Wilson's legitimacy barrier, they generally remained on the agenda.

Causes of the Great Broadening

We found that time trends of our measures of broadening that follow the horseshoe pattern follow similar time traces of the standard causes proposed by political scientists as critical to policy change in democracies—elections, public opinion, and partisan control of government. But we find a consistent inconsistency—the effects don't seem to occur as disjunctures when one party wins a big electoral victory or captures control of government. Contemporaneous dynamics do not show up in the manner predicted by the standard models. Nonetheless, these political variables seem to have effects on the velocity of change, accelerating and decelerating the curves that describe the broadening process.

It is also clear from our work that the standard political variables do not explain the sequencing of issues as they reach the federal agenda. Social movement activists motivated by creedal passions infused the system with energy, focus, and a comprehensive view across agencies and programs. In particular, we found distinct roles for liberal social movements in the sequencing of the issue components of the Great Broadening—from civil rights to environmentalism, consumer safety, and women's rights. Plus we found strong evidence of a counter-mobilization of business interests that occurred in reaction to the liberal social movements, giving specific quantitative evidence to a thesis argued by other scholars.

Causation within the Vortex of the Great Broadening Differed from the Stability that Followed

The Great Broadening exerted a strong magnetic influence on the forces that normally structure politics. The key was the sudden ascension of many new issues clamoring for policy action virtually simultaneously. The old structures of federal intervention on economic policy issues (established by the New Deal) and international affairs (required by the Cold War), along with the implicit understanding that race relations in the South were not to be questioned, all collapsed within a handful of years.

Not only were the old structures destroyed, the opening created by this collapse encouraged activists to urge a panoply of new issues on the federal government for resolution. These issues included environmentalism, women's rights, and consumer safety, along with other, less organized issues. Issues previously settled within relatively decoupled policy subsystems were swept up into the macropolitical debate because social movements spanned these areas. Civil rights activists raised not just denial of voting rights to minorities and the legal segregation of schools and public facilities in many states, but activist policies from the New Deal that maintained discrimination, such as veterans' benefits and agricultural policies (Katznelson 2005). Civil rights activists targeted other matters, such as housing and segregated restaurants and lunch counters, where segregation was enforced more by custom than law. Addressing the problem required a comprehensive approach, one that spanned policy subsystems.

Environmentalism, consumer safety, and (to a lesser extent) women's rights also spanned policy subsystems designed to address specific industries. Indeed, it is in the very nature of social movements to find unity in the causes of the problem; consumer safety did not just address automobiles, but a whole host of products and services. Out of necessity, policy subsystems evolved into networks of actors (Heclo 1978; Meier 1985). This broadening of networks across policy subsystems resulted in a series of punctuated equilibria (Baumgartner and Jones 2009; Padgett and Powell 2012) that led to a transformation of policy-making, of the structures within which policy-making occurs, and of the political system more broadly. Baumgartner and Jones (2009, 6) wrote that "policy subsystems are continually being created and destroyed in American politics," but it is clear in hindsight that destruction or radical change in subsystems based on rate regulation of trucking, railroads, airlines, and energy had already begun to fade (but financial deregulation was still on the horizon). A better description of policy-subsystem development would be a burst of destruction and creation during the Great Broadening and immediately thereafter, and a quieter period following.

New issues appeared on the formal policy agenda rapidly over a short period of time in a manner not obviously connected to the typical dynamics of politics, such as elections or party control of Congress. Social movements had an outsized influence on the nature and sequencing of the public debate, and hence on the appearance of issues on the formal agenda. Causal processes differed within the Great Broadening from those established in the wake of the period. Within the period, feedback effects intensified, a series of rapid punctuated equilibria in policy subsystems occurred, and the legislative parties forged more cooperative arrangements than before and afterward.

Congress: Lawmaking during the Great Broadening, Oversight After

During the Great Broadening, Congress passed many landmark statutes, but passed fewer afterward. It created many agencies and programs during the broadening period, but did so with much less frequency afterward. Perhaps most striking is Congress's shift from using the hearings process predominantly to legislate to using it almost exclusively for oversight.

Congress was experiencing other major changes, many of which were due to the expanding governmental agenda. During the Great Broadening, Congress decentralized, giving increased power to subcommittees. While congressional scholars properly viewed this as a response to the conservative, mostly Southern Democratic, oligarchic committee chairs, it was also a device to allow increased parallel processing of the increasing number of issues requiring congressional attention. Proponents saw it as an energizing period, full of opportunities to use government to address social wrongs. It was also a period of commitment to analytical approaches to public policy. Under Comptroller General Elmer Stats, the General Accounting Office focused increasingly on policy analysis. Under the Legislative Reorganization Act of 1970, the Congressional Research Service (formerly the Legislative Reference Service, renamed in the act) added analytical capacity. Congress added new analytical agencies—the Office of Technology Assessment in 1972 (dismantled in 1995), and the Congressional Budget Office in 1975. Critics saw a chaotic, undisciplined, and uncoordinated public policy response that confused lines of authority. They advocated for centralized and disciplined legislative parties.

That is what these critics got. Centralization began during the 1980s, but accelerated after Republicans took control of Congress in 1995. Democratic control of the House from 2007 to 2011 maintained this centralization, and it continued apace afterward. More centralized, disciplined parties led to a shift to centrally developed laws, undermining the roles of committee chairs in the development of legislation. These developments, in turn, encouraged committees to turn increasingly to oversight as floor time, rigidly controlled by the speaker, became limited (Lewallen 2017). Interestingly, as the Republican Party developed a factional politics after the 2010 election, the centralized pattern of the development of legislation continued. Centralization led to more oversight but a lessening of the previous commitment to analysis in the forging of legislation. It also led to hearings that were more partisan and one-sided in their information-processing roles (Lewallen, Theriault, and Jones 2016).

Many of these developments are far downstream from the Great Broadening, and it would be folly to attribute too much of the institutional development of the legislative branch today directly to it. But it would be a mistake not to recognize the fundamental role of the dramatic increase in the scope of the governmental agenda in the 1960s and 1970s in the subsequent development of the institution. In particular, we point to the rapid development of the capacity of policy analysis to cope with the flood of new issues during the relatively bipartisan era of the 1970s, and its decline as the reactions to the Great Broadening developed.

Thickening Follows Broadening

We distinguished the addition of new issues to government's portfolio of policies from the addition of more activities (or increasing their intensity) within both the old and newly added issues. The former we termed *broadening*; the latter, *thickening*. This thickening can be traced in a number of ways, the most obvious being funding growth in established functions. But we explored other avenues as well. As the broadening proceeded, government added competencies. Congress expanded its analytical capacity and created new agencies and programs to implement the mandates established by a broadened legal code (see chapters 3 and 4). Funding categories expanded as the policy-making agenda increased in scope. The corpus of US law first broadened and then thickened. We assessed these processes by looking both at the issue content of statutes and of titles within statutes. The broadening process added new issues, assessed by the adoption of new Policy Agendas Project subtopics. The thickening process built on both the established and new issues, but we found more thickening in the freshly established issues (see chapter 8). This thickening was a consequence of attempts to adjust mistakes in the new laws, to extend them incrementally, and to reverse some of their provisions. Great thickening also occurred when Republicans adopted the cause of bigger government, as was the case in crime control, where Democrats joined in as partners (chapter 13).

Weak Political Polarization during the Great Broadening, Strong Polarization Afterward

Following the Great Depression, the New Deal, World War II, and the Cold War, the parties' voting records had converged more than at any point after the founding of the Republican Party. Even as the government's agenda began to expand, party divergence was minimal. Why didn't the parties begin polarizing, given the explosion in the scope of the agenda? Our research supports the thesis that the issues bombarding Congress were hard to categorize within the existing conflict structure. That structure centered on economics and federalism: how much should the federal government intervene in economic affairs, and how much should be left up to the states? Some of the new issues, particularly civil rights, had been deliberately structured out of politics. As these issues emerged as serious contenders for attention, they raised complex trade-offs. Pro-business Republicans faced the choice of fighting discrimination versus defending property rights in the Civil Rights Act of 1964. It was also obvious that federalism had failed to solve what was clearly a severe moral problem, so conservatives faced the national-local trade-off as well.

Other choices brought up trade-offs that were similar, if not as intense. Protecting the environment versus traditional prerogatives of business. Ensuring the safety of consumers versus the freedom of business to make decisions regarding products. Promoting the movement of women into larger economic roles versus the demands imposed by the still-common large families for traditional structures to manage the home.

In the face of these challenges, both Democrats and Republicans had trouble figuring out just how issues were defined. What the data show is that both parties during this period were fairly evenly involved in putting new issues on the agenda. In our examination of decision-making within Congress, we found that votes on old issues (those on the agenda for some time) exhibited more of a partisan structure than votes on new ones (those joining the agenda during the Great Broadening). As these new issues worked their way through the legislative process, they enjoyed the support of both parties. If opposition arose, it came, again, from members of both parties, as was clearly true in the case of dismantling the systems of price regulation in transportation. Only after the Great Broadening did the partisanship that so dominates the system today began revealing itself.

Downstream Arms Races?

In some cases the broadening process provoked sustained reactions that cannot be called either retrenchment or path-dependent; rather, they resembled an arms race. This pattern seems particularly true in the cases of polarization and the proliferation of interest groups. The Great Broadening and its associated expansion of the regulatory state provoked the business interest groups to react, which was a central part of the counter-mobilization by conservatives. Recent scholarship on interest groups has detected a more sustained pattern of mobilization, in which different business interests mobilized in the face of mobilization by other business groups. Whether the earlier broadening process had much to do with this pattern is not at all clear, but surely it was a precondition of the much more complex interest-group environment that prevailed.

Such an arms race also developed in the increases in partisan polarization. Our increased political tribalism had its roots in the period following the peak of the Great Broadening and clearly continues to this day. Once born of differing positions on issues, today it consumes our political debate far beyond differences on issues. Indeed, some policy solutions to acknowledged problems were developed by conservatives and then adopted by pragmatic Democrats, only to be jettisoned by Republicans who saw them tainted by their association with Democrats. These policies included cap-and-trade as a technique for addressing environmental pollution, market-based insurance exchanges in health care, and pay-as-you-go rules to maintain the federal budget. In the case of crime, Democrats adopted conservative approaches and contributed to an overinvestment bubble in crime control. In the case of pollution control, Democrats adopted cap-and-trade, and Republicans responded by claiming that government should not address the problem, but should allow the private sector to conduct business as it sees fit.

Is the Great Broadening Solely a US Phenomenon?

The Great Broadening was both a massive historical trend altering the course of American politics and a set of underlying processes that interacted to generate the historical trend. On the one hand, the Great Broadening was a unique historical happening, but on the other it was a consequence of dynamic processes that could potentially happen anywhere—social changes, positive-feedback effects, spillovers from subsystem to subsystem, and a predictable push-back from political actors harmed by the cascading changes.

Was this particular combination of factors unique to the United States, or could it have also occurred in other political systems? Western democracies could be subject to the same configuration of dynamics, and because of contagion or historical developments along similar lines could have experienced them during roughly the same time period.

We have at least one case that can serve as a starting point for such an examination. The Comparative Policy Agendas Project deploys a common coding scheme, basically the one that we have used in this book, to provide a common frame of reference in examining policy change across countries. Although parliamentary systems are not always directly comparable to the government of the United States, with care we can make some judicious comparisons. Using the Danish team's data, Christoffer Green-Pederson (2011) has measured the length of plenary debate concerning four basic elements of parliamentary activity in Denmark (bills, motions, interpellations, and government accounts) to construct an index of debate activity. He measured the number of Policy Agendas subtopics used to code the debates, as well as the total length of the debates during parliamentary sessions. The number of subtopics used is not quite the same measure as our measure of broadening, but it suffices for our purposes. The length of the debate could be thought of as a rough indicator of thickening. In a manner similar to the broadening in the United States, Danish broadening expands rapidly in the 1960s and 1970s, plateaus in the mid-1980s, and drifts upward only gradually afterward. Thickening also plateaus, but it resumes its upward trend after the early 1990s (see fig. 14.1).

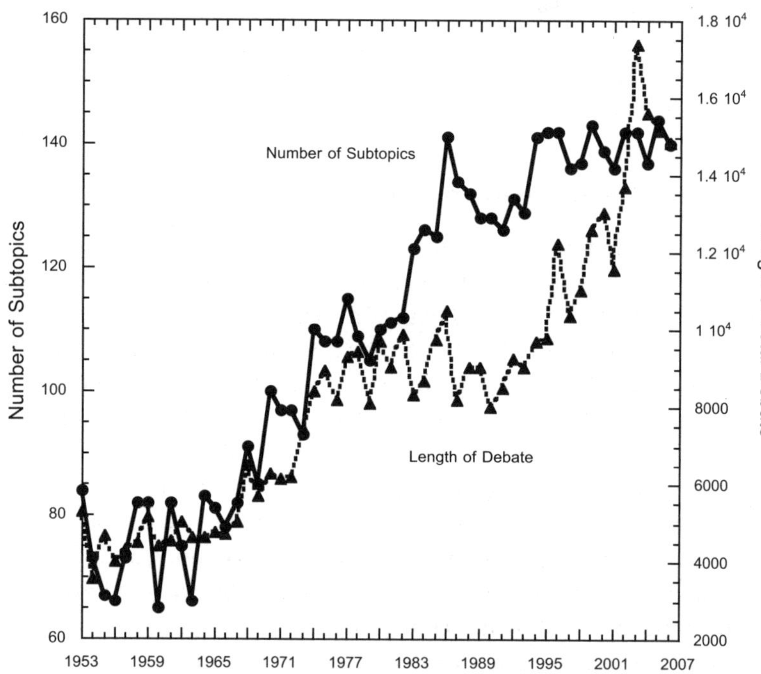

FIGURE 14.1. Number of subtopics addressed and the length of parliamentary debates in Denmark

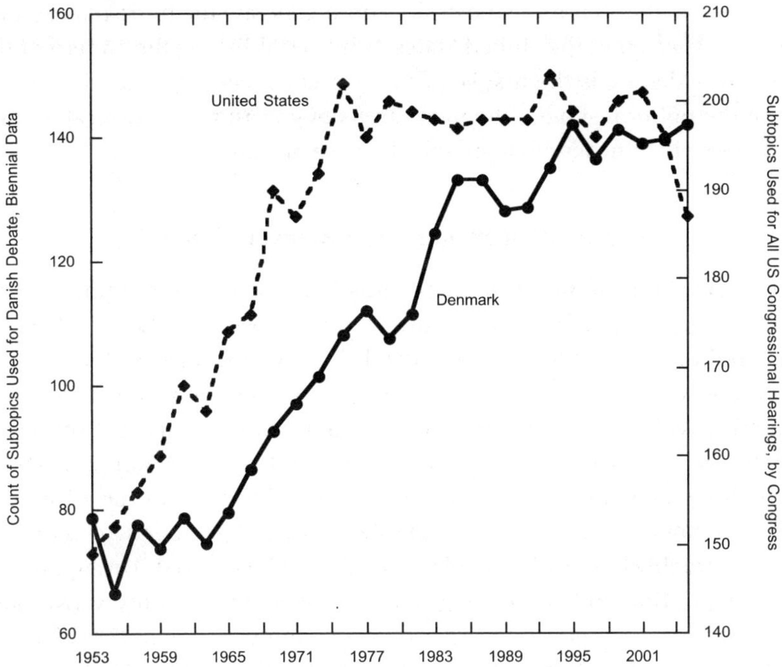

FIGURE 14.2. Number of subtopics addressed, Danish parliamentary debate, biennially, and US congressional hearings by congress

Legislative procedures in parliamentary democracies do not correspond uniformly to those used by the US Congress. Nevertheless, legislative procedures in any political system must involve the consideration of policy issues, even if they are handled somewhat differently. So the scope of issues considered may be compared across political systems with the proper data.

If we compare the number of Policy Agendas subtopics addressed in the Danish parliamentary series with the number addressed in US congressional hearings, we observe a remarkable, if rough, correspondence (see fig. 14.2). Both series experience a period of rapid growth in the scope of government. Both experience plateaus during which little changed. While the US series begins and peaks earlier than the Danish series, they both generally occur in the same period—in particular, the 1970s was a period of growth in the reach of government, while the 1990s and beyond involved consolidation.

We cannot say whether these trends are mimicked in other Western democracies beyond Denmark, as we lack comparable data for appropriate time spans. But what we have is intriguing. It suggests that similar processes are at work, and that these dynamics could generate the burst-plateau pattern we observed in the United States. While establishing the pattern of the Great Broadening is the first step, the consequences it has are dependent upon the political system, the institutions of government, political parties, and mass-elite linkages that are specific to each country.

Is the Great Broadening Relevant Today?

Surely the effects of the Great Broadening have weakened over time. Nevertheless, some major facets of the broadening period continue to affect today's politics. These effects are not trivial. The language of the 1960s politics continues today, but the content packaged by those almost archaic terms are filled with new meanings. The old arguments by conservatives about smaller, less intrusive government continue, but much of politics is about something quite different. According to many of today's conservatives, private companies ought to assume the role of providing public services, while the presumably less efficient civil service should be reduced. The arguments for privatization and contracting out run the gamut, as conservatives and business interests argue that such arrangements are more effective, efficient, and less expensive. Competition supposedly raises quality and reduces cost. Unfortunately most of these arguments have not held up well in the many evaluation studies conducted that compare public provision with private provision. Moreover, while the Hatch Act prohibits public servants from lobbying, private contractors can lobby members, who use the quid-pro-quo to finance their elections.

Today a major target of conservative groups is the Department of Veterans Affairs. The attack is two-pronged: first, claim that the VA is inefficient and cannot meet the demands of the veterans returning from Iraq and Afghanistan. Second, cut the funding of the VA or at least limit its growth to a level insufficient to meet the demand (under the guise of smaller government). Then create a new program, Veteran's Choice, requiring the VA to pay for private care for now-underserved veterans (Fandos 2017).

Interest groups have used this playbook many times over, although the targets differ. Advocates for school reform, municipal services, and the generalized contracting out of specialized services by the federal government have repeated very similar arguments in different guises. These arguments can have merit, but in most cases the benefits are vastly overstated. Study after study casts deep doubt on privatization as an effective mechanism in school reform. Charter schools provided by the private, for-profit sector have proved less effective than charters provided by nonprofit organizations.

Medicare choice plans have proved adept at adverse selection—offering services that attract the healthiest elderly. Insurance brokers compete with nonprofit organizations to help people choose health insurance plans on the Affordable Care Act insurance exchanges.

The debate about privatization rather than limitation of public service provision has become a major fault line in modern American politics. That division stems in large part from the increased federal role that was established during the Great Broadening. We need not reprise the merits of the privatization movement to establish that the terms of the debate have shifted from whether government should assume the role of service provider to what mechanisms should be employed to deliver those services. That has shifted conflict in part from partisan contests to interest-group politics, resulting in more business interests supporting a role for government than in the past. It also represents a recognition of the expanded role of government in service provision, shifting the conflict terrain from the relative roles of civil society and government to the mechanisms of delivery for those services. Moreover, it is unlikely that political conflict involving the mechanism of service provision reduces the scope of government, as contracting and privatization are no less expensive than the direct provision of services.

The new aspects of these old debates on the proper role of the federal government in the delivery of services have their roots in the Great Broadening. As we argue, Republicans initially signed on to the Great Broadening, because the increasing scope benefited their allies. As the ground shifted, the terms of the debate did as well, as conservatives began to try to put the proverbial genie back in the bottle. The Republican struggles to repeal the health care benefits provided by the Affordable Care Act (aka, Obamacare) simply underscore the difficulty of shrinking the scope of government's activity. A simple change in budgets is nothing compared to extricating the federal government from a policy area in which it has encroached.

Policy Feedback and Complex Systems

Policy feedback, with politicians, interest groups, voters, and policy entrepreneurs all reacting to past policies, is endemic to current politics. These past policy settlements provide the basic content for current debates. They interact in surprising ways with current institutional and political arrangements, often by providing new incentives for political actors. We have argued that the Great Broadening probably generated not just a policy terrain for future political battles, but actually deflected the internal causal dynamics driving the policy-making system. Until we appreciate the nonlinear and highly contingent dynamics of complex causal systems, we will consistently misestimate effects and misattribute causes in our attempts to forge a more systematic political science. We hope that our graphical and intuitive approach to these complex dynamics provides a springboard for future thought and study.

Our claims, which not infrequently run counter to the prevailing approaches, are put forward as simply plausible, not definitive. But for every claim we have made in this book, we have provided documentation in data and a plausible narrative to support that claim. We hope to be questioned on what we have asserted, but we ask that any counterclaim be held to standards that are at least as strong as those we have imposed on ourselves.

Final Thoughts

The power of this book is in giving name and context to an idea that everyone—Democrat or Republican; elected official, bureaucrat, or voter—recognizes, but few have ever seriously considered. The very contestation of ideas in politics today cannot be understood without an appreciation for how the federal government's scope grew from the late 1950s to the late 1970s. Both Democrats and Republicans propelled federal government action in areas of the law that would have been unthinkable even thirty years before. Once James Q. Wilson's (1979) legitimacy barrier had been crossed, it was and remains exceedingly difficult to withdraw government's attention from these policy areas.

It is the pervasiveness of the federal government across all facets of our economic, social, and political lives that animates today's debate between Democrats and Republicans and between liberals and conservatives. The differences between these groups on taxes and spending—and even government action and inaction—is constrained to a relatively small part of the policy space relative to the debate between the parties in the past and parties in other governments in the world.

Yet the sides of the debate perversely shift in a manner oblique to ideology and party. Republicans and conservatives supported a strong military and aggressive crime policies. Liberals argued for less government when it came to regulations on marriage or abortion and, over time, less aggressive crime policies. Facing demands concerning information relevant to national security, libertarians and liberals, but not conservatives, supported less intrusive government. Both supported veterans' benefits, but conservatives wanted the private sector to deliver them. During the Great Broadening, conservatives and liberals both attacked price regulation. The federal government broadened in the end because a part of every political philosophy desired it, while a part did not.

The Great Broadening triggered the Great Debate: What is the proper reaction to the federal government's encroachment on so many facets of our lives? Our aim in this book has been to define the Great Broadening and to suggest some causes of it, but mostly to delineate its consequences, which continue to persist even today. Most importantly, the Great Broadening altered the policy terrain, so that most political arguments about what the government is doing involve the mechanisms of service delivery, not the scope of government. We hope that we have provided a context for a more meaningful debate about politics in the United States—both the politics of the last fifty years and the politics of the next fifty.

NOTES

CHAPTER ONE

1. Data series are from the Policy Agendas Project (https://www.comparativeagendas.net). The arcs are statistically fitted quadratic curves. The goodness of fit correlation between the *NYT* arc and the data is 0.90; for the *CQ* arc, it is 0.71. The numbers for the *New York Times* are estimates based on a sample of articles; those for the *Congressional Quarterly* are direct counts of articles in the *CQ Almanac*.
2. Since then, several other scholars have developed other estimation techniques. As we show in chapter 3, these approaches all reach similar conclusions about the lawmaking surge. Mayhew continued his estimates though the 113th Congress, presenting them on his website, but we limited figure 1.1 to the 102nd Congress. The later part of the series levels out and never rises to the levels of the lawmaking surge.
3. If we model laws as a linear equation with a positive slope to describe the expansionary forces, and laws as a linear equation with a negative slope to represent the resisting forces, and multiply these equations together to capture their interacting effects on lawmaking, we get a quadratic equation of the form $Y = a + bX + cX^2$, with $b > 0$ and $c < 0$. As can be seen in the figures, the quadratic actually underestimates the lawmaking surge. The correlations between the arc and the actual data points are 0.84 for figure 1.2 and 0.74 for figure 1.3.
4. One does not really require a histogram to see the extreme events in the lawmaking case—it is a simple but important illustration of a process. In the stochastic budget studies, many budget series are combined, resulting in a more stable distribution. This lowers the probability of confusing an error in measurement or a meaningless outlier with major budget change.

CHAPTER TWO

1. Precise cut-points are somewhat difficult to specify, as we demonstrate in chapter 4, where we provide more detailed analysis. That analysis shows that the patterns are clear, even if the specific cut-points are a little fuzzy.
2. In the study of urban politics, under the guidance of Clarence Stone (1980, 1988, 1989), the stratificationist perspective was revived, modified, and given an observational base.

CHAPTER THREE

1. The Policy Agendas coding system was established long after the peak of the Great Broadening, in the 1990s, so the coding system cannot be responsible for an artificial peak. Moreover, codes are added when new issues emerge.
2. See http://campuspress.yale.edu/davidmayhew/datasets-divided-we-govern/ for his updates (accessed February 20, 2017).
3. All measures in figure 3.2 include those by Mayhew; Grossmann; both measures of Howell et al. (which they term a1 and a2); and the Policy Agendas estimates.
4. Part of what explains the rise and decline of figure 3.4 is a change in cosponsorship rules in the House. From the 90th Congress (1967–68) through the 95th Congress (1977–78), House bills were limited to twenty-five cosponsors. By the time the House changed the rule, up to 44 percent of the bills were duplicate bills (Thomas and Grofman 1993). While this rule change makes figure 3.4 appear more dramatic than it otherwise would be, what is clear is that the numbers grew while the limit was in place and declined even after bills could have unlimited cosponsors.
5. CQ changed its annual format in the mid-2000s, making comparisons with earlier versions not practicable. So we cannot completely rule out the possibility that changes in format affected the measure in figure 3.7, but we believe it to be unlikely, given the correlation with law hearings data.
6. Expenditures (or outlays) occur when the agencies actually spend the money. Budget Authority reflects the appropriations process and hence captures congressional decision-making. Expenditures reflect both the initial decision and the demands of writing contracts and other factors that can cause expenditures to occur over several years. The correlation for the fit for an exponential curve to total Budget Authority is 0.978. See Jones, Zalányi, and Érdi (2014).
7. Paul Pierson (1994) argued that the dismantling of the welfare state is highly unlikely because of this dynamic—which suggests the cumulative nature of issue development that we find.
8. Some of the lawmaking series have larger "tails" than others—particularly the Howell et al. (2000) series.

CHAPTER FIVE

1. Chris Wlezien and Hans Noel suggested this possibility to us independently.
2. We use Stimson's biennial measures to correspond to our congressional data.
3. Platform data was initially collected, parsed, and coded by Christine Wolbrecht and updated by the Policy Agendas Project staff. We are indebted to Christina for making her data on platforms available to the Policy Agendas Project.

CHAPTER SIX

1. The newspaper numbers are relative, as they are from a systematic, random sample of articles constructed by the Policy Agendas Project from the *New York Times Index*. Data are aggregated by congress to facilitate comparison with indicators of legislative activity.
2. A similar pattern is evident in Spain (Chaques Bonafont and Palau 2011). This pattern seems to be typical in the policy process.
3. The measure of certs accepted is a ratio of Supreme Court cases to a 10 percent sample of certs denied.
4. Here we use the Policy Agendas major topic for Civil Rights, which incorporates all forms of discrimination, rather than the two subtopics we used in the analysis of civil rights above. This works for minority discrimination, because it accessed the agenda first.

5. The Minority Rights count is a sum of three Policy Agendas subtopics under the topic of Civil Rights: Minority Discrimination, General, and Voting Rights. Gender Discrimination is that subtopic.

CHAPTER SEVEN

1. Part of the trend for bill introduction is due to the cosponsorship rules of the House, which changed in the 96th Congress (1979–80). It is clear is that the trend was increasing even as the rule was not in place and it was decreasing even as the rule was in place. The inflection point in the data series occurred three congresses before the rule-change went into affect.
2. Again, part of the trend in the House can be explained by a rule-change. At the start of the 93rd Congress (1973–74), the House began voting by electronic device. Until then, roll-call votes in the House could take up to an hour. The time for an electronic roll-call vote is rarely more than fifteen minutes and can be as short as five minutes. The number of votes increased after the introduction of electronic voting, but it had been increasing even before the rule-change. Likewise, even under the electronic voting rule, the number of votes went up and then down. The pattern is valid even in light of the rule-change.
3. That belief already motivates many citizens today in the United States and other Western democracies; in Europe it is sometimes termed the *democratic deficit*.
4. We thank Matt Grossmann for making this data available to us.

CHAPTER EIGHT

1. Congress passes two types of laws: private laws, which have a limited impact, often affecting a single citizen, and public laws, which apply evenly to all citizens of the United States. The literature that examines congressional productivity focuses only on the latter, a practice that we adopt in our analysis as well.
2. Law length and the use of titles over the period are correlated: $r = 0.67$, $p < .000$.
3. Some laws include but a single title. That title may have different substantive content than the rest of the law. This is the case with 159 of our laws. Generally, the law opens with the name of the act, has a few pages related to that central topic, and then includes a title that has a few more pages on a different subtopic.

CHAPTER NINE

1. The quadratic fit for an upward-opening parabola is 0.83.
2. Another consequence of moving the nexus of policy-making from Congress to federal agencies is that it encourages the proliferation of organized interests. Groups that have the requisite policy expertise, bureaucratic connections, and the time it takes to monitor the *Federal Register* for new regulations and organize writing campaigns during public comment periods are more likely to have their views represented in public policy, compared to the average citizen. In chapter 11, we investigate another plausible consequence of the Great Broadening: the proliferation of interest groups in our political system.

CHAPTER TEN

1. The units are arbitrary, derived from a scaling algorithm. There relative values are reliable, however, so they may be directly compared.
2. The curves are quadratics, which fit slightly better than exponentials. The quadratics fits move more steeply than exponential fits. For polarization, $r = 0.990$; for the ratio of non-law to law, $r = 0.985$.

3. We use Mann and Ornstein's (1980) tabulations. Later data are from https://www.brookings.edu/multi-chapter-report/vital-statistics-on-congress/.
4. This positive-feedback system may be limited. Sufficiently high levels of polarization and gridlock may render Congress unable to pass any laws, even omnibus bills. Once such a theoretical limit is reached, productivity will necessarily decline; the federal government, however, will still be compelled to conduct maintenance in existing policy areas. This demand may conceivably move the nexus of policy-making closer to the executive. As we've demonstrated in chapter 9, the majority of modern law that citizens must obey takes the form of federal regulations.

CHAPTER ELEVEN

1. We use the standard we established in chapter 4 of being on the agenda. Any subtopic on which a hearing has been held in two of the three previous congresses is considered as being on the congressional agenda. Any subtopic on which a hearing was held in only one (or none) of the previous three congresses is considered off the agenda. Any issues that have been on the agenda are considered old issues. Issues that are added but had not previously been on the agenda are called new issues.
2. For purposes of this chapter, the Great Broadening takes place from the 86th to the 93rd Congresses (1959–74).
3. The difference between the Republican proportion in the majority (–7.2) and the minority (–3.6) is not statistically significant.
4. The difference between the Republican minority outside of the Great Broadening and the Republican majority is statistically significant.
5. Due to the low number of congressional hearings in the dataset on new issues during the Great Broadening, the percentages are not statistically significantly different from each other at conventional levels, though they are different at slightly relaxed levels (0.8 percent confidence versus 0.95).
6. For our purposes, these scores present other troublesome features. Poole and Rosenthal's algorithm only analyzes votes that contain some information. For example, a vote in which nearly all members vote on one side or the other does a poor job of differentiating one member's voting record from another's. Poole and Rosenthal therefore delete unanimous and nearly unanimous votes from their computation of DW-NOMINATE scores; they use a 5 percent dissent as the minimum for inclusion in the computation. If differentiating scores among members is the task at hand, this decision makes sense, because the votes contain little information to differentiate more than just a few members. If, however, the task is to compare the differences in how the parties vote across time, this decision has important ramifications. Take an extreme hypothetical as an example. Suppose that each Congress has only one hundred members, who, over the course of the Congress, take only ten votes per Congress. If on nine of those votes, all members vote together, and on the tenth vote, they split 50-50, the DW-NOMINATE algorithm would show that the Congress is highly divided because the first nine consensual votes are deleted from the analysis, and the highly contentious 50-50 vote is the only one used in the calculation. A set of votes like this would show more division than another set of ten votes from another hypothetical Congress in which every vote was split 60-40. DW-NOMINATE scores would show the former as being more divisive, yet any outside observer would recognize that the more divisive Congress was the latter one.
7. We use the VOTE variable from the Political Institutions and Public Choice (PIPC) Roll-Call Database (Crespin and Rohde 2017). We coded 1–19, 30–34, and 65 as final passage votes.

CHAPTER TWELVE

1. Walker's survey did not include private businesses, only trade associations representing businesses, although fewer firms engaged in lobbying at the time.
2. These estimates are from very different sampling schemes, but they at least give us some indication of changes in the system.
3. The *Encyclopedia* is a bit inconsistent during the early part of the series, but the totals are generally reliable. Furthermore, they are the best source of data we have for the number and kinds of interest groups that were active at different time intervals.
4. The *Encyclopedia* was coded in four-year intervals, beginning in 1966, so the Policy Agendas Project interpolates for the intervening years.
5. Frank Baumgartner provided the total number of associations from his analysis of the *Encyclopedia of Associations*. Because of the sampling method for the *Encyclopedia*, we have to be careful in imputing a particular year for the start of the counter-mobilization.

   The regression estimates are $y = -659900 + 340.36x$; $r^2 = 0.978$ for 1961–78; and–1.659500 + 845.62x; $r^2 = 0.993$ for 1979–88. The fit for the full series, 1961–88, is $r^2 = 0.940$, significantly poorer than either segment separately. Moreover the series winds around the best-fit line in a manner that further indicates poor fit.

CHAPTER TWELVE APPENDIX

1. If the conditional distribution of the dependent variable is overdispersed, as is the case here, the confidence intervals for the negative binomial regression are likely to be narrower as compared to those from a Poisson regression model (Hilbe 2011).

CHAPTER THIRTEEN

1. We examined hearings within the Policy Agendas subtopic Highways, under the topic Transportation, selecting those involving either economic regulation or vehicle safety regulation. Figures 13.1 and 13.2 reflect this data.
2. These bills include the Railroad Revitalization and Regulatory Reform Act of 1976, the Motor Carrier Act of 1980, the Household Goods Act of 1980, the Staggers Rail Act of 1980, the Bus Regulatory Reform Act of 1982, the Surface Freight Forwarder Deregulation Act of 1986, the Negotiated Rates Act of 1993, the Trucking Industry Regulatory Reform Act of 1994, the ICC Termination Act of 1995, and the Airline Deregulation Act of 1978.
3. Data difficulties in FBI reporting are regularly noted because they rely on reports from a variety of agencies and governments nation-wide. A second source, the National Crime Victimization Surveys conducted by the Bureau of Justice Statistics, is able to assess both reported and nonreported crime but has been conducted only since 1973 and experienced a redesign in 1993 (Federal Bureau of Investigation, *Uniform Crime Reporting Statistics* 2018b).
4. Congress passed the crime package as an amendment to a must-pass continuing appropriation. The House took a vote on attaching the amendment. The Senate never separately considered the crime package as such, so a party difference score cannot be determined.
5. Sources: Federal Budgets: US Policy Agendas Project; Prisoners: Bureau of Justice Statistics, Prison Population Counts.

REFERENCES

Adler, E. Scott, and John D. Wilkerson. 2012. *Congress and the Politics of Problem Solving*. Cambridge: Cambridge University Press.

Allaby, Michael, ed. 2014. "S-shaped Growth Curve." *Dictionary of Zoology*. 4th ed. Oxford: Oxford University Press. Online at http://www.encyclopedia.com/earth-and-environment/ecology-and-environmentalism/environmental-studies/s-shaped-growth-curve.

Anderson, James E. 1975. *Public Policy-Making*. New York: Praeger.

Ansolabehere, Stephen, Maxwell Palmer, and Benjamin Schneer. 2014. "Divided Government and Significant Legislation: A History of Congress from 1989–2010." Working paper.

———, James M. Snyder, and C. Stewart. 2001. "Candidate Positioning in US House Elections." *American Journal of Political Science* 45 (January): 136–59.

Anzia, Sarah, and Terry M. Moe. 2016. "Do Politicians Use Policy to Make Politics? The Case of Public Sector Labor Laws." *American Political Science Review* 110:763–77.

———. 2017. "Polarization and Policy: The Politics of Public-Sector Pensions." *Legislative Studies Quarterly* 42 (July): 33–62.

Arthur, W. Brian. 1994. *Increasing Returns and Path Dependence in the Economy*. Ann Arbor: University of Michigan Press.

Bachrach, Peter, and Morton S. Baratz. 1962. "Two Faces of Power." *American Political Science Review* 56:947–52.

———, and Morton S. Baratz. 1963. "Decisions and Non-Decisions: An Analytical Framework." *American Political Science Review* 57:632–42.

Barabasi, Albert-Laszlo. 2010. *Bursts: The Hidden Order Behind Everything We Do*. New York: Dutton.

Barber, Benjamin. 1986. "America as a Monumental Gamble." *New York Times*. November 16. Online at http://www.nytimes.com/books/00/11/26/specials/schlesinger-cycles.html. Accessed 6/22/2014.

Bates, Robert H., Avner Grief, Margaret Levi, Jean-Laurent Rosenthal, and Barry R. Weingast. 1998. *Analytic Narratives*. Princeton, NJ: Princeton University Press.

Baumgartner, Frank R. 2005. "The Growth and Diversity of US Associations, 1956–2004." Working Paper.

———, Jeffrey M. Berry, Marie Hojnacki, David C. Kimball, and Beth L. Leech. 2009. *Lobbying and Policy Change*. Chicago: University of Chicago Press.

———, Jeffrey M. Berry, Marie Hojnacki, David C. Kimball, and Beth L. Leech. 2014. "Money, Priorities, and Stalemate: How Lobbying Affects Public Policy." *Election Law Journal* 13 (1): 194–209.

———, Christian Breunig, Christoffer Green-Pederson, Bryan D. Jones, Peter Mortensen, Michiel Nuytemans, and Stefaan Walgrave. 2009. "Punctuated Equilibrium in Comparative Perspective." *American Journal of Political Science* 53:602–19.

———, and Bryan D. Jones. (1993) 2009. *Agendas and Instability in American Politics*. 2nd. ed. Chicago: University of Chicago Press.

———, and Bryan D. Jones. 2015. *The Politics of Information*. Chicago: University of Chicago Press.

———, and Beth L. Leech. 1998. *Basic Interests*. Princeton, NJ: Princeton University Press.

Bernstein, Marver H. 1955. *Regulating Business by Independent Commission*. Princeton, NJ: Princeton University Press.

Bevan, Shaun, Frank R. Baumgartner, Erik W. Johnson, and John D. McCarthy. 2013. "Understanding Selection Bias, Time Lags, and Measurement Bias in Secondary Data Sources: Putting the *Encyclopedia of Associations* Database in Broader Context." *Social Science Research* 42:1750–64.

"Black Americans in Congress: The Civil Rights Movement and the Second Reconstruction, 1945–68." N.d. In *History, Art, and Archives,* the web page of the House Historian, U.S. House of Representatives, online at http://history.house.gov/Exhibitions-and-Publications/BAIC/Historical-Essays/Keeping-the-Faith/Civil-Rights-Movement/.

Boushey, Graeme. 2010. *Policy Diffusion Dynamics in America*. Cambridge: Cambridge University Press.

Brady, David and Craig Volden. 1998. *Revolving Gridlock*. Boulder CO: Westview.

Buckley, William F. 1957. "Why the South Must Prevail." *National Review*, August 24. Online at http://www.xoxohth.com/thread.php?forum_id=2&thread_id=2845379.

Bureau of Justice Statistics, Office of Justice Programs. 1994. *Fact Sheet: Drug Related Crimes.* Online at https://www.bjs.gov/content/dcf/duc.cfm.

Bureau of Justice Statistics, Office of Justice Programs. 2015. *Drug Offenders in Federal Prison.* Online at https://www.bjs.gov/content/pub/pdf/dofp12.pdf.

Burstein, Paul. 2002. "The Impact of Political Parties, Interest Groups, and Social Movements on Public Policy." *Social Forces* 81:381–408.

Calabresi, Guido. 1982. *A Common Law for the Age of Statutes.* Boston: Harvard University Press.

Campbell, Andrea. 2003. *How Policies Make Citizens: Senior Political Activism and the American Welfare State*. Princeton, NJ: Princeton University Press.

———. 2007. "Parties, Electoral Participation, and Shifting Voting Blocs." In *The Transformation of American Politics*, edited by Paul Pierson and Theda Skocpol, 68–102. Princeton, NJ: Princeton University Press.

———, and Kimberly J. Morgan. 2005. "Federalism and the Politics of Old-Age Care in Germany and the United States." *Comparative Political Studies* 38 (8): 887–914.

Capoccia, Giovanni, and R. Daniel Kelemen. 2007. "The Study of Critical Junctures." *World Politics* 59 (June): 341–69.

Carmines, Edward G., and James A. Stimson. 1989. *Issue Evolution: Race and the Transformation of American Politics.* Princeton, NJ: Princeton University Press.

Carter, Jimmy Earl. 1979. *Public Papers of the Presidents of the United States: Jimmy Carter, 1978.* Washington DC: Office of the Federal Register.

Chaques Bonafont, Laura, and Anna M. Palau. 2011. "Assessing the Responsiveness of Spanish Policy-Makers to the Priorities of Their Citizens." *West European Politics* 24:706–30.

Chong, Dennis. 1991. *Collective Action and the Civil Rights Movement.* Chicago: University of Chicago Press.

Clinton, Joshua, and John Lapinski. 2006. "Measuring Legislative Accomplishment, 1877–1994." *American Journal of Political Science* 50:232–49.

Cobb, Roger, and Charles D. Elder. (1972) 1983. *Participation in American Politics.* 2nd ed. Baltimore: Johns Hopkins Press.

———, Jennie-Keith Ross, and Mark Howard Ross. 1976. Agenda Building as a Comparative Political Process. *American Political Science Review* 70:126–38.

———, and Mark Howard Ross, eds. 1997. *Cultural Strategies of Denial.* Lawrence: University Press of Kansas.

Cohen, Michael D., James G. March, and Johan P. Olsen. 1972. "A Garbage Can Model of Organizational Choice." *Administrative Science Quarterly* 17 (1): 1–25.

Cohn, Bob. 2011. "Scalia: Our Political System Is 'Designed for' Gridlock." *The Atlantic,* October 6. Online at https://www.theatlantic.com/national/archive/2011/10/scalia-our-political-system-is-designed-for-gridlock/246257.

Cox, Gary W., and Mathew D. McCubbins. 1993. *Legislative Leviathan: Party Government in the House.* Berkeley: University of California Press.

———, and Mathew D. McCubbins. 2005. *Setting the Agenda: Responsible Party Government in the U.S. House of Representatives.* New York: Cambridge University Press.

———, and Keith T. Poole. 2002. "On Measuring Partisanship in Roll-Call Voting: The U.S. House of Representatives, 1877–1999." *American Journal of Political Science* 46 (July): 477–89.

Crandall, Robert. 2008. "Extending Deregulation: Making the Economy More Efficient." In *Opportunity 08: Independent Ideas for America's Next President,* edited by Michael E. O'Hanlon. Washington DC: Brookings Institution.

Crenson, Matthew. 1971. *The Un-Politics of Air Pollution.* Baltimore: Johns Hopkins University Press.

Crespin, Michael H., and David Rohde. 2017. "Political Institutions and Public Choice Roll-Call Database." Online at http://cacexplore.org/pipcvotes/.

———, David W. Rohde, and Ryan J. Vander Wielen. 2013. "Measuring Variation in Party Unity Voting: An Assessment of Agenda-Effects." *Party Politics* 19 (3): 432–57.

Dahl, Robert. 1956. *A Preface to Democratic Theory.* Chicago: University of Chicago Press.

———. 1961. *Who Governs?* New Haven, CT: Yale University Press.

———. 1963. *Modern Political Analysis.* Englewood Cliffs, NJ: Prentice-Hall.

———. 1966. "Further Reflections on the Elitist Theory of Democracy." *American Political Science Review* 60:296–305.

Derthick, Martha, and Paul J. Quirk. 1985. *The Politics of Deregulation.* Washington DC: Brookings Institution.

Dodd, Lawrence C. 1979. *Congress and the Administrative State.* Wiley: New York, New York.

———. 2012. *Thinking About Congress.* New York: Routledge.

———. 2015. "Congress in a Downsian World: Polarization Cycles and Regime Change." *Journal of Politics* 77 (February): 311–23.

———, and Scot Schraufnagel. 2009. "Reconsidering Party Polarization and Policy Productivity: A Curvilinear Perspective." In *Congress Reconsidered,* ed. Lawrence Dodd and Bruce Oppenheimer, 393–418. 9th ed. Washington, DC: CQ Press.

Drutman, Lee. 2015. *The Business of America Is Lobbying.* Oxford: Oxford University Press.

———, and Steven Teles. 2015. "A New Agenda for Political Reform." *Washington Monthly,* March/April/May.

Easton, David. 1953. *The Political System.* New York: Knopf.

Edwards, Ezekiel, Will Bunting, and Lynda Garcia. 2013. *The War on Marijuana in Black and White.* New York: American Civil Liberties Union.

Ellis, Christopher, and Christopher Faricy. 2011. "Social Policy and Public Opinion: How the Ideological Direction of Spending Influences Public Mood." *Journal of Politics* 73:1095–1110.

Érdi, Péter. 2008. *Complexity Explained*. New York: Springer.

Erikson, Robert S., Michael B. Mackuen, and James A. Stimson. 2002. *The Macropolity*. Cambridge: Cambridge University Press.

Evans, C. Lawrence, and Walter J. Oleszek. 1997. *Congress Under Fire: Reform Politics and the Republican Majority*. Boston: Houghton Mifflin.

Fandos, Nicholas. 2017. "With Obamacare Fight Lost, Conservatives Turn to Veterans' Care." *New York Times*, November 10. Online at https://www.nytimes.com/2017/11/09/us/politics/obamacare-veterans-affairs-koch-brothers-health.html.

Farhang, Sean. 2008. "Public Regulation and Private Lawsuits in the American Separation of Powers System." *American Journal of Political Science* 52:821–39.

Faricy, Christopher. 2015. *Welfare for the Wealthy: Parties, Social Spending, and Inequality in the United States.* New York: Cambridge University Press.

Federal Bureau of Investigation. 2018a. *Uniform Crime Reporting*. Online at https://ucr.fbi.gov/.

———. 2018b. "The Nation's Two Crime Measures." In *Uniform Crime Reporting Statistics*. Online at https://www.ucrdatatool.gov/twomeasures.cfm.

Federal Bureau of Prisons. 2018. "Inmate Offenses." Online at https://www.bop.gov/about/statistics/statistics_inmate_offenses.jsp.

Feltzenberg, Alvin. 2017. "How William F. Buckley, Jr., Changed His Mind on Civil Rights." *Politico Magazine*, May 13. Online at https://www.politico.com/magazine/story/2017/05/13/william-f-buckley-civil-rights-215129.

Free, Lloyd, and Hadley Cantril. 1967. *The Political Beliefs of Americans: Study of Public Opinion*. New Brunswick, NJ: Rutgers University Press.

Gamson, William A. 1968. "Stable Unrepresentation in American Society." *American Behavioral Scientist* 12 (November/December): 15–20.

Gell-Mann, Murray. 1994. "Complex Adaptive Systems." In *Complexity: Metaphors, Models, and Reality*, edited by George A. Cowan, David Pines, and David Meltzer, 17–45. Santa Fe Institute Studies in the Sciences of Complexity, no. 19. Cambridge, MA: Perseus Books, 1999.

General Accounting Office. 1996. *Airline Deregulation*. Report to the Chairman, Committee on Commerce, Science, and Transportation, U.S. Senate.

Grant, J. Tobin, and Nathan J. Kelly. 2008. "Legislative Productivity of the US Congress, 1789–2004. *Political Analysis* 16 (3): 303–23.

Greenstone, David, and Paul E. Peterson. 1973. *Race and Authority in Urban Politics*. Chicago: University of Chicago Press.

Green-Pederson, Christoffer. 2011. *Partier I Nye Tider*. Aarhus, Denmark: Aarhus Universitetsforlag.

Grossbeck, Lawrence J., David A. M. Peterson, and James A. Stimson. 2006. *Mandate Politics.* Cambridge: Cambridge University Press.

Grossmann, Matt. 2014. *Artists of the Possible*. Oxford: Oxford University Press.

Hacker, Jacob, and Paul Pierson. 2010. *Winner-Take-All Politics: How Washington Made the Rich Richer and Turned Its Back on the Middle Class*. New York: Simon and Schuster.

———. 2012. "Presidents and the Political Economy: The Coalitional Foundations of Presidential Power." *Presidential Studies Quarterly* 42 (1): 101–31.

———. 2014. "After the 'Master Theory': Downs, Schattschneider, and the Rebirth of Policy-Focused Analysis." *Perspectives on Politics* 12:643–62.

———. 2016. *American Amnesia*. New York: Simon and Schuster.

Harbridge, Laurel. 2015. *Is Bipartisanship Dead? Policy Agreement and Agenda-Setting in the House of Representatives*. New York: Cambridge University Press.

Hayes, Ron D. and Phyllis L. Ellickson. 1990. "Longitudinal Scalogram Analysis." *Behavior Research Methods* 22:162–66.

Heclo, Hugh. 1978. "Issue Networks and the Executive Establishment." In *The New American Political System*, edited by Anthony King, 115–24. Washington, DC: American Enterprise Institute.

Hetherington, Marc J. 2001. "Resurgent Mass Partisanship: The Role of Elite Polarization." *American Political Science Review* 95 (3): 619–31.

Hilbe, J. M. 2011. *Negative Binomial Regression*. 2nd ed. New York: Cambridge University Press.

Hojnacki, Marie, Kathleen M. Marchetti, Frank Baumgartner, Jeffrey M. Berry, David C. Kimball, and Beth L. Leech. 2015. "Assessing Business Advantage in Washington Lobbying." *Interest Group and Advocacy* 2 (4): 205–224.

Howard, J. H. 1984. "Perspectives on 'Overloaded Government.'" *Australian Journal of Public Administration* 43:332–403.

Howell, William, Scott Adler, Charles Cameron, and Charles Riemann. 2000. "Divided Government and the Legislative Productivity of Congress, 1945–94." *Legislative Studies Quarterly* 25:285–312.

Huntington, Samuel. 1952. "The Marasmus of the ICC: The Commission, The Railroads, and the Public Interest." *Yale Law Journal* 61 (4): 467–509.

———. 1981. *American Politics: The Promise of Disharmony*. Cambridge, MA: Belknap Press of Harvard University Press.

IresearchNet. 2018. Criminal Justice Research and Reference. Sentencing. Online at https://www.iresearchnet.com/.

Jacobs, Lawrence R. 2014. "Health Reform and the Future of American Politics." *Perspectives on Politics* 12:631–42.

Jenkins, Jeffery A., Michael H. Crespin, and Jamie L. Carson. 2005. "Parties as Procedural Coalitions in Congress: An Examination of Differing Career Tracks." *Legislative Studies Quarterly* 30 (August): 365–90.

Jessee, Stephen A., and Sean M. Theriault. 2014. "The Two Faces of Congressional Roll-Call Voting." *Party Politics* 20 (October): 836–48.

Jochim, Ashley, and Bryan D. Jones. 2013. "Issue Politics in a Polarized Congress." *Political Research Quarterly* 66 (August): 1–16.

Jones, Bryan D. 2001. *Politics and the Architecture of Choice: Bounded Rationality and Governance*. Chicago: University of Chicago Press.

———. 2016a. "The Comparative Policy Agendas Projects as Measurement Systems: Response to Dowding, Hindmoor, and Martin." *Journal of Public Policy* 36 (May): 31–46.

———. 2016b. "A Radical Idea Tamed: The Work of Roger Cobb and Charles Elder." In *Handbook of Public Agenda-Setting*, edited by Nikolaos Zahariadis, 25–34. Cheltenham, UK: Edward Elgar.

———, and Frank R. Baumgartner. 2004. "Representation and Agenda Setting." *Policy Studies Journal* 31, no. 1: 1–24.

———, and Frank R. Baumgartner. 2005. *The Politics of Attention*. Chicago: University of Chicago Press.

———, and Frank R. Baumgartner. 2012. "From There to Here: Punctuated Equilibrium to the General Punctuation Thesis to a Theory of Government Information Processing." *Policy Studies Journal* 40 (1): 1–19.

———, Frank Baumgartner, Christian Breunig, Christopher Wlezien, Stuart Soroka, Martial Foucault, Able Francois, Christoffer Green-Pederson, Chris Koski, Peter John, Peter Mortensen, Frederic Varone, and Steffan Walgrave. 2009. "A General Empirical Law of Public Budgets." *American Journal of Political Science* 53:855–73.

———, Frank R. Baumgartner, and Jeffery C. Talbert. 1993. "The Destruction of Issue Monopolies in Congress." *American Political Science Review* 87:657–71.

———, Frank R. Baumgartner, and James L. True. 1998. "Policy Punctuations: U.S. Budget Authority, 1847–1995." *Journal of Politics* 60:1–33.

———, Heather Larsen-Price, and John Wilkerson. 2009. "Representation and American Governing Institutions." *Journal of Politics* 71 (January): 1–14.

———, Tracy Sulkin, and Heather Larsen. 2003. "Punctuations in American Political Institutions." *American Political Science Review* 97:151–69.

———, Herschel Thomas, and Michelle Wolfe. 2014. "Policy Bubbles." *Policy Studies Journal* 42 (March): 146–71.

———, James L. True, and Frank R. Baumgartner. 1997. "Does Incrementalism Stem from Political Consensus or from Institutional Gridlock?" *American Journal of Political Science* 41:1319–39.

———, and Walter Williams. 2008. *The Politics of Bad Ideas: The Great Tax Cut Delusion and the Decline of Good Government in America.* New York: Longman.

———, László Zalányi, and Péter Érdi. 2014. "An Integrated Theory of Budgetary Politics and Some Empirical Tests: The US National Budget, 1791–2010." *American Journal of Political Science* (July): 561–78.

Jones, Charles O. 1970. *An Introduction to the Study of Public Policy*. Belmont, CA: Wadsworth.

———. 1979. "American Politics and the Organization of Energy Decision Making." *Annual Review of Energy* 4:99–121.

Katznelson, Ira. 2005. *When Affirmative Action Was White*. New York: W. W. Norton.

Kingdon, John W. (1984) 1995. *Agendas, Alternatives, and Public Policies*. 2nd ed. New York: Harper Collins.

Koger, Gregory, and Matthew J. Lebo. 2017. *Strategic Party Government: Why Winning Trumps Ideology.* Chicago: University of Chicago Press.

Krehbiel, Keith. 1998. *Pivotal Politics: A Theory of U.S. Lawmaking*. Chicago: University of Chicago Press.

Krouse, Richard W. 1982. "Polyarchy and Participation." *Polity* 14:441–63.

Krutz, Glen S. 2000. "Getting Around Gridlock: The Effect of Omnibus Utilization on Legislative Productivity." *Legislative Studies Quarterly* 25:533–49.

———. 2001. *Hitching a Ride: Omnibus Legislating in the U.S. Congress*. Columbus: Ohio State University Press.

Lee, Frances E. 2009. *Beyond Ideology: Politics, Principles, and Partisanship in the U.S. Senate.* Chicago: University of Chicago Press.

———. 2016. *Insecure Majorities: Congress and the Perpetual Campaign*. Chicago: University of Chicago Press.

Lee, Taeku. 2002. *Mobilizing Public Opinion*. Chicago: University of Chicago Press.

Leech, Beth L., Frank R. Baumgartner, Timothy M. La Pira, and Nicolas Semanko. 2005. "Drawing Lobbyists to Washington: Government Activity and the Demand for Advocacy." *Political Research Quarterly* 58 (March): 19–30.

Lewallen, Jonathan. 2014. "The Decline of Subsystem Government." Working Paper, Austin, Texas: US Policy Agendas Project, University of Texas.

———. 2017. *You Better Find Something to Do: Lawmaking and Agenda-Setting in a Centralized Congress*. PhD diss., Department of Government, University of Texas at Austin.

———, Sean M. Theriault, and Bryan D. Jones. 2016. "Congressional Dysfunction: An Information Processing Perspective." *Regulation and Governance* 10 (May): 179–90.

———, Sean M. Theriault, and Bryan D. Jones. In press. "The Issue Dynamics of Congressional Capacity."

Levi, Margaret. 1997. "A Model, a Method, and a Map: Rational Choice in Comparative and Historical Analysis." In *Comparative Politics: Rationality, Culture, and Structure*, edited by Mark I. Lichbach and Alan S. Zuckerman, 19–41. Cambridge: Cambridge University Press.

Light, Paul. 1995. *Thickening Government: Federal Hierarchy and the Diffusion of Accountability*. Washington, DC: Brookings Institution.

———. 2004. "Fact Sheet on the Continued Thickening of Government." Washington, DC: Brookings Institution. Online at https://www.brookings.edu/research/fact-sheet-on-the-continued-thickening-of-government/.

Lipton, Douglas, Robert Martinson, and Judith Wilkes. 1975. *The Effectiveness of Correctional Treatment: A Survey of Treatment Evaluation Studies*. New York: Praeger.

Lowi, Theodore. 1964. "American Business, Public Policy, Case-Studies, and Political Theory." *World Politics* 16:677–93.

———. 1967. "The Public Philosophy: Interest-Group Liberalism." *American Political Science Review*: 61:5–24.

MacWhinney, Brian. 2005. "The Emergence of Grammar from Perspective." In *Grounding Cognition*, edited by Diane Pecher and Rolf A. Zwaan, 198–223. New York: Cambridge University Press.

Mann, Thomas, and Norman Ornstein. 1980. *Vital Statistics on Congress*. Washington, DC: Brookings Institution.

———. and Norman Ornstein. 2006. *The Broken Branch: How Congress Is Failing America and How to Get It Back on Track*. New York: Oxford University Press.

Marone, James A. 2003. *Hellfire Nation: The Politics of Sin in American History*. New Haven, CT: Yale University Press.

Matthews, Donald R. 1959. "The Folkways of the United States Senate: Conformity to Group Norms and Legislative Effectiveness." *American Political Science Review* 53: 1064–89.

Mayhew, David. 1991. *Divided We Govern: Party Control, Lawmaking, and Investigations, 1946–1990*. New Haven, CT: Yale University Press.

———. 2005. *Divided We Govern: Party Control, Lawmaking, and Investigations, 1946–2002*. New Haven, CT: Yale University Press.

McCarty, Nolan. 2007. "The Policy Effects of Political Polarization." In *The Transformation of American Politics*, edited by Paul Pierson and Theda Skocpol, 223–55. Princeton, NJ: Princeton University Press.

———, Keith T. Poole, and Howard Rosenthal. 2006. *Polarized America: The Dance of Ideology and Unequal Riches*. Cambridge, MA: MIT Press.

Meier, Kenneth. 1985. *Regulation: Politics, Bureaucracy, and Economics*. New York: St. Martin's.

Mettler, Suzanne. 2005. *Soldiers to Citizens: The G.I. Bill and the Making of the Greatest Generation*. New York: Oxford University Press.

———. 2011. *The Submerged State*. Chicago: University of Chicago Press.

Moore, Thomas G. 1993. "Trucking Deregulation." In *The Concise Encyclopedia of Economics.* Library of Economics and Liberty. Online at http://www.econlib.org/library/Enc1/TruckingDeregulation.html.

Noel, Hans. 2013. *Political Ideologies and Political Parties in America.* New York: Cambridge University Press.

Novak, William J. 2014. "A Revisionist History of Regulatory Capture." In *Preventing Regulatory Capture,* edited by Daniel Carpenter and David Moss, 25–48. New York: Cambridge University Press.

Office of the Historian, United States House of Representatives. n.d. History, Art, and Archives: "The Civil Rights Movement and the Second Reconstruction." Online at http://history.house.gov/Exhibitions-and-Publications/BAIC/Historical-Essays/Keeping-the-Faith/Civil-Rights-Movement/.

Owens, Ryan J., and David A. Simon. 2012. "Explaining the Supreme Court's Shrinking Docket." *William and Mary Law Review* 53:1219–86.

Padgett, J. 1980. "Managing Garbage Can Hierarchies." *Administrative Science Quarterly,* 25 (4): 583–604.

Padgett, John F., and Walter W. Powell. 2012. *The Emergence of Organizations and Markets.* Princeton, NJ: Princeton University Press.

Patashnik, Eric M. 2008. *Reforms at Risk: What Happens After Major Policy Changes Are Enacted.* Princeton, NJ: Princeton University Press.

Patterson, James T. 1996. *Grand Expectations: The United States, 1945–1974.* Oxford: Oxford University Press.

Pew Charitable Trusts. 2015. *Prison Time Surges for Federal Inmates.* Online at http://www.pewtrusts.org/en/research-and-analysis/issue-briefs/2015/11/prison-time-surges-for-federal-inmates.

Pew Research Center. 2014. "Political Polarization in the American Public." June 14. Online at http://www.people-press.org/2014/06/12/political-polarization-in-the-american-public/.

Pierson, Paul. 1993. "When Effect Becomes Cause: Policy Feedback and Political Change." *World Politics* 45:595–628.

———. 1994. *Dismantling the Welfare State?* Cambridge: Cambridge University Press.

———. 1996. "The New Politics of the Welfare State." *World Politics* 48:143–79.

———. 2000. "Increasing Returns, Path Dependence, and the Study of Politics." *American Political Science Review* 93:251–67.

———. 2004. *Politics in Time.* Princeton, NJ: Princeton University Press.

———. 2007. "The Rise and Reconfiguration of Activist Government." In Pierson and Skocpol 2007, 19–38.

———, and Theda Skocpol, eds. 2007. *The Transformation of American Politics.* Princeton, NJ: Princeton University Press.

Polsby, Nelson W. 1963. *Community Power and Political Theory.* New Haven, CT: Yale University Press.

———. 1968. "The Institutionalization of the U.S. House of Representatives." *American Political Science Review* 62:144–68.

Poole, Keith T., and Howard Rosenthal. 1997. *Congress: A Political-Economic History of Roll-Call Voting.* New York: Oxford University Press.

Redford, Emmette S. 1969. *Democracy in the Administrative State.* New York: Oxford University Press.

Riker, William. 1980. "Implications of the Disequilibrium of Majority Rule for the Study of Institutions." *American Political Science Review* 74:432–46.

Roberts, Jason M., and Steven S. Smith. 2003. "Procedural Contexts, Party Strategy, and Conditional Party Voting in the U.S. House of Representatives, 1971–2000." *American Journal of Political Science* 47:305–17.

Rochefort David, and Roger Cobb, eds. 1994. *The Politics of Problem Definition*. Lawrence: University Press of Kansas.

Rohde, David W. 1974. "Committee Reform in the House of Representatives and the Subcommittee Bill of Rights." *Annals of the American Academy of Political and Social Science* 411:39–47.

———. 1991. *Parties and Leaders in the Postreform House*. Chicago: University of Chicago Press.

Sabatier, Paul A., and Hank C. Jenkins-Smith. 1993. *Policy Change and Learning: An Advocacy Coalition Approach*. New York: Avalon.

Salisbury, Robert. 1984. "Interest Representation: The Dominance of Institutions." *American Political Science Review* 78:64–76.

Schattschneider, E. E. 1935. *Politics, Pressures, and the Tariff*. New York: Prentice-Hall.

———. 1957. "Intensity, Visibility, Direction, and Scope." *American Political Science Review* 4:933–42.

———. 1960. *The Semisovereign People*. New York: Holt, Reinhardt, and Winston.

Schickler, Eric. 2016. *Racial Realignment*. Princeton, NJ: Princeton University Press.

Schlesinger, Arthur, Jr. 1986. *The Cycles of American History*. New York: Houghton Mifflin.

Schneider, Anne, and Helen Ingram. 1993. "Social Construction of Target Populations: Implications for Politics and Policy." *American Political Science Review* 87:334–47.

Schumpeter, Joseph. 1942. *Capitalism, Socialism, and Democracy*. New York: Harper and Row.

Segal, Ehud. 2016. *Patterns of Gradual Change in Public Policy*. PhD diss., Hebrew University of Jerusalem.

Sentencing Project, The. 2018. *Criminal Justice Facts*. Online at https://www.sentencingproject.org/criminal-justice-facts/.

Shepsle, Kenneth A. 1989. "The Changing Textbook Congress." In *Can the Government Govern?* edited by John E. Chubb and Paul E. Peterson, 355–68. Washington, DC: Brookings Institution.

Shpaizman, Ilana. 2014. "Ideas and Institutional Conversion Through Layering: The Case of Israeli Immigration Policy." *Public Administration* 94: 1038–53.

———. 2017. "Policy Drift and Its Reversal: The Case of Prescription Drug Coverage in the United States." *Public Administration* 97: 698–712.

Simon, Herbert. 1996. *The Sciences of the Artificial*. 3rd ed. Cambridge, MA: MIT Press.

Simon, Jonathan. 2007. "The Rise of the Carceral State." *Social Research* 74:471–508.

Sinclair, Barbara. 1989. *The Transformation of the U.S. Senate*. Baltimore: Johns Hopkins University Press.

———. 2011. *Unorthodox Lawmaking: New Legislative Processes in the U.S. Congress*. 4th ed. Washington, DC: CQ Press.

Skocpol, Theda. 1995. *Protecting Soldiers and Mothers: The Political Origins of Social Policy in the United States*. Cambridge, MA: Harvard University Press.

———. 2007. "Government Activism and the Reorganization of American Civic Democracy." In Pierson and Skocpol 2007, 39–67.

Smith, Mark A. 2000. *Business and Political Power: Public Opinion, Elections, and Democracy*. Chicago: University of Chicago Press.

Snyder, James M., Jr., and Tim Groseclose. 2000. "Estimating Party Influence in Congressional Roll-Call Voting." *American Journal of Political Science* 44:193–211.

Soroka, Stuart, and Christopher Wlezien. *Degrees of Democracy*. Cambridge: Cambridge University Press. 2010.

Soss, Joe. 1999. "Lessons of Welfare: Policy Design, Political Learning, and Political Action." *American Political Science Review* 93 (2): 363–80.

Sparrow, Bartholomew. 1996. *From the Outside In: World War II and the American State*. Princeton, NJ: Princeton University Press.

Stone, Clarence N. 1980. "Systemic Power in Community Decision-Making: A Restatement of Stratificationist Theory." *American Political Science Review* 74:978–90.

———. 1988. "Preemptive Power: Floyd Hunter's 'Community Power Structure' Reconsidered." *American Journal of Political Science* 32:82–104.

———. 1989. *Regime Politics: Governing Atlanta, 1946–1988*. Lawrence: University Press of Kansas.

Strolovitch, Dara. 2007. *Affirmative Advocacy*. Chicago: University of Chicago Press.

Taleb, Nassim. 2008. *The Black Swan: The Impact of the Highly Improbable.* New York: Random House.

Teles, Steven M. 2007. "Conservative Mobilization Against Entrenched Liberalism." In Pierson and Skocpol 2007, 160–88.

Theriault, Sean. 2008. *Party Polarization in the U.S. Congress*. New York: Cambridge University Press.

———. 2013. *The Gingrich Senators: The Roots of Partisan Warfare in Congress*. New York: Oxford University Press.

———, and Barry R. Weingast. 2002. "Agenda Manipulation, Strategic Voting, and Legislative Details in the Compromise of 1850." In *Party, Process, and Political Change in Congress,* edited by David Brady and Mathew McCubbins. Stanford, CA: Stanford University Press.

Thomas, Scott, and Bernard Grofman. "The Effects of Congressional Rules about Bill Cosponsorship on Duplicate Bills: Changing Incentives for Credit Claiming." *Public Choice* 75 (March): 93–98

Truman, David. 1951. *The Governmental Process*. New York: Knopf.

Turley, Jonathan. 2013. "The Rise of the Fourth Branch of Government." *Washington Post,* May 24, 2013. Online at http://www.washingtonpost.com/opinions/the-rise-of-the-fourth-branch-ofgovernment/2013/05/24/c7faaad0-c2ed-11e2-9fe2-6ee52d0eb7c1_story.html.Vogel, David. 1989. *Fluctuating Fortunes*. New York: Basic Books.

Walker, Jack L. 1966. "A Critique of the Elitist Theory of Democracy." *American Political Science Review* 60:285–95.

———. 1983. "The Origin and Maintenance of Interest Groups in America." *American Political Science Review* 77:390–406.

Wamsley, Roy. 2016. *World Prison Brief*. 11th ed. London: Institute for Criminal Policy Research. Online at http://www.prisonstudies.org/sites/default/files/resources/downloads/world_prison_population_list_11th_edition_0.pdf. Accessed 4/11/2018.

Whyman, Michelle. 2011. "Disproportionate Attention on the Supreme Court, 1948–1990." Department of Government, University of Texas at Austin Masters Report.

———. 2014. "Designing for Durability." Paper Presented at the Annual Comparative Policy Agendas Conference. Konstanz, Germany. June.

———, and Bryan D. Jones. 2012. "Building Blocks and Bursts in US Lawmaking." Paper presented to the Comparative Agendas Project, Reims, France. June 14–16.

Wildvasky, Aaron. 1979. *Speaking Truth to Power: The Art and Craft of Policy Analysis*. Boston: Little, Brown.

Wilson, James Q. 1975. *Thinking About Crime*. New York: Basic Books.

———. 1979. "American Politics, Then and Now." *Commentary* (February): 39–46.

Wlezien, Christopher. 1995. "The Public as Thermostat." *American Journal of Political Science* 39:981–1000.

Wolbrecht, Christina. 2000. *The Politics of Women's Rights: Parties, Positions, and Change.* Princeton, NJ: Princeton University Press.

Wolfinger, Raymond E. 1971. "Nondecisions and the Study of Local Politics." *American Political Science Review* 65:1063–80.

Workman, Samuel. 2015. *The Dynamics of the Bureaucracy in the U.S. Government.* New York: Cambridge University Press.

———, and JoBeth Shafran. 2015. "Communications Frameworks and the Supply of Information in Policy Subsystems." In *Policy Paradigms in Theory and Practice,* ed. Michael Howlett and John Hogan, 239–68. Basingstoke, UK: Palgrave MacMillan.

Wright, Valerie. 2010. *Deterrence in Criminal Justice.* Washington, DC: Sentencing Project.

Zelizer, Julian E. 2007. "Seizing Power: Conservatives and Congress Since the 1970s." In Pierson and Skocpol 2007, 105–34.

INDEX